THE INKY DIGIT OF DEFIANCE
Selected Prose 1966–2016

TONY HARRISON

The Inky Digit of Defiance

Selected Prose 1966–2016

EDITED BY EDITH HALL

FABER & FABER

First published in 2017
by Faber & Faber Limited
Bloomsbury House
74–77 Great Russell Street
London WC1B 3DA
First published in the USA in 2017

Typeset by Ian Bahrami
Printed and bound in England by CPI Group (UK) Ltd, Croydon CR0 4YY

A CIP record for this book
is available from the British Library

ISBN 978–0–571–32503–0

2 4 6 8 10 9 7 5 3 1

Contents

CONTENTS

Foreword: An Inky Tribute
by Edith Hall

In his *Apology for Poetry* (1595), Philip Sidney explains that he never consciously set out to be a poet. But he could not help writing poetry: 'over-mastered by some thoughts, I yielded an inky tribute unto them'. This is my inky tribute, albeit in prose, to Tony Harrison. Ink is the physical liquid in which he writes his poems, using his fountain pen. And ink is an image binding these essays across the eight decades of his life, from a storybook he read in his childhood to his speech accepting the PEN Pinter Prize in 2009.

Harrison has never explained the title of a short essay he wrote in 1971, included in this collection, 'The Inkwell of Dr Agrippa'. The essay illuminates some of the poems in *The Loiners* (1970), because in it he describes some of his earliest memories of growing up in Leeds. Understanding the full significance of Dr Agrippa's inkwell for Harrison requires looking at an illustrated children's book which made a profound impression on him when he was small. 'The Story of the Inky Boys' is told in *The English Struwwelpeter, or Pretty Stories and Funny Pictures for Little Children*, first published by Friedrich Volckmar of Leipzig in 1848. A copy of this much-reprinted English-language text was possessed and read by Harrison. It is anonymous and in rhyming couplets. Although Heinrich Hoffmann's striking pictures are reproduced without alteration, the words offer a free version rather than a translation of Hoffmann's original German verses of 1845. Despite being rebuked by Dr Agrippa, three racist little white boys are cruel to a black boy:

> Then great Agrippa foams with rage –
> Look at him on this very page!
> He seizes Arthur, seizes Ned,
> Takes William by his little head;
> And they may scream and kick and call,
> Into the ink he dips them all;
> Into the inkstand, one, two, three,
> Till they are black as black can be . . .

Harrison has told me that he particularly likes the grave expression on Dr Agrippa's face in the drawing reproduced opposite: putting the naughty boys morally right is a serious business.

Curiously, in the German version the tall bearded sage is named Saint Nicholas – Santa Claus. It was the anonymous author of the English text who changed him to Dr Agrippa, a mythologised version of the famous early-sixteenth-century German polymath and occultist Heinrich Cornelius Agrippa von Nettesheim. This learned Dr Agrippa was in 1848 culturally familiar, having recently featured in works by both Mary Shelley and Søren Kierkegaard. But by the 1940s none of this will have concerned a little boy in Leeds. What is fascinating is the way that the image and the story stayed in Harrison's mind,

Then great Agrippa foams with rage—
Look at him on this very page!
He seizes Arthur, seizes Ned,
Takes William by his little head;

And they may scream and kick and call,
Into the ink he dips them all;
Into the inkstand, one, two, three,
Till they are black as black can be:
Turn over now, and you shall see.

to re-emerge in the title of his short psycho-biographical essay thirty years later. The rhyming couplets of English popular verse, typified in this children's book, fundamentally affected his evolution as a poet. He explains this process in his essay here on translating Molière.

Such a fusion of 'high' and 'low' culture – the significance of children's rhymes to the translation of canonical French drama – has been central to all Harrison's work, above all *The Trackers of Oxyrhynchus*. It is here personified in the august figure of Dr Agrippa. The celebrated Renaissance man of letters, a representative of elite intellectual culture, appears as a moral exemplar in a popular book for children and speaks like a good fairy in a pantomime. Baptism by ink in the inkwell of an illustrious thinker is, moreover, a suitable image for a poet's initiation rite. A poet whose voice has always been activated in the cause of the voiceless and oppressed will have been drawn to the 'moral' of the tale: that ink can be instrumental in the exposure of racism or any other narrow-minded form of prejudice or inhumanity. And Arthur, Ned and William are made to realise, through their submersion in Dr Agrippa's inkwell, that, as human beings, they are indistinguishable from their black victim; their rite of passage could symbolise the progress of the human soul as it learns about universal human values by being refined through experiencing fine poetry. This collection of Harrison's essays could, therefore, just as well have been entitled *The Inkwell of Dr Agrippa* as *The Inky Digit of Defiance*.

A visual memory from his youth which Harrison *does* describe, in the same 1971 essay, is of the windows over the altar in the chapel of Leeds Grammar School. There were figures, he writes, representing possible professions that the pupils might later follow. One was MILES ('soldier') and another MERCATOR ('businessman'). In my favourite sentence in this volume, Harrison writes that he can't remember the figure portrayed between them, but in adulthood,

> when I close my eyes now I see *Poeta*, the poet,
> sometimes as poised, saintly and acceptable as his
> worldly flankers, sometimes like some half-naked

shaker in the throes of a virulent *scribendi cacoethes*, being belaboured by public-school angels wielding gamma minuses like immense shillelaghs over their glossy Cherry Blossomy hairstyles, driving the poet from the Garden of Eton.

The vocation of POETA and Harrison's working-class identity were thus indissoluble from the start. But it turns out that there were in fact *two* other figures portrayed in the chapel window: an academic, SCHOLASTICUS, and a BENEFACTOR ('philanthropist').

The chapel has long since been turned into the Business School of Leeds University. The British educational system, in which underprivileged children like Harrison could once hope for free grammar-school and university educations, has been taken over by commercial interests, like England in Shakespeare's *Richard II*, 'bound in with shame, / With inky blots, and rotten parchment bonds'. But the two figures in the window which Harrison had forgotten are not irrelevant to his achievements. He is certainly a scholar: the range and depth of his reading and research are staggering, as the notes at the end of this volume, detailing the sources of most of his rich range of quotations and citations, reveal. He is also a benefactor. It is true that in the public imagination he is primarily associated with his most snarling poetic voice – his characteristic, embittered railing against stupidity and injustice, which made him identify with the cynical epigrammatist Palladas from the fourth century AD. Palladas' biting epigrams, a selection of which are reprinted here, along with

Harrison's essay introducing them, scoffingly deprecate the fall of pagan literary and artistic culture to the intolerant theocrats of the new Christian regime. Yet for all his bitterness, the fundamental outlook of Harrison's poetry is always humane and benevolent. There is a philanthropic 'charity' in the best sense, a non-judgemental, inclusive social vision, even in his most superficially harsh and most controversial poem, *v.* (1985).

As an example of his breathtaking erudition, the title of his 'Newcastle Is Peru' (1969) was drawn from an obscure poem attributed to John Cleveland, 'News from Newcastle; or, Newcastle Coal-Pits'. Cleveland was a seventeenth-century satirical poet, little read today, whose scathing tone (although not his Royalist politics) Harrison admires. Cleveland's biographer said that he struck people as a '*Vates* in the whole Import of the Word, both Poet and Prophet'. *Vates* is the oldest Latin word for a creator of poetry. In 1977, the retired Regius Professor of Greek at Oxford, E. R. Dodds, wrote in his autobiography:

> With the possible exception of Louis MacNeice, Yeats is the only poet I have known or encountered who looked just like what he was, a poet – no mere rhymester, but a *vates*, a poet in the full, ancient, arrogant meaning of the term. He behaved like the consecrated priest of a mystery – the mystery of words, which alone are certain good.

All four of these men – Cleveland, MacNeice, Yeats and Dodds, who himself wrote poetry as a young man – are quoted approvingly by Harrison in this book. I gasped when I read Dodds's description, because it fits Harrison perfectly. Charisma, magnetism, a human energy field – none of this language is adequate to describe the effect of his physical presence and his way of talking. He habitually speaks in a manner not too far removed from the sound of his poetry – intermittently elated or playful, but dominantly sardonic and caustic, uncompromisingly honest, sometimes explicit, and always in the resounding Leeds accent of his northern childhood.

The difference lies in the matter of rhythm, for he does not normally converse in metre. But he has devoted his whole life to writing poetry, and has made every penny of his livelihood from it, as a true 'consecrated priest' of 'the mystery of words'. He has published, in comparison, little prose. This makes this volume unique and indispensable to understanding the man, his voice in conversation, his methods and biography. Its title alone, *The Inky Digit of Defiance* (the title also of the published version of his speech on accepting the PEN Pinter Prize in 2009), is informative. He tells us in the eponymous essay that he first heard the phrase on radio in 2009. In Afghanistan some courageous women exercised their right to vote. This was in the face of intimidation, even though the Taliban's ban on women entering polling centres had supposedly been rescinded following the fall of the Taliban government in 2001. Listening to the BBC World Service, Harrison heard the reporter speak 'of women coming from the polling booth proudly displaying fingers marked with indelible ink to show they had voted. "The inky digit of defiance", the reporter called it.' This reminded Harrison of his Uncle Harry, who was deaf and dumb and needed to use signs to communicate. A famous teacher of rhetorical gesture was praised in a 1644 poem for using his hands so eloquently that 'every Digit dictates and doth reach / Unto our sense a mouth-excelling speech'. But Uncle Harry also used a dictionary to communicate, licking his finger to flick through the pages and point to words, often to express anti-Tory opinions. The ink in which the dictionary was printed stained his digit-tip.

These two anecdotes, unified by the image of the inky finger, speak volumes about Harrison's attitude to human life. He has been consistent in his defiantly dissident stance in a class-ridden, sexist world. He has always used his poetic gift as a public vehicle to give voice to the poor and the oppressed. The essays here reveal him speaking up for women everywhere abused, insulted or repressed by men, but also for causes less frequently espoused by the Establishment liberal left. We hear his praise of Cuban poets of the 1960s for their revolutionary project and the insights they gained from Marxism; we feel his sympathy with socialism and his support for the highly unfashionable cause of the British miners during the 1984–5 strike; we come to understand his uncompromising dislike of monarchy and the parts of the Establishment that fawn upon the British royal family; we respect his sense of fellowship and a project shared with all the other republican, rebellious and revolutionary wordsmiths who have used their art as a vehicle for public dissent, and often suffered marginalisation, ridicule or even persecution for it: Milton and May, Shelley and Hugo, Heine and Brecht, Holub, Ritsos, and Zargana,

the imprisoned Myanmar poet with whom Harrison chose
to share the PEN Pinter Prize in 2009.

Dodds's word for describing Yeats as a poet, '*vates*', is
suitable for Harrison in other senses. Dodds, as a Classics
professor, was aware that '*vates*' was the primordial Latin
word for a poet, related in the most remote human antiquity to the Sanskrit verbal root *vad*, 'speak' or 'utter'. The
Romans used the word '*vates*' to describe not just singers or
the composers of songs, but also the sacerdotal men in what
they saw as the barbarian countries to their north, such as
Britannia. It was to the barbarian *vates* that communal rites
were entrusted; his role included safeguarding the tribe's
understanding of 'the philosophy of nature'. In this volume,
Harrison is seen most intensely in touch with his 'barbarian' northern roots in the chapter 'Egil and Eagle-Bark',
describing his quest for a poetic diction in which to translate Aeschylus' *Oresteia* for the National Theatre. This took
him back beyond the language of the medieval mystery
cycle to Old English and early Teutonic poetry, and thence
to the visceral 'kennings', new words compounded out of
two existing elements, in Old Norse and Icelandic. He discovered a linguistic ancestor for his own raw, compounded,
consonantal version of Aeschylus, 'eagle-bark' and all, in the
tenth-century Icelandic poet Egil Skalla-Grimsson, who
once lived in England himself.

The word '*vates*' fell out of use for a time amongst the
culturally insecure ancient Romans. They came under the
spell of Greek literature, began to distrust their prehis-
toric Italian heritage with its 'vatic' priests, and instead
used their Greek word '*poeta*' when they meant a civilised

'poet'. The term '*vates*' was reintroduced by Virgil, a poet with whom Harrison has had a long and intense relationship. In the 1960s, he published, as 'T. W. Harrison', two academic articles on the eighteenth-century reception of Virgil; much more recently, he served as president of the Virgil Society. But he has moved, as he explains in this volume in the essay 'The Tears and the Trumpets', from admiration and emulation of Virgil's craftsmanship to an increasing unease with his political stance as celebrator of the Augustan imperial project.

Virgil liked the term '*vates*' because it has a visionary connotation, meaning 'seer' as well as 'poet', and he wanted to convey the idea of a bard with a sacred task of transcending time to gaze into the future imperial destiny of the Romans. Harrison, who is not a religious man, makes no such oracular claims. He is constitutionally incapable of using poetry to celebrate any political regime, let alone an empire on a massive scale. But his work, if not oracular, has nevertheless proved consistently prescient. Those scholarly articles on the 'reception' of Virgil in the eighteenth century prefigured the emergence in the 1980s of Classical Reception Studies, now a central sub-discipline of academic Classics. In the 1960s, when he was writing them, and in the 1970s, he visited and lived in places that few British poets have ever experienced: Nigeria immediately after it secured full independence from Britain in 1960; Cuba in the early years of the revolutionary government; cold war Czechoslovakia during the Prague Spring; Brazil at the height of the hard-line dictatorial regime. His prose pieces provide shrewd and humane witness to these places at momentous historical moments. They are both prescient and riveting.

Aikin Mata, his 1964 adaptation of Aristophanes' comedy *Lysistrata* to fit local north Nigerian voices, performance styles and social structures, was years ahead of its time. With student actors at Ahmadu Bello University, Zaria, he evolved an unprecedented theatrical language transcending the cultural divisions between Europe and Africa. Within Africa this subsequently encouraged indigenous writers, especially those from Nigeria, to consider the ancient Greek plays when mounting new stage productions. This in turn led to a flowering of homegrown adaptations by writers including Ola Rotimi and Femi Osofisan. Globally, it anticipated the explosion of interest in performing Greek drama, which is now in the professional repertoires of significant theatres in every continent, a development which has been traced precisely to the last years of the 1960s. But in grafting the Aristophanic situation of a war between Athens and Sparta onto the contemporary tribal rivalry between the Yoruba and Ibo peoples, and utilising their indigenous rituals and performance traditions, *Aikin Mata* broke new ground. It anticipated by a decade the 'intercultural' or 'transcultural' trend in world theatre, which saw directors abandoning narrow ideas of national or ethnic theatre traditions to mingle 'eastern' and 'western' repertoires, performance styles, rituals and ethnology: the Japanese director Tadashi Suzuki using Noh conventions to realise Euripides from the late 1970s; and the Russian-French-English Ariane Mnouchkine harnessing Kathakali, Kabuki and Balinese mask and dance traditions to Aeschylean tragedy in her *Les Atrides* in 1990.

Harrison's production was infinitely less well funded and far less widely reported, but he and his collaborator, James Simmons, were some of the earliest pioneers of 'intercultural' Greek theatre.

In *Aikin Mata*, Harrison required some of his male actors to perform female roles. A mixed group of Yoruba and Ibo *men* were required to forget their tribal rivalries and merge identities as a chorus of old Hausa *women*. Such gender-role-inverting or 'gender-blind' practices are familiar enough in serious theatre today, but in the 1960s and 1970s, they were regarded as shockingly avant-garde or vulgarly suggestive of the drag roles in children's pantomimes inherited from the Victorian music-hall tradition of *burletta en travesti*. So when Harrison insisted on using an all-male cast for the *Oresteia* at the National Theatre, being convinced that the full misogyny of the trilogy could only be realised by having all the female roles delivered by male actors, as they had been in the ancient theatre, he encountered opposition from a range of viewpoints. Feminists objected to female actors being deprived, as they saw it, of the opportunity to star in an important production, and aesthetic aficionados disliked seeing men in female costumes, which they felt inappropriate to the dignity of 'high art'. But Harrison's fascination with the light that cross-dressing can throw on restrictive gender ideology has persisted. His most recent play, *Iphigenia in Crimea* (to receive its premiere on BBC Radio in 2017), features British soldiers in 'drag' taking female roles, in a burlesque version of Euripides' *Iphigenia in Tauris*. For the performance they wear frocks that they have looted from a deserted aristocratic house near Sebastopol – something which Harrison, with typically scrupulous research, has discovered actually happened in the British camp, located on the site of the ancient Greek city of Tauric Chersonesos, during the 1854–5 siege.

The unfair treatment of women in professional theatre, as in society, is something of which he is well aware. His account of *Aikin Mata* ends with the wry observation that 'the most enthusiastic reception of the play came from the small, embattled group of female students'. I have always thought of Harrison when I read the magnificent line in Sophocles' *Antigone* about Haemon, who is supporting Antigone and her insistence on burying her dead kin in the face of his father Creon's fury: 'ὅδ᾽, ὡς ἔοικε, τῇ γυναικὶ συμμαχεῖ᾽ ('It seems that this man fights as an ally of the woman') (740). Harrison planned to conclude the all-male *Oresteia* with a satyr play, as Aeschylus' trilogy was originally followed by a satyric *Proteus* (which sadly did not survive the centuries). He wanted women to 'play the half-men/half-goats and wear the phalluses as a mode of comment and redress'. This was made impossible by industrial disputes at the National Theatre, but Harrison's determination to have women play male roles eventually found fruition in *Square Rounds* (1992), which he had started planning as early as 1975, and in which women took almost all the roles. Using female voices to explore the invention of TNT and chlorine gas had the obvious advantage of exposing the intimate relationship between militarism and the masculine identity endorsed by patriarchal society, a synergy which Harrison also exposed in his second adaptation of *Lysistrata*, combined with Euripides' *Hecuba* and entitled *The Common Chorus*. This was set at the women's peace camp outside the US missile base at Greenham Common, Berkshire. It has never been performed in full, although Glenda Jackson delivered some of the speeches in a programme, 'The Memory of Troy', broadcast on BBC Radio 4 on 28 August 1988. *Square Rounds* was staged at the National Theatre, and some critics slammed it for its affinities with vaudeville and cabaret. But the twenty-one women and two men performing in *Square Rounds* were a huge success at the Taganka Theatre in Moscow, where non-realist theatre has historically been rather better understood and appreciated.

Harrison's profound originality can also be seen in his idea of creating a new play out of the fragments of an ancient drama in his *The Trackers of Oxyrhynchus*, which was voted one of the best hundred plays of the twentieth century in the National Theatre Millennium Poll. His essay in this volume explains his lifelong attraction to the almost lost genre of satyr drama, in which august heroes and gods were forced to revel in subversive musical-comedy versions of mythology with a chorus of satyrs – half men and half goats – wearing huge, semi-erect, artificial phalluses. But in piecing together, translating and augmenting the fragments of a satyr play, *The Trackers*, by Sophocles, Harrison was, once again, way ahead of his time. Constructing a powerful modern drama out of the fragments of ancient Greek plays subsequently became a familiar practice. *Trackers*, which premiered in Delphi in 1988, was swiftly followed by Timberlake Wertenbaker's *Love of the Nightingale* (1989, based on Sophocles' *Tereus*) and Silviu Purcărete's *Les Danaïdes* (Avignon, 1996), which supplemented the surviving parts of Aeschylus' *Danaids* trilogy.

The essays here, presented in the chronological order in which they were written, provide unparalleled insights into Harrison's development. 'Fellowship' and 'Shango the Shaky Fairy' show him experimenting with the prose essay as an art form. But they also reveal his urge to dramatise – to write direct speech bringing the conversation with people he had encountered to life, breaking through his first-person narrative, especially where the subject matter is painful. The speech he writes in 'Shango' for the Cuban revolutionary exploring his hopelessly reactionary views on homosexuality is a fascinating case in point. Reading these essays also illuminates his working methods – the endless drafts and the voluminous scrapbooks, now housed in the Brotherton Library in Leeds, into which he pastes quotations, newspaper cuttings, photographs and ideas as he writes. Harrison's prose reveals a candid, sometimes frustrated and disappointed creative artist. He has often not received the funding he needed for important projects, especially film poems. He has frequently suffered attacks by critics who have meretriciously disguised political disagreement as aesthetic judgement.

These prose works also enrich our knowledge of Harrison's personal biography. Although many of his important memories and relationships feature in his poetry, in his prose we catch different glimpses of his early life with his uncles and neighbours in Leeds, of travel with a young family in Cuba and Nigeria, and of innumerable thought processes and conversations with collaborators over delicious bottles of wine. His insights into his friendships with giants of twentieth-century culture are required reading: Hollywood titan George Cukor, stage designer Jocelyn Herbert, writer Harold Pinter, as well as directors and actors including Richard Eyre, Diana Rigg, Peter Hall, Glenda Jackson and his own long-term partner in private life, Sian Thomas. But his accounts of encounters that shaped him with individuals enjoying no such fame are equally significant: with Terezinha, a homeless little girl living under the exit ramp of the National Theatre of Brazil; with the elderly Yorkshire woman who gave him a bust of the poet John Nicholson after seeing *Poetry or Bust*, saying, with mordant Yorkshire wit, that it was as much use to her 'as a chocolate fireguard'.

In a touching paragraph, he tells us that he learned a great deal about the use of cameras in film from his son Max, before Max was afflicted in early adulthood with a cruel psychiatric illness. The least familiar works of Harrison are those using a camera: his film poems. All the scripts have been published, but most of the films themselves, for complex copyright reasons, have not been made widely available and have therefore not been properly understood and valued. This makes his precious essay 'Flicks and this Fleeting Life', as well as the others which talk extensively about film, even more valuable. Although he was an ardent movie-goer as a child and saw every classic of world cinema that was shown when he was studying at Leeds University, his first experience of editing came with the montage of martial clips from documentaries and newsreels with which his Nigerian *Lysistrata*, *Aikin Mata*, had opened in 1964 – once again proving his prescience and appetite for innovation. Although it is now ubiquitous, the incorporation of video within live theatre, while not altogether unprecedented in eastern European performances, was unheard of in Britain in 1964. In that production, Harrison tells us, his Lysistrata put a sudden stop to the filmed combatants by throwing a water pot at the screen on the back wall, thus exploiting the power of the 'hard cut'. Years of experimentation with mutually reinforcing both word and image through careful editing of clip against metre, producing what he calls 'the scansions of edited sequences', came to a climax in his powerful 1998 feature film *Prometheus*. This confronts the viewer with 'a procession of arresting images leading from northern England to eastern Europe and Greece, via the bombing of Dresden, the collapse of socialism and the Holocaust. This procession advances – its sequential logic dictated by poetic values rather than strict chronology – with a measured pace enhanced by Alastair Cameron's meticulous camera work and by precision editing.'

Alongside his creation of the moving images of film, flickering through time at twenty-four frames per second, these essays reveal the extent of Harrison's engagement with 'static' works of visual art. The reader of almost any of his poetry will have noticed his fascination with statues and sculpture and their political uses and abuses. In the film poem *The Gaze of the Gorgon*, he adopts a statue of Heine as narrator, exploring the tragic history of European warfare in Heine's own verse form, the couplet. He knew that the statue of the poet, who was Jewish, was removed from the Bavarian royal family's summer palace on Corfu on the orders of Kaiser Wilhelm II. Harrison's play *Poetry or Bust*, performed at Salts Mill in Bradford in 1993, uses the bust of the 'wool-sorter poet' John Nicholson as a symbol of a poet who 'sells out' his political principles in return 'for the praise of genteel admirers, money or fame'. But the essays here reveal the extent to which Harrison's imagination has been aroused by contemplating artworks from all over the world. They include carved wooden images of Shango (the hermaphroditic thunder spirit in the Yoruba religion) and the depictions of the poets Arion and Orpheus painted in the fifteenth century by Andrea Mantegna on the ceiling of the bridal chamber of the Ducal Palace in Mantua. Harrison's poetry has been informed equally by a fresco in the National Archaeological Museum in Naples depicting a verdant Mount Vesuvius *before* the eruption which destroyed Pompeii; by Rembrandt's *Descent from the Cross*; and, in *Phaedra Britannica*, his translation of Racine's tragedy to India under the British Raj, by erotic eighteenth-century art from Rajasthan in north-western India.

Harrison has adapted works by all four great classical Athenian dramatists: Aeschylus, Sophocles, Euripides and Aristophanes. Yet he has not translated any tragedy by Sophocles, held by Aristotle and the Victorians to be the most 'perfect' of the tragic poets. He relished, rather, working on Sophocles' theatrical style as exemplified in the more boisterous, rowdy, comical key of satyr drama, as he explains here in 'The Trackers of Oxyrhynchus'. Yet there is much that is Sophoclean about Harrison's own theatre: a pleasure in the 'plain words' for which Sophocles was admired in antiquity, in letting poetry work its own effect without overelaborate visual effects, in unflinching acknowledgement of the absolute unfairness of human life and the undeserved extremes of human suffering. The famous view of Matthew Arnold – that Sophocles 'saw life steadily, and saw it whole' (in the sonnet 'To a Friend', 1849) – often comes into my mind when I read Harrison's writing. This may seem incongruous. The anger and demotic verve of Harrison's poetry may seem a world away from Arnoldian elegiac wistfulness and urbanity. But his poetry reveals that he has stared at the best and worst that human existence affords, if not with absolute steadiness, then with unflinching steadfastness. He has seen it steadfastly and he has certainly seen it 'whole'.

For everything he has ever done, said and written is underpinned by an unerringly consistent and coherent intellectual structure. He looks at the material world from a perspective that is fundamentally informed by Marxist analysis, which is in turn grounded in the ancient atomism of Epicurus and Lucretius. Harrison's cosmos is in constant flux; plants, humans and other organic bodies are in a perpetual process of coming to be and passing away, the matter that constitutes them dispersing, as they die, back into the environment. He is intrigued by horticulture, compost, cooking, alimentary processes and decomposing rubbish heaps. While his work is located in real, specific places, and gains much of its power from its physical particularity, his geopolitical perspective as a human being is never less than global. He is fascinated by cartography, physical geography, geology and the history of science, the latter being most clear in his fascination with the way chemistry, physics and technology have been used in the development of weapons – machine guns, explosives, chlorine gas and nuclear bombs. He has no religion and believes in no afterlife; there is no providential god for Harrison, and all his work laments that life is short and too often brutal, that human history has consistently disappointed utopian dreamers, and that apparent 'progress' takes us backwards away from the light. For these reasons, like the ancient Greeks who have so consistently inspired him, he believes in savouring happiness and sensory pleasure from landscape and sunshine, food and wine, love, sex, friendship and literature.

Harrison's passion for the products of human artistic creativity is inexhaustible. To say 'passion for the Arts' would be a ludicrous distortion, since 'the Arts' are not normally taken to include all the countless forms taken by words and images, across the social and cultural spectrum, that he has enjoyed and that have enriched his imagination. As Richard Eyre has put it, 'Tony wants the whole body of society, not just its head, to be involved in art.' These essays complement his poetry by detailing the sheer diversity of his cultural experiences and how they have informed his own creative output. The most canonical high operas by Monteverdi, Verdi, Smetana and Orff jostle here with working-class entertainers George Formby and Vesta Tilley. Films seen only in art-house cinemas, by Eisenstein, Torre Nilsson and Tarkovsky, appear alongside James Cagney in *White Heat* and Disney's *Bambi*. Almost forgotten translators like Edward Powys Mathers and minor novelists like Nancy Bogen rub shoulders with Dryden and Dostoyevsky. The work in which he offered his most eloquent exploration of the way the Arts have been used to create and maintain social divisions was *The Trackers of Oxyrhynchus*, where the human–animal hybridity of the satyr, and what Adrian Poole has aptly called the 'ribald generic indeterminacy' of satyr drama, allowed Harrison to meditate on the chasm in his own previous theatre between the supposedly 'high' culture of the *Oresteia* and the folk culture of *Bow Down* (1977) and *The Mysteries*. But Joe Kelleher points out that Harrison had previously chosen, for the cover of his translations from Martial, a photograph of a carved stone satyr, serving as a kind of mask for Harrison's persona as a translator. This persona is neither neutral nor self-effacing, but has 'a diabolically gleeful grin', suggesting that the transformation of poetry from the ancient language to modern vernacular is the work of a personality with 'an inscrutable agenda' of his own. The same applies to the satyrs in *Trackers*. His clog-dancing satyrs perform his own manifesto not only on the gulf that separates elite art from popular culture, but on the system of social stratification that has always silenced the poor, the hungry, the oppressed and the persecuted (represented in the flayed body of Marsyas, above all) and excluded them from the rights and privileges enjoyed higher up the class system.

It is no accident that Harrison has found in classical antiquity his most fruitful medium for discussing the class politics of art. The boys at Leeds Grammar School studied Latin and Greek to make them feel superior to other children, but it did not work on the Loiner Poet. Harrison has faced up to the quandary of working in a medium whose consumers are not of the same class as that into which he was born – and to which he remains loyal – through his own brand of classicism. His radical treatment of classics has underpinned his quest for a public role for a poet who never forgets the way the upper and middle classes' prosperity has been built on the working class's deprivation. Harrison uses classical myth in the attempt to forge an inclusive public poetry rather than an exclusive curriculum. He uses a classical tradition of public poetry in a way that is consistently class-conscious and oppositional: it is, in Patrick Deane's acute formulation, 'the deft and opportunistic annexation of classical authority by a poet not born to it'. These essays, especially those on the *Oresteia*, *Phaedra Britannica* and *Prometheus*, show Harrison dipping his pen into his inkwell to use ancient Greek and Roman culture in ways that help us confront the darkest, most tragic elements of human experience.

Yet, in the final analysis, it is the exuberance of his classicism for which he may be best remembered. I have always felt that much of his work shares an attitude with the final scene of Jacques Offenbach's uproarious *Orpheus in the Underworld* (1858), where the Olympian gods hold a party in Hades. Bored by Zeus's old-fashioned taste in sedate dances, they invent the riotous 'infernal gallop', better known as the cancan. Critics were appalled by the irreverence Offenbach had shown towards ancient Greek culture, his 'profanation of holy and glorious antiquity'. But another way of looking at it is that Offenbach was using the

Greeks to take society and entertainment into the future, or, as Harrison puts it in 'Facing Up to the Muses', to take the human race *forward with the Greeks*. To use his own inimitable phrase from another essay, '*The Misanthrope*: Jane Eyre's Sister', the whole life's work of this *vates* from Leeds has truly been 'a *Jack and the Beanstalk* act'. He has braved 'the somnolent ogre of a British classical education to grab the golden harp'.

December 2016

Edith Hall is Professor of Classics at King's College London. She regularly broadcasts on the BBC and has been a consultant for professional theatre companies, including the RSC, the National Theatre, Shakespeare's Globe and the ENO. She has published more than twenty books on Greek and Roman culture and their reception. Her most recent books are *Adventures with Iphigenia in Tauris* (OUP, 2013) and *Introducing the Ancient Greeks* (Random House, 2014). She is the recipient of the Erasmus Prize of the European Academy and an Honorary Doctorate from the University of Athens.

Introduction: Inkless and Digital

I am sitting in the same room in Delphi that has been my creative base for the poems I keep writing here, like 'Wasted Ink', begun in August 2008 and published in the *London Review of Books* in October that year, and 'Polygons', worked on here obsessively through 2013 and 2014, until finally published in the *London Review of Books* in February 2015, to coincide with my being awarded the David Cohen Prize for Literature. It was also the Cohen Foundation that helped to fund *The Trackers of Oxyrhynchus* here in Delphi. This is a room where I've never found it difficult to think that everything I do is poetry – for the page, the stage or the screen – because it still reverberates with the poetry and the strong rhythms of the plays I have written and directed for spaces in Delphi:

1988: *The Trackers of Oxyrhynchus* in the stadium above for the one-performance world premiere. Among the people who saw it there was Piero Bordin, who invited me to bring it to his newly started venue in Austria, on the Danube between Vienna and Bratislava. I took the version I revised in 1990 for the NT's Olivier and then did an original piece, *The Kaisers of Carnuntum*, in the ancient amphitheatre in the manically busy year of 1995.

It was this revised version of *Trackers* that I took to Salts Mill in Saltaire, where Jonathan Silver afterwards commissioned a new piece for the mill. This became *Poetry or Bust*, which I wrote and directed in 1993, about the Airedale poet John Nicholson, who drowned drunk in the Aire a few minutes away from the wool-sorting shed we used as our theatre.

1995: *The Labourers of Herakles*, to initiate the building site for a new ancient-style theatre to be built in the grounds of the Cultural Centre of Delphi. This piece, with its chorus of nine cement mixers and a vast Herakles cement silo out of which voices and music came, was based on some fragments of Phrynikos. I came on myself as the spirit of Phrynikos to remind the audience that drama has its responsibilities in the face of the savageries of war, like that just over the mountains in Bosnia. I went to Bosnia after the play and wrote poems from Donji Vakuf and Sarajevo.

2005: *Hecuba* of Euripides, as the inauguration of the newly completed theatre, to be called, appropriately enough after my piece of ten years before, the Theatre of Phrynikos.

It was also here in Delphi that I began to think of my film of *Prometheus*, partly because of the costumes and masks still displayed in the house of Angelos Sikelianos and his American wife Eva Palmer, who revived the use of the ancient theatre in 1927 with their *Prometheus Bound* of Aeschylus. One story of that performance always haunted me: that the cries of the chained and suffering Prometheus could be heard echoing from the Phaedriades all the way down to Galaxidi, which I'm looking at now from my room. Two years ago, at every sunset for four days, we shared the balcony and the view (and some local wine from Distomo) with Peter Symes, with whom I've had a long and hugely fruitful collaboration on my four film poems on graveyards, *Loving Memory*; one on Alzheimer's, *Black Daisies for the Bride*, which won the Prix Italia in 1994; *The Gaze of the Gorgon*, shot in Corfu and Germany; and, finally, a collaboration with Peter and me and Oliver Taplin, with whom I have shared many earlier times in Delphi, on the journey of the severed head of Orpheus along the Hebrus through Bulgaria and into the sea and finally to Lesbos.

There are many loving memories in the pages that follow about my great and much-missed collaborator Jocelyn Herbert, with whom I first went to Greece for the two performances in Epidaurus of the NT's *Oresteia* in 1981, and who went on to design almost all the plays I wrote and directed. I came with Jocelyn and with my partner Sian in 1996, and we all came together a second time in 1998, Jocelyn's last visit before she died in 2003. I remember the three of us held hands and stood in the centre of the ancient theatre of Delphi. As we did so, Jocelyn raised her head towards the looming Phaedriades and saw an eagle. It was, of course, two eagles sent by Zeus meeting up above that defined Delphi as the *omphalos* – 'the navel of the earth'. For the last twenty years Sian and I have come here together, and we always remember Jocelyn in the same way by commemorating the three of us standing on the ancient stage and holding hands. This year, 2016, Sian and I stood in the same theatre, and as we whispered the name of Jocelyn (Joc!) an eagle appeared high up above us in the same place as before. Jocelyn was eighty-one on her last visit. And next year I will reach my eightieth year, when I hope I will sit and brood and compose again in this same room, though various physical afflictions have made an inevitable question mark loom a little larger as the months go by.

This room is between two places where I have asked my loved ones to scatter my ashes when I can no longer make the journey to Delphi as a living being. The first is a steep climb up above, to the now unused stadium where I put on *The Trackers of Oxyrhynchus* for the first time in 1988. Thirty years ago, I used to run up and down from here to the stadium at least three times a day. Now it takes me almost half the day to go up once. The second place I'd like my ashes scattered in is a forty-minute drive down below, beyond the sea of olives in Amphissa and the port of Itea to the sea and the small town of Galaxidi, where we go to swim and from the sea look up to see Delphi far above, and over Delphi the peaks of Parnassus, the home of the Muses, with Melpomene, the Muse of Tragedy, the most supreme.

I wrote a poem half down in Galaxidi but finished in this room in 2006 called 'Galaxidi':

> Those golden hairs I'm stroking on your thigh
> I only get to glimpse in this Greek light,
> and only here do claw-snags on my hand
> (from grappling with our lunch of *garavides*,
> the Greek word for the local langoustines),

the back of which has those dark freckle marks
my grampa called his 'grave-spots', catch
on your glittering Galaxidi-gilded hairs.

The only year for many I did not spend some time in this
room was 2011, when I began a version of the *Iphigenia in
Tauris* of Euripides, encouraged by funding organised by
Edith Hall, who also accompanied me, Sian, my daughter Jane, an archaeologist, and David Braund, a classicist
and Crimean specialist, to the Crimea to recce the most
northerly ancient Greek theatre near Sebastopol, not far
from the ruins of the temple of Artemis, where Iphigenia
was priestess after being saved by the goddess from being
sacrificed by her father Agamemnon at Aulis. This was one
of what I call my 'kamikaze' projects. I wanted, as always, to
imagine it in the specific space of the ruined theatre, made
more than slightly awkward by the presence of the ruins of
a small early Orthodox church considered by contemporary
Crimeans as probably more important than the ancient
Greek ruins, which were discovered in 1954 but were not
very accessible until the end of the cold war, as the area was
where the Soviets had their nuclear-submarine base.

In the Crimea we all bathed in the Black Sea and looked
across at the lights on the shores of Russia. I had to buy
a towel, and it had on it a colourful map of the Crimea
showing Sebastopol, with the ancient site of Chersonesos
near by, and Kerch and Yalta, where the house of Chekhov
is, which we visited and was where we were given tea sweet-
ened with a cherry jam made from Chekhov's orchard. That
swim in the Black Sea later gave me my poem 'Black Sea

Aphrodite', which I also worked on in this very room when I again came to Delphi.

All the negotiations with the Crimeans finally came to nothing and Putin's annexation of the Crimea made a performance of *Iphigenia* unlikely. I had a very welcome workshop at the National Theatre Studio, the place where I had started *Trackers* and *The Labourers of Herakles*, but no further interest from the present NT management in any of my work. I had finally chosen to set it in 1854, during the Crimean War, with the tragedy enacted by all-male soldiers playing Iphigenia and the female chorus. Happily, this intrigued Emma Harding at the BBC, and it will be performed on Radio 3 about the time this book comes out and I have finally made eighty, and hopefully before the scattering of ashes above in the stadium and below in the sea at Galaxidi.

A number of things I use for swimming in the sea at Galaxidi dry on the balcony railings of this room. After a swim down at Galaxidi, and maybe a meal, and the drive back up to Delphi, I spread my damp Crimean towel out to dry on the railings of my balcony and reflect on the Russian script derived from Greek: Херсонес – 'Chersonesos' – founded by the Greeks in the fifth century BC, where an ancient theatre exists near to the ruins of the temple of Artemis, where the play is set. Alongside the Crimean towel is a white T-shirt also with Cyrillic script, saying, Пловдивски античен театър – 'Plovdiv Ancient Theatre' – which I bought in Bulgaria while making the Orpheus film with Peter Symes and Oliver Taplin. Our film, titled *Metamorpheus*, followed the severed head of

Orpheus down the Hebrus and over the sea to Lesbos. This is the one white T-shirt I possess, as all the others are black with the Greek text of Nikos Kazantzakis: Δεν ελπίζω τίποτα. Δεν φοβούμαι τίποτα. Είμαι λέφτερος – 'I hope for nothing. I fear nothing. I am free.' There are usually two of them drying on the balcony railing. And they found their way into my poem 'Polygons', all five of them.

There is also a battered baseball cap with a Florida gator on it in an orange T-shirt. Its peak is shredded. I use it when swimming to protect my bald head with the spreading 'grave-spots' from the sun. As it dries on the balcony I remembered with Peter two unrealised projects imagined for Florida. One was to be set in Gainesville, near to where I had lived in the late 1970s and early 1980s with my then wife Teresa Stratas. The film was to be called *Fast Forward* and was about the Florida Gators football team, and Halloween with its pumpkin lanterns, and the fact that a serial killer had been at large around the campus at the same time, and that my son Max, who had chosen to study in the university there, had a serious breakdown because of it all. The other unrealised project was set in Arcadia, Florida, where the first rattlesnake canning factory had been set up by George End in 1931. He claimed to have canned every part of the snake 'except the hiss'! It was also the place where a prototype flying bomb had been devised. The film we never got to make was to have been called *Et in Arcadia Ego*.

There are other rooms and balconies where I've sat in Delphi, especially in the Cultural Centre, which I can see to the right if I stand up on this balcony. Seamus Heaney and I had adjoining rooms and balconies when we attended the performances and conference at the centre and spoke about our own work on Greek tragedy (and, in my case, the satyr play!). Now, his death haunts me here, though it was down in the village that I first knew of it. On 31 August 2013, Sian and I had gone down to eat under the plane tree where we often eat. Next to the taverna is a kiosk that used to sell foreign newspapers but now only sells Greek ones. Hanging up secured by a clothes peg was the Greek paper *Ethnos*, with a large picture of Seamus on the front. That could only mean one thing: that he had died. The kiosk was opposite a derelict building that was the first hotel in Delphi, the Vouzas, where Jocelyn Herbert told me she had stayed with George Devine in the 1950s. Sometimes dinner was arranged in the hotel for guests of the Delphi Festival, and I had eaten there with Seamus. My poem 'Polygons' grew from this moment into something else, though it wasn't finished until 2014.

Exactly one year later, we were sitting here on this balcony when the room's phone rang and Michael Kustow's partner, Jane, told us he was dead. The following is what I said at his memorial:

MICHAEL KUSTOW (1939–2014)
I have labels attached by drawing pins to the shelves that carry the hundreds of notebooks of all my projects in poetry, theatre and film. And there is a large, ever-growing section labelled 'Unrealised Projects', which I was forced to add to last year with some bitterness after being given a two-year runaround by some nameless (for now!) BBC commissioning editor. I slammed the

notebook for work on the new but never to be realised
film poem onto the shelf with a curse and went off to
Delphi in Greece, where over the last thirty years I'd
done a number of theatre projects, and where I could
recuperate from my disappointment. Soon I found
myself thinking of Michael Kustow, who, though he'd
had no direct involvement in these Delphi projects,
nonetheless took the trouble to come to Greece to see
them and be supportive. And I began to think of the
notebooks next to the 'Unrealised Projects' labelled '*The
Mysteries*' or '*The Oresteia* at the National Theatre', both
of which Michael had been instrumental in bringing to
Channel 4. And there was the opera *Yan Tan Tethera*,
about shepherds and sheep-counting, for which I'd
written the libretto and Harrison Birtwistle the music.
It was an opera the BBC had commissioned and then
chickened out of, which Michael snapped up. In his
book *One in Four: A Year in the Life of a Channel Four
Commissioning Editor* [London: Chatto & Windus,
1987], Michael remembers that Harry Birtwistle
had rung him to say that we had both decided that
we'd like the opera dedicated to him. 'I can hardly
say how pleased and proud I am [he writes] . . . It's
a true reward when artists . . . acknowledge that you
have some special gift as an encourager, a sustainer,
an eliciter, a fellow spirit.' Michael was all those – 'an
encourager, a sustainer, an eliciter, a fellow spirit'. And
he was all those things when he brought Richard Eyre's
film of my reading of my poem *v.* to Channel 4, which
brought the front-page fury of the *Daily Mail* down on

our heads. I found myself almost every day thinking of
Michael in Delphi in August 2014, when we had a call
on this room's phone to say that he had died.

Every time I went to Delphi I sent him a postcard
of the ancient stadium in Delphi where *The Trackers of
Oxyrhynchus* had its world premiere in 1988. Michael
had helped to try and find me backing to take it there
and to have it filmed, though even his enthusiastic
eloquence didn't manage that one. Unlike others, he
saw nothing strange in my being a poet in film or in the
theatre and directing my own, what I called 'kamikaze'
performances. Michael the 'encourager' encouraged me,
and what is more, unlike anyone from the NT, actually
came to them all, whether in Salts Mill, Yorkshire, the
ancient Roman stadium in Carnuntum in Austria on
the Danube for *The Kaisers of Carnuntum*, or in Delphi
again for *The Labourers of Herakles* on a building site.
Not only was he one of the few who came from Britain
to see the productions, he later wrote an enthusiastic
Introduction to Volume 3 in the Faber collection of
my plays, in which these 'kamikaze' productions were
eventually printed.

It was during and after this project in 1995 that
Michael began to perform his 'eliciter' and 'encourager'
roles again by urging me, after a number of film poems
I'd made for the BBC and Channel 4, to write and
direct a film for the cinema. And eventually, for Film
Four, in 1998, I did and made *Prometheus*, with Michael
as executive producer, which translates in Michael's case
into 'encourager, sustainer, eliciter, fellow spirit'.

Another notebook in the 'Unrealised Projects' is
for a film which I regret not making but which was in
nobody's power to retrieve. But for me it shows how
Michael could respond enthusiastically to the briefest,
even craziest of suggestions, on one page faxed from
the Amazon. I'd gone to Colombia to do a reading
in Medellín, and then went south to Leticia on the
Amazon and got a boatman to take me up the river
between Colombia and Brazil. In that year, 1994, the
two neighbouring countries were expecting to play each
other in the football World Cup final. I went past a
wooden house tied by lianas and ropes to trees to stop it
drifting away. A boy and a girl, both wearing the blond
afro wig of '*El Pibe*' Valderrama, were kicking a football
and balancing on floating logs, until the river carried
the ball away. On the veranda snuffled a *chiguero*, a
giant kind of rat the size of a wild boar. Inside, two men
in hammocks were watching the football on TV. Also
watching were six macaws, which are, of course, red,
blue and yellow – the colours of the Colombian team.
Whenever Colombia scored, the macaws squawked,
'*Gol! Gol! Gol!*' As soon as I got off the river, I sent a fax
from the small hotel on its banks with only these details
to Michael, saying it would make a great film if the
final were between Brazil and Colombia, knowing that
there was no one else who would respond. He didn't
attribute my sketched suggestions to the influences of
Colombian powders. He was on the case immediately,
encouraging and sustaining, but sadly Colombia didn't
make the final and we never made the film, but I can't

imagine anyone else taking up that brief hint of a project with such encouraging alacrity. I now feel there are more people helping to unrealise projects than helping to realise them, and it makes me miss Michael even more. He sent me his *One in Four* book, inscribed: 'For Tony, comrade and chum'. And that was how I felt about him. He asked me for my view of his book, and I remember I wrote to say he should stop writing apologetically about being carried away by his own 'enthusiasm' or 'earnestness', as I was always amazed how undiminished his enthusiasm could be. He was a rare and utterly warm enabler.

He helped me to realise some of my most cherished projects. I'll always be grateful to him, 'encourager, sustainer, eliciter, fellow spirit'.

On this Delphi balcony death is part of all my sunset thoughts, of those I have mentioned and all the actors and collaborators, recalled in the various introductions that are gathered in this book, who are no longer here. I remember seeing on an English balcony off a hospital room the actor Walter Sparrow, who played the chain-smoking ex-miner who was my Prometheus, with his fennel stalk/constantly lit fag. I went to the hospital with Alistair Cameron, who'd been the cameraman on my film. Walter was dying from lung cancer caused by a lifetime's heavy smoking. He struggled out of bed, and we helped him to his chair on the balcony. He sat down and lit up a fag, and with it held in his nicotine-stained digits of defiance he did the whole of the smoking speech at the end of *Prometheus* from memory:

You just get t'first drag down your throat 'n
some bugger's barking it's *verboten*.
Dictators, deities, they're all t'same
forbidding men fags, fruit or flame.
First Zeus wi' t'fire then t'God of t'chapel's
obsession wi' forbidding apples.
One crunch into that contraband
gave men t'knowledge God had banned.
We've got t'knowledge, we've got t'fire,
we've raised ussens up out of t'mire.
Diso-bloody-bedience got us over
t'barbed-wire fences of Jehovah.
But men thesens bring back barbed wire
round t'Bramleys and round t'bakehouse fire.
There's not one joy but what some berk'll
want it ringed wi' a red circle.
Gods or men or summat similar,
'ermes or some town hall 'immler,
those in power'd like red ring
round almost bloody everything.

He died a few days later.

Then there are this year's deaths down below. Christophoros, who had a place for coffee just round the corner
from the Castalian Spring and overlooking the gymnasium
where the column lay that Byron had etched his name on
in 1809, which is totally neglected and will soon disappear.
I took Christophoros down to see it. He never had. I tried
to get the Delphi mayor of the time to do something about
the column for the 2009 bicentenary of Byron's visit, but

nothing happened and the neglect and fading away continues. Like the stadium above, no one is allowed in the
gymnasium, as they once were, due to dangerous rockfalls.
When we walked to the Castalian Spring to fill up our bottles, we always used to have a coffee with Christophoros.
He died a few months ago. As did Panagiotis, who in the
old days of the Delphi Festival ran the taverna Gargantuas,
where all the performers went to eat and drink into the
small hours after a show. I can never forget walking down
the steps with Jocelyn and my actors after the *Labourers of
Herakles*, and the gathered diners, led by Yuri Lyubimov,
all rising to give us a standing ovation. Lyubimov later
invited me to do something at his theatre, the Taganka, and
so I went to Moscow a few times to prepare and direct a
Russian version of *Square Rounds*, which finally redeemed
the play for me. I'd done it in the NT's Olivier in 1992,
but most of the actors were stuck in television naturalism,
which for me still ruins most of the theatre I see. One of the
exceptions was Sian Thomas, now my partner. Panagiotis
had to leave the old premises and cross the road, to have
a few tables inside the small new space and four or five
outside on the pavement. We stayed loyal to him and his
wife, Panagiota, and his son, Stephanos, and eat down
the hill on a lot of our nights. He died a few months ago.
Each meal we take there keeps Panagiota's grief still raw,
though Panagiotis had been very ill for ten years. As she
takes our orders, we talk about him. On the night he left
the old taverna, we were his final and only customers. We'll
probably be at the new place tonight, on a shaky pavement
table facing the mulberry trees from the old taverna, and

opposite a kiosk that was run by Andreas, who had been my production manager on *Hecuba* and who would always come across and share some wine with us. Now, the kiosk is shuttered and a 'For Rent' notice painted on it, like many of my other favourite Delphi haunts, as one by one they close. Stephanos, the son of Panagiotis, always asks at the end of our meal if he can drive us back up the steep hill. I always say, 'It is better for my heart if I go on foot.' It becomes a ritual, especially after the times he had given us a lift before I had my dodgy damaged knees replaced at the brilliant Freeman Hospital in Newcastle, when I couldn't get up the hill at all and it took me all day to shuffle with a stick down to the Castalian Spring, which I saw as essential to my recovery. I couldn't even think of climbing to the stadium to remember my manic self of thirty years before, running up there sometimes three times a day.

My moods on the balcony are often now very elegiac. Which is probably appropriate also for the reason that this collection of introductions to my theatre and film projects seems to me to be almost like a set of obituaries, sometimes affectionate enough, sometimes defensive. The doing of it, that manic energy I used to have for these projects, I have often been asked or gently bullied into describing, works only in the transience of the performance itself.

I look down at Galaxidi, where I took Vanessa Redgrave and the whole *Hecuba* company for a swim and lunch at Tasos's tavern. Tasos is now dead, but yesterday Sian and I ate at his *psarotaverna*, now run by his son Panagiotis and every bit as delicious, with its beetroot leaves, octopus and mussels, which come from a place I can see here from the room's balcony. It is the setting for the poem written here I've mentioned above, 'Wasted Ink'. And here I would be wasting even more ink if I were using, as I always did, my fountain pen and paper to draft poems or plays and be left with my digits typically inky. As the sun sets over the mountains I no longer climb but celebrate in front of me, I hope that my defiance isn't diminishing, though this text is inkless and digital. As the sun sets, the cicadas fall suddenly silent. So do I.

Tony Harrison
224 Amalia Delphi
August 2016

Aikin Mata

1966

'The Greeks'
They care for the outward show of this life,
but of the life to come they are heedless.
The Koran

THE LYSISTRATA OF ARISTOPHANES

Aristophanes (*c.*450–385? BC) is the only writer of Greek old comedy whose work survives in more than isolated fragments. Eleven of his plays are extant. Aristophanes wrote *Lysistrata* in 412 BC, at a time when Athens was on the brink of total disaster in the prolonged Peloponnesian War with Sparta and her allies, which Thucydides called 'the greatest disturbance in Greek History'. The play was produced in 411 BC, at one of the great Athenian religious festivals. It is one of the most admirable things in Greek culture that, at the worst time of a bitter war, which would eventually mean the collapse of the Athenian Empire in 404 BC and the downfall of Athenian civilisation, this play, which mocks the whole concept of war and makes an 'indecent' but deeply pacifist plea for an immediate truce between Athens and Sparta and for peace in general, was performed at a public festival. 'The Greeks', said Werner Jaeger, 'placed laughter on the same plane with thought and speech as an expression of intellectual freedom.' A culture without such laughter, however progressive or religious, is an inadequate one, and it is a kind of measure of later European societies that the *Lysistrata* has often been considered too licentious to perform. The *Lysistrata* of Aristophanes is now well over 2,000 years old, but its laughter and its purpose are perennially meaningful.

More recently, Professor Erik H. Erikson, the Freudian psychologist and Professor of Human Development at Harvard University, looking for a solution to the desperate problems of war and general human aggression, came to a similar conclusion:

> It may well be that war cannot be banned until women, for the sake of worthwhile survival, dare to recognise and to support the as yet undeveloped power of unarmed resistance.

It is a long time since Aristophanes said the same thing, but it would be difficult to say it better.

FOREWORD

Aikin Mata was written for a specific group of student actors at Ahmadu Bello University, Zaria, in northern Nigeria. The year before, the same group had won the first prize in the Students' Drama Festival at Ibadan with a production of Wole Soyinka's *The Lion and the Jewel*. This group and other local groups had, between them, performed most of the published plays by modern Nigerian dramatists, and they wished to do something different, and yet they were not prepared to tackle Shakespeare or any of the classics of English theatre. They liked the mixture of drama, mime, music and dance in *The Lion and the Jewel*. An adaptation of a Greek comedy seemed the best solution, and in particular the *Lysistrata* of Aristophanes, with its great basic comic plot, particularly relevant in a country where women have not yet reached political equality with men, and where the 'sex war' is a recurrent source of humour. It seemed to us too that an adaptation of the play into Nigerian terms would not only draw fully upon the various acting, dancing and musical talents we had available, and exploit relevant or potentially relevant comic themes, but also that, by restoring music and dance to an integral place in a production of a Greek comedy, the play itself could be performed in a manner nearer to the Greek than the kind of productions one has in European theatre and on radio, with effete angelic choral speaking and emasculated dancing. Masquerades like the Yoruba *Egungun* of Oshogbo, with their dual sacred and profane functions as ancestor spirits and as comic entertainers, seem closer to Greek comedy than anything one has in modern Europe. The particular brand of satire of different ethnic groups in the Oshogbo *Agbegijo*, with its *Gambari* (Hausa man), *Tapa* (Nupe man) and *Oimbo* (Europeans), and in the popular Yoruba travelling theatres like the Afolayan Ogunsola Theatre, seemed particularly suited to the *Lysistrata*. For this reason we had Yoruba and Ibo actors playing Hausa and Fulani characters and a mixed group of Yoruba and Ibo *men* as the chorus of old Hausa *women*. The masks that were used were a studied compromise between Nigerian and Greek traditions. The music and dance was evolved from various traditional dances and an inter-tribal variety of instruments were used, just as Attic and Doric modes were mingled in Greek comedy.

A basic linguistic division exists in the original Greek play between Attic Greek and the Doric Greek spoken by the Spartans, which the Athenians never tired of mocking as a substandard form of their own 'received pronunciation'. Existing translations of the *Lysistrata* have used either a Scots dialect or the accent of the American 'Deep South' to recreate this linguistic division. In Nigeria we had a ready-made distinction between 'standard' English and pidgin English, and the northerners in the play speak 'standard' and the southerners speak pidgin. This helped to emphasise the spirit of inter-tribal parody as a basic ingredient of the comedy of the adaptation, and since we had no real wars to draw upon for a parallel to the Peloponnesian War, we had to make it imaginary, drawing upon latent or blatant tribal rivalries. The whole play is, of course, a plea for mutual goodwill, and all tribes in the play have their fair share of parody and lampoon.

While *Aikin Mata* was being auditioned and rehearsed, a number of European members of the university made objections to the performance of such a play, which has a notorious reputation in Europe, especially amongst those who have neither read it nor seen it produced, and has often been the source of prurient scandal and attempts at censorship. All kinds of fearful speculations about the effects of such a frankly bawdy play were aired, ranging from the farcical – that outbursts of self-indulgent sexuality would occur on the campus – to the traditional outcries levelled against the stage since the theatres were closed in England during the seventeenth century. The basis of the objection was that the plot of the play presumed in the audience a knowledge that husbands sleep with their wives and are likely to suffer if their wives refuse sexual intercourse over a prolonged period. In the society of Lysistrata woman's only weapon was her sexual attraction, as Pope writes:

Power all their end and beauty all their means.

Finally, a deputation was made to the Vice-Chancellor, Sir Norman Alexander, who would not entertain any of the objections, and made it quite clear that censorship in any form was inimical to the whole idea of a university.

After the play was performed in March 1964, to capacity audiences from the university and the town, there were none of the expected dreadful consequences or deputations either Christian or Muslim. The would-be censors had suggested, among other things, that Muslims would seriously object to the spectacle of Muslim women taking an oath over a calabash of wine, since the consumption of alcohol is forbidden in Islam. In actual fact, the audience, which contained a great many devout Muslims, accepted the scene in the spirit of comedy as just one more outrageous way in which the women could demonstrate their defiance of a male-dominated society. In any case, jokes about Muslims drinking are frequent in Hausa and several neologisms among 'initiates', like *jajaye hiyu* and *Krolar Kaduna*, refer-ring to the lacing of soft drinks with something more intoxicating, have found their way into the language.

Significantly enough, the most enthusiastic reception of the play came from the small, embattled group of female students.

Fellowship

1969

I had always been under the naïve impression that
UNESCO was a surefire incantation for the raising of international goodwill. Driving from the airport in Havana at
three in the morning past the VIETNAM VENCERÁ posters with the secretary of the Cuban National Commission
for UNESCO, I said that I hoped to travel into the interior,
as they called it, and maybe see the initiation of the *zafra*
(sugar cane harvest), in which the Soviet fleet were to par-
ticipate so nobly instead of whoring round Havana like the
imperialist marine. 'No,' he said, 'you look too much like a
Yankee.' No one else thought so. Whenever I walked along
the Malecón (esplanade) I was followed by boys shouting,
'*Hey, Ruso,*' or '*Hey, Tovarich, da me chicle.*' So much so that
after almost two months of it I finally delivered a lecture
to one persistent got-any-gum-chummer. Didn't he realise
that chewing gum was a North American confection and
didn't he know the insult he offered to a Soviet comrade by
begging for imperialist *chicle*? He seemed chastened, then
said, 'Give me your belt then.' If I wasn't a Russian I was
Czech. I was walking up and down in old Havana, waiting for the bank to open to draw my UNESCO pittance,
when a workman beckoned me over to the welding yard
and asked me if I'd like to see the shop. There was an oldish,

deliberately distinguished-looking man standing guard over a former Coca-Cola fridge. *Coca-Cola el refresco de la Amistad*. He gave me a bottle of orange and clearly fancied himself as the 'professor' of the works. '*Checo?*' '*Sí,*' I lie. Then he explained to his workmates that Czechoslovakia was divided into three parts, '*Slovakia, Moravia y . . . y . . .*' 'Bohemia,' I said. '*Sí, Bohemia.*' When I had drained the *refresco*, they asked how much I wanted for my sunglasses. 'I am afraid they are not for sale. Thank you for the welcome refreshments, comrades.' Many Cubans rationalise the Soviet occupation of Czechoslovakia, and Fidel's support, by saying things like, 'The Czechs are taking advantage of the imperialist blockade to sell us shoddy goods at high prices,' or 'The Czechs feel your clothes . . . enviously.' In Havana, they didn't feel our clothes, but we were always being asked to sell them. In the end we had to. The money given by some kids' pants, and a dress or two to pay off our bill. We could have left Cuba in barrels and braces if we had wanted.

In Brazil my stipend had been raised, and we managed a little better for a while. Things went reasonably, until in the north-east of Brazil I paid a visit to Dom Hélder Câmara, the Archbishop of Recife, who is 'in quarantine'. He agreed to meet me later that day at the archbishop's palace. Suddenly, I was summoned to the president of the EMPETUR (the state tourist bureau of Pernambuco) and told my programme was cancelled. 'Such a person', he said to a colleague, 'must not be allowed to visit Dom Hélder. The man has worked a whole year in Czechoslovakia. He has been to the Soviet Union by invitation. He has come from Cuba. He has been to China.' I hadn't been to China. I had told a train-enthusiast employee of EMPETUR that once you could go all the way to Peking by train. UNESCO, I murmured. But it was no good. It was the day that the hostages for the kidnapped American ambassador had arrived in Havana and sworn to return to Brazil armed for the struggle. The army had been jumpy all day. 'The war is against the people,' explained a poet. Ambassador Elbrick had been kidnapped the day I flew from Rio to Bahía, and when I made my contact in the Afro-Oriental Institute, he said, 'It's the CIA. Brazilians could never plan anything like that.' I began to see what he meant after two weeks, when my promised programme of Afro-Brazilian attractions had not materialised. I ran out of money, waiting. UNESCO, UNESCO, I murmured to EMPETUR. That made matters worse, I was later told by a monk when, being again penniless, I had sought refuge in a monastery. 'In Latin America,' he said, 'UNESCO is highly suspect. The Americans think that there is too much European influence and so restrict its activity. I had two friends who did literary campaign work. They were paid and told to do nothing.' I was glad to hear that they had been paid. I was having some difficulty. But as a UNESCO Fellow I did have one invitation to eat from a UNESCO expert, a Canadian, and his wife. When the wife heard that we had just been in Cuba, the flesh between her bikini shook and she said, 'Everybody in the world knows that North America has the best food in the whole world.' Then she said, 'When they start getting their filthy communist literature translated into French and putting it for sale in

Canada . . .' She tailed off and sighed, 'How awful it must be not to feel free.' And as an afterthought and a warning, I thought, to me she said, 'In UNESCO we just do a job and never meddle in politics. We have no political opinions.' 'Of course,' I said. Then, changing the distasteful subject, she went on to speak of what she felt she lacked in Brazil. 'I lack bilberries. I lack gooseberries. I lack loganberries.' 'But fruit is plentiful.' 'Have you tasted the apples?' she shouted back. We preferred to rely on monks and nuns. Habitless now, radical, they lead dangerous lives. Their hero is Dom Hélder, whom I was prevented from seeing, whose house has been often machine-gunned, and their martyr is the young Padre Henrique, who chose to work among the students of the north-east and was found with bullet holes in his head, the nails broken off his fingers, cord marks round his throat and wrists. His funeral all but provoked a violent confrontation between the military and the radical church. As I was seen off on my way to Brasilia, two nuns listed the terrible diseases prevalent in the north-east and concluded, 'But the worst disease here is hunger.'

In Brasilia my first human contact was with Terezinha, a little girl of five whose family, six in all, were living under the fancy exit ramp of the National Theatre. It met the ground at an angle like a bushman's windbreak. It had the advantage of being near the bus station, where they could get water, and being near the foyer, where Terezinha could hold her lice-ridden two-year-old sister up to the playgoers, coming out of *The Devil Is a Woman*, and beg for *centavos*. Culture. The 'C' of my incantation, UNESCO, was the half-open womb I had to huddle into. In UNESCO we do our job and don't meddle in politics. My job was culture. I looked at the brave new architecture, the flat-topped pyramid of the National Theatre, with Terezinha's family flopped at the bottom like broken-backed Aztec sacrifices. I looked at the architecture. The CHEs, seven storeys high, that they had in the Plaza de la Revolution in Havana would do even better in Brasilia.

When I got back to Rio, UNESCO in Paris had still not authorised the payment of the *cruzeiros* still owed to me. We left Brazil for West Africa penniless, although a French Mother Superior offered us some money. When we arrived in Dakar in Senegal, we found UNESCO had not authorised our payment there either. Fortunately, the marabout of the Grande Mosque in Dakar offered us all spoons to dip into the communal bowl of rice and peppers, which we did with an alacrity that must have startled the old man, otherwise we would have gone very hungry. We eventually got enough to pay for our stopover in Dakar and left on the first stage of our journey to the Gambia, with £37 for fifteen days. The cheapest hotel, the Adonis, owned by a Lebanese called Kamal Milky, cost three times as much for a single person. I asked a Wolof steward where Africans stayed in Bathurst. He said with their brothers. We had no brothers in the Gambia. I cabled UNESCO in Paris: 'MUST ABANDON FELLOWSHIP UNLESS STIPEND INCREASED.' There was no reply. 'If the British taxpayer knew how much money was wasted by these international organisations,' said the secretary of the UN regional advisor, 'there would be real trouble.' She told me of a Swede, a UNESCO expert, who had not been paid for over three months and was living on an overdraft with a 10 per cent interest rate. My case looked hopeless. 'It's bad enough', she said, 'working for an African government. But I'd sooner work for an African government', she added loyally, 'than work for the UN.' I cabled home for enough money to pay off our debts to Mr Milky and borrowed £2 from the British High Commission. We had two months of Fellowship still to go, and today I was returning to England penniless.

Penniless, we caught the airport bus at the terminal in Wellington Street, near the British Information Office, where all the library chairs were full, and slowly all the heads went down over the pink *Financial Times* and the *Oxford Atlas* upside down, and Dembo went round waking the sleepers. I tipped the Gambian porters and paid for the airport bus in useless Cuban pesos. One peso equals one US dollar, I said. From now on Swissair would look after us. That night in the Hotel N'gor, Dakar, the crews of Lufthansa, Swissair and Air France were getting drunk together on the table next to us, as we ate our free alcohol-less transit passengers' meal. They laughed uproariously at trilingual jokes. It was 24 October . . . United Nations Day.

Shango the Shaky Fairy

1970

Where are you now, O Shango?
Two-headed, powerful
Man and woman, hermaphrodite
Holding your quivering thunderbolts
With quiet savage malice;
Brooding over your domain,
Africa, Cuba, Haiti, Brazil,
Slavery of mind is unabolished.
Always wanting to punish, never to love.

This question was posed by Abioseh Nicol, the Sierra
Leonean poet, in a poem called 'African Easter', and it's a
question I've often asked myself after my first acquaintance
with Shango, that god of many parts. I am also worried to
the point of madness by punishment and love. I have an
oshe Shango, a Shango staff, I picked up in the country of
the Nigerian Yoruba, whose god of thunder he is. Like all
foot-or-so-high Yoruba wood carvings, my Shango staff is
good to feel, pick up, think and worry with. I am a chronic,
inveterate feeler. I was once evicted from the Musée d'Art
Moderne for stroking Brâncuși's *Le Phoque*, which surely
was what it was made for. Later, in the National Gallery of
Prague, I discovered with the help of a Czech friend that if

you carried a white stick, wore dark glasses and took someone to guide you round, you could handle the extremities
of the Rodins and insinuate your connoisseur hand just
wherever you wanted, even essay a bit of hesitant frottage,
if you fancied. My *oshe Shango*, like the Yoruba twin figures (*igbeji*) of the same height, is a very feelable piece of
wood, and it is my own. At my worst moments of tension
I polish or fondle it, shove it under my oxter like a swagger
stick, twirl it about like a bastard New York cop, or even
waddle, to my children's delight, with it stuck between my
legs, until we all collapse in ribald laughter and my anxiety is eased. My daughter, Jane, has an appliquéd cloth I
bought in Dahomey. It hangs on the wall above her bed,
and when she almost lost her leg in an accident, she had
to gaze at it for months during her recuperation. There is a
man carrying a double axe and a ram's head belching fire,
emblems of Shango, god of the storm for the Yoruba of
Dahomey as well as Nigeria. So when I went looking for
Shango, to investigate his status in the socialist island of
Cuba and under the military dictatorship of Brazil, Jane
came with me, along with her mother and her brother Max.
The unbalanced poet and the lame daughter. Jane tires easily, and when she does I carry her piggyback like an African
woman, like that Shango figure in the D'Harnoncourt collection of New York, which William Fagg has called 'one of
the finest African sculptures extant'. When I carried her in
this way, people stared, and I remembered that when I produced a new translation of the *Lysistrata* of Aristophanes
into a Nigerian setting, nothing caused more raucous
laughter than when the Fulani herdsman I had made the

equivalent of Cinesias came to claim his wife with the baby swaddled on his back, unless it was his great red phallus they were laughing at. The actor who played the part was so embarrassed by his costume he tried to wear it back to front. I remember only two other similar moments of high excitement in largely male Nigerian audiences: one in the film version of Lawrence's *Sons and Lovers*, where Morel turns on his wife and throws her out of the house; and the other when Olivier's Hamlet castigates Ophelia. Anxiety over the definition of the sexual scope and role creates this humour, and its related despairs and prejudice. In this field Shango has had more experience than old Tiresias, and in crossing the Atlantic to the New World, has come to acquire more drag and quick changes than Danny La Rue.

To search for Shango in Cuba is to search for that Africa I came to know and love. To search for Africa is to discover and create Cuba. Shango is just one of many, but one of the most powerful, and certainly the most widely travelled, of the *orishas* in the Yoruba pantheon, which is every bit as rich if not richer than that of the Greeks. In the middle passage, in the dark hold of the slaver and in the slave barracks of the sugar plantations, Shango, the thunder god, the king, who, in one version of his legend, is human and hangs himself in the forest, becomes Santa Bárbara in that syncretism of the Catholicism of the Spanish colonist and the *orishas* of the Yoruba, who were shipped over to Cuba in their thousands after the extermination of the gentle Taino and Siboney Indians. Santa Bárbara is the patron saint of artillery, arsenals, powder magazines, and is invoked against lightning (*quand le tonnerre tombera*, Ste.

Barbe nous préservera) because when her wicked father, the king of Nicodemia, struck off the head of the virgin for refusing to renounce newfangled Christianity, lightning struck him dead. In Cuba she was an army patron too, but her black devotees address her in Lucumí, that form of the Yoruba language still used in the island cults like a liturgical Latin, as *Changó* (Shango). He/She/It is central to the understanding of *cubanidad*. And true *cubanidad* is as much an effort of the revolutionary as the 1969/70 sugar harvest of 10,000,000 tons. Nicolás Guillén, now president of the Union of Artists and Writers, wrote of Cuba in 1931:

> *. . . esta tierra mulata*
> *de africano y español*
> *(Santa Bárbara de un lado,*
> *del otro lado, Changó)*

One on either side, like a coat of arms, the black god and the white virgin. But they are one and the same person. A concept like the Trinity, only there are (for the moment) only two, and certainly more complex, and perhaps more kinky, but in the end fuller of potential salvation. A mulatto country, a mulatto culture, and much of this notion can be found in the apostle Martí's idea of *cubanidad*. Though now the official report to the United Nations in 1968 can say that 'the real Cuban culture is, and cannot but be, mulatto', and though now, when the Soviet fleet made a courtesy visit to Havana in July 1969, the hands that held the Cuban flags on the posters that greeted them were of two shades of brown only, it needed the Castro revolution to make the recognition of this visibly obvious cultural fact about Cuba respectable. About some aspects of the mulatto religion, however, the revolution is decidedly uneasy.

It is true that in the period clearly defined in Ramón Guirao's anthology *Orbita de la poesía afro-cubana, 1928–1937* (Havana, 1937), there existed a movement known variously as *poesía afro-cubana, poesía negra* or *negrista*. Of its various practitioners only one, Marcelino Arozarena, was actually black, and only Guillén himself mulatto. It was, like many similar movements – 'gaucho' poetry in South America, 'Maori' poetry in New Zealand – basically white, cultivated, urban and primitivistic. Its verses chime with rumba dancers and the onomatopoeia of the sun-dried gourd maraca. It owes much to the movement in Europe which brought to such artists as Picasso, Braque, Derain and Vlaminck the knowledge of African masks; and to the theories of Leo Frobenius, mentor of Spengler, dabbled in by both Pound and Lawrence, and whose ideas were much prevalent in the Hispanic world after the translation of *Schwarze Dekameron* into Spanish in 1925, and after the master himself had toured Europe and had been well expounded in the *Revista de Occidente*, a Madrid journal, very influential with Cuban intellectuals of the time. It is a movement wide enough to include Tarzan of the Apes, and what is behind it is what the Allied Supremacies of Africa declared in their Proclamation in the equally symptomatic novel of Charles Williams, *Shadows of Ecstasy*, that 'the great age of the intellect is done'. Europe, cerebral Europe, trapped in its grey matter, is done for. The two poems that initiated the movement in Cuba in 1928 are both by white poets, Ramón Guirao and José Z. Tallet, and they are both about a negress dancing the rumba, mildly sexotic, with surface sound effects as awful as Vachel Lindsay's *Congo* or, even worse, Edith Sitwell. It was Africa in the head. Now, we mustn't say, said Guillén, Afro-*Cuban* but Afro-*Spanish*.

Today's Cuban poets, who are again turning to the Yoruba myths 'in a revolutionary context', dismiss the old 1930s Afro-Cuban stuff as '*pintoresquismo*'. They make an occasional exception: say, for Regina Pedroso, who was half Chinese, and who very appropriately complained in her poem '*Hermano negro*':

Are we nothing more than rumbas . . . and carnivals?

And the new 'Afro-Spanish' poets, Miguel Barnet, Pablo Armando Fernández, whose book *Libro de los heroes* (1964) J. M. Cohen credits with giving modern Cuban poetry a new beginning, Nancy Morejón, Excilia Saldaña and Rogelio Martinez Furé also make an exception for 'Nicolás' their president. Guillén's *Motivos de son* appeared two years after the start of the Afro-Cuban movement in 1930. This poetry is also marred by facile onomatopoeia like:

> *Tamba, tamba, tamba, tamba,*
> *tamba del negro que tumba;*
> *tumba del negro, caramba,*
> *caramba, que el negro tumba:*
> *yamba, yambo, yambambe!*

But what was to distinguish Guillén from the exoticists pure and simple was his Marxism, his commitment to causes outside the poetry, where it was obvious that the exploited negro was more than rumba and carnival.

In the preface to his next volume of poems, *Sóngoro cosongo* (1931), subtitled *poemas mulatas*, Guillén says that the spirit of Cuba is '*mestizo*', and it is his own awareness of his dual origins that was to produce some of his best poems, like '*Balada de los dos abuelos*' from *West Indies Ltd* (1934), where he calls together his white Spanish ancestor and his black slave ancestor and presents them in a synthesis of anguish and celebration:

> *Los dos del mismo tamaño,*
> *ansia negra y ansia blanca;*
> *los dos del mismo tamaño,*
> *gritan, sueñan, lloran, cantan.*

> The two are on the same scale,
> black anguish and white anguish;
> the two are on the same scale,
> they shout, they dream, they weep, they sing.

The components of what Jean Price-Mars called the '*ajiaco*', the goulash of Cuba, stirred together by colonial oppression and foreign investors. His poems move beyond Cuba to the rape of Abyssinia by Mussolini and to the activities of the Mau-Mau in Kenya. It is the sustained anti-colonialism which made him the obvious choice for president of the Writers' Union of the new Cuba. Although the critic Cintio

Vitier praised Guillén's 'afro-cuban' style as being produced, unlike that of his contemporaries, *desde adentro*, 'from the inside', the one failing the new Cuban poets attribute to him is his only superficial knowledge of the negro culture of Cuba. Unlike themselves, he doesn't know the cults from the inside. And in all the poetry of rumba and maraca of the 1930s Shango himself makes only a rare appearance, once in a shrine before yet another rumba dancer (this time that of Emilio Ballagas), whose navel gazes on the god like a solitary, adoring eye, and apart from when he is set beside Santa Bárbara, again in Guillén, when his power is invoked to protect Stalin:

> *Stalin, Capitán,*
> *a quien Changó proteja . . .!*
> (1937)

After the revolution most of this was to change. An editorial in the important journal *Casa de las Américas*, in a special issue devoted to *Africa en América*, proclaimed in 1966, 'now we are more Cuba, we are more Africa'. But only seven years before, Lydia Cabrera, one of the few researchers, apart from the great Fernando Ortiz, dedicated to the collection and description of *Afro-Spanish* folklore and culture, complained in her study of the secret society *Abakuá* of Efik origin that it was perfectly acceptable to be an Indianist in Cuba because there was none left, but to delve into the rich complexities of negro culture was considered 'antipatriotic' and a 'subversion of national dignity'. This is thankfully no longer so – up to a point. Caballero

Calderón said of the whole search for national cultures in Latin America, '*para crear es necesario conocer*', 'to create it is necessary to know', something that applies equally to the creation of national cultures in independent Africa. If Guillén did not know the Yoruba cults from the inside, the new poets do, and there is that intimate connection between sociological research and creativity that Calderón thinks essential. Miguel Barnet (b. 1940), for example, worked for five years in the Havana Institute of Ethnology and Folklore, as well as doing a perhaps over-edited and directed Oscar Lewis-type job on the 108-year-old runaway slave Estaban Montejo's *El Cimarrón*. He writes poetry which often invokes the Yoruba orishas and includes chants in Lucumí. In two slim pamphlets, *La piedra fina y el pavorreal* (1963) and *Isla de Guijes* (1964), there appear Oggun, Eleggua, Oya, one of Shango's wives, Osain and Shango himself. He dedicates his first book to Tonde, a *santero* of Palmira in the Las Villas province of Cuba, 'in memory of my first visit to a lucumí temple'. Impatient with the *pintoresquismo* of the Afro-Cuban poetry (so-called) of the 1930s, Barnet began travelling, researching and living with *santeros* in Palmira and Jovellanos in Matanzas, in order to *know* and create Cuba, correct the imbalance that an education in a North American college had given him. Rogelio Martínez Furé (b. 1937) is a translator of Yoruba poetry through the English of such collectors as Ulli Beier, and also a compiler of the stories and songs of Yoruba origin in Cuba. His book of translations, *Poesía anónima Africana* (Instituto del Libro, 1968), is immensely popular among the poetry-reading public and with other poets, and like most popular books in Cuba, is unobtainable in bookshops. He has a similar background of Institute of Ethnography and Folklore, was a founder of the *Conjunto Folklorico* of the National Theatre, and was responsible for the introduction of the study of African art in some of the colleges. To know is to create. '*We use the myths*', said one or the other of them to me at different times, '*in a revolutionary context.*'

> The *orishas* become modern Cubans. Eshu, say, can be
> a bastard and bugger things up. They are boozy *orishas*
> and lecherous *orishas*, like Cubans, though they'd be
> hard put to it to be boozy these days. And Shango, well
> Shango is a guerrilla like El Che.

And that made me recall the righteous indignation of the nineteenth-century *Herald* correspondent James O'Kelly, after his travels in Mambiland, as he called the island in the first stages of becoming *Cuba Libre* in the 1870s:

> The planters grow enormously rich, and become
> millionaires at the expense of the tears and misery
> of the wretches who toil for their benefit. That
> such a system can be permitted to exist among
> men pretending to be civilized is an outrage on the
> common conscience of mankind. When one sees the
> representatives of this abomination kneeling before the
> altar of the God of the Christians, he must regret the
> thunderbolts of the grand old gods of the past, who, the
> poets tell us, smote in their indignation such criminals.

And about eighty years later along came Shango El Che. Down from the mountain, where all the *orishas* dwell, and from where they are summoned to the aid of the revolution by such poets as Pablo Armando Fernández:

> *Duermen en la tierra de los antiguos mitos,*
> *doce presagios de los ríos, doce*
> *augurios de la primavera.*
> *Cuando despierten serán guerreros*
> *de olvidada tradición. Sus memorias inauguran*
> *el tiempo señalado por los poetas.*
> *Caballos y leones misteriosos en la casa*
> *de Orisha,*
> *doce rayos invisibles que cambian el signo*
> *de los meses.*

> They sleep in the land of ancient myths,
> twelve omens of the rivers, twelve
> portents of spring.
> When they wake up they will be warriors
> of forgotten tradition. Their memories inaugurate
> the time signposted by the poets.
> Mysterious horses and lions in the house
> of Orisha,
> twelve invisible flashes that change the mark
> of months.

The twelve. The twelve invisible lightning flashes are Shango's, and in the poem '*Epiphanía*' the thunder that changes the age is Shango's too:

Revolución,
naces y veo la edad cambiada, el trueno
furia y sangre y unas aguas de miedo,
arrasadoras, pasan.
En el futuro halla el hombre su límite.

Revolution,
you are born and I see the age changed, the thunder
fury and blood and waters of terror,
devastating, they pass.
In the future man finds his limit.

An epiphany of Shango, but not here the protector of Stalin.
That the revolution is still keeping *el hombre* within certain
limits, and *la mujer* within others, is no fault of Shango's,
who can pass from one into the other and back again.

'*Para crear es necesario conocer.*' This is even more apparent
in the work of the theatre in Havana. The Teatro Nacional
as early as 1960 presented under the direction of Argeliers
León, who is director of the institute where Barnet and
Martínez Furé studied, four successful programmes of
Afro-Cuban (Afro-*Spanish*) ceremonies: *Abakuá*, with the
rites, legends, drumming, songs and dances of the secret
cult of Calabar Efik origin; *Bembe*, of Yoruba origin,
including as finale the magnificent chant to Shango; and
Yimbula, rites and music of Bantu origin. In his programme
notes to the presentation of *Abakuá*, Argeliers León speaks
of the timid and irregular process of *mestizaje* in Cuba,
but adds that now in 1960 the door to ultimate integration had been opened by the triumph of the revolution. The

National Theatre, pursuing the policy of research and creation, also sponsored the folklore monthly in 1961, *Actas del
Folklore del Teatro Nacional de Cuba*, which published both
new essays on Cuban folklore, mostly of African origin,
and reprints of inaccessible articles, like those of Romulo
Lachatañere on the religious beliefs of the Cuban Yoruba.
This work and the presentations in the theatre were content with simply reporting on the rituals or with displaying
them with only the minimum of direction. In the Teatro
Nacional de Guiñol, an inspired group of puppet and mask
players for adults and children, the legends of the Yoruba
have found a true *dramatic* representation. This work has
been encouraged and fostered by the directors Pepe and
Carucha Camejo and the dramaturg Pepe Carril. Since the
theatre's inauguration in 1963, it has presented *Chichereku*
(1966), based on some of the Afro-Cuban stories collected
by Lydia Cabrera, who is now, to everyone's regret, living
in Miami, and in the following year *La Loma de Mambiala*,
adapted by Sylvia Barros from the same rich source material. In 1966, Pepe Carril wrote *Shangó de Ima*, subtitled 'a
Yoruba mystery', which is a chronicle of the life and loves
of Shango. One spectator compared Shango to a black
Don Juan, and since Ulises Garcia (Shango) was the only
unmasked actor in the play, it was inevitable that the main
review of the play by the poetess Belkis Cuza Malé should
be titled '*Shangó Hombre*'. She praised the play as a true
'work of our people and the revolution', and one which confirmed the search for what was truly *Cuban* through the
medium of the negro, rather than a search for the negro
himself. No *négritude*, that is.

But at the same time the Teatro Mella was mounting a production of Aimé Césaire's play *Une Saison au Congo*. The free programme was admirably educative, in a way that the theatre programmes of socialist countries tend to be and ours don't. There were essays on Césaire and Lumumba, by René Dépestre, the Haitian poet now living in Cuba, and by Sartre; the hair-raising betrayal of Lumumba was set out in ruthless detail, and the characters of the international intrigue carefully annotated. But on the stage all the characters shouted at the top of their voices the whole time, so that the only serious thing in the end could have been said in a whisper. The costumes were 'African', garish, carnival, and the faces of the Congolese were painted in bright hues. Lumumba did sexual athletics as he delivered his principal orations. One could almost hear that old Afro-Cuban rhythm coming in . . . rumba Lumumba, rumba, the jungle jangle of the congo bongo. It was embarrassing to learn that the producer Roberto Blanco had spent a year in Ghana. It was all, except for Césaire's indictment of the Congo episode, an Africa of the mind, in the head. Actors and producers of other theatres tended to shrug and say there was '*demasiado movimiento, movimiento gratuito*', 'too much movement, gratuitous movement'. The one visual thing that saved the spectacle were the back projections painted on glass by the Cuban negro artist Manuel Mendive, and a remark I heard in the stalls:

Che was in the Congo, you know. That was quite a surprise when his book came out. But they say he couldn't get on with the blacks.

The spectacle I really wanted to see, though, was that of Shango possessing, 'mounting' his worshipper, as Apollo used to 'mount' the Sybil at Cumae. *Yes, it still goes on*, everybody assured me, *all over the place*, but a curious unhelpfulness entered into our relations. Granted that in an island where rationing is absolutely total, what food there is, what clothes there are, paper, toys, pencils, a whole goat or a sheep as a sacrifice for Shango might seem a huge extravagance, even for a god, even for a god who had seen service in the Sierra Maestra. But under Cuban socialism even the gods are equal.

Everyone believes here in Cuba. Look, see that guy there with sort of sacking pants. He's wearing them for Baba-lu-aye, that's San Lazaro. And that woman we saw; she had a red and white necklace, those red and white beads. She's a daughter of Shango. Those are his colours, red and white. Blood and bandages. You'll see necklaces like that on even very high up people in the revolution. Or a little thing of beads round the ankle. Cubans can't live without it, *Santeria*, black and white. Our socialism is now a third ingredient in the *mestizaje* of beliefs. You wait, in ten, twenty years Che will be an *orisha*, if he's not already in Oriente Province. Already, well, you know, he was a doctor, a healer. He tended not only the wounded guerrillas, but the hurt Batista pigs as well. There were twelve when they came down from the mountains, twelve *barbudos*. Che was a great man, an important man . . . a minister. Maybe he was tempted . . . but he died a lowly death in the jungle. They hung his body from a helicopter. That was a mistake. You know, the Ascension and all that, Che will be an *orisha*. They'll be calling him Jesus. The drums will bring El Che back. They might call him Shango or one of those. Or Jesus. Ten or twenty years. You must think our revolution is very primitive. Notice when you go into any office of the UJC, almost any, you'll find almost always the table pushed against a wall, and up there above the table, three photos, Fidel, Che, Camilo. There you are already, your altar. Do you think we are very primitive? It's usual socialist practice to name streets, factories, etc., after heroes of the revolution. When they do that here, Frank Pais, say, they believe that guy's right there getting on with the work. Really there. It helps the revolution no end.

On 13 August 1969, Commandante René Vallejo Ortiz died. He had been chief medical officer to the army, a hero of the Sierra Maestra, and Fidel's right-hand man. It had been generally known that he was dying for some weeks before, as a consequence of a cerebral haemorrhage. Some weeks before he died a huge totem pole appeared implanted in the pavement of 23rd Street, '*La Rampa*', outside a cinema. I thought it was some sort of exotic restaurant sign, like the one for the *Carabali* (Calabar) almost opposite. But it had been erected, everyone whispered, to preserve the spirit of the *Commandante*, but by whom no one would say.

He was born in Manzanillo in Oriente, noted for its spiritualism and its communication with the dead.

Outside Manzanillo itself there's a house where 12 *santeros* live, black and white, who join hands and sing songs in a language none of them knows or understands. But probably African. Commandante Vallejo used to visit them every week. Everyone believes in Cuba, even Fidel. Well, he's not a true believer but he listens . . . listened to everything Vallejo told him that the *orishas* communicated. But Vallejo really believes, believed. He was a famous surgeon, a lung specialist, but some days, you know, he just wouldn't operate if the spirits said that it wasn't a good day for it. It was he, well, Vallejo and the *orishas* who told Fidel to move the army from Oriente to nearer the centre of the island, where the imperialist attack would come. That was at the time of the Bay of Pigs. The *orishas* advised it. They also say . . . said that Fidel wouldn't long survive Vallejo. We don't know what Fidel will do without him.

So although Shango is culturally integrated, politically he still remains only the power behind the *trueno*. His presence among the *barbudos*, bearded revolutionaries, makes Cubans lapse into a kind of inferiority feeling, which is deeply rooted in their colonial past. *Do you think our revolution is primitive?* And where these feelings exist one has to create a compensatory superiority feeling. I was talking to a middle-aged negro woman from Santiago in Oriente, on holiday in the capital with her family, and when I told her I had lived in Africa for four years, she nodded in that direction with a worried face and said, 'But over there, aren't they very backward, uncivilised?' So I didn't get to see much of Shango in Cuba, except when he zoomed from the hurricane with ostentatious flashiness and lodged in the *palma real*, the tree that most distinguishes the island's landscape, which is his throne and lookout post. And his symbols were unintentionally there in the double axes of the old ironwork of the Paseo José Martí; double axes stuck into a bundle of *fasces*, like those near a small war memorial near the Prado Museum in Madrid, or, to the acute embarrassment of some Muscovites, in the railings round the Kremlin Park. And as in the famous and beautiful Shango figure of the D'Harnoncourt collection, where the indispensable double-axe motif is left out, it asserts itself in the divided, exaggerated cleavage of the *cubana*, the *doble hacha* carved in the iconography of breasts and buttocks that, swaying or bouncing, inevitably turn the head of the Cuban *macho*. The tighter the skirt or trousers, the better, it seemed, the bigger the arse, the better, rolling like something from our 1940s, when men were men and women were women, before the outrages of unisex. The oddity about the tight garment that accentuates the eye-catching arse is that the zip, even on the female militia uniform, is neither tucked discreetly to the side, nor imitates the masculine fly (that would never do in Cuba), nor is discreetly flapped, but shines and glitters and divides the mountainous buttocks like a rich vein of silver. Odd. My Joycean kids coined an apposite word for the underwear of such Latin flesh: ANDES.

The figures of Shango, even in West Africa, are of ambiguous sex, but in Cuba, once he is syncretised with Santa Bárbara, the Cuban male worries about him/her/it, as if as well as helping to overthrow the Batista regime, he were undermining *machismo* itself. The anxiety extends even into 'scientific' anthropological enquiry. One researcher tries to account for Shango's association with Santa Bárbara by recounting one Nigerian legend which has him escaping his enemies dressed in the clothes of his wife, Oya. 'This legend', he says, 'has led to the belief that Shango is really a *woman*. But', he adds, 'we have seen *un macho muy macho* under the skirts.'

And so sometimes the iconography of Shango has to depict the genitalia not *debajo las sayas*, 'under the skirts', but actually *over* the skirts, as in Manuel Mendive's drawing of Shango. In the same drawing Shango is holding a sword, a cup and stands by a tower. Mendive went through formal art school education, where he 'had to draw Greek beauties', and eventually reacted against the European images towards Africa, and he began painting the legends of the *orishas* worshipped in his own house. I asked about the tower in the picture. A phallus, he said. And the goblet, I didn't need to ask, would be a vagina. But, of course, it isn't and the tower isn't. They are part of the centuries-old paraphernalia of Santa Bárbara. Her father imprisoned her in a tower. She had a third window put in it *in honorem Trinitatis*. He cut off her head with a sword, which is why Mendive's Shango holds one. The tower can be seen in the Van Eyck St Barbara in Antwerp, where the virgin also holds a branch of palm, Shango's and the martyr's tree. And the cup? Ah, and here scholarship salivates at the coincidence of History. History *is Finnegans Wake*. The cup is, of course, the chalice and can be seen in Holbein's picture of the saint on the St Sebastian altarpiece, in the Pinakothek, Munich, *but* she did not earn the right to carry it until after 1448, and all due to one Kock. Henry Kock was nearly burnt to death and called upon the saint, who preserved him long enough to receive the last sacraments. So Shango carries the chalice and the host. Kock's near immolation took place at Gorkum in Holland. I can feel it starting, the great poem on racial integration in Cuba, my masterpiece. It will be called 'Burnt Gorkum'. But Mendive doesn't do many drawings. The ones he gave me were all done in hospital, when he was waiting for an operation and couldn't use other materials. His right foot was crushed under one of our Leylands. He and Jane compared sufferings and became immediately close, *ansia negra y ansia blanca*. He showed her a huge painting on wood of his accident. Above the bus, the injured Mendive, and the spectators crowded round the *orishas* in all their brilliance, and above them, the whole thing giving the effect of El Greco's *Burial of the Count of Orgaz*, the *Egungun*, the ancestors, the dead, who in African societies are continuous with the living, who are behind such ideas as 'African socialism', who share the earth *now* with the living and the unborn. In other paintings Shango sat at table with the Mendive family. Jane was wearing red and white. She is the daughter of Shango, Mendive said.

If Cubans are learning and creating their *cubanidad* from a new discovery of the Afro- part of their Afro-Spanish inheritance, it is likely that it is from both strains that they inherit *machismo. Machismo*, the stereotype of the big guy, with lots of *cojones*, or at least two big ones, like money bags full of doubloons. One of the favourite Spanish curses is, 'By the twenty-four balls of the twelve apostles'. So they were all right. I thought that maybe the greatest blasphemy one could produce in Cuba might be something like, '*Por los veintitrés cojones de los doce barbudos*'. *Machismo* which makes a journalist attack a poet as a pederast for wearing a psyche-delic tie given to him by Adrian Mitchell. A *machismo* every bit as suspicious and on the defensive as the *Andycappismo* of northern England. That *machismo* can undermine the revolution is the suggestion of the third part of that prize-winning film, the trilogy on Cuban womanhood, *Lucia*, where a country *macho* resists his wife's attempt to learn to read with the young *alfabetizador* during the great literacy campaign of 1962 and, the film clearly states, resists her tak-ing part, her true part, in the revolution. It must have been a great source of anxiety to the Cuban man when he first saw his woman in the olive-green militia uniform, carrying that dreadful penis symbol, the rifle. *Machismo*:

Sure, sure, we're scared of homosexuality. It's a historical problem. *Machismo*, all the bullshit culture of Catholic Spain. God, they've even corrupted the negroes. They're the worst exponents of *machismo*. And those fucking, bullshit Panthers. They only come here to bum around and screw. Eldridge Cleaver's here in Havana, though nobody's supposed to know. He sends notes round to women he fancies, saying who he is and that he'd like to meet them. He signs himself *MADRUGADOR HACHA*. You know, even our fags are backward. Greenwich Village, sure they're a gas, but here . . . But anyway, last September they rounded up thousands on the Rampa and shoved them inside incommunicado for ten days, all kinds of people, just everyone out there on the street, candidates for party membership, a second lieutenant, a mother with three daughters. Crazy! It was because of pimping for foreigners, payment in radio sets, clothes, and it wasn't just prostitution of the genital organs either! Well, all the queers, all those they said were queers, they sent to a UMAP in Camaguey. Military psychology . . . give them some hard graft, put some muscles, put some *cojones* into, onto them, make them real guys. They showed them porn, hetero porn, movies, and they just laughed themselves silly, the homos, and the colonel couldn't count one damned erection in the whole goddam camp. *Then* the queers retaliated. They cut up their mosquito nets, and dyed them a pretty pink with mercurochrome, and hung up Priscilla curtains all over the place. They made wads of the netting, and put spots of mercurochrome on them, and went off to the medic complaining of aches and pains, and saying their periods had started. *(Note: red and white: Shango, I noted.)* They ogled the handsome guards. They drew up a directory of Camaguey fags. And in the end the military, the big, butch *machos*, just had to let them go, released them. Yes, even now, after that gaff, the military keeps its big, brotherly eye on potential fag centres like art schools. Makes sure they get some real hard cane-cutting in their *trabajo productivo* and no tomato picking. One *girl* I know, plays violin, gets her hands so bad out there in the country that she can hardly touch her instrument for weeks, and she can't be a fag . . . can she?

Machismo: the reverence for old man Hemingway. If the *orishas* can open one's eyes to the Cuban landscape, the official tourist agency, INIT, only seems able to show you the *Casa Hemingway*. The house 'just as he left it'. All the whisky bottles a big guy gets through. The obsessive pencilling of his weight on the bathroom walls. The awful bull-fight posters like a ladies' training college or a 'fifties' coffee bar. The stuffed heads of his kills. On the way back, with all the Russian tourists, my kids divide up the rooms between them, impressed by the house, its green setting, its views, its clutter: *You can have the tower with the big-game guns and the war picture books. And I'll have the lion's head and the fishing rods and I want the room where he kept the hundred cats.* Then, as we turned a corner into the Plaza de la Revolucíon, with its Che seven storeys high, one of them yelled: *Look, there's the SHAKY FAIRY!* But I am thinking all the way back of Hemingway's last kill, and Shango hanging himself in the forest, like Okonkwo in Chinua Achebe's *Things Fall Apart* (1958), and of our room on the eighth floor of the Hotel Nacional, with the one bed for the four of us. Already I am bequeathing *habitacíon* 844 to the revolutionary government 'just as he left it', still with the bits of mousy hair in the sink, his, because, although it barely covered his ears, he had been stared at, and even pointed at and tutted at by the lift girl, between *ocho* and the cafeteria, and his son's the same colour, also cropped after standing in one of those endless Havana queues, this time for ice creams at the zoo, in front of two kids, a boy who said Max was a girl, and a girl who said he was a boy:

Macho!
Hembra!
Macho!
Hembra!
Macho!
HEMBRA!

The boy clinched the argument.

What about Che, then, I wanted to say, *didn't he have long hair?*

Just as the following exchange used to take place, at least once a year, between me and mi mam:

Get your hair cut. Boys don't have long hair.
What about Jesus, then, didn't he have long hair?
Don't talk to me like that!

So the bits of hair as he left them and, in the wardrobe, a purple crimplene shirt he'd worn only once, and all the heads in *sombrero de yarey*, on the tops of bodies belted with sheathed machetes and/or holstered pistols, swivelled, gawped and guffawed. The lobby rang with the studs of their boots. It was then I evolved the perhaps counter-revolutionary concept of *machetismo*.

I was sitting one day in the Public Library in the Academy of Science building in Carlos III reading Lydia Cabrera's absolutely unobtainable book *El Monte* (1954), a book which apportions the Cuban flora to the various *orishas*, and is acknowledged by many writers to be one of the strongest influences on their work. This is especially true of

those poets I have already mentioned who are seeking to
create a specifically Cuban mythology for the revolution.
I was reading how Shango inhabited the silk cotton tree,
and the *palma real*, and the incandescent flame tree, and
opposite me was a man taking copious notes from a book
called *Destilacíon de alcoholes*. And well he might, for Cuba
is pretty boozeless. I hadn't had a drop in all the two months
I'd been in Havana, except a gnat-piss beer named after the
rebellious Indian Hatuey. The heat of the afternoon made
me drowse in my seat under the bust of Cervantes, and
suddenly I was myself again, pissed, on palm wine, Shango
juice, wearing my purple crimplene shirt (Jan Hus's colour,
Miroslav Holub once told me) and my hair flowing in the
wind off somewhere near Key West, and I strode along the
wall of the Malecon, Malecon, and the shouts, Malecon, or
was it *Morejón* or *Marejón*, but there was I, Shago (*stet*) the
Shaky Fairy tilting a huge padded red phallus at all the military bureaucracies of the world. But, curiously, for all their
African inheritance they don't make palm wine in Cuba.

As we left Havana, on our way to Brazil to find Shango
there, Jane bought a doll in the airport. One of those things
– costumes, beefeater, guardsman – a nation projects something of its image into, and there was nothing else to buy
except those lovely brown phalluses of tobacco with names
like Romeo and Juliet. But I don't smoke, though my wife
had developed a taste for cigars in Havana and we were
entitled to two cheap, definitely not hand-rolled ones per
male person per evening meal. So I used to get the ration
for Rosemarie. But she was tutted at by the same lift-lady
who tutted at my hair, when she was smoking one. *Women*

don't do that. And Jane's doll was none other than the hooded *diablito* of the *Abakuá* cult, noted, as Lydia Cabrera tells us in the study of the rites we have already mentioned, for its '*agresividad*' and dedicated, above all, to Afro-Cuban (-Spanish) *machismo*. 'To be a man', one of their refrains goes, 'you don't need to be an *Abakuá*, but to be an *Abakuá* you need to be a man.' And the innermost secret of this cult, the *sanctum sanctissimorum*, the *Fa Ekue*, as they say in Efik, and as El Macho Hemingway could no doubt tell us, behind the black curtain, is a skull. But *machismo* had the last word on me. I noticed with a sudden panic that in my Mexican visa, opposite 'profession', and no doubt misled by my pre-Havana days haircut, the consular authorities had written: '*escritora*'. I masculinised it discreetly on the short flight over to Mexico City, but fluttered a bit as *they* went through my papers, the toads in dark glasses who shoota de espiders in Mejico. One said, the other nodding at me, and I was terrified they were going to put the deleted '-*a*' to the test:

Profesión?
Escritor.
Escritor?
Sí, you know, *The Children of Sanchez* and all that shit!

In Brazil, in Salvador, Bahia de todos os Santos, there was a boutique called *Xangô, moda masculina*, and it sold purple crimplene shirts. The African cults were on display for tourists. The hotels advertised TODAY, CANDOMBLÉ or TODAY, CAPOEIRA, that ritualistic foot fighting, of

Angolan origin, that has given such a distinctive style to Brazilian football. Further north in Recife, in Pernambuco, all the cults are called *xangôs* after Shango, and at one I was given a medallion to wear round my neck by Pai Apolinário Gomes da Mota. It said that I was a *filho do Xangou*, a 'son of Shango', and when Shango came to possess the poor, ugly, worn women who were yet so graceful in their dancing, and became their joy, he was *Xango meninho*, 'young Shango', and *Xangô velho*, 'old Shango', and they were both St John the Baptist. The iconography of the double axe had survived on my red and white medallion, but had been metamorphosed over the years into a crutch, like Mendive's hung on the wall of his house, like Jane's. Researchers of the local Sociological Institute were doing studies of the relation between *xangôs* and pederasty, and on the high incidence of mental instability among the devotees, and a psychiatrist was using the drums of Shango in his patients' therapy. I wore my medallion on the plane from Recife to Brasilia, and the bits of red paint came off on my almost hairless chest. In Brasilia all the buildings were El Che high and the ground plan was like a double axe. At night a violent storm swept across the surrounding desert. The lightning came out of the sky, first white, then red. It lit up all night the pyramid of the National Theatre, where they were playing *The Devil Is a Woman*.

I arrived back in England, unisex rampant, a son of Shango the Shaky Fairy, Santa Bárbara, St John the Baptist, suicidal king, virgin martyr, man, woman, young, old, black, white, god and guerrilla, and when I got back to Newcastle on the edge of the Roman Wall, I remembered how Tacitus had described Britain as *bipennis*, 'double-axed' (*Agricola* 10.3). I huddle over the fire, my flesh mottling to Shango's colours, fondling my *oshe Shango*, staring into the flames of the Shilbottle cobbles, flushing in Shango's honour as I brood on punishment and love, and invoke his epiphany, here and now, in Britannia, bold but gentle, brave but neutral, an *orisha* in touch with the dead, the living and the yet to be, and with only double axes to grind.

The Inkwell of Dr Agrippa

1971

When I search my childhood for something to explain what drove me into poetry, something like Pablo Neruda's story of the silent exchange of a toy lamb and a pine cone between himself and an unseen boy through a hole in a fence, I can find nothing quite so significantly beautiful, but there are things which brought to me, early but obscurely, the same precious idea 'that all humanity is somehow together'. 'To feel', Neruda says, 'the affection that comes from those unknown to us who are watching over our sleep and solitude . . . widens out the boundaries of our being and unites all living things!' My images are all to do with the war. One of my very earliest memories is of bombs falling, the windows shaking, myself and my mother crouching in the cellar listening, me begging to be allowed to rush out into the lit-up streets, the whistlings sounded so festive. The next morning, I found the overgrown tennis courts in the local park pitted with bomb craters. As I rooted around in one for shrapnel, I heard someone talking to a policeman utter the still haunting but no longer so puzzling phrase 'humane bomber'. Another is the contact I had with German prisoners of war in a work party near our street. I remember only we children talked to them much. I introduced them to the pleasures of smoking cinnamon sticks, and bought their supplies from the chemist. Another is of a street party with a bonfire and such joy, celebration and general fraternity as I have never seen since. As I grew up the image stayed, but I came to realise that the cause of the celebration was Hiroshima. Another is the dazed feeling of being led by the hand from a cinema into the sunlit City Square after seeing films of Belsen in 1945, when I was eight. Around all these too is a general atmosphere of the inarticulate and unmentionable, a silence compounded of the hand-me-down Victorian adage, 'Children should be seen and not heard,' and the mock-Yorkshire taciturnity of 'Hear all, see all, say nowt.' Even now when I have finished a poem I have bouts of speechlessness in which that fireside atmosphere again casts dark shadows in my skull. When I began my travels, I converted that into a third part of my small-time self-dramatisations of 'silence, exile and cunning'.

In our street in Hoggarty Leeds I was the only one who used his literacy to read books, the only 'scholar', and so every kind of cultural throwaway from spring-cleaned attics and the cellars of the deceased found its way to me. I acquired piles of old 78s – George Formby, the Savoy Orpheans, Sophie Tucker, Sandy Powell, Peter Dawson – and sometimes the odd book – an old guide to Matlock, the *Heckmondwike Temperance Hymnal*, stamped *Not to Be Taken Away*, and, above all, a Livingstone's *Travels* so massive I could barely manhandle it. Somehow it seems that my two early ambitions to be Dr Livingstone and George Formby were compromised in the role of poet, half missionary, half comic, Bible and banjolele, the Renaissance *ut doceat, ut placeat*.

Although there were strenuous and exhausting years under formal education, my vividest memories of enthralled achievement are in minor closet dramas of midnight or dawn autodidacticism in the style of Thomas Cooper the Chartist poet. In some ways I still re-enact this when I write a poem. My school, Leeds Grammar School, to which I won one of six scholarships for the plebs, seemed to me like a class conspiracy. When I left, my final report said: 'He possesses something of the poetical imagination, but suffers from the waywardness of that gift.' The windows behind the altar in the school chapel were dedicated to *Miles*, the soldier, and *Mercator*, the merchant. Somehow I can't recall the pig in the middle. But when I close my eyes now I see *Poeta*, the poet, sometimes as poised, saintly and acceptable as his worldly flankers, sometimes like some half-naked shaker in the throes of a virulent *scribendi cacoethes*, being belaboured by public-school angels wielding gamma minuses like immense shillelaghs over their glossy Cherry Blossomy hairstyles, driving the poet from the Garden of Eton.

It was probably no less a pressure than the whole weight of the Protestant ethic in its death agonies, a monstrous north of England millstone grit, that made me pit myself against the most difficult traditional verse forms. It had to be hard work, and it was, and it still is. I learned by what Yeats called 'sedentary toil and the imitation of great masters'. I still find it all almost impossibly difficult, but the difference now is that, again in the words of Yeats, 'difficulty is our plough'. Nothing encourages me more than the progress from a first to a final draft in Yeats. Some of my poems in *The Loiners* went through as many as forty or fifty versions. The forms I taught myself, through use and an enormous amount of translation, none of which I kept, are now enactments of unresolved existential problems, of personal energies in ambiguous conflict with the stereo-type, sexual, racial, political, national. The themes, like Zárate's *History of Peru*, are about discovery *and* conquest; celebration and defeat.

The myth of Virgil, whose *Aeneid* I read and re-read for some five years and still read often, and whose labo-rious mother-bear methods of composition I adopted as a heroic posture of my own, is a constant threat to the most hubristic poetic self-confidence. Virgil asked for his 'botched' epic to be burned at his death. The example of Rimbaud is also disturbing. Fracastorius, part of whose *Syphilis* (Verona, 1530) I translated in *The Loiners*, was born literally without a mouth and died speechless. And there is that most haunting epigraph in the whole of literature, the sentence from Azedinne El Mocadecci, prefixed to Edward Powys Mathers's masterly and beautiful rendering of the Panchasika of Chauras, *Black Marigolds*: 'And sometimes we look to the end of the tale that there should be mar-riage feasts, and find only, as it were, black marigolds and a silence.' With these examples in mind and haunted by recent history on which speech gags, the choice, especially in an environment where poetry was only for the 'lassy-lad', seemed to lie between making my poetry important against all odds or giving it up, renouncing all this fiddle for the more important thing. I can't see myself achieving the first, and however hard I try, I don't seem to be able to manage the second, so I expect that like Virgil I'll put off the final renunciation until my deathbed. Meanwhile, I go on trying, wavering between a parody of heroic effort I learned in the hushed attic of my childhood and an equally mock-heroic vow of silence.

The Loiners (citizens of Leeds, *citizens* who bear their loins through the terrors of life, 'loners') was begun in Africa, after I had thawed out my tongue on a Nigerian version of the *Lysistrata*, which I translated and adapted with James Simmons, the Irish poet. Shortly after the publication of *The Loiners*, I was killing time in Hereford Cathedral before catching a train home after giving a reading from the book, and suddenly I found myself standing before the *Mappa Mundi*, a thirteenth-century map of the world like a golden brain with a tumour somewhere near Paradise. If you look at Africa on it, you see all its prodigies, the Hermaphrodites, the Himantopodes, the four-eyed Marmini, the Psylli, the Troglodytes, and the kin of Fracastorius the mouthless race of Ethiopia and all their strange brothers. But in great gold letters the Dark Continent is labelled EUROPE. Prebendary A. L. Moir, writing on this incredible error, suggests either that the names were added erroneously by a later hand, or, and I like to think that this is the truth, that it is 'an attempt to represent Africa–Europe as a single entity with interchangeable names'. I felt the same almost unbearable excitement staring at the *Mappa Mundi* (with no New World as yet) as I felt when I first read the words of Thomas Browne which I use as an epigraph to the African poems in *The Loiners*: 'There is all Africa and her prodigies in us; we are that bold and adventurous piece of nature.' Or when about to move to Newcastle-upon-Tyne, where I am

now living, after four years in Africa and a year in Prague, I
read in a poem attributed to John Cleveland:

Correct your maps: Newcastle is Peru.

That accident (I had my head split open by a laundry van at
the age of three), *that accident, Mrs 'Arrison,* I overheard a
neighbour say to my mother, *all that there reading. It'll turn
'is 'ead.* Now I hear her saying: *I told you so.*

The Misanthrope

1973–4

JANE EYRE'S SISTER

This version of *Le Misanthrope*, commissioned by the National Theatre for production in 1973, the tercentenary of Molière's death, sets the play in 1966, exactly three hundred years after its first performance. One of the focuses for mediating the transition was the famous series of articles that André Ribaud contributed to the French satirical paper *Le Canard enchaîné*, under the title of *La Cour*, with Moisan's brilliant drawings, interpreting the régime of General de Gaulle as if he were Louis XIV. The articles were continued under M. Pompidou as *La Régence*. There are some obvious advantages to such a transposition: characters can still on occasions refer to 'the Court', but it is intended in the sense of M. Ribaud: the subversive pamphlet, foisted on Alceste in the same way as one was foisted on Molière by enemies angered by *Tartuffe*, can be readily accepted in a period during which, from 1959 to 1966, no fewer than three hundred convictions were made under a dusty old law which made it a crime to insult the head of state; above all, it has the advantage of anchoring in a more accessible society some of the more far-reaching and complex implications of Alceste's dilemma, personal,

social, ethical, political. Once the transition had been made
other adjustments had to follow. The sonnet I first wrote
for Oronte has now been replaced by something closer to
my own experience of today's poetaster. To adapt what John
Dryden, one of my masters and mentors in the art of the
couplet, said of his great translation of Virgil's *Aeneid*, 'I
hope the additions will seem not stuck into Molière, but
growing out of him': no more intrusive, that is, than the
sackbut, psaltery and dulcimer the Jacobean translators of
the Bible introduced into the court of Nebuchadnezzar, or
the Perigord pies and Tokay that the anonymous translator
of 1819 introduces into his version of *Le Misanthrope*. That
same version seems to base its Clitandre on Lord Byron.
I have used contemporary, but less talented, models. The
version itself is my form of exegesis.

I was 'educated' to produce jog-trot versions of the
classics. Apart from a weekly chunk of Johnson, Pitt the
Younger and Lord Macaulay to be done into Ciceronian
Latin, we had to turn once living authors into a form of
English never spoken by men or women, as if to compensate our poor tongue for the misfortune of not being a
dead language. I remember once making a policeman in a
Plautus play say something like '*Move along there,*' only to
have it scored through and '*Vacate the thoroughfare*' put in
its place. This tradition lingers in the verse versions of the
nineteenth and twentieth centuries. This is a typical piece
of ripe Virgilian translation:

> Penthesilea furent, the bands leading
> Of lune-shield Amazons, mid thousands burns,

Beneath exserted mamma golden zone
Girds warrior, and, a maid dares cope with men.

That would have earned some marginal VGs from my mentors. With the help of Gavin Douglas, John Dryden, Ezra Pound and Edward Powys Mathers I managed to escape from all this into what I hope is a more creative relationship with foreign tongues. So my translation, when I do it now, is a *Jack and the Beanstalk* act, braving the somnolent ogre of a British classical education to grab the golden harp.

The problems of the academic coming to grips with a classic of foreign literature, in this case some three centuries old, puts me in mind of Francis Galton, the cousin of Charles Darwin, on his travels in Damaraland, southern Africa, in 1851, who, wishing to measure the phenomenon of steatopygia in what he called 'a Venus among Hottentots', but restrained by Victorian *pudeur*, took a series of observations with his sextant, and having obtained the base and angles, proceeded to work out the lady's intriguing 'endowments' by trigonometry and logarithms. The poet, and the man of the theatre, has to be bolder and more intimate.

The salient feature of Molière's verse is its vigour and energy, rather than any metaphorical density or exuberant invention, and it is this which gives his verse plays their characteristic dramatic pace. In *Le Misanthrope* the effect of the rhyming couplet is like that of a time bomb ticking away behind the desperation of Alceste, and Célimène's fear of loneliness. The relentless rhythm helps to create the tensions and panics of high comedy, and that *rire dans l'âme* that Donneau de Visé experienced on the first night of the play in 1666. The explosion never comes. But the silence, when the ticking stops, is almost as deafening. There is an almost Chekhovian tension between farce and anguish. To create this vertiginous effect, verse (and *rhymed* verse) is indispensable. Neither blank verse nor prose will do. I have made use of a couplet similar to the one I used in *The Loiners*, running the lines over, breaking up sentences, sometimes using the odd half-rhyme to subdue the chime, playing off the generally colloquial tone and syntax against the formal structure, letting the occasional couplet leap out as an epigram in moments of devastation or wit. My floating *'s* is a way of linking the couplet at the joint and speeding up the pace by making the speaker deliver it as almost one line, not two. And so on. I have made use of the occasional Drydenian triplet and, once in Act III, of something I call a 'switchback' rhyme, a device I derive from the works of George Formby, e.g. in 'Mr Wu':

> Once he sat down – those hot irons he didn't spot 'em.
> He gave a yell – and cried, 'Oh my – I've gone and
>   scorched my . . . singlet!'

or:

> Oh, Mister Wu at sea he wobbles like a jelly,
> but he's got lots of pluck, although he's got a yellow . . .
>   jumper!

I have also tried both before and during rehearsals to orchestrate certain coughs, kisses, sighs and hesitation mechanisms into the iambic line. These are sometimes indicated by (/) in the text.

An American scholar (forgetting Sarah Bernhardt) said of rhymed translation that it was 'like a woman undertaking to act Hamlet'. A similar, though much more appropriate, summary of the kinship between my version and the original was given by my six-year-old son, Max. 'I know that Molière,' he said, with true Yorkshire chauvinism, though he was born in Africa. 'She's Jane Eyre's sister.'

MOLIÈRE NATIONALISED

I

Even the *Pictorial Record of the National Theatre 1963–71* on sale at the Old Vic bookstall was discouraging. 'Molière', it says curtly of the National's production of *Tartuffe* in 1968, 'rarely works in English and the National failed to find the key.' I began to feel that I had involved myself in a masochistic enterprise. What the key to Molière in English was I had no clear idea, but I had vague notions of what it wasn't. The trouble with many versions of verse plays done by poets is that publication tends to be primary and performance secondary. It has obvious effects on the resulting text. Despite the growth of public poetry readings in the last ten years and the obvious feedback of oral performance into some of the poetry now being written in Britain or the USA, the poet is still very much bound to the private pleasure of the solitary literate. This doesn't help much when it comes to writing for the theatre. I had to re-examine a great many rhetorical presuppositions. Above all, it seemed to me that if Molière was to work in English, the verse, while retaining his sort of formality, should be as speakable as the most colloquial prose. The negative idea of rhyme as an obstacle one tried to surmount as best one could I discarded, and tried to think of it in positive terms as a way of continuously throwing the action forward, accelerating the pace of the play when necessary, and controlling the flow in a way that prose could never do. The playing time of a verse version tends to be shorter than an equivalent version in prose, and this is a considerable advantage. From the very earliest drafts of my *Misanthrope* I resolved that publication would be as secondary to my purpose as providing a printed score for the concert-goer would be for the composer.

When I first met the director John Dexter in September 1971, he had asked me for a version for seventeenth-century costume, accurate, speakable, no anachronisms, no jarring slang, but in 'modernish' colloquial English. An almost impossibly paradoxical request, I thought at the time. My earliest drafts tried to create the illusion of the colloquial by syntactical means rather than by lexical. Deprived of a really up-to-date lexicon and with a barrier across my choice of image at 1666, the date of the play's first performance, the energy of the spoken lines had to come largely from the syntactical contractions and elisions of modern speech. Some of these problems tied up with those I was trying to cope with in my own poems. I have always listened closely to speech and noted down the devices of relaxed informal styles. I took long walks and spoke the drafts aloud to myself, going over and over the lines to make them as naturally speakable as I could, and at the same time as formally impeccable as possible. I counted lines like the following as an early success with the diction I was aiming for:

> But what I'd like to know's what freak of luck's
> helped to put Clitandre in your good books?

> *Mais au moins dites-moi, Madame, par quel sort*
> *Votre Clitandre a l'honneur de vous plaire si fort.*
>   (vv. 475–6)

Or this kind of exchange between Alceste and Célimène:

> CÉLIMÈNE: I can't not see him. He'd be most upset.
> ALCESTE: I've never known you 'not see' people yet.

The elision of *is*, as in the first example, in positions natural to English speech, though uncommon in representations of that speech in English verse, was one of the first devices I hit upon to create the illusion of the colloquial and to capture some of the pace of the original, a recording of which I played continuously as I worked, as a way of keeping my mind on performance rather than on the page. Here is an example of the same elision used in a position which enables the speaker to run the couplet together:

>   and what I mean to do
>   's find out what her love is: false or true.

The same device can be extended over four lines without violating natural English usage:

> what use would all our virtues be, whose point,
> when all the world seems really out of joint,
> 's to bear with others' contumely and spite,
> without annoyance, even though we're right.

Sometimes my contractions can look, as the 'Commentary' column of the *TLS* (16 March 1973) put it, 'messy on the page', quoting as an example Célimène's line:

> Surely I'd've thought it wouldn't've mattered . . .

but adding that 'English isn't well equipped to point out its vernacular elisions.' I have, for a long time, felt that it ought to be better equipped. One has great need of notations as these things must be scored for the actor in a form as metrically tight as the heroic couplet. The work wasn't written for the page but to be spoken. I wanted the illusion of real people talking and arguing, in a context where we have come to expect declamation and verse arias. The rigorous form of the verse, though, is necessary to create the detachment from reality so essential to the workings of comedy. I worked in this way from the beginning of November 1971 to the end of January 1972, more or less all day every day. As well as the problem of idiomatic speech rhythms which had to be free from slang, I tried to vary the rhythm of the couplet, which is capable of a great deal more variety than it is often given credit for, so that I could give elements of a characteristic rhythm to each actor: the rather rocking rhythm of Philinte, both conciliatory and somewhat complacent; the barbed wit of Célimène, where the end-stopped couplet of Pope was effective; the sly insinuating rhythm of Arsinoé; the staccato oiliness of Oronte; and leaving a much wider scale of variations for Alceste – implacability, satirical outrage, baffled love. Another problem, and one which is perennial in translating from French poetry, is the greater degree of physical concretisation characteristic of the genius of English poetry. I did feel the need to anchor sentiments and statements much more closely to the specific, but I had been very careful, at this stage, to research my concretisations so that they remained in period and I introduced nothing into the text after 1666. John Dexter's reaction to the first draft was that it was very speakable; at the same time, it was so free of vocabulary exclusively modern that Sir Laurence Olivier picked out only two words, 'manic' and 'randy', and the phrase 'so what?' as being too modern to be spoken in period costume. I revised the text only a little between January and August, and then only in a direction away from anything I thought a mere gesture to the dubious permanence of the printed page. In early August, I had a letter from John Dexter saying that he had decided to produce the play in 'modernish dress'. We met for a discussion, and I felt somewhat worried that his decision to transfer the setting had rather marooned my text in the seventeenth century. There were so many references to things specifically of the period: clothes, customs, institutions, the king and the Court with all its etiquette and protocol.

II

The problems of translating a classic of the stage seem to me inextricable from the problems of production. The problems with a version of *Le Misanthrope* are vastly different from those of producing an English play of the seventeenth century in modern dress. There the text is fixed. With a translation the text need not be fixed, and when the collaboration was as close and open as ours was, the words could anchor the production in its chosen time as much as the clothes and the setting. It seems to me now, after the experience of creating a version of the *Lysistrata* for Nigerian actors (unplayable outside West Africa) and of *Le Misanthrope* for the National, that the best way of creating a fresh text of a classic is to tie it to a specific production rather than aim, from the study, at a general all-purpose repertory version. This undoubtedly gives a limited lifetime to the version, but this is no bad thing, as I believe that a 'classic' needs to be retranslated continuously. It seems to me that one could do worse than treat a translation as one does décor or production, as endlessly renewable. Indeed, one could say that one of the marks of a literary classic is its capacity for change and adaptation. I have been very impressed by (and all translators could learn from) the probably obscure but indefatigable labours of John Ogilby (1600–76), who did two *entirely different* translations within a short space of time of a poem as vast as Virgil's *Aeneid*, nearly 10,000 lines, five times as long as *Le Misanthrope*. His first version was in 1649 and his second in 1654. What happened to change not only his but the whole period's focus on the poem were the momentous events leading up to the execution of Charles I in 1649. Ogilby's second version is a far more explicitly Royalist version than the first. History had shocked him into a fresh appraisal of a complex poem, capable of many interpretations, though some of them mutually exclusive. Here, for example, is a piece of Virgil's Latin about the activities of the subversive Fury Alecto:

> *tu potes unanimos armare in proelia fratres*
> *atque odiis versare domos, tu verbera tectis*
> *funerasque inferre faces, tibi nomina mille,*
> *mille nocendi artes, fecundum concute pectus,*
> *disice compositam pacem, sere crimina belli;*
> *arma velit poscatque simul rapiatque iuventus.*
> (*Aeneid* VII, 335–40)

Here is Ogilby's version of 1649:

> Thou loving brothers canst provoke to War,
> Houses destroy with hate, both sword and flames
> Bring to their roofs; thou hast a thousand names,
> As many nocent arts; then quickly shake
> Thy pregnant breasts, and peace confirmed, break;
> Lay grounds for cruel war, make with thy charms
> Their wilde youth rage, require, and take up arms.

Five eventful years later, the same translator sees the same passage through the disturbances of his own times:

> Unanimous Brothers thou canst arm to fight,
> And *settled Courts* destroy with deadly spight;
> Storm *Palaces* with Steel, and Pitchy Flames,
> Thou hast a thousand wicked Arts: and Names,
> Thy Bosom disembogue, with Mischief full,

And Articles concluding Peace annull.
Then raise a War, and with bewitching Charms
Make *the mad People* rage to take up Arms.

The implications of those changes are obvious. Civil war
has become a vision of revolution. Dryden's version of 1697
is informed with the same Hobbesian fears. Momentous
events, and even minor, less spectacular shifts in our *mores*
and environment, give us new attentions and demands on
the long-surviving classic, whose very survival is dependent on its being, in the widest possible sense, retranslated.
History gave Simone Weil her sudden, illuminating insight
into the *Iliad* as 'the poem of force', and made Shakespeare
a 'contemporary' in eastern Europe. If we were to expand
a usual organic metaphor for a work of art, we could say
that, like the rose, for example, in a state of nature, a work
is constantly throwing up new growths. Into these new
growths it gradually directs its sap, and the older growths
become starved out. The activity of pruning, in our case the
historical consciousness at work in the mind of the director or translator of the classic, is to hasten the rejection
of the old wood and to encourage the instincts for producing new growths *especially* (the gardening manuals tell
us) *from the base of the plant.* And pruning of this kind is a
regular, recurrent task. In the oral cultures of Africa, when
words or phrases no longer signify, thrill or seem relevant
to the hearers of a recitation in a particular society, they
tend to become changed. There is in this sort of culture
a homeostatic process at work which we in our museum
culture must often envy, that which the anthropologists call

'structural amnesia', a form of constant, often barely conscious, pruning that keeps a work continuously alive. In our conditions of literacy and individualism this 'structural amnesia' is frustrated by a concern for the text that is almost fetishistic. We update Shakespeare; we clothe him in modern dress; we give his words new emphases, but those words are fixed. It is precisely because of this rigidity in the text that we have come to expect fluidity in the changing focuses of production. The American linguist Charles Hockett has drawn some rather disturbing implications from the objective comparison of oral and literate cultures, and he says:

> In an illiterate society the precise shape of a poem may be gradually modified, a word replaced here, a rhythm or rhyme brought up to date there, in such a way as to keep pace with the changing language. On this score the introduction of writing has some implications which might be called unfortunate. Once a poem is written down it is fixed; it has lost its ability to grow with the language. Sooner or later, the poem is left behind.

We then, even in our own language, have to translate. The implications for an essentially oral art like the theatre are even more interesting. It is in theatrical production and translation that we of a late literate culture can in some measure reassert our lost instincts for 'structural amnesia'. The original is fluid, the translation a static moment in that fluidity. Translations are not built to survive, though their original survives through translation's many flowerings and decays. The illusion of pedantry is that a text is fixed. It cannot be fixed once and for all. The translation is fixed but reinvigorates its original by its decay. It was probably on these lines that Walter Benjamin was thinking when he said in his *The Task of the Translator* that 'the life of an original reaches its ever-recurring, latest and most complete unfolding in translation'. It was with thoughts such as these in the back of my mind that I took away my version of *Le Misanthrope* to revise. Between then and 22 February 1973, when the play opened, I must have rewritten over half the play, though the basic *stylistic* choices had already been made.

III

The first things to be updated were the clothes. The *grands canons, vaste rhingrave* and *perruque blonde* of the foppish Clitandre became, in Alceste's mockery to Célimène:

> What makes him captivate the social scene?
> Second-skin gauchos in crêpe-de-chine?
> Those golden blow-wave curls (that aren't his own)?
> Those knickerbockers, or obsequious tone?
> Or is it his giggle and his shrill falsett-
> o hoity-toity voice makes him your pet?

Clitandre's 'knickerbockers' came in only very late, after I had seen what Tanya Moisiewitsch had given him to wear in the last act. Clitandre's *ongle long*, the long fingernail of seventeenth-century fashion, I found hard to contextualise, as I only knew of Brazil where the fashion persists into our own day. Finally, I made Clitandre an habitué of Angelina's tea shop on the rue de Rivoli:

> What amazing talents does the 'thing' possess,
> what sublimity of virtue? Let me guess.
> I'm at a loss. No, let me see. *I know!*
> It's his little finger like a *croissant*, so,
> crooked at *Angelina's* where he sips his tea
> among the titled queens of 'gay' Paree!

I had one couplet in the first draft which went:

> proof of all the mean and dirty tricks
> of Mankind circa 1666.

I changed this to 1966, thinking, I suppose, to execute a circle of three hundred years for the Molière tercentenary. A fetishistic gesture, perhaps, and at this stage little more than that. Then I was reminded of André Ribaud's series of articles in *Le Canard enchaîné*, which adopted the style of Saint-Simon's *Mémoires* and under the title of *La Cour* satirised the autocratic regime of de Gaulle as if he were Louis XIV, under whose reign, of course, *Le Misanthrope* was first performed. The pieces were reissued in a paperback collection by Juillard in 1961. The series continued under M. Pompidou as *La Régence*. The point is that these articles in *Le Canard enchaîné* appeared regularly over a long period and terms such as '*le roi*' and '*la cour*' in M. Ribaud's sense were as current as, say, 'grocer' was with us. Now the phrase 'circa 1966' seemed exactly right and *La Cour* gave me cues for the rewriting of all the many references to 'the Court' and 'the king', etc. As I rewrote in this way some of the implications of *Le Misanthrope*, so often concealed under the frills of the traditional courtier, became much clearer to me. I let two references to 'the Court' stand but put them in the inverted commas of *Le Canard enchaîné*. Some became 'the Élysée', and others more knowingly became 'over there' and the king a whispered confidential 'HE'. One, if not the sole, cause of the guarded, wary *politesse* of court society was precisely its autocratic nature. '*La Cour*', wrote Saint-Simon, '*fut un autre manège de la politique du despotisme.*' Perhaps, I thought, by concentrating less on the *forms* of this *politesse* and more on its *meaning* I would be able to clarify a little the discrepancy between Alceste's violent attacks on the *symptoms* of social corruption and his complete lack of an objective *diagnosis*. The outer Court of real power is reflected in the brilliant mirror of the 'court' of Célimène's *salon*. It seems more than a linguistic accident that makes many commentators refer to Célimène's *salon* as a 'court'. Lionel Gossman brings out some of the inferences in *Men and Masks: A Study of Molière* (Baltimore, MD: Johns Hopkins University Press, 1963).

The court of Célimène with its urbanity, wit and formal civility masking subterranean rivalries and resentments calls to mind a passage in Saint-Simon's *Mémoires* which describes another and more celebrated court:

Les fêtes fréquentes, les promenades particulières à Versailles, les voyages furent des moyens que le Roi

*saisit pour distinguer et pour mortifier en nommant
les personnes qui à chaque fois en devaient être, et pour
tenir chacun assidu et attentif à lui plaire. Il sentait
qu'il n'avait pas à beaucoup près assez de grâces à
répandre pour faire un effet continuel. Il en substitu
donc aux véritables d'idéales, par la jalousie, les petits
préférences qui se trouvaient tous les jours, et pour ainsi
dire à tous moments, par son art. Les espérances que ses
petites préférences et ces distinctions faisaient naître,
et la consideration qui s'en tirat, personne ne fut plus
ingénieux que lui à inventer . . .*

The frequent fetes, the private promenades at
Versailles, the journeys, were means on which the
King seized in order to distinguish or mortify the
courtiers, and thus render them more assiduous in
pleasing him. He felt that of real favours he had not
enough to bestow; in order to keep up the spirit of
devotion, he therefore unceasingly invented all sorts
of ideal ones, little preferences and petty distinctions,
which answered his purpose as well.

While it would be ludicrous to suggest that Molière
deliberately dressed Louis XIV up as Célimène, it is
worth noting that some acute observers discovered
in the supreme social reality of Molière's own time
the same structure of relations as that which binds
Célimène and her world together in the supreme
comedy of that same time.

It seems very worth noting, though the last thing I wanted to suggest was that Diana Rigg was Charles de Gaulle in drag. The *roi soleil* shines on some and leaves others in outer darkness. It was written of de Gaulle quite recently that 'he was so narcissistically self-absorbed in being the Idea of France on the international plane that a great many Frenchmen came to feel half-consciously that they were only anonymous fodder for his representational ego'. The sense of intrigue is strong in the play, outside and inside, even in the minor off-stage characters, impaled only on the spike of Célimène's wit in the portrait scene, Timante 'the cloak-and-dagger-ite', and the resentments of Adraste 'the utter megalomaniac'. There is an off-stage autocratic power 'over there', and once the rehearsals got onto the set this became literally so, for the Élysée Palace was through the window and over the way. This power continually enters into the conversation of the *salon*, in its consciousness of being 'in', its knowingness. Later, the power irrupts into the room in the threat of arrest for a subversive pamphlet. Both Oronte and Arsinoé are tempters in that they offer Alceste 'influence', they will 'oil the wheels' or obtain a 'place' or a 'sinecure', if only he will admire a piddling poem or show some sexual interest. Acaste and Clitandre come to Célimène's 'party' directly from the Élysée. There is a constant feeling of the nearness of political power. There is also something in the restless gaiety of such a *salon* that conceals defeat and desperation. It seems to be a recurrent phenomenon in all periods of impending change. One recalls Gérard de Nerval's comment on a similar brilliance of his own set in *Sylvie*:

. . . où toute mélancolie cédait devant la verve intarissable
. . . tel qu'il s'en est trouvé dans les époques de rénovation
ou de décadence, et dont les discussions se haussaient à ce
point, que les plus timides d'entre nous allaient voir parfois
aux fenêtres si les Huns, les Turcomans ou les Cosaques
n'arrivaient pas enfin pour couper court à ces arguments . . .

. . . with the sense of bitter sadness left by a vanished
dream . . . Periods of renewal or decadence always
produce such natures, and our discussions often
became so animated that timid ones in the company
would glance from the window to see if the Huns, the
Turkomans or the Cossacks were not coming to put an
end to those disputations . . .

It is difficult with this reading of the background of the
play to assent to the Romantic interpretations of it, though
they have helped to focus on the obvious *subjective* anguish
of Alceste. The play is not a tragedy, not even the *tragédie
bourgeoise* that Brunetière called it, and certainly it is utterly
absurd to call it 'an uncompromising left-wing play', as one
critic did. It is too complex a play to be claimed by either
left or right. Alceste is not a political radical, and far from
being a proto-Marxist, and certainly, as he wavers between
the *salon* of a coquette and a country estate, no activist.
One has to clear *désert* of its Romantic accretions and go to
Madame de Sévigné and the Furetière dictionary of 1690
for the meaning: country estate. Alceste's *désert* is rather
like an inverted image of the Moscow of the *Three Sisters* of
Chekhov. I have already said how the modern background

helps to show the absence of real objective social analysis in Alceste's outbursts, though it by no means should exclude his subjective pain and anguish, which make him a both comic and moving figure. Others have been less lenient with Alceste. Mauriac said of him that 'in a world where injustice is rife, he is up in arms against trivialities'. Against this judgement Martin Turnell in *The Classical Moment* asks us to set Stendhal's view of Alceste:

> His mania for hurling himself against whatever appears odious, his gift for close and accurate reasoning and his extreme probity would soon have led him into politics or, what would have been much worse, to an objectionable and seditious philosophy. Célimène's *salon* would at once have been compromised and soon become a desert. And what would a coquette find to do in a deserted *salon*?

One must also remember how horrified he is to have a subversive pamphlet foisted onto him by his enemies, in the way that Molière himself had by *dévots* angered by *Tartuffe*. It seems to me that the production at the National took cognizance of both these extremes of opinion, and while recognising Alceste's *potential* for political thought, is faithful to Molière in leaving in ambiguity any fulfilment of that potential. If the play is set 'circa 1966', the spectator worried by these issues can always ask himself the question, 'What would the position of this Alceste be in *les événements* of May 1968?' The transposition, in my view, helps to make the background more important, though none the less *background* to the central human relationship, than the stereotypes of period costume perhaps allow.

Erich Auerbach's brilliant study of the meaning of *La Cour et La Ville* in the seventeenth century shows that real power has bypassed such people as Acaste and his whole class, 'meaningless, without economic or political or any other organic foundation'. Alceste is only partially or potentially liberated from this milieu. With Gossman I find something almost Chekhovian in *Le Misanthrope*. 'Chekhov', he writes, 'joins hands over the centuries with his great predecessor, for Molière's *Misanthrope* is the first profound statement in modern terms of the world's silent indifference to those who no longer have any significant place in it or relation to it.'

IV

We began rehearsals in late December 1972, with a text that was for me still only partially anchored in the recent past. I felt that I had by no means solved all the problems of the transposition, but we had decided to leave the text as it stood as a 'springboard' into the play, and we hoped that I would be able to do what rewriting seemed necessary in a concentrated way after hearing the actors' reactions and earliest interpretations. The best way to illustrate what happened during rehearsals and how much the text owes to the close collaboration of director, actors and poet is to take a few examples. I had earlier objected to John Dexter that since we were now in the '60s of this century a poetaster like Oronte was unlikely to produce a sonnet. Others agreed, and Kenneth Tynan felt that a parody of a modern style would be better. The more I heard the sonnet in rehearsals, the more convinced I became that it wasn't right. I had originally given Oronte a sonnet in octosyllabics, as in Molière:

> Hope can ease the lover's pain,
> make anguish easier to bear,
> but, Phyllis, that's a doubtful gain
> if all that follows hope's despair.
>
> Great kindness to me once you showed.
> You should have been I think less kind.
> Why so much so soon bestowed
> if hope was all you had in mind?
>
> With all eternity to wait
> a lover's zeal turns desperate
> and looks for hope in last extremes!
>
> Lovely Phyllis, I'm past care
> but lovers like me all despair
> if offered only hope and dreams.

I planted deliberate excrescences for Alceste to pick up in his outburst when it finally comes, making the criticism a little more specific than in the original:

> You followed unnatural models when you wrote;
> your style's stiff and awkward. Let me quote:
> 'last extremes' tautologous, the rest, hot air;

it goes in circles: *bear/care, despair/despair,*
wait/desperate, all pretty desperate rhymes.
It's repetitive: hope you use five times.

When the sonnet went, that went too. I had earlier rewritten all the entrances in the first three acts to adapt to John Dexter's idea of running those acts together with a party going on downstairs, as a means of overcoming the perennial problem of 'visiting' in seventeenth-century plays. This also led to the brilliant juxtaposition of Lully's music to the same music transposed into a modern pop idiom by Marc Wilkinson. We had still not solved the problem of an equivalent for the Marshalsea of France, an office of the seventeenth century created to arbitrate in quarrels between gentlemen after the abolition of duelling. It is an obscure enough office to warrant a note in all editions and translations. The dramatic point lies in the discrepancy between the machinery brought to bear and the triviality of the quarrel between Alceste and Oronte over the trifling poem in question. I made the Marshalsea the *Académie Française* at John Dexter's suggestion. Kenneth Tynan had suggested that Oronte should threaten to have Alceste blackballed from *Le Jockey Club*, which though socially plausible hadn't, we decided, the right imposing sound for an English audience unacquainted with French high life. But I had tried a version with *Le Jockey Club.* I imagined Oronte coming over to Célimène's party, a little drunk and overfed, from Maxim's, where the Club Committee, say, had been dining, with his poem, clearly intended for Célimène, doodled on the Maxim's menu, which he turned this way and that as he reconstructed the jottings as he recited. I tried to retain the theme of the original sonnet, with its contrast between a lover's hope and despair, while trying to draw the metaphors from the new context. It went something like:

> That kiss was my *apéritif*,
> that cuddle the *hors d'oeuvres*.
> Now I'm wanting the roast beef
> that's something you won't serve.
>
> Passion's a sort of super chef
> and you his *spécialité*.
> Fulfilment the head waiter's deaf
> and never looks my way.
>
> And so alone at Love's *Maxim's*
> I gnaw the empty air.
> Here's my plate of hopeless dreams,
> my drained glass of despair.

Neither Alec McCowen nor Diana Rigg, whose insights into comedy were a constant inspiration for me to produce them better lines, thought the new Oronte poem appropriate. I could see that they were right and I rejected it there and then. Diana Rigg went to her dressing room and brought back a 'little magazine' of poetry, and said that she thought Oronte was more likely to write something like the poems in it. We all read them aloud and decided she was right. Memories of editing little magazines came

back to me, and that evening after rehearsals, prompted by
the magazine Diana Rigg had given me 'for inspiration', I
wrote Oronte's poem as it now stands, again preserving the
theme, if nothing else:

> Hope was assuaging:
> its glimmer
> cheered my gloomy pilgrimage
> to the gold shrine of your love . . .
>
> a mirage of water pool and palms
> to a nomad lost in the Sahara . . .
>
> but in the end it only makes thirst worse.
>
> Darling, if this hot trek
> to some phantasmal Mecca
> of love's consummation
> is some sort of Herculean Labour
> then I've fallen by the wayside.
>
> A deeper, darker otherwhere
> is unfulfilment . . .
>
> we who have bathed in the lustrous light
> of your charisma
> now languish in miasmal black despair
> and all we hopeless lovers share
> the nightmare of the bathosphere.

Alceste's outburst, to correspond to Oronte's new literary excrescences, I felt had to be somewhat ruder than before:

> Jesus wept!
> It's bloody rubbish, rhythmically inept,
> vacuous verbiage, wind, gas, guff.
> All lovestruck amateurs churn out that stuff.
> It's formless, slack, a nauseating sprawl,
> and riddled with stale clichés; that's not all.
> 'Thirst worse' cacophonous, and those '*ek eks*'
> sound like a bullfrog in the throes of sex.

The bullfrog, of course, came partly from Aristophanes and partly from the grotesque appearance of the huffing, much-padded Gawn Grainger as Oronte.

Another passage that was rewritten in rehearsal was Eliante's speech beginning:

> *L'amour pour l'ordinaire, est peu fait à ces lois.*
> *Et l'on voit les amants vanter toujours leur choix.*
> (vv. 711–12)

Many editors, I think wrongly, find the dramatic justification of this speech a little doubtful, and try to explain its presence by saying that Molière was using up an old version of Lucretius' *De rerum Natura* (IV, 1160–69) that he had written in his youth. The piece has a relevance I haven't the space to dwell on, but one cannot escape the feeling that the lines have the air of a prepared set piece, as though Eliante were only able to be witty through the proxy of quotation, as opposed to Célimène's spontaneous crackle. I decided to take those critics head-on and allow Eliante to call her speech 'not inapposite' to the situation. I also went back to the Latin of Lucretius for the examples of love's euphemisms and made Eliante introduce her speech with the admission that what was to follow was a quotation from a well-known source:

> How does that bit in old Lucretius go,
> that bit on blinkered lovers? O, you know . . .

I could give many examples of lines, phrases, whole couplets, words which I revised in collaboration with the actors, when they were reaching for something better, or funnier, or simply dramatically more effective. Often I went away and produced a set of possible alternatives for one couplet, and the actor in question and John Dexter and maybe others involved in the scene would test them and vote on which was best. The last alteration to be made was in the same Eliante speech. It was something I had felt to be wrong but, I suppose, had hoped that at this late stage no one would notice. I had all along tried to maintain the illusion of 'Frenchness' by making use of French words, not necessarily in the original, which were common currency in English, often as rhyme words to stress their presence, phrases like: '*au fait*', '*bons mots*', '*mon cher*', '*entrée*', '*ordinaire*', '*enchanté*'. But in Eliante's speech I had:

> The 'svelte gazelle''s the girl all skin and bone.
> 'Majestic, regal' means, say, fifteen stone.

Sir Laurence Olivier noticed it at the first dress rehearsal and said it jarred, so two days before the opening the lines became:

> The loved one's figure's like Venus de Milo's
> even the girl who weighs a hundred kilos.

Palladas

1974

One of the disadvantages of the traditional organisation of those 4,000-odd epigrams that make up *The Greek Anthology* is that the poems are arranged according to subject matter and type, thus obscuring the singularity of individual poets. Peter Jay's decision to rearrange the poems by poet and period for his selection of modern versions allowed distinctive talents to emerge clearly from the welter of reiterated themes; among the most notable of them, that gloomy epigrammatist of the fourth century AD, Palladas of Alexandria.

Gilbert Highet places Palladas among the world's great pessimists – with Juvenal, Swift, Nietzsche, Bernard de Morval (the author of *De Contemptu Mundi*) and Ecclesiastes; while J. W. Mackail, somewhat tantalisingly, as he felt unable actually to print the poem in his selection, regards poem 1, sometimes known as 'The Descent of Man', as 'one of the most mordant and crushing sarcasms ever passed upon Mankind'. His dates are usually given as AD 360–430, but C. M. Bowra, in an essay 'Palladas and Christianity', argues fairly plausibly for putting his birth at about 319, and – since we know from poem 40[1] that he lived at least seventy-two years – for placing his death around the end of the century. This would make him an old man

at the time of the savage anti-pagan riots and destruction
of Greek temples, the looting and burning of pagan objects
of worship by Christian mobs given licence by the edicts of
the Emperor Theodosius in 391, and inflamed by the rabble-
rousing Bishop Theophilus. That his last years should have
coincided with the virtual destruction of the system of
beliefs to which he owed his always precarious living as a
schoolmaster gives us an added insight into the bitter force
of his poetry. The new dates calculated by Bowra also mean
that he died before he could witness the dreadful murder
of the Hellenistic teacher and intellectual Hypatia, whose
flesh was scraped from her bones by Christians wielding
oyster shells like razors. But there is no doubt that he must
have witnessed similar events, even though the well-known
poem 18[2] seems to me more gnomic than specifically about
the persecution of non-Christians. I have included the
poem (67[3]) which Palladas was supposed to have addressed
to Hypatia since their two names, the martyr of Hellenistic
culture and the poet of its last exasperated gasp, have been
traditionally associated in the drama of its extinction.

Palladas, when noticed at all, is generally regarded as the
last poet of paganism, and it is in this role that I have sought
to present a consistent dramatic personality in this selection of slightly less than half the poems ascribed to him in
The Greek Anthology. His are the last hopeless blasts of the
old Hellenistic world, giving way reluctantly, but without
much resistance, before the cataclysm of Christianity. It is
difficult, if not impossible, at this time of sectarian violence,
pagan hopelessness and Christian barbarity to characterise
Hellenism as worldly sanity, or Christianity as sweetness

and light. Poor Palladas seems to be in the predicament of his murderer in that rather nasty poem 'The Murderer & Sarapis' (70[4]). There seems to have been little or no moral sustenance or sense of identity left in the one, and little sense of hope in the other. The choice was between a crumbled past and a future of specious regeneration. This is the conflict of the following rather mysterious poem of his (*Greek Anthology* 10.82) about the Christian attitude to the Hellenes:

> We non-Christians are dead, and only seem
> alive; the life we're living's a bad dream,
> or so THEY say. My version of it's this:
> *we're* alive but wonder if life is!

The irony of Palladas' image as 'the last of the pagans' gloomily watching the Christian world view assert itself, even, as I have imagined, in the person of his own wife (see poem 52[5]), is that his is a paganism so turned in on itself that in its hatred of life and the senses, and its scorn of worldly goods and endowments, it seems very like the spirit of early Christianity; 'a Father of the Church', Palladas has been called, 'who has all the proper characteristics except faith, hope and charity'.

His bitterness is compounded of historical pessimism, the poverty of a poor teacher dependent on rich Hellenes for his very precarious existence (see poem 31[6]), and a bad marriage which seems to have led to general misogyny. His ironic poems (such as 63[7]) on the new time-serving roles of the old gods show that bitter sense of humour which prevents a man from toppling over into the abyss of his own creation. There is no sense of joy in his few poems on the *carpe diem* theme. He recommends drink as oblivion. The sense of death is stronger than any urge to sensual life. The tone of his bitterness ranges from common-room bitchiness (e.g. poem 37[8]), still so much a part of the 'humanist' tradition, the donnish moue and pedantic repartee, to a cosmic derision like an orchestrated death rattle. What is unique and even invigorating about Palladas is that there is no sense at all of 'gracious' surrender either to the inevitability of death or to historical change. Even the fatalism of poems like 10[9] seems grudging. If there is only the bleakest of Epicurean attitudes, there is certainly nothing Stoical about Palladas. He is one of those embarrassing but heroic figures who are not dignified in despair, refusing to be noble on the gallows or to make peace with their maker. It is perhaps this aspect of his tone, his 'raging against the dying of the light', that makes commentators like Mackail refer to his 'harsh thought and half barbarous language', or like Gilbert Highet to regret his lack of 'great verbal dexterity'. He is certainly not elegant (and most certainly not in that false sense often wished onto the classics by classicists); his is not the stylish after-dinner despair of the high table, the sighing gestures of surfeit, but the authentic snarl of a man trapped physically in poverty and persecution, and metaphysically in a deep sense of the futile. He is not, as it happens, incapable of the dexterous play on words, the pedantic pun or the neat turn (e.g. poem 51[10]). For all his complaints about life as a *grammatikos* teaching children to learn Homer by rote, he must have been familiar enough with the Greek traditions to have produced any amount of passably smooth imitations, and so we must assume that the undeniable roughness of his tone was worked for. His epigrams are much more 'pointed' than most of his predecessors' in *The Greek Anthology*, and 'point' is somehow the formal equivalent of despair. There is a strong sense of form in Palladas, and it is something which barely seems able to contain the apoplectic energy of his nihilistic scorn. It is as if the formal endeavour and metrical tension were all that stood between Palladas and choking silence, sheer cosmic exasperation and what Beckett's Lucky calls 'divine aphasia'.

1.

40
A lifetime's teaching grammar come to this –
returned as member for Necropolis!

2.

18
Death feeds us up, keeps an eye on our weight
and herds us like pigs through the abattoir gate.

3.

67. Hypatia
Searching the zodiac, gazing on Virgo,
knowing your province is really the heavens,
finding your brilliance everywhere I look,
I render you homage, revered Hypatia,
teaching's bright star, unblemished, undimmed.

4.

70. The Murderer & Sarapis
A murderer spread his palliasse
beneath a rotten wall
and in his dream came Sarapis
and warned him it would fall:

Jump for your life, wretch, and be quick!
One more second and you're dead.
He jumped and tons of crumbling brick
came crashing on his bed.

The murderer gasped with relief,
he thanked the gods above.
It was his innocent belief
they'd saved him out of love.

But once again came Sarapis
in the middle of the night,
and once more uttered prophecies
that set the matter right:

Don't think the gods have let you go
and connive at homicide.
we've spared you that quick crushing, so
we can get you crucified.

5.

52

Cuckolded husbands have no certain sign
that trusted wives are treacherous, *like mine*.
The ugly woman's not *de facto* pure,
nor every beauty fast. You're never sure.
The beddable girl, though every bidder woos
with cash and comfort's likely to refuse.
There's many a plain nympho who bestows
expensive gifts on all her gigolos.

The serious woman, seemingly man-shy
and never smiling, does that mean chastity?
Such gravity's worn only out of doors;
at home, in secret, they're all utter whores.
The chatty woman with a word for all
may well be chaste, though that's improbable.
Even old age gets goaded into lust;
senility's no guarantee. What can we trust?

I've got twelve gods to swear my honour by,
she, convenient Christianity!

6.

31

It's grammarians that the gods torment
and Homer's fatal wrath's their instrument.

Monthly (if that!) the grudging nanny wraps
their measly pittance in papyrus scraps.

She nicks some, switches coins, and not content
holds out her grasping claws for 10 per cent,
then lays at teacher's feet a screw of stuff
like paper poppies on a cenotaph.

Just get one loving father to agree
to pay (in decent gold!) a yearly fee,
the eleventh month, just when it's almost due,
he'll hire a 'better teacher' and fire you.

Your food and lodging gone, he's got the gall
to crack after-dinner jokes about it all.

7.

63. *On a Temple of Fortune Turned into a Tavern*
i
Agh, the world's gone all to fuck
when Luck herself's run out of luck!

ii
Fortune, fortune-maker/breaker,
human nature cocktail-shaker,

goddess one, and now a barmaid
's not too drastic change of trade!

You'll do nicely where you are
behind the counter of The Fortune Bar,

metamorphosed to 'mine host'
the character that suits you most.

iii
Fortune, can you hear them making fun,
all the mortals, now you're one?

This time you've really gone too far
blotting out your own bright star.

Once queen of a temple, now you're old
you serve hot toddies to keep out the cold.

Well might you complain, now even you
suffer from yourself as mere men do.

8.

37
You brainless bastard! O you stupid runt!
Such showing off and you so ignorant!
When the talk's linguistics, you look bored;
your specialism's Plato. Bloody fraud!
Someone says, 'Ah, Plato!' then you duck
behind some weighty new phonetics book.

Linguistics! Plato Studies! Dodge and switch,
you haven't a clue, though, which is which.

9.

10

If gale-force Fortune sweeps you off your feet,
let it; ride it; and admit defeat.

There's no point in resisting; it's too strong –
willy-nilly, you'll get swept along.

10.

51

You invite me out, but if I can't attend
I've had the honour and I'm more your friend.

The heart's no gourmet, no, it feels
honour stays hunger more than meals.

Phaedra Britannica

1975

Prétends-tu m'éblouir des Fables de la Grèce? . . .
Quoiqu'au-dessus de nous ils sont ce que nous sommes,
Et comme nous enfin Héros sont des Hommes.

Do you pretend to dazzle me with the fables
    of Greece? . . .
Though above us they are what we are,
And for us heroes are finally men.
      Pradon, *Phèdre et Hippolyte*, 1677

I

Racine took two years to write *Phèdre*, and I took two
years to adapt it for the English stage. My methods, such
as they are, a mixture of what Dryden called metaphrase
and paraphrase, are no more original than Johnson's *Vanity
of Human Wishes* or than Racine's, who made his play out
of the Greek of Euripides and the Latin of Seneca, as
well as earlier dramatic versions of the myth in his own
tongue. In a pre-Romantic age I would feel little need for
self-justification, nor feel I need be defensive about the
poet's role as adapter. Nothing better could be said on that
issue than what was written by Lion Feuchtwanger in his
poem 'Adaptations' (1924), composed after collaborating

with Brecht on their version of *Edward II* after Marlowe:

I, for instance, sometimes write
Adaptations. Or some people prefer the phrase
'Based on', and this is how it is: I use
Old material to make a new play, then
Put under the title
The name of the dead writer who is extremely
Famous and quite unknown, and before
The name of the dead writer I put the little word 'After'.
Then one group will write that I am
Very respectful and others that I am nothing of the sort
    and all
The dead writer's failures
Will be ascribed
To me and all my successes
To the dead writer who is extremely
Famous and quite unknown, and of whom
Nobody knows whether he himself
Was the writer or maybe the
Adaptor.

Critics of *Phaedra Britannica* have provided a spectrum of opinion as wide and as contradictory as that in the Feuchtwanger poem, from the English critic (to whom Racine was, no doubt, 'quite unknown') who accused me of taking a 'crowbar' to the original, to the French critic Jean-Jacques Gautier, writing in *Le Figaro* and finding that in my version '*la noblesse linéaire, la flamme, la grandeur de l'ouvrage original est préservée*'.

II

When a play becomes a 'vehicle' only, the greater part of it has died. 'If we go to see *Phèdre*,' wrote Roland Barthes, 'it's on account of a particular great actress, a certain number of felicitous lines, some famous *tirades* set against a background of obscurity and boredom. We tolerate the rest.' Barthes was writing after the production by Jean Vilar at the TNP in 1957 with Maria Casarès, and his reluctant conclusion was prominently displayed in the programme of a production I saw in Paris in 1974 at the Théâtre Essaion: *'Je ne sais pas s'il est possible de jouer Racine aujourd'hui. Peut-être sur scène ce théâtre est-il aux trois-quart mort.'* Similarly, Jean-Louis Barrault in his *Mise en scène de Phèdre* (1946) writes that audiences went to see Sarah Bernhardt as Phèdre, but they didn't go to see the *piece*. They didn't even go to see the divine Sarah in the *entire* role, but the two scenes in which she excelled: the declaration of Act II and the despair of Act IV. *'Phèdre n'est pas un concerto pour femme,'* Barrault warns us, *'mais une symphonie pour orchestre d'acteurs.'* The solution to the problem offered by Barrault could well apply to the revival of any classic play that has become simply a one-role play by coming adrift from its social origins: *'Phèdre femme doit de nouveau s'incorporer dans Phèdre tragédie.'* A play is 'about' everyone who sets foot on the stage, principals and mutes alike. The way to re-energise *Phèdre*, setting aside for the moment the well-nigh insuperable problems of doing that for an English audience, is to rediscover a *social* structure which makes the tensions and polarities of the play significant again. To make the roles, neglected for the sake of the 'vehicle' role, meaningful again. To grasp the *play* entire. It is only when the characters around her are duly reinstated that the central figure can be seen in her true light. One can begin by going back to the title displayed on the original edition of Racine's text in 1677: *Phèdre et Hippolyte*. In order to correct the theatrical imbalance and sharpen the focus, one needs such, perhaps overloaded, assertions as Leo Spitzer's that Thésée is the most important person in the play. He is, after all, left alive with the awareness of the consequence of his actions, and the knowledge of the deaths of his wife and son. He has the last word.

III

There is a mode of literary criticism, built upon the ruins of neoclassicism, and deriving from a period which was beginning to value intensity of experience at the expense of structure, a mode of criticism that extracts the principal 'beauties' of a work, Arnoldian 'touchstones', as though the essence of poetry resided in a few reverberant lines, and long works like Homer's were nothing more than a handful of titillating monosticha, rooted out of grey unappealing tracts by Romantic truffle-hounds. It's an attitude represented at its extreme by Poe's opinion that 'there is no such thing as a long poem'. It made assayer Matthew Arnold call Dryden and Pope 'classics of our *prose*'. Racine has suffered similarly in France. Henri de Montherlant thought that there were only twenty-seven lines of 'poetry' in the whole *oeuvre* of Racine, some 20,000 lines. Jean Dutourd thought that Racine's alexandrines were 99 per cent rhetoric and 1 per cent 'poetry'. One line which has consistently seemed to glitter from all this dross is one which Flaubert thought the most beautiful line in the whole of French literature, and which Proust valued for its *beauté dénuée de significa-tion*. It's a line which, typically, can only be understood, like most of Arnold's rhapsodical nuggets, by referring it back to the total context from which it was prised, by reconstructing the strata from which it was hastily lifted. One has to assume the responsibility of the archaeologist among so many opportunist treasure-seekers. The line in question is the famous one spoken by Hippolyte describing Phèdre as:

La fille de Minos et de Pasiphaé.

Admittedly, it is a crucial line. A line full of mythical reverberations. For those who know the myth. And it's not enough to refer the *reader*, as most French editions do, to the *tableau généologique* or the *index mythologique*. For one thing, we are preparing a piece for the stage and not the study. Tableaux and indices are not theatrical, at least in a would-be Racinian recreation. The line is the key to the inner struggle of Phèdre, to her essential torment. For those who are at home in the obscure genealogies of Crete! As an eighteenth-century commentator puts it, this line '*semble préparer le spectateur à ce caractère mélangé de vices et de remords que le poète donne à Phèdre*'. The key word in this is '*mélangé*'. Many simply stress that the line signals the bad heredity of Phèdre, as if it were simply a case of the mother, Pasiphaë, though R. C. Knight tentatively suggests that 'Minos *may* perhaps stand for moral conscience'. Both elements of Phèdre's parentage are of equal importance. The problem about expanding the line, and absorbing into it the facts given in study texts by genealogies impossible to project theatrically, is that the line occurs in a context of nervous reticence. It is an old story for Hippolyte and Théramène. Théramène cuts off Hippolyte with an abrupt '*J'entends*'. The line foreshadows the causes of Phèdre's shame and her need to break through the barriers of shame; it articulates her tension, without Hippolyte having to transgress his own sense of propriety by being specific. It is an 'enough said' situation. The polarities represented by Minos and Pasiphaë are those which maintain the tension of the whole play and not simply the character of Phèdre. Minos and Pasiphaë, an emblematical marriage, are the opposite poles of the human consciousness. Minos (whose function we cannot ignore and who is given a disastrously misleading emphasis in Robert Lowell's epithet 'homicidal') is one of the three judge figures in Greek mythology. He is the judge who *punishes* crime, as opposed to Aeacus, who represents division of property, and Rhadamanthus, the rewarder of virtue. Interiorised psychologically, as he is in Phèdre, he is that part of our selves which is judgement, prescription, that part that creates moral codes, imposes laws, fixes limits, the 'frontiers' of experience, defines the acceptable and punishes transgression. Pasiphaë is the transgressor of the codes created by Minos, that part of our selves that hungers for every experience, burns to go beyond the frontiers of current acceptability, specifically, in her case, to gratify her sexuality with a bull, incur the guilt of forbidden bestiality. She is what Henri de Montherlant made of her in his play

Pasiphaé (1928): the woman who wants to transcend morality, accept *every* part of her nature, however 'animal' or 'bestial' it has been branded by the law-makers, to assert that nothing is unhealthy or forbidden. She rejects the codes of her husband Minos. The Minos/Pasiphaë duality is yet another statement of 'civilisation and its discontents'. In that sense we are all children of Minos and Pasiphaë. The wedlock of Minos and Pasiphaë is a dynamic power struggle for the upper hand fraught with matrimonial tension, uneasy even in brief armistice. The struggle lives on in their daughter Phèdre, with the father Minos continually more assertive. I have isolated the function of Minos and made him simply 'the judge', who represents internally the moral conscience and is, in the exterior political world, a representative of 'the rule of reason', like the ambiguously placed Governor himself, only utterly unimpeachable:

> a judge so unimpeachable and just
> to have a wife destroyed by bestial lust!

That may well seem a far cry from the cherished

> *La fille de Minos et de Pasiphaé*

and it is not intended as its formal equivalent. I have had to redistribute the energies of that renowned line over my whole version, surrender the more obvious nugget for a concession to work the whole seam more painstakingly.

The problem, then, of Phèdre, as of us all, is that she contains within herself both Minos *and* Pasiphaë. That is the essence of the genealogy. She condemns the mother/ female/accepter/'transgressor' in herself with the voice of the father/the male voice of punishment/repression/rigid social code. That is the psychological dynamic of the character. As with the outer political dynamic, I have sought to create an equivalent, but redistributed, nexus of imagery for the internal tensions. The 'bestiality' of Pasiphaë is seen as part of the threat of the alien, of that personified, often apostrophised India upon which the exiled British projected all that was forbidden in their own culture. The temple sculpture and painting of India depict, in a spirit of acceptance, what one particular picture reproduced in the National Theatre programme for *Phaedra Britannica* called 'the love of all creatures'. It is a painting from Rajasthan of circa 1780 showing not only pairs of animals copulating, but women in joyful congress with a variety of beasts. One could well apply to it the long passage of the power of Venus from Seneca's *Phaedra*:

> The dolphin of the raging sea doth love:
> the elephants by Cupid's blaze do burn:
> Dame Nature all doth challenge as her own,
> And nothing is that can escape her laws.

That in the translation of John Studley, 1581, the first English version of Seneca's play. But the Indian picture goes just a little further, extends the frontiers of Venus into bestiality. This is quite beyond the limits of acceptability for the British in India, totally alien, though no doubt present in the dark recesses of the imagination. To Western eyes India seemed actually to celebrate a world where everything was sexually possible. The Western reaction was both fascinated (Pasiphaë) and repressive (Minos). It is the voice of Minos we hear speaking through Lieutenant General Sir George MacMunn:

> In the description of the astounding indecency which to Western eyes the temples of Conjeveram, of Jaganath and the Black Pagoda offer, mention has been made of the bestiality recorded: the mingling of humans and animals in intimate embrace . . . The ancient religions did permit such terrible abominations and India has always apparently been more openly acquainted with such matters than the rest of the world.

When the guilt of Pasiphaë, which, it should be noted, is never specifically referred to in Racine, although it is, characteristically, in Seneca, is mentioned in my version it is intended with reference to what is depicted in the temples listed by Sir George MacMunn:

> Mother! Driven by the dark gods' spite
> beyond the frontiers of appetite!
> A *judge's* wife! Obscene! Such bestialities
> Hindoos might sculpture on a temple frieze.

And the monster which kills Thomas Theophilus (Hippolyte) and seems to represent the suppressed passions of all the principal characters is described by Burleigh as being

like one of those concoctions that one sees
in dark recesses on a temple frieze.

But on the faces of the women in the painting from
Rajasthan, women being joyfully pleasured by everything
from a peacock to an elephant, we have the spirit of
Pasiphaë seeking the total joy that seems to lie beyond all
remorse and moral codes. One senses the Yeatsian cry:

> When such as I cast out remorse
> So great a sweetness flows into the breast
> We must laugh and we must sing,
> We are blest by everything
> Everything we look upon is blest.

The nearest my Memsahib ever gets to understanding such
a mood is, ironically, in her envy of the young lovers she
imagines untrammelled by the agonies that destroy her:

> To follow one's feelings through nature's course
> without recriminations and remorse,
> not to feel criminal, and meet as though
> the sun shone on one's love and watched it grow!
> Ah! Every day they must wake up and see
> vistas with no black clouds, and feel so free!

The tensions of the Minos/Pasiphaë polarity are maintained
too in my images of the hunter, the Victorian type, pro-
jecting his inner repressed desires onto the fauna of India,
amassing tiger pelts, covering his walls with animal heads,

collecting obsessive proof that he is in control of his own animal nature, that he is the fit representative of 'the rule of reason'. The Governor himself is renowned as a great hunter, naturally, often scorning the rifle with its distant, rationally controlled despatch for closer gladiatorial combat with a bayonet. The images of the hunt are maintained, in one degree or another, in all the versions of the story: Euripides, Seneca, Racine. At the beginning of the Euripides play Aphrodite (Venus) herself complains of Hippolytus that he denies her not only by ignoring women, but also by driving wild animals off the face of the earth. Venus, the principle of generation, replenishes the stocks exhausted by the hunter. The nurse in Seneca tells the destructively chaste young man as much, imagining the world as an unpopulated desert without the influence of the love goddess:

> *Excedat, agedum, rebus humanis Venus,*
> *Quae supplet ac restituit exhaustum genus;*
> *Orbis iacebit squallido turpis situ;*
> *Vacuum sine ullis piscibus stabit mare;*
> *Alesque coelo deerit, et silvis fera . . .* (ll. 469–73)

Come now, if Venus withdraws from human life, Venus, who makes our race complete and restores it when it is depleted, then the whole world will sprawl squalidly in a foul condition; the sea will come to a standstill, empty of fish; there will be no birds in the sky nor wild animals in the woods.

The first speech of the Seneca play is one in praise of the excitement of hunting and a list of quarry. Ironically, one of the beasts listed – '*latis feri cornibus uri*', 'wild bison with wide-spreading horns', probably some sort of buffalo – is described in an edition of 1902 as 'extinct' owing to the untiring perseverance of the hunter! There is another element to the obsessive animal-slaying. What is part of human nature, but not acknowledged, tends to be labelled 'animal'. Even in today's papers behaviour which does not even transcend the limits of acceptability as much as Pasiphaë's is labelled by the Minos voice of judgement from the British bench as 'animal' or 'bestial'. We are very nervous of our status on what used to be called 'the scale of Creation'. And this is the point of the animal abuse with which the Memsahib finally rejects her 'lower' self in the shape of her ayah, or with which the Governor denounces Thomas Theophilus, when he tries to reimpose *within* his household the rigid limits he himself has clearly gone beyond outside the home.

The Governor's own position on this shifting scale of transgression and animality, with Minos at one end and Pasiphaë at the other, is decidedly ambiguous. The Governor both accepts and represses, he is both law and transgression. He is in many ways the classic male hypocrite. He avidly seeks experience outside the limits of his own code, or the code his society ostensibly subscribes to, but to do so he finds it necessary, as many Victorians did, to adopt 'native costume'. Sir Richard Burton is only one of the most well known of models for such behaviour. In some ways the Governor carries the whole burden of the male Victorian dilemma. I wanted to state the conflict at a social and political level as well as at the psychological, as it is in Racine in slightly different form. Another redistribution. I took the clues for this from what the Victorian imagination found not only in its Indian experience, but also in its assessment of the Theseus legend itself. All ages have used the long-surviving classical heroes like Odysseus, Aeneas, Theseus to realise their own natures and preoccupations. W. B. Stanford's *The Ulysses Theme* (Oxford: Blackwell, 1954) has charted the fortunes of Odysseus from Homer to Joyce, and Anne C. Ward's *The Quest for Theseus* (London: Pall Mall Press, 1970) has done more or less the same for the hero of our present play. To the Victorians, who often cast themselves into the roles of classical heroes reborn, Theseus was a type of Victorian. John Ruskin, in Letter XXII dated 1872 of *Fors Clavigera*, sees in Theseus:

> The great settler or law-giver of the Athenian state; but he is so eminently as the Peace-Maker, causing men to live in fellowship who before lived separate, and making roads passable that had been infested with robbers and wild beasts. He is that exterminator of every bestial and savage element.

With this as a guide one may specify merely from those combats with monsters, grotesques, giants and brigands that Racine uses:

> *Les monstres étouffés et les brigands punis,*
> *Procuste, Cercyon, et Scirron et Sinnis,*
> *Et les os dispersés du giant d'Epidaure,*
> *Et la Crète fumant du sang du Minotaure.*

The accounts of early 'law-giving', the establishment of 'the rule of law' in British India, read like a British version of the same kind of heroic, semi-mythical exploit. And not simply the obvious sources like Sleeman's account of the suppression of Thuggee, legendary brigands and murderers worthy of any Theseus, but others mentioned always in mythologising tones by, for example, James Douglas in his *Bombay and Western India* (London: Sampson Low, Marston & Co., 1893): 'England is the St George that has slain the great dragon of infanticide which among the Jhadejas ravaged Kach and Kathiawar', 'Jauhar, that Cyclopean monster of self-immolation', 'the Hashashin' (from whom we derive our word 'assassin'), 'Dacoits', 'Aghori Cannibals', 'the anthropophagous Mardicura'. Douglas is also typical when he dramatises in a mythological, almost hagiographical way the tiger slaughter of, for example, Sir James Outram, who in ten years was present at the deaths of 191 tigers, fifteen leopards, twenty-five bears and twelve buffaloes. He doesn't mention what Aphrodite thought of Sir James Outram, but he hails him as 'another St Paul, [who] had been a day and a night in the deep and fought with wild beasts'. 'The wild beasts and wilder men' of accounts like Douglas's of the establishing of 'the rule of law' in British India represent the same stage of civilisation of the Greeks before Theseus, and the Victorians saw their own confrontation in his. So the Governor in *Phaedra Britannica* is, as John Ruskin wrote, 'that exterminator of every bestial or savage element', but, at the same time, he is also, as Sir Richard Burton was described, 'an authority on all that relates to the bestial element in man'. This authority is acquired, of course, as the Governor, who represents 'the rule of reason' and suppresses alien bestiality, while, at the same time, as his other ('lower') self he explores his own animality in his forays 'in native costume'. It is with these two contrasting elements in his father that Thomas Theophilus has to struggle. In an article in *MacMillan's Magazine* for August 1889 Walter Pater adds an important qualification to a summary of the character of Theseus that, in other respects, is similar to Ruskin's. His Theseus

> figures, passably, as a kind of mythic shorthand for civilisation, making roads and the like, facilitating travel, suppressing various forms of violence, *but many innocent things as well.*

As law-giver, then, Theseus/Thésée/the Governor shares an element of repression with the father of Phaedra/Phèdre/ the Memsahib. But only part. The other side of his nature, the seeker of new experiences, especially sexual, often 'in disguise' precisely because he cannot relate the two halves of his nature, goes hand in hand with the hunter of beasts and the suppressor of bestial custom. That which he is most fascinated by he represses most ruthlessly. He is a kind of mythic shorthand, if you like, for civilisation *and* its discontents.

The Khan who imprisons the Governor in my version of 'a season spent in Hell' lies, on this scale of transgression, somewhere between the Governor and Pasiphaë. There is even a slight note of envy perhaps in these lines of the Governor's:

My captor was a beast, obscene, perverse,
given to practices I won't rehearse,
to crude carnalities that overrode
every natural law and human code.
He'd draw the line at nothing. No taboo
would stop him doing what he wanted to.

The Governor has gone beyond 'the frontier' both geo-
graphically and psychologically. Some of the vocabulary
of territory from our Anglo-Indian experience marks the
boundaries very well. 'The frontiers of appetite . . . of virtue
. . . of blood.' The Governor has gone beyond 'the frontier', beyond the Indus, known everywhere as 'the forbidden river'. H. Bosworth Smith in his *Life of Lord Lawrence*
speaks of the Khyber Pass as 'the forbidden precincts over
whose gloomy portals might well have been inscribed the
words of Dante':

'All hope abandon, ye who enter here.'

So the hellish overtones, the Stygian symbolism were created for me by those with some historical experience of the
Anglo-Indian period I chose for my setting. Whatever the
Governor has experienced, and he is, possibly through fear
or shame, vaguely unspecific, he has finally seen the limits
of the acceptable. His version of hell is being subjected to
another's unlimited will, and suffering in the way that many
victims of his casual sexual whims might well have suffered. His experience is a vision of the monstrous, the non-
human other, beyond all human access and control, even

for a 'law-giver', something more terrible than mere animal or beast, something that cannot finally be suppressed or mounted on a Residency wall, nor even physically embraced. This monster defeats both Minos and Pasiphaë. A monster to whom victims must be fed. ('Is there not a home among us that has not paid blood tribute to that relentless monster?' writes an Anglo-Indian lady, meaning India.) The Governor's vision is probably a glimpse of the monster that finally destroys his son. Whatever the experience he has had of Hell, it is one which makes him long for the circumscribed, apparently ordered world of his marriage and home. But the boundaries of that he finds are now shaken, the barriers in need of reconstruction, the edges blurred between inner and outer, Hell and earth . . .

> A season spent in Hell, I've no desire
> for whiffs of brimstone from the household fire.

IV

Neoclassical plays are about sex and politics. From as early as classical times there has been a healthily vulgar if slightly overdone satiric scorn for Phaedra's problems. The taboo of incest between stepmother and stepson seems irrelevant in societies with different kinship restraints. It is easy for us to feel self-satisfied at what we think of as our own permissiveness and to sneer at sexual problems which were at the time agonisingly real. If literature is what Ezra Pound said it was, 'news that stays news', then dramatic agony should stay agony, but this is difficult when the tensions involved have come adrift from their social origins. To Ovid, the

Roman poet of sexual opportunism, Phaedra's passion was not only not incestuous, Hippolytus had to be chivvied by her beyond *his* consciousness of taboo (*Phaedra to Hippolytus*, *Heroides* 4.129–32):

> *Nec, quia privigno videar coitura noverca*
> *Terruerint animos nomina vana tuos.*
> *Ista vetus pietas, aevo moritura futuro,*
> *Rustica Saturno regno tenente fuit.*

> Don't be alarmed by vain fears that intercourse between son-in-law and stepmother is disreputable. Such kind of out-of-date piety, which had no future, was appropriate to the rustic age of Saturn.

And this in the translation of poet/dramatist Thomas Otway (1683), who also did a version of Racine's *Bérénice* into heroic couplets:

> How can'st thou reverence thy Father's Bed,
> From which himself so Abjectly is fled?
> The thought affrights not me, but me enflames;
> Mother and Son are notions, very Names
> Of Worn out Piety, in Fashion Then
> When old dull Saturn rul'd the Race of men.
> But braver Jove taught pleasure was no sin,
> And with his sister did himself begin.

These attitudes to a 'Worn out Piety', repeated often enough throughout the ages, are mild enough compared with a version of the story published only four years after Racine's play by Alexander Radcliffe (also author of *Terrestrial Hymns and Carnal Ejaculations* (1682)). This is a Phaedra Britannica, isolated in 'a Farm-House in Putney in Surrey', who has no feelings of restraint whatsoever, either Euripidean Greek or neoclassical French:

> When Young, I cou'd have cur'd these am'rous stings
> With Carrots, Radishes, or such like things;
> Now there's no pleasure in such Earthly cures,
> I must have things apply'd as warm as yours.
> Where lies the blame, art thou not strong, and young?
> Who would not gather fruit that is well hung?

In this case Pasiphaë has triumphed over Minos, and re-working the passage already quoted from Ovid and Otway, Radcliffe has:

> We'd no such opportunity before:
> Your Father is at London with his Whore.
> Therefore I think 'tis but a just design,
> To cuckold him, and pay him in his coin.
> Besides he ne're was marry'd to your Mother,
> He first whor'd her, and then he took another.
> What kindness or respect ought we to have
> For such a Villain and perfidious Knave?
> This should not trouble, but provoke us rather
> With all the speed we can to lye together.
> I am no kin to you, nor you to me,
> They call it Incest but to terrifie.

Lovers Embraces are Lascivious Tricks
'Mongst musty Puritans and Schismaticks.

This is that 'Anglo-Saxon irreverence' that Michael Billing-
ton mentioned in his review of *Phaedra Britannica*. One sees
it too in Stevie Smith's poem 'Phèdre'. And very necessary
it is too, though it scarcely helps to recreate the Racinian
mode in modern English. We read such pieces in early
rehearsals, partly for the couplets, but also to draw the fire
of cheerful vulgarity before we tackled the main text. It's an
irreverence not confined to our attitude to inaccessible foreign classics, and I associate it in my mind with one of my
culture heroes, the comedian 'Professor' Leon Cortez, who
offered his own cockneyfications of Shakespeare, reduc-
ing the high-flown poetry of kings to an earthy demotic.
Nor is such irreverence purely Anglo-Saxon, even towards
Racine. Far from it. In June 1974, I saw a production of
Phèdre I have already referred to, directed by Régis Santon
at the Théâtre Essaion, which played the Racinian text as
vulgar farce, a compound of Buñuel, Racine and Feydeau,
with *Tristan and Isolde* as background music, and a vaguely
Latin American setting, something like Torre Nilsson's film
La casa del ángel (1957). The production had simply given
up the struggle to present the play on its own terms, and
enjoyable as it was as a lively piece of juvenile iconoclasm,
very necessary for the French classic theatre, it gave no help
whatsoever to one desperately seeking access to the play for
equally, if not more, irreverent English audiences. With this
constant sense of total subversion I had, even more carefully, to consider solutions to the play which would place

the problem in a society where the sense of transgression was once more an agonising burden. Sexual problems do not occur in a vacuum, in a theatrical never-never land, but are created by social codes. The period I chose eventually, after many false starts and crablike researches, envisaged a particular society, early Victorian Britain, with a rigid code made even more formally defensive by being placed in the alien environs of sensual India.

The politics of the play are also obscured by genealogical complications, with which we no longer have any spontaneous rapport, and distanced by our distaste for the absolute monarchy of the court of Louis XIV. Even the translator cannot shirk his responsibility for historical criticism.

Everywhere in the imagery of seventeenth-century poetry, prose and drama, in England and France, the psychological structure of man is seen as an interiorisation of the political. 'The Government of Man', writes the Cambridge Platonist, Benjamin Whichcote, 'should be the Monarchy of Reason; it is too often a Democracy of Passions.' Passions are elsewhere in Dryden:

> unreasonable things
> That strike at Sense, as Rebels do at Kings.

When Dryden came to paraphrase the famous Latin hymn 'Veni Creator Spiritus', the simple lines

> infirma nostri corporis
> virtus firmans perpeti

become a typical piece of the politically expressed psychology I mean:

> Our Frailties help, our vice controul;
> Submit the Senses to the Soul;
> And when Rebellious they are grown
> Then lay thy hand and hold 'em down.

The alignment of political synonyms in such imagery is: Reason/King/Rule/Monarchy/(to which series we can add *raj* = rule) on the one hand and what they restrain on the other: Passions/Mob/Democracy/('the Natives'). As Martin Turnell, the best English commentator on Racine, points out: 'there are only two classes in Racine: masters and servants, the rulers and the ruled, royalty and the people'. Elsewhere, discussing the psychology of Corneille and Racine, he writes that 'reason has to operate *tyrannically* and repress by force an uprush of the senses'. Hence 'the rule of law'; the use of words like 'seditious' and 'mutinous' of the passions, hence also the time of the piece, defined as taking place a few years before the Mutiny. As I used the prospect of *les événements* of 1968 in Paris as a political, historical 'measure' of the realities of my setting of *Le Misanthrope* and of Alceste's status as a critic of society, so in *Phaedra Britannica* I imagine the tensions of the play continuing into the Indian Mutiny, 1857 (the year also of the Obscene Publications Act). My text demands that the political realities of Racinian society are reinterpreted physically, realised literally in 'black and white'. I sought to re-energise critically the political content by aligning it with the British 'Imperial dream', which like Goya's dream of reason, 'produces monsters'.

V

Aphrodite speaks in Euripides. In Seneca, Venus is merely addressed. But even in Euripides the gods are, as his translator Philip Vellacott puts it, 'no more than dramatic fictions'. The gods in Racine, as Martin Turnell points out, are 'projections of basic human impulses, which means that in *Phèdre* they belong to the realm of psychology rather than theology'. '*Venus, c'est Phèdre, c'est Hippolyte . . . Neptune est dans Thésée,*' writes Jean-Louis Barrault in his production notes. The British projected their own suppressed nature onto the continent they subdued, personifying a destructive India, devastating to those who gave in to its powers, who were seduced by its nakedly obvious allure. Personification is general throughout the literature and memoirs of British India. Everything psychologically alien or suppressed becomes 'India' or 'the dark gods' or, not detached enough to be theologically accurate, an apostrophised Hindu deity like Siva or some other menacing god from a bewilderingly diverse pantheon. Here, for example, is an Englishwoman writing about the 'hot weather':

One has to experience the coming of the Hot Season to understand something of the worship of Siva – Creator and Destroyer – the Third Person of the Hindu Trinity. For its approach – swift, relentless and inevitable – is like that of a living and sensate force – like the visible work of that terrible yet withal beneficent God who destroys and tramples all things beneath His feet in an ecstatic harmonious dance, that He may create them anew. For in a sense there is a necessity for the hot weather. The intensity of the sun's power cracks and cleaves the dry, obdurate earth, in order that the blessed rains of the Monsoon may irrigate and revivify the whole, jaded, exhausted face of the land.

And as Jean-Louis Barrault speaks of the tragedy of *Phèdre*, giving the arc and cathartic trajectory of the play the same kind of cumulative, meteorological image, as '*un de ces orages de fin août*', 'a late August thunderstorm', it seems to make Siva, as present in the British imagination, particularly fitted to preside over the passion of *Phaedra Britannica*. The same woman goes on to describe her feelings of helplessness in the Indian heat (which another woman, Mrs B. M. Croker, likens to some 'cruel vindictive animal') in terms which, typically, create the sense of powerful alien forces:

> And finally there is the close, hot evening, and an airless night of tossing and turning, of trying to find one cool spot in one's bed, giving it up in despair, and lying in still resignation to look up at the uncaring stars above the gently flapping punkah, helpless beneath the destroying feet of Siva.

Such projections onto an alien divinity are very common in Anglo-Indian writing, and they tend to stand for those things that are felt to be outside the sphere of reason, order and justice (or the current concepts of them), which it is the function of tragedy, according to George Steiner, to reveal as 'terribly limited'. It was to insist on the role of the gods as projections that I conflated the functions of Venus and Neptune in Racine. The sea which in Racine is the symbol of the uncontrolled, the formless, becomes in my version 'the jungle', almost a synonym for chaos. I have unified the psychological projections represented in Racine and ascribed them both to Siva, as he was imagined by the British, not necessarily as a complex component of the Hindu pantheon. Contemplating the attributes of Siva, though, one can see that the god can well bear the parallels, being at once the god of regeneration and sexuality, and of destruction. He contains opposing forces. He is associated both with asceticism (Hippolyte) and yet is everywhere reverenced under the symbol of the phallus or *lingam*. He is Destroyer/Creator, birth and death, Apollo *and* Dionysus, to use the Nietzschean pair that forge the tragic dialectic. Even the minor parallels can be maintained, to authenticate the transfer, as Siva has a bull as a vehicle, and as a weapon the *trisula* or trident. But the matchings at this level hardly matter, even if they aid the metamorphosis. What matters is the function of projection, the use of pagan gods in a culture that dramatises itself as an age of reason, and its equivalent in the British apostrophisation of the dark gods of India.

VI

I don't remember the exact point at which I decided on a nineteenth-century Indian setting, but in retrospect there seem to have been catalysts and clues about me from the start, though I did begin with versions ostensibly in ancient Greece and in the period of Louis XIV. Of all the many elements I now can recognise the following as particularly prominent:

1. Maria Casarès, who played Phèdre in Jean Vilar's production at the TNP in 1957, said of her character: '*j'ai toujours imaginée étendue dans l'ombre d'un chambre closé, dans un lieu où le soleil explosé*' ('I always imagined lying in the shadow of a closed room, in a place where the sun exploded'). India! The all-pervading presence of the sun, either seen as light or felt as heat in a darkened room, became also a physical counterpart for Phèdre's mythological kinship in the original.

2. There was an equivalence, felt intuitively at first and then researched, between the way critics write about the character of the confidante, Oenone, and the way in which Anglo-Indian memoirs and fiction write of the ayah figure. Jean-Louis Barrault calls Oenone the '*valeur noire*' of Phèdre, and in my version she is literally that (the Anglo-Indians used the inaccurate and deliberately insulting adjective 'black' of Indians). Racine also speaks, too aristocratically and high-handedly for my liking, of the *bassesse* of Oenone, and the servile propensities which make *her* able to accuse Hippolyte, and not her mistress as was the case in the Euripides version. As I have made it a Memsahib-and-ayah relationship, it is a way of absorbing into my version, without doing violence to the sense, my social reservations about Racine, and it makes the Memsahib's final outburst

of racialist rejection of her faithful servant a terrible one, and one that is linked to the outside world of alien domination, of which the psychological is a mirror aspect.

3. I felt the need of making the Amazon mother of Hippolyte physically present in the son, a constant reminder of the past of Thésée. My Hippolyte, Thomas Theophilus, becomes a 'half-caste' embodying the tensions between Britain and India within himself, as much as he embodies the two conflicting selves of his father. The occurrence of marriage between British men and Indian women was by no means uncommon in nineteenth-century India, and if we need historical authentication, it is enough to cite only the more well-known examples, like James Achilles Kirkpatrick, Resident at Hyderabad; Job Charnock, who rescued a Brahmin widow from suttee and lived with her happily until her natural death fourteen years after; Colonel Gardiner; and Sir Charles Metcalfe, who had three Eurasian sons by an Indian princess probably related to Ranjit Singh. The railways were to bring the Memsahibs to India and put a stop to that. I have assumed that transition in *mores* to be taking place, creating a new distance between ruler and ruled that was to harden to a more rigid apartheid after the Mutiny of 1857. The Victorian male couldn't permit his women the same intimate insights into India which he had allowed himself before his ladies made the crossing over the 'black water'.

4. Assailed as the British felt on all sides by an irrational India with its dark sensual gods and 'primitive' customs,

they created in their imagination defensive roles for themselves as the inheritors of rational civilisation. They constructed residencies and public buildings in classical style,
attempting to realise in external marble what they felt
unable to realise internally in their far from securely sta-
ble minds. The books of the period are full of engravings
showing proud classical facades in clearings in dense jungle, with creeper and mangrove festooning the edges of the
scene. It is an eloquent juxtaposition. Mark Bence-Jones,
in his *Palaces of the Raj* (London: Allen & Unwin, 1973),
describes the Residency at Hyderabad, with its Durbar
Hall lined with Ionic columns, and a staircase which 'was
adorned with sculpture: the Apollo Belvedere, Leda and
the Swan' (not Pasiphaë and the Bull to complete the circle
but almost there!) and 'Venus Rising from the Sea'. 'The
mirrors in neoclassical frames, reflected the Durbar Hall to
infinity.' It reads almost like the description of a traditional
set for *Phèdre* at the Comédie-Française!

It is more than a convenient point of contact. It represents the effort of one era, with its values threatened, to
define itself in terms borrowed from another, which would
seem best to support and prop up what was felt to be most
shaky. The drama of Britain and India was constantly seen
in these terms. Even as late as 1924 (the year of *A Passage
to India*), Bennet Christian Huntingdon Calcraft Kennedy
could write: 'We are here to govern India as delegates of a
Christian and civilised power. We are here as representatives
of Christ and Caesar to maintain this land against Siva and
Khalifa.' And the cleaned-up classicism of the corresponding
architecture, deriving as it does from Greece and Rome via

Palladio and Wren, is still, as David Gebhard writing about Lutyens's New Delhi Residency has it, 'a favourite political symbol in our century ranging from the megalomania of Albert Speer and Hitler to the New Deal of Roosevelt'. This belief in our being the chosen heirs of Greece and Rome gives a special poignancy to those pictures of the classical facade of the Lucknow Residency after the Mutiny, shattered by rifle-fire and shell, and littered with skulls. This kind of Residency and the life lived within it seemed to fit almost exactly Martin Turnell's summary of the dramatic and political function of the palace in the plays of Racine. They are 'not simply impersonal buildings which provide a setting for the tragedy . . . They represent a particular *order* . . .'

We are aware from the first of an almost suffocating tension in the air, combined with a desperate effort to maintain some sort of control, which frequently breaks down. The tension is pervasive; it is also contagious. It is the atmosphere which produces fascinating and frightening revelations about human nature – about ourselves.

The palaces vary in style . . . they have one thing in common. There is something of the prison about them. We have the impression that the community is somehow confined within their walls. The sense of confinement is partly psychological, but in some parts of the palaces we shall find one or two members of the community are literally prisoners . . .

The palaces are huge, dark, claustrophobic. They give the occupants the alarming impression that they are constantly being watched, that their lives are in danger in that disaster may overtake at any moment.

There are winding corridors with innumerable rooms leading off them. But we, the visitors, are only admitted to a single room. The whole of the drama is concentrated inside it . . . at the same time we are aware that the room, or more accurately, the palace, is a world within a world it is trying to dominate.

VII

Couplets keep the cat on the hot tin roof. Each spirit has its own custom-built treadmill. After the metronome, the comic pacemaker of the *Misanthrope* couplet, I wanted a more organic model for my iambics. I wanted to return the iamb back to its sources in breath and blood. In the silences one should hear the heart beat. Jean-Louis Barrault, writing of the alexandrine in *Phèdre*, says:

Le coeur, qui egrène, jusqu'à la mort, les deux temps de son tam-tam obsédant: systole–diastole; systole–diastole. Brève–longue; brève–longue etc: le coeur bat l'iambe.

The heart, which echoes, until death, the two times of its obsessive tom-tom: systole–diastole; systole–diastole. Short–long; short–long etc.: the heart beats the iambic . . .

It was this heartbeat, this bloodthrob that marked the time of my metric. The heart as '*tam-tam obsédant*' leads us straight back too to British India, where, another woman writes in her memoir, 'the throbbing tom-toms became almost like our heartbeats':

I sensed the gods of India were there
behind the throbbing heat and stifling air.
Heart beat like a tom-tom, punkah flapped
backwards and forwards and my strength was sapped.
I felt you mocking, India, you brewed
strange potions out of lust and lassitude,
dark gods mocking, knowing they can claim
another woman with the Judge's name,
picking off the family one by one,
each destroyed by lust and Eastern sun.

Facing Up to the Muses

1988

μουσάων Ἑλικωνιάδων ἀρχώμεθ᾽ ἀείδειν

From the Muses of Helicon let us begin to sing.
Hesiod, *Theogony*, line 1

Let's kick off with the Muses – and I use the words 'kick off'
advisedly, as I want to make a revelation about the sporting
interests of the Muses that may well surprise you. For the
last four years I've been to Delphi for the annual symposium on ancient Greek drama, and I've just returned from
Delphi, where I'm preparing, for the ancient stadium, for
this year's Festival a sort of reconstruction of that fragmentary satyr play of Sophocles, the *Ichneutae*, 'The Trackers'.
My piece is called *The Trackers of Oxyrhynchus* as it is also
an account of the discovery of the tattered papyrus in the
deserts of Egypt by the Oxford papyrologists, Grenfell and
Hunt. I am giving Delphi the doubtful privilege of hosting
a *thiasos* of British satyrs.

Last year, I went to Delphi in the company of my friend
and unflagging inspirer Oliver Taplin. We were both going
to speak at the symposium, from our different, though
related, vantage points, on Greek theatre, he as the scholar,
me as the poet and man of the theatre with his smattering

of ancient Greek. Our journey together made me think of that anonymous Elizabethan play, *The Pilgrimage to Parnassus* (1598), in which there are two pilgrims, like us, going to Parnassus, called Philomusus and Studioso, said to be 'well met in faith in the field of Poetrie'. We had a day free before we were supposed to be under the shadow of Mount Parnassus in Delphi to give our talks on and to debate Greek drama, so I suggested that we make a pilgrimage of our own and we hired a car at the Athens airport and drove out into the country rather than spend a night in the noise and poisonous *nephos*. So we drove slowly to Delphi and looked at Boiotia and Mount Cithaeron, where Oedipus had been exposed as a baby and where the Maenads had torn Pentheus to pieces, and the turning off to Distomo, near which is the famous crossroads where Oedipus had unwittingly killed his father, Laius. I had also suggested that we use the spare time to visit the Archaeological Museum of Thebes, which I had been to four times before, but which Dr Taplin had not yet visited. I don't need to dwell on our overnight stop at Porto Germano, on the Corinthian Gulf under Cithaeron, where we swam and ate charcoaled crayfish and drank retsina drawn from a great barrel. I wouldn't want you to think that we were waylaid, as were Philomusus and Studioso in their Pilgrimage to Parnassus, by the aptly named Madido, who tells them:

This Parnassus and Helicon are but the fables of the
poetes, there is no true Parnassus but the third lofte
in a wine taverne, no true Helicon but a cup of brown

bastard. Will youe travell quicklie to Parnassus, do but
carrie your drie feet into some drie tavern, and straight
the drawer . . . will bring you a cup . . . that will make
you speak leaping lines and dauncing periodes.

The blandishments of Madido have been the ruin of many
a poor poet, and though we were not seduced by our way-
layer, we thoroughly enjoyed the retsina of our Boiotian
'drawer'. And I should like to remind you, in passing, of
how that great Greek scholar, and former president of the
Classical Association, E. R. Dodds, wrote in his autobiography, *Missing Persons*, of a day which he called 'one of the
most unalloyed satisfactions of my life', ending, as it did,
with 'the pleasures of drinking retsina in the late sunshine'.
On the way back to his ship he whispered to his companion, 'I know now what happiness is − today I have been
completely and without qualification happy.' These 'unalloyed satisfactions', these days of 'happiness . . . without
qualification' are very important to us when we have to, as
we all do, face up to tragedy, and I mention these things
only to contrast with a Classics don (of all people!) whom
I overheard after a week's open-hearted generosity from his
Greek hosts expressing himself 'glad to be going back to
civilisation'. And he didn't mean Periclean Athens but Mrs
Thatcher's Britain.

The next morning, after another swim in the Corinthian
Gulf, we set off for Thebes and the museum. On the way
I was enthusing about some of the objects that I'd seen
in this collection: the red-figure *skyphos* by the Brygos
painter, with a leopardskin-clad satyr brandishing a long

phallic ramming stick, which had been one of the images
I had pasted into my notebook when I began work on the
fragmentary *Ichneutae*, as had the rather pawky terracotta
Silenus, who is saluting the viewer with his right hand and
otherwise engaged with his left. I was also enthusing about
the clay *larnax* from Mycenean Tanagra, whose calcified
contents were borne aloft into immortality by a dragonfly
poised on each corner. I gave a detailed guide to the treasures we were about to see and had thoroughly whetted
the appetite of my companion by the time we drove into
Thebes to find, as so often can happen in Greece, that the
museum was mysteriously closed. This was very disappointing, and it put us in the mood for some other side pilgrimage on our way to Parnassus, but after looking at a map
of the region we decided to forget about it and drive on
directly to Delphi. But not too long afterwards we passed
a sign reading 'ASKRI'. 'That must be the ancient Askra
where Hesiod was born,' said Dr Taplin, and braked. 'Let's
go there!' cried Philomusus and Studioso together, and we
turned left into a dusty side road. The drive to Askri took us
longer than we expected, but we passed by timeless Greek
images that gave me a sense of happiness 'without qualification', that sort of 'unalloyed satisfaction' that E. R. Dodds
derived from his wild cyclamen and sun-filled retsina: the
blue bee boxes; the tins strapped to the pine trees catching
the oozed resin to flavour the retsina; four goats on their
hind legs stretching their necks to gobble figs from the tree,
an image I'd seen on a fifth-century vase. But then, as if
to remind us that happiness without qualification can only
exist in Golden Ages that are mythical or locked in Hesiod,

we were suddenly jolted out of our Boiotian well-being back into our times by a vast, untended, smouldering pile of rubbish and old lorry tyres giving off a foul Phlegraean smell. The fire had obviously been burning for days. It was probably that jolt into mephitic modernity and because we were making our new pilgrimage to the birthplace of Hesiod that made Dr Taplin quote those lines from the poet's *Works and Days* about the Fifth Age of mankind, the Age of Iron, when Zeus would destroy the whole race of *meropon anthropon*, 'men gifted with speech' (lines 180–1):

Ζεὺς δ᾽ ὀλέσει καὶ τοῦτο γένος μερόπων ἀνθρώπων,
εὖτ᾽ ἂν γεινόμενοι πολιοκρόταφοι τελέθωσιν.

And Zeus will destroy this race of men gifted in
speech when they come to have grey hair on their
temples when they are born.

We both fell quiet, I remember, our 'unalloyed satisfactions' somehow undermined by these thoughts, and I think we were both thinking the same thing, that even if it hadn't been the Fifth Age, the Age of Iron, for poor old Hesiod, then we of the late terrible twentieth century would certainly have to say:

νῦν γὰρ δὴ γένος ἐστὶ σιδήρεον (176),

'This really is the Age of Iron.' After some moments of this brooding, suddenly troubled silence, Oliver turned to me and said did I know there had been *poliokrotaphoi*, babies born *literally* with their hair already grey, in Japan as a result of the A-bombs dropped on Hiroshima and Nagasaki. And with these chilling thoughts we arrived at a village with three *kapheneia*, all facing outwards towards the square, all full of men drinking coffee, clicking their worry beads and reading the newspapers (the two activities go together in the Age of Iron!) and looking out and watching life passing by, which now happened to be Philomusus and Studioso. The village sign had said 'Panaghia', so I leaned out of the car and said, 'Where is Askri, please?' 'It's here,' said one old man. There was little evidence of poor old Hesiod, and in any case, come to think of it, didn't the poet himself write pretty grudgingly and dismissively about his birthplace, a 'miserable hamlet near Helicon' (*Works and Days*, 639–40):

... ἄγχ' Ἑλικῶνος ὀιζυρῇ ἐνὶ κώμῃ,
Ἄσκρῃ, χεῖμα κακῇ, θέρει ἀργαλέῃ, οὐδέ ποτ' ἐσθλῇ.

'Askri, lousy in winter, terrible in summer and not much good at any time.' Scarcely approvable by the local tourist board. It was probably the remembered curmudgeonly, grousing voice of old Hesiod that induced Dr Taplin to turn the car round and begin to head back the way we came. At that point, the man I'd asked directions of made one of those eloquently economical Greek gestures that managed to convey with a slight movement of the wrist, 'Why the hell have you come to Askri only to turn your car round?' His gesture rather shamed us into stopping, and we got out and ordered a coffee and maybe (though still mindful of the blandishments of Madido), *maybe* an *ouzaki* and began talking to the men. 'Why had we come to Askri? Had we lost our way?' Dr Taplin, whose modern Greek puts mine to shame, explained that he was a teacher of ancient Greek at Oxford and that I was a poet, and that we had wanted to pay homage to the birthplace of Hesiod. One of the men pointed to me and said, 'He *is* a *synadelphos Hesiodou*, a brother of Hesiod.' 'Of course,' said another, 'Hesiod's actual brother, Perses, he was a lazy bugger like me. Spent all his time in the *kapheneion!*' Then they said, like a chorus, if we'd come so far, and were really making a pilgrimage to Hesiod, we should go a little further still to the Valley of the Muses, and the Mouseion. They began to draw maps of various complicated tracks on cigarette packets, until finally, unable to transfer the directions to paper, one of the men said he'd come with us. We all got into the car and went along a very rough road for quite some time, until we came almost to the end of the valley and could make out on the left a hollowed-out space covered with vegetation and thorns but with the unmistakable shape of an ancient theatre.

It turned out to be the Mouseion, where the ancient *Mouseia*, the poetry festivals in honour of the Muses, were held. It was quite a climb up once we left the car behind and the mountainside was covered with sharp thorns. Our guide, who was sensibly shod in good boots, went ahead of us and kept shouting, '*Agathai, agathai!*' – 'Thorns, thorns!' There was nothing we could do to avoid them. We were both wearing sandals bought from Melissonos, the poet/sandal-maker of Pandrossou Street in Monastiraki (I give you his address as this is an unashamed commercial break!), and although they are the best and most poetical sandals you can buy, they were the least appropriate footwear for our present steep pilgrimage through thorns, and very soon our feet were cut and bleeding and we were beginning to wonder why we had bothered. But when we finally stood in the overgrown place that would have been the orchestra, I realised that we had been led there for our inspiration. As perhaps befits our different though intimately related vantage points on ancient theatre, we both stood in that orchestra, Philomusus and Studioso, 'well met in faith in the field of Poetrie', but facing in opposite directions. Dr Taplin, who has gained his insights by gazing deeply in his direction, looked over the thorn-covered orchestra and over to the level plains of Boiotia and what would have been Lake Copais, the source of juicy eels and juicy Aristophanic jokes, and across to Aulis, where the Greek fleet was stalled until Agamemnon had his daughter, Iphigeneia, butchered, and from where Hesiod made his one and only sea voyage to Chalcis, where he won a tripod for his poetry at the funeral games of Amphidamas, and brought his prize back to his valley and had it dedicated in the spot where we were now actually standing. He was excited by the view, but I scarcely heard his catalogue of discoveries as I was transfixed by one of my own. We were standing almost back to back, and I was trying to imagine what it would have been like to read my poems in that place when it had been a theatre with an audience looking over my head towards Boiotia. I tried to cover the sweep of the auditorium now bristling with the thorns that had scourged our feet, and I raised my head to take in what would have been the very back row and found myself facing up to the ridge of a mountain, and my hair literally began to stand on end. The mountain was, of course, Helicon and the spectators on the ridge none other than the Muses. They looked down on the poet performing his work. And the poet had to face up to the Muses.

In that *Pilgrimage to Parnassus* where I found Philomusus and Studioso, Ossa is not piled on Pelion but Helicon is piled on Parnassus, so that to reach the summit one would have needed a whole *thiasos* of sherpas. On their gruelling climb the two pilgrims have this conversation:

PHILOMUSUS
Thinks thou oure softe and tender feet canne bide
To trace this roughe, this harsh, this craggie waye
That leadeth unto fair Parnassus Hill?

STUDIOSO
Why man, each lazy groom will take the paine
To drawe his slow feete ore the clayie landes,
So he may reste uppon a faire greene banke.
These pilgrims feete which now take weary toile
Maie one day on a bedd of roses rest
Amidst Parnassus shadie laurell greene.

This is pretty miserable stuff from the same year as *Hamlet*. And it's probably due to the fact that the author thought of the abode of the Muses as a 'bedd of roses'. What we later pilgrims had discovered was no bed of roses, only unending thorns. And could we say that the laurels were still green in this Fifth Age of mankind? Hadn't Christopher Marlowe written, only five years after Philomusus and Studioso had made their ascent of Helicon/Parnassus, that 'burned is Apollo's laurel-bough'? And were the Muses still up there in the Fifth Age of mankind? Or had they left the earth as Hesiod predicted Aidos and Nemesis would do when there would be no remedy against evil? In the *Theogony*, Hesiod describes the flow of sweetness of the Muses as 'inexhaustible', but nearer our time Byron called the Muses 'the weary nine', and Keats had looked to Helicon and found that:

> . . . all is dark
> Around thine aged top . . .
> (*Endymion*)

'The sun of poetry is set,' he said. There have been discouraging reports also about the fountain of inspiration on Helicon, the spring of Hippocrene, from George Wheler in the seventeenth century, who found 'the famous haunt of the nine Sisters . . . frozen up', to the American Paul W. Wallace in 1973, who drank from the fountain of the Muses and found its taste 'so foul that we drank it only because nothing else was available'. How much wearier the nine will be a hundred and fifty years on from Byron in the latter end of the twentieth century, how much darker the summit of the Muses' haunt. This weariness of the nine, this erosion of the affirmative spirit in our times, this darkness, this *nephos* on Helicon has been made darker by two world wars, the terrors of Nazism and the fearful conflagrations unleashed on Hiroshima and Nagasaki in 1945, creating the literal *poliokrotaphoi* of Hesiod's Fifth Age. These years which I described addressing Keats over the time that divides us:

> . . . years, like an open crater, gory, grim,
> with bloody bubbles leering at the rim;
> a thing no bigger than an urn explodes
> and ravishes all silence and all odes.
> Flora asphyxiated by foul air,
> unknown to either Keats or Lemprière,
> dehydrated Naiads, Dryad amputees,
> dragging themselves through slagscapes with no trees,
> a shirt of Nessus fire that gnaws and eats
> children half the age of dying Keats . . .
>
> ('A Kumquat for John Keats')

It's not only our lateness in history but the dark catastrophes of our century that undermine creativity at its very roots. Exactly sixty years ago to this day in April the then Regius Professor of English Literature at Glasgow, a man called Macneile Dixon, stood in the very same area on Helicon as we were standing. He had been prompted to go there by an 'unaccountable firm determination' to visit, what others have found frozen or foul-tasting, the spring of Hippocrene. He was led, as we seemed to be, by something outside his control. He stood on that spot on Helicon and he *mused*:

> Is there anywhere in human history to be found a more
> charming conception than this of the Muses . . . which,
> like so many of our most fruitful thoughts we owe to
> the Greek imagination? . . . They stand apart . . . alone
> and peerless, without parallel, look where we will in

the many mythologies . . . [They make] a direct appeal
to the modern spirit . . . remaining, even in a world of
change, eternally acceptable.

And what he really found unique about these deities was
that

in honour of these, unlike other divinities, no blood
was spilt; . . . flute and voice became the substitutes of
victim and burnt offering.

The problem, true as this may be, is that the Muses have
to inspire work in a world where the many other 'divinities', the personifications and the ideologies, continually
have the blood of victims spilled and holocausts created.
And Macneile Dixon knew this too, although he was
writing sixty years ago. And if he himself had a favourite
Muse among the nine it would be Melpomene, the Muse
of Tragedy, and he wrote an interesting book on tragedy
in 1924. In it he says about tragedy that it 'must deal with
the most monstrous and appalling that life can offer when
it turns upon us its Medusa-like countenance of frenzy
and despair'. It's the frenzy and despair of the Fifth Age
of mankind, the iron age, and the gaze turns men to stone
and numbs their sources of affirmation. Sixty years since
Macneile Dixon saw life turn its Medusa-like gaze on us,
there have been greater quantities of blood spilled, greater
horrors, and it has created a very 'weary nine' and a darker
and darker Helicon.

At the time I began feeling my way in life as a poet,

there was, in reaction to our century's terrible events, what George Steiner has characterised as 'a retreat from the word'. Unfortunately for me, while this retreat from the word was happening, I was beginning to acquire what Harold Pinter called my 'voracious appetite for language'. I acquired this appetite for language both from my background and my education. People often ask me who my 'influences' were, and when a poet is asked that question the expected answer is usually a roll call of distinguished literary mentors, great models of eloquence. Of course there were those, and they have included the great names of Greek drama. But I have always related that particular question to the puzzlement my mother always felt as to 'where it all came from', as there had never been any artists in the family before. So I wrote a short poem to answer both questions, and it's called 'Heredity':

> 'How you became a poet's a mystery.
> Wherever did you get your talent from?'
> I say: 'I had two uncles, Joe and Harry,
> one was a stammerer, the other dumb!'

I was born into an uneducated working-class family in Leeds, and at the age of eleven I won one of those scholarships created by the Education Act of 1944, to Leeds Grammar School, where, as 'scholarship boys' were considered 'bright' if nothing else, I was set almost automatically, it seems to me now, to study the classics. And I was very conscious at the same time as I was being shepherded towards these great founts of eloquence that I had family about me, with an uncle who stammered and an uncle who was dumb, and others who were afflicted with a metaphorical dumbness and lack of socially confident articulation; and also their forebears, who, although their mouths had been shaped for speech like all *meropes anthropoi*, had been silenced and went unrecorded in the chorus of history. And so it seemed to me then that the greatest gift that I could acquire for myself was the gift of articulation, the treasure of eloquence, the power over words, the power of words. I had a hunger, an appetite for all modes of articulation, for English and for other languages, and even in those very early days, though the teaching was often horrendous, for Latin and Greek, and above all a hunger for that supreme form of articulation, the highest eloquence, poetry. So when I discovered that there was supposed to be a 'retreat from the word', I wasn't prepared to retreat. And when I heard about the 'death of tragedy', I wasn't prepared to attend the funeral, because at that time of my life when I most hungered for articulation and models of eloquence, at the maximum point of my need and hunger I was brought face to face with Greek tragedy, in which, I think, the primacy of language is paramount. I had quite a wrestle, however, with those who taught me. I have described in one of my poems from *The School of Eloquence* called 'Them & [uz]' how one English teacher wouldn't allow me to read Keats aloud because of my Leeds accent. Much of my writing has been a long, slow-burning revenge on the teacher who taught me English when I was eleven or twelve, and full of retrospective aggro. I think that to these feelings are due my reclamation of the Mystery Plays for northern speech and actors, and why there's a strong northern character to the language I used for the National Theatre *Oresteia*, which proved too much for some people. One critic wrote that the chorus 'sounded like fifteen Arthur Scargills'! I make no apologies. There's no earthly reason why a Greek chorus should sound like well-bred ladies from Cheltenham in white nighties. I had also some problems with my Classics teachers, one of whom was engaged in a campaign to keep all colloquial language out of the translations his pupils were required to do from Latin and Greek. It's easy to deny the colloquial roots of a dead language. The upshot of what seemed to me like a conspiracy was to pretend that the language had never been alive or spoken at all. I wish I could remember the piece of Latin that I was translating, but I think it was Plautus and there was some official or other moving a group of people on in a crowded street. My translation went something like: 'Move along there!', true to constabulary vernacular. I do remember that this was crossed out with a heavy red pen, and the alternative I was offered in the margin by the teacher was: 'Vacate the thoroughfare!' I'm sure that such terrible things of forty years ago don't happen today, even if the National Curriculum permitted the possibility of translating Plautus. I gave expression in another poem which I'll read to you about some of the frustrations I had as a working-class boy with a Leeds accent translating upper-class English into patrician Latin and vice versa. It's a poem called 'Classics Society (Leeds Grammar School 1552–1952)'. The grammar schools were founded in the belief that poor old English hadn't the benefit of being a dead language, and the poem begins with a quotation from 1552, the year of my school's foundation, from one who felt humbly cowed by the gracious eloquence of Ciceronian rhetoric:

The grace of Tullies eloquence doth excel
any Englishmens tongue . . . my barbarous stile . . .
The tongue our leaders use to cast their spell
was once denounced as 'rude', 'gross', 'base' and 'vile'.

How fortunate we are who've come so far!

We boys can take old Hansards and translate
the British Empire into SPQR
but nothing demotic or too up-to-date,
and *not* the English that I speak at home,
not Hansard standards, and if Antoninus
spoke like delinquent Latin back in Rome
he'd probably get gamma double minus.

So the lad who gets the alphas works
the hardest in his class at his translation
and finds good Ciceronian for Burke's:
a dreadful schism in the British nation.

That dreadful schism regrettably still exists in the British nation, and an awareness of it has helped to make me the kind of poet I am and the kind of translator I have become when I approach the classics. The tensions in that schism made me into the kind of poet who uses an immensely formal classical prosody against colloquial diction and against the working-class speech of Leeds and even the language of street aggro and graffiti, as in my much-reviled (and, I'm glad to say, much championed!) poem *v.*, where the language of the Beeston graveyard ranges from Latin and biblical to obscene graffiti and four-letter words. And the same tensions between my background and my education, between my awareness of the inarticulate on the one hand and being presented with the models of eloquence from the ancient world on the other, at a time of my maximum need to discover utterance, also made me into the kind of translator that I am.

My earliest experience among people I loved who felt hugely inadequate when it came to using language made me value the word above all, even though there seemed to be a 'retreat' from it under the Medusa-like gaze of the Fifth Age of mankind, and the pressure of other media. My feeling was then, and still is, although I have every poet's despair at times, that language could take on anything and everything, the worst things perhaps above all, and this lesson I learned at that impressionable period of my life in Greek tragedy. However galling it could be at the time, the fact is that I learned ancient Greek, and the sad thing about the new National Curriculum is that no one from my kind of background especially, with my kind of hunger and appetite for language, will have the chance to make his own way to those founding models of European eloquence. While the world of expression was losing its belief in the word, I was busily acquiring mine. 'Words! Words! for me, alas, there was no other salvation!' as the great Cretan writer Nikos Kazantzakis wrote.

This doesn't mean that I haven't had other intimations that not everything was well on Helicon. I have had intimations of the mortality of the Muses that may surprise you. The Muses can have other homes than the mountain top in Boiotia, 'the Grove of the Muses', as Pausanias calls it. It may astonish you, but for the last twenty years, on and off, in Newcastle-upon-Tyne, I have lived not only in The Grove but no. 9 The Grove. And that's not all. This may be harder to believe, but I swear to you it is true and can produce evidence to prove it. For some years I have been receiving mail, which I assumed had been misdirected, addressed to Mrs Muse, 9 The Grove! I was very alarmed, but it was more than my existence as a poet was worth to put it back in the letter box marked 'Not Known at this Address'. After a while I had to open one of these missives to the Muse. I opened one (and I said at the very beginning I was going to make a revelation about the Muses) and inside the envelope was a football coupon! Why not, I thought, after contemplating it for some moments, why not? The ancients, after all, didn't have our problem about reconciling culture and sporting activities. The oppositions and divisions I partly drama-tised in my poem *v.* would have been incomprehensible to the spectators of the Pythian Games at Delphi. So why shouldn't the Muse receive her football pools? Good luck to her, I thought. I went on receiving these missives from time to time, and only a few days ago, addressed to Mrs Muse, 9 The Grove, there was a brown envelope franked 'Newcastle Health Authority'. I had to open it, and it said that 'the doctor will see Mrs Muse at 9.15'. I thought, is this then the last ailing survivor of that *thiasos* on Helicon who inspired my Boiotian *synadelphos*, Hesiod? You will remember that in Hesiod's time, the Muses, though he gave them names which he probably invented himself, were represented as an indissoluble chorus, holding hands in their dance and not yet presiding over the specialisms that they were later to be credited with. I prefer to think of them like that: Tragedy and History holding hands with Lyric and Music, because some of the work I do, which I regard as all *poetry*, seems to be critically unclassifiable and resistant to being placed under the care of any specific Muse of the distinguished nine. It's all poetry to me, whether it is for the printed page, or for reading aloud, or for the theatre, or the opera house, or concert hall, or even for television. But if there were to be only one Muse left of all the 'weary nine', one silent, ailing Mrs Muse with an early appointment to see the doctor, and with a poste restante address at my house, 9 The Grove, which one is it? I think I would have to choose, like Macneile Dixon, Melpomene, the Muse of Tragedy. She may be ailing, but I think the announcement of her death is premature.

This is the Muse, as Macneile Dixon wrote sixty years ago, who deals 'with the most monstrous and appalling that life can offer, when it turns upon us its Medusa-like countenance of frenzy and despair'. Whatever it was in my early experience that didn't allow me to despair of the word turned me also towards tragedy. This frenzy and despair of the Fifth Age is that terror that tragedy allows us to gaze into, as Nietzsche said, 'yet' (and this is a very important yet), Nietzsche added, 'without being turned to stone by the vision'. In an age when the spirit of affirmation has almost been burned out of us, more than ever we need what Nietzsche also called tragedy in *Ecce Homo*, 'the highest art to say yes to life'. The mother of the Muses, or of the one frail, ailing, afflicted daughter still surviving, is Memory, so that we can't celebrate our existence, we can't have those 'unalloyed pleasures', that 'happiness . . . without qualification' that E. R. Dodds wrote about, simply by forgetting the terrors of the recent past or by ignoring the frightening future. Robert Jay Lifton, the American Professor of Psychology, who has charted the effect of the Nazi concentration camps and the nuclear holocaust on our imaginations, and the deeply numbing effect of what must be the most petrifying Medusa-like gaze of all on our sense of futurity, has called for artists to discover a 'theatre that can imagine the end of the world and go beyond that . . . [a theatre] that can believe in tomorrow', what he later was to call 'a theatre of faith'. It sounds to me like a call for the *rebirth* of tragedy. And this theatre he calls for, this tragedy has to believe in the primacy of the word. I think my obsessive concern with Greek drama isn't about antique reproduction, but part of a search for a new theatricality and also a way of expressing dissatisfaction with the current theatre, where I want to work as a *poet*. There are a number of occasions when an obsession with Greek drama has been used to focus dissatisfaction with theatrical cliché and create new forms of expression. The Camerata in Florence thought they were reviving ancient tragedy, and discovered opera with Peri and Rinuccini's piece about Orpheus leading to Monteverdi's *Orfeo* in 1607. And there was Wagner's obsession with Greek tragedy, especially the *Oresteia*, which gave him not only a form to search for new theatricality, but also the means to express his total impatience with the theatre that he found about him. And he did create a new form which was finally realised in the festival theatre at Bayreuth. And I should say, since these examples both produced operatic results, that when I began my long and very fruitful collaboration with Harrison Birtwistle on the *Oresteia*, I said to him that Greek tragedy was opera, but I added hastily, with a poet's understandable nervousness, opera where the *words* are primary.

None of this means going 'back to civilisation', a going 'back to the Greeks', a reactionary cry I sometimes hear at the Delphi drama meetings, but 'forward to the Greeks', or 'forward *with* the Greeks'. What are some of the things I think when I stand facing up to the Muses in an ancient theatrical space? What are some of the resources from which a poet of the Fifth Age can learn from the Greeks? How was it, I ask myself, that the Greeks could present the worst things they could imagine, gaze into terror, as Nietzsche said, and yet not be turned to stone? From his vantage point in that same theatrical space Oliver Taplin has posed many difficult questions and come out with brilliant answers which are of enormous help to us in the theatre. The questions I ask when I face in the opposite direction up to the Muses are very simple ones, and you might even find them simple-minded, but it's in such simple first questionings that we can create theatre.

The first and most obvious fact about Greek tragedy is that it was played in the full light of day. To this is due a great deal of its unique character. It helped first and fore-most, to create what Harbage also found in the theatre of Shakespeare and called 'an obvious reciprocity'. This ancient theatre, this *theatron*, this place for seeing was not only where the audience saw actors bringing dark events *eis to phōs*, 'to the light of day', as Sophocles himself puts it in *Oedipus Tyrannus*; the audience also saw each other, everyone else, so that the bearing of terror was not only shared but seen to be shared, and that is very important. As it was seen to be shared so was it communally endured. The audience were not segregated by armrests and darkness into individual pockets of anxiety and troubled thought in the face of tragedy. Our lights are always dimmed, except by fire regulations for the 'EXIT' signs, which I've always found a great inhibitor of theatrical concentration. And fire regulations can be great inhibitors otherwise. I had to go to court with Peter Hall, and with the wonderful support of R. P. Winnington-Ingram, to persuade a judge to allow us to use real fire for the conclusion of the *Oresteia* at the National Theatre. Elias Canetti in *Crowds and Power* says how spurious the sense of community is in a modern audi-torium if fire breaks out! When a dramatist like Brecht, in his poem 'The Lighting', writes: 'Give us some light on the stage, electrician . . .', or the poet/dramatist Yeats longs for 'a Shakespeare play with all the stage lights in every scene', or we leave the house lights on in our modern auditori-ums it is partly from a deep nostalgia for the theatre of full daylight. Prometheus can cry out at the end of *Prometheus Bound*:

ὦ μητρὸς ἐμῆς σέβας, ὦ πάντων
αἰθὴρ κοινὸν φάος εἱλίσσων,
ἐσορᾷς μ᾽ ὡς ἔκδικα πάσχω. (1091–3)

O you heavens who roll around the light that is
    common to everything,
you witness the injustices I suffer.

– confident that the full light of day not only illuminates
his suffering and the collective audience, but also the landscape and life beyond the imagined realities of the stage.
Not only by this light that was 'common to all' were the
tragic events, the actors, the sea, the valley, Lake Copais,
Euboea illuminated; the actors could also see the audience.
This shared space and shared light makes an enormous difference to the sense of theatrical communication. It creates 'obvious reciprocity'. It is harder to slide into some of
the self-indulgences of obscurity and some of the audi-
ence-dodging evasions of much modernism. And remember, and we should always remember this, though I am not
suggesting that their use is essential in modern productions
of Greek drama, all these plays were performed in *masks*.
Masks have the curious ability to look many people in the
eye at the same time. They had the effect of that famous
Lord Kitchener recruiting poster, where it seemed impossible for the unenlisted to avoid the pointing finger and
the staring eye. A chorus of twelve or fifteen could patrol
(if that's the right word) the concentration and attention
of those spectators on the curved cavea because they were
wearing masks. If you think you are being looked at, if you

think you are being addressed personally and directly, you listen. And masks make an audience feel exactly that. You can bet your life that when the Furies in the *Oresteia* talk about individual guilt, no one in the audience felt let off the hook of moral scrutiny. There is a British TV documentary about the great Greek actress Katina Paxinou, who is appearing currently, I am happy to see, on Greek postage stamps. She talks about playing in the theatre of Epidaurus with 18,000 people. She was distracted by a man at the back scribbling in a pad, obviously a critic (or the correspondent of *The Times*!). She said: 'I looked at him, and I spoke my next lines to him, and he stopped scribbling.' And if an unmasked human face can effect that renewal of attention, how much more so the mask that seems to look at many people at the same time, in the same shared light and the same shared space.

I'd like us to think about masks for a while because I have the sense that when you scholars consider masks, if and when you do consider them, it only occurs to you as a rather embarrassing afterthought, and it's been my contention that masks are central to the understanding of the style and language of ancient drama. Although, as I have said, I am not of the opinion that masks are obligatory gear in modern productions, I have to maintain that we cannot understand the action or verbal style of Greek theatre without continually reminding ourselves that it was a theatre of masks. Perhaps you leave masks out of your dramatic considerations because you have never had the opportunity, as I have, of experimenting with masks and actors. Some of you may recall Jocelyn Herbert's beautiful masks for the

NT *Oresteia*. They were the result of much experiment and workshops with actors, which were to find out, as much as anything, what kind of language would be spoken by masks in this theatrical situation of 'obvious reciprocity' in a shared space and a shared light. I don't think you need me to tell you that it wasn't the language of Noël Coward. Agamemnon and Clytemnestra didn't have a 'little chat in front of the palace', though I have heard it actually described like that by a distinguished classicist. And, once and for all, we should dismiss a fallacy which must still be current because I saw in Brussels only two months ago in a museum section where they had depictions of Greek theatrical masks the explanatory caption that a mask performed the *office de porte-voix*, the 'function of a megaphone'. I'm actually quite attached to this little delusion. When I was a schoolboy studying Greek and the class was about to be subjected to a harrowing test on the conjugation of *histēmi*, one of the unfailing ways of distracting Dr Wilson from his horrible purpose was for one of us to point to the picture of the Theatre of Dionysus on the wall and ask innocently, 'Please, sir, how could people hear at the back?' The teacher would go off into a long, complicated explanation, the gist of which was that the masks were a sort of megaphone. Since I no longer have to undergo the ordeal of tests on the conjugations of *histēmi*, I am glad to jettison the megaphone theory of the Greek theatrical mask. There's another kind of red herring too when we have to consider the language that masks use. In the last six months, I have sat and brooded in a number of ancient theatres, in Athens and Epidaurus, Delphi, and Priene, and Bergama and Ephesus and the beautiful 'chamber' theatre at the top of a mountain on the site of ancient Thera in Santorini. In all of them there was always a crowd of people with or without a guide dropping drachmas, or yen or deutschmark or pence or dimes, or crying loudly, 'Yoohoo!' to one of their number strategically placed on the very back row, to 'test the acoustics'. And although I believe with W. B. Yeats that 'first of all there must be visibility and audibility and if these are absent nothing can be right', it's even more important than testing the fine acoustics to remember that the texts that were spoken there by masks had a built-in 'performability'. This performability had a rhythmical energy that was designed to fill such spaces, to communicate in such conditions of full daylight. We will discover more about the texts by thinking of them first in this way than through years of drachma-dropping. It's probably fortunate that Oedipus wasn't required to drop the brooch he blinded himself with or it would have been taken as irrefutable evidence that you could hear a pin drop. You have only to compare the amount of artificial and external rant that has to inflate a *prose* translation of a Greek tragedy with a real metrical pulse to begin to address the problem. The reason that Peter Hall and Jocelyn Herbert and I had to spend so much time in workshops on masks for our *Oresteia* was that there really is nowhere to turn for help. Even when some practical work has been done there exists a generalising stylistic confusion between Noh drama and *commedia dell'arte* and the full Greek tragic mask. There is no help either in what little writing there is on masks. When Susan Harris Smith, in her recent book *Masks in Modern Drama* (University of

California Press, 1986), writes about masks, even though she has the NT Furies on the cover of her book, she gets it almost 100 per cent wrong when she writes:

> The mask challenges the primacy of language that is undisputed in realistic and naturalistic drama.

This is absolutely the wrong way round, as the mask actually reinforces the primacy of language, at least in the theatre of ancient Greece. The mask reinforces that primacy by continuing to speak in situations that 'normally' or in realistic or naturalistic drama would render a person speechless. It is exactly the primacy of language that allows us to gaze into terror and not be turned to stone. Adrian Poole, in another recent book, *Tragedy: Shakespeare and the Greek Example*, gets it wrong in a related way when he writes that 'tragedy represents the critical moment at which words fail'. Words might fail you or me at such critical moments when we see the city burned to the ground, our children slaughtered, devastation and horror in all their worst forms, but words do not fail the mask. It is designed with an open mouth. To go on speaking even at 'critical moments'.

Let's juxtapose the naked human face that you and I have with a tragic mask and ask three questions to get a feel of the difference between life and theatre.

1. What does a human face do, what do we tend to do, when we're presented with real or very realistically filmed versions of blood, death, violence and terror? We tend to close our eyes in psychic self-preservation. The psychiatrist

Anthony Clare wrote in *The Listener* not long ago that 'the portrayal of Ulster violence has only numbed viewers into anaesthetised silent voyeurs'. They've looked into terror and been turned to stone. The Medusa-like countenance of the Fifth Age has petrified them. Silent voyeurs!

2. What does the human face do, what do we do, when we gaze on such terrors? We become silent. We are speechless with anguish or grief. We have no words to describe them. 'There can be no poetry after Auschwitz,' the familiar and utterly dispiriting adage of Adorno. *Das Wort ist tot.* 'The word is dead.' For my new piece for the Delphi stadium in July 1988 I have been reading papyri and studying their fragments, and I found one the other day which is an appeal to a Roman general to come and save the inhabitants of Egyptian Thebes from a barbarian tribe thought to be the Blemyes, of whom the pleader writes:

> οὐ μία τις βιότοιο γὰ[ρ ἔμ]φασις, οὐ χορὸς αὐτοῖς,
> οὐχ Ἑλικών, οὐ Μοῦσα·

For such people life has no emphasis, no significance. They have no dance, no Helicon, no Muse.

The mask, facing up to the Muses, refuses to surrender *emphasis*.

3. What does the head do when it suffers or witnesses suffering? It tends to bow down.

And now we should imagine the Greek mask in the same three situations. If a mask gazes on the same horrors, the same terrors, it goes on gazing. It is created with open eyes. It has to keep on looking. It faces up to the Muses. What does a mask do when it suffers or witnesses suffering through these continually open eyes? Words never fail it. It goes on speaking. It's created with an open mouth. To go on speaking. It has faith in the word. The chorus in *Agamemnon* might say:

τὰ δ᾽ ἔνθεν οὔτ᾽ εἶδον οὔτ᾽ ἐννέπω (248)

What happened next I did not see and will not tell.

but what they *have* seen they will tell you about, and in such spellbinding language that you have to listen. The open eyes and open mouth of the mask come together very powerfully in the figure of Cassandra, in the same play of Aeschylus. For almost three hundred lines of the *Agamemnon* she stands gazing silently into the terrors she has already witnessed in the destruction of Troy and gazing into the terror she sees in the future, her own bloody death and Agamemnon's. Her silence establishes the seeing, and the seeing prepares the way for her bursting into speech. The open-eyed silence is full of seeing. The mask creates that expectancy. If the human head bows down when it suffers, the mask keeps its head upright. It is created to stay upright. It's created to present itself. In this theatre of 'obvious reciprocity' the mask is created to see, to speak and to present itself so it can be seen. Even Oedipus has to present his bloody sockets to be seen. When he enters blinded, the messenger introduces him as a *theama,* something to be seen in the *theatron.* '*Theama*' is also the word Prometheus uses of himself to direct the *theatēs* to the injustice of his Zeus-imposed suffering. When Oedipus, this *theama,* enters, Sophocles has the chorus draw attention to what we must see by saying how terrible it is to regard:

> ὦ δεινὸν ἰδεῖν πάθος ἀνθρώποις,
> ὦ δεινότατον πάντων ὅσ᾽ ἐγὼ
> προσέκυρσ᾽ ἤδη. τίς σ᾽, ὦ τλῆμον,
> προσέβη μανία; τίς ὁ πηδήσας
> μείζονα δαίμων τῶν μακίστων
> πρὸς σῇ δυσδαίμονι μοίρᾳ;
> φεῦ φεῦ, δύσταν᾽:
> ἀλλ᾽ οὐδ᾽ ἐσιδεῖν δύναμαί σε, θέλων
> πόλλ᾽ ἀνερέσθαι, πολλὰ πυθέσθαι,
> πολλὰ δ᾽ ἀθρῆσαι:

> O dread fate for men to see, O most dreadful of all that I have set my eyes on! Unhappy one, what madness has come upon you? Who is the unearthly foe who, with a leap of more than mortal range, has made your ill-starred life his prey? Alas, alas, you hapless man! I cannot even look on you, though there is much I desire to ask, much I desire to learn, much that draws my wistful gaze.
>
> (trans. R. C. Jebb)

I'm not enough of a Greek scholar to say, but it seems to me that the progression in that speech from one word for 'seeing' to the next, from *idein* to *esidein* to *athrēsai*, help to make the audience continue their gazing, and focus on the mask, with its now blood-glued eyes, when it starts to speak from its still open mouth. Words have not failed the mask of Oedipus. The head stays unbowed for us to see the terrible sockets and also to register the carriage of survival. One could almost say that the first words of Hecuba in the *Trojan Women* of Euripides, *ana, dysdaimon*, is a kind of motto for the tragic mask, an injunction to present itself suffering and all to the audience:

ἄνα, δύσδαιμον, πεδόθεν κεφαλή.

Lift your head, unlucky one, from the ground.

The mask of Hecuba presents itself to the audience, faces up to its suffering, speaks, and carries from this first act of presentation an existential meaning that survives in the last words of the *Trojan Women*. The very final scene of the play could be said to have been prepared by this *ana, dysdaimon*, that survives into the play's ending and brings us back full circle to the act of raising the head and facing up to the life of the future, with all its horrors. Euripides deliberately brings Hecuba, and the chorus with her, back down to the earth we first see her prostrated on, just before the very end of the play:

Ἑκάβη
γεραιά γ' ἐς πέδον τιθεῖσα μέλεα καὶ
χερσὶ γαῖαν κτυποῦσα δισσαῖς.

Χορός
διάδοχά σοι γόνυ τίθημι γαίᾳ
τοὺς ἐμοὺς καλοῦσα νέρθεν
ἀθλίους ἀκοίτας.

(*Trojan Women*, 1305–9)

HECUBA
I'm stooping my ageing limbs to the ground
and pound the earth with both my hands.

CHORUS
I kneel down too, calling my poor husband
from the world below.

My dramatic instincts tell me that Euripides brings his Trojan women low to the ground not only to take a last leave of their dead, but in order that they again had to raise their heads like Hecuba at the beginning of the play, and stand, in order to make an exit. And the bearing of that exit and the deportment of the mask are reasons why we are able to gaze on the terror and not turn to stone. What is Hecuba's last word, if not the final word of the play?

ἴτ᾽ ἐπί, τάλανα,
δούλειον ἁμέραν βίου. (1329–30)

Come on, poor woman, slavery is now your life.

For all the future is slavery the mask's last word and vision is of *biou*, 'life'. And the chorus add to this:

ἰὼ τάλαινα πόλις: ὅμως δὲ
πρόφερε πόδα σὸν ἐπὶ πλάτας Ἀχαιῶν. (1331–2)

Oh my miserable city. But none the less start
walking to the ships of the Achaeans.

In that little word *homōs*, in that 'none the less' so strategically placed at the beginning of a new sentence and at the end of a verse line, is a reinforcement of, a commitment to the last word of Hecuba, *biou*, 'life'. These are small words but crucial, and spoken in masks, with their necessarily upright bearing, they resonate with existential survival that is at the heart of tragedy and make it impossible to agree with Jean-Paul Sartre that the play ends in 'total nihilism'.

These are some of the simple questions that I put to myself standing with a fellow pilgrim in an ancient theatrical space on the slopes of Helicon in the Valley of the Muses. They are part of a search for the means to face up to the Fifth Age of mankind. One of my new projects for the National Theatre, which will hopefully be brought *eis to phōs*, though not, alas, to the full light of day, in 1989, bears all the marks of these recent broodings. I have combined two ancient plays written within a short time of each other as a response to the same political events in Athens, and I have placed them in a setting which makes all our spiritual struggles and cultural endeavours face up to the impasse of the Age of Iron. It is a place that mocks our inner adventures either in reimagining the past or shaping the future. One play is a comedy, the other a tragedy: the *Lysistrata* of Aristophanes and the *Trojan Women* of Euripides. I intend to play them both on the same evening. In my study at 9 The Grove, where I write my poems and plays and create my versions of Greek drama for the National Theatre, I have on the wall some inspiring pictures of the Muses. I have a copy of a vase painting of the Muse sitting on Helicon with a lyre. I have a reproduction of the Muses dancing on their mountain by Giulio Romano, from the Pitti Palace in Florence. And next to them I have what looks like a similar group of women holding hands and dancing in an 'indissoluble chorus'. The mountain they are dancing on is in no way *zatheon*, 'holy', like the mountain of Hesiod we happened on last year. It is in no way sacred or holy, though it has blind worshippers. It is a hellish Helicon more appropriate, perhaps, to our Age of Iron. In front of this mountain is barbed wire and razor wire and police cars. This chorus of 'Muses' is a picture of women dancing on the top of a nuclear silo at the Greenham Common US missile base in January 1983. It is here that my two plays, which I have combined and call *The Common Chorus*, are set. The mountain that these Muses dance on is where our extinction is stored, an extinction that even Memory, the mother of the Muses, will not survive to make our sufferings a story like those of Hecuba and the women of Troy, an extinction that will mean no going 'back to civilisation', even for one learned in the classics. Life will have no emphasis, no significance. There will be no dance, no Helicon, no Muses. This 'scenario', as it is called by strategists speculating over the future of Europe, sometimes called the 'theatre' of war, is probably the worst thing that our imagination can and, I'm afraid, must conceive. And on the brink of the silo and the extinction it represents, this chorus of Muses of the late Age of Iron affirm life, and celebrate it by dancing in the face of the ultimate darkness on Helicon. Our way not back to civilisation but forward might begin by facing up to these Muses. My play *The Common Chorus*, combining the *Lysistrata* and the *Trojan Women*, is set outside one of the gates to the Greenham Common missile base. It begins with the guards behind the wire shouting sexual abuse at the women's peace camp, with its 'benders', where they live their continually disturbed existence, made from bent branches and polythene. The women's response to the guards' abuse is to play, with very limited theatrical resources, first the comedy of Aristophanes and after it the tragedy of Euripides. The threat of extinction contained in the weapons the guards are protecting make the real and the imagined interdependent, as we of this Fifth Age bear in our memory all responsibility now for the struggles and aspirations of the past, of all ages, not only fifth-century Athens. This idea casts its shadow over the whole piece. When it became known that I was preparing this piece for the theatre, I was asked to send a draft of the *Lysistrata* to an American magazine, with a view to publishing it before the performance. Although my texts for the theatre are never finished until they are performed, I sent the draft. The magazine was a well-known, once 'radical' American journal. They hung on to the text for a long time, as is the way with these magazines, and to tell the truth I forgot about it. Then I had a letter saying that, after due consideration, etc. etc., while they found the version 'wonderful', they had come to the conclusion that it was 'too pacifist, and too obscene' to publish. God knows what the *Daily Mail* will make of it if the *Partisan Review* takes this attitude. God knows also what the member for Cannock and Burntwood and the member for Bury South will find to say in their outrage to the *Daily Mail* about a play over two thousand years old. I mention this now only to remind you, when you are debating the threatened future of your subject, that the book-burners are abroad again. There are grave threats to Greek studies besides the new National Curriculum. Some people are trying to create a climate of opinion in this country also where it might soon not be beyond the realms of fantasy to foresee such brilliant and human books as that by another former president of your association, the great Greek scholar Sir Kenneth Dover, on Greek homosexuality falling foul of the infamous Clause 28. When the Regius Professor of Greek at Oxford reviewed this book in the *New Statesman* ten years ago, he wrote that Sir Kenneth Dover gave 'an excellent selection of illustrations, all the more welcome because museums are often unwilling to exhibit and scholars to reproduce the works of art most relevant to this purpose, some of which are not only interesting but delightful'. Can delightful pictures be said to promote homosexuality? There are certainly some very happy and unashamed couplings in the pages of Sir Kenneth Dover's book. Are the vases, I wonder, even now being re-relegated to the dusty basements and cellars of our museums? The homosexuality of ancient Greece is as essential to its understanding as its tragic drama. I have had my problems with the book-burners of Cannock and Burntwood, and Bury South, and I know many of the ancient poets I admire would have similar problems if they were alive in Britain today, and I would be proud to be hounded in their company. I have said that I am in the process of reconstructing the fragmentary satyr play of Sophocles, the *Ichneutae*, and I have a feeling that I'd better hurry round the museums with my *thiasos* to seek inspiration from the satyrs depicted on vases before they too are sent 'back to civilisation' in some basement. I don't quite know where satyrdom will stand under Clause 28, but I have witnessed them coupling not only with Maenads (which might well pass muster!), but also with each other, even with gratefully surprised donkeys, not to mention the Sphinx handle of the wine jar they are cavorting on. I'm not sure how buggering the Sphinx would fare either under this infamous clause.

To conclude, I would like to read a short scene from *The Common Chorus*, Part I, the *Lysistrata*. The Greenham woman playing Lysistrata (which I hope will be Glenda Jackson) faces the magistrate, or in this case a Police Inspector who has come to find out why, as actually happened, the women have put huge padlocks on the main gate to the missile base, that 'Acropolis' whose very existence and cost undermine our national education as much as anything:

INSPECTOR
We let laxness in the home and when we're on the beat
they're giving someone else our little midnight treat.
We're out and about enforcing British law

and they first learn whoredom and then denounce war.
If this is what happens when you treat her
like an equal, don't give her a millimetre
or she'll take six inches and it won't be yours.
Then they try to castrate us by stopping wars.
Domestic leniency, believe you me
first it's sensuality then it's CND!
First it's going out alone with made-up faces
then, the next thing that you know, surrounding missile
    bases.
One day it's taking classes, ancient bloody Greek!
Then it's aerobics and building a physique.
What's next, you wonder. Well, one thing that's next
is getting our missile systems hexed
with their witchcraft, wailing, all this, all this,
because in domestic matters men have been remiss.
You know we've given them far too free a hand
and the upshot of it is, they'll destroy the land.
In my opinion they'll undermine the state
and as for Great Britain, you can forget the Great.
It's my belief we're on the slippery slope
because we've given women far too much rope.
Now they've gone too far. They've cooked their goose.
Their necks are going to feel the tightening of the noose.
HE's on our side. He's a bloke is ZEUS!

Well, ladies, I think you should be knowing
that this is as far as Liberation's going.
Sorry to spoil your little fun, but from today
the only way you're going is Holloway.

I'm rather afraid that we're going to get tough.
The gentlemen of Britain have had e-bloody-nough!

(*to* LYSISTRATA)
You've locked these gates, madam. May we enquire why?

LYSISTRATA
Because the weapons in there bleed the country dry.

INSPECTOR
Locking the gates, though. It doesn't make any sense.

LYSISTRATA
It's a protest against the money wasted on Defence.

INSPECTOR
O so we're a paid-up economist are we, miss? I see.
The FT index is all Greek to me.
Tell me then, if you're an economist, miss,
about the money that gets wasted policing all this.
Ever thought about the cost to the nation
of policing your protest and your little demonstration?

LYSISTRATA
You won't need to do it once they withdraw
the missiles, and we've put an end to war.
The money stockpiled in that Acropolis . . .

INSPECTOR
Acro . . . Acro . . . is that some foreign lingo, miss?

English is all I ever need to speak.

LYSISTRATA
OK, then, no more references to anything Greek!
The money represented by this wire fence
could be used on education if men had any sense.
The millions of pounds in your barbed-wire barricade
could go on education here, or Third World aid.
The billions committed to your missile base
could go towards helping the human race.
These destructive systems waste enormous wealth
better spent on Housing, Education, Health.
The billions behind that guarded silo door
would feed more than five thousand if we got rid of War.
Those millions in missiles and US personnel
could be spent on health, on making people well.
Those millions on missiles that you pour
along with human blood down the open drain of War.
Those millions, those billions stored in that concrete
could let the world's hungry learn to eat.
We protest against those billions that are poured
into payloads the nation can't afford,
cash that's needed to house, feed, clothe, heal, teach.

INSPECTOR
Just open the bloody gate. Forget the Budget Speech!

LYSISTRATA
Inside blast-hardened bunkers housing Cruise
are millions the nation's being forced to misuse.

These palatial missile bunkers almost halve
the nation's resources and people starve.
Even if you never use your boyish little toys
by taking from the needy deterrence destroys.
With Cruise-missile money you could create jobs
for kids your kind will end up calling 'yobs'.
Their lives of unemployment don't make any sense,
and the money needed is squandered on 'Defence'.
And by jobs I mean some profession other
than killing the sons of a Spartan mother.

INSPECTOR
Now you've lost me. Where the hell is Sparta?

LYSISTRATA
Where your payloads are pointing. The Peloponnese.

INSPECTOR
Didn't catch the last bit.

LYSISTRATA
                    Forget it, it's in Greece.
And if you want to know my name it's Lysistrata.

INSPECTOR
Well, miss, is it? Lysistrata, or do we say Ms?

LYSISTRATA
When I've finished with your armies it'll be DisMs!

INSPECTOR
Your geography's confused me, Ms. I do hope
your little ladies' commune's not into dope.

POLICEMAN
Shall we search them, Inspector? They look the type
that have their peace pow-wows with the hashish pipe.

OLDER WOMAN
I'll kick his knackers for him, the cocky little devil!

LYSISTRATA (*restraining her*)
No! That would be descending to their male level.

(*to* INSPECTOR *again*)
There's no confusion. My mind's completely clear
and there's no difference between there and here.
Since Hiroshima what we've done,
paradoxically, 's to make the whole earth one.
We all look down the barrel of the same cocked gun,
one target, in one united fate
nuked together in some new hyperstate.
So Greece is Greenham, Greenham Greece,
Poseidon is . . . Poseidon, and not just for this piece.
Not just all places, all human ages too
are dependent on the likes of us and you.
In the Third World War we'll destroy
not only modern cities but the memory of Troy,
stories which shaped the spirit of our race
are held in the balance in this missile base.

Remember, if you can, that with man goes the mind
that might have made sense of the history of Mankind.
It's a simple thing to grasp, when we're all dead
there'll be no further pages to be read,
not even leaflets, and no peace plays like these,
no post-holocaust Aristophanes.
So if occasionally some names are new
just think of the ground that's under you.
If we're destroyed, then we
take with us Athens 411 BC.
The world till now up to the last minute
and every creature who was ever in it
go when we go, everything men did or thought,
never to be remembered, absolutely nought.
No war memorials with the names of dead on
because memory won't survive your Armageddon.
So Lysistrata, Glenda Jackson, it's one name.
Since 1945 past and present are the same.
And it doesn't matter if it's 'real' or a play.
Imagination and reality will go the same way.
So don't say it's just a bunch of ancient Greeks.
It's their tears that will be flowing down your cheeks.

In Lady Falkender's memoirs of the Harold Wilson years
she has this to say about the election of 1964:

Before the Election I had been leafing through the
Radio Times to check which television programmes
might interfere with public response to our campaign-
ing. To my horror, I discovered that on polling day itself

Steptoe and Son was due on an hour before the polls closed. This is the time during which, traditionally, the largest number of Labour voters come out and Steptoe was very popular at the time. I told Harold Wilson, and he explained to the then Director General of the BBC, Sir Hugh Greene, that the programme might reduce the number of people who voted, Conservatives as well as our own supporters. Sir Hugh Greene accepted the general point that the BBC should not put temptation in the way of voters of any political loyalty, and wryly asked Sir Harold what programme he thought would be suitable. The reply was: 'Greek drama, preferably in the original.'

I have a dream that we might devise a drama, not Greek drama in the original, but deeply inspired by it and drawing some energy from that inexhaustible source, that might push Mrs Thatcher, and her spokesman on defence, and education, not to mention the members for Cannock and Burntwood, and Bury South, way down the ratings, so that on my way back from Delphi this July with my *thiasos* of British satyrs I might be able to go to Askri again, and Hesiod's valley, and face up to the Muses, look the Muses in the face, and say, 'See you again next year. I'm going back to a little bit of civilisation.' And maybe hear the quavering voice of the ailing Mrs Muse, recuperating on Helicon, say, '*Kalo taxidi!*'

The Trackers of Oxyrhynchus

1989

INTRODUCTION TO THE DELPHI TEXT

I

Something prepared me for Greek drama long before I knew a word of ancient Greek or had ever heard the names of Hecuba or Oedipus. It began with the creation of what I call my 'orchestra', in the sense I later learned for that Greek word meaning 'circular dancing place'. This 'orchestra' became my first brooding ground and, I think, the first intimation of what for me is the basic struggle of art. I was eight. We were celebrating what was called VJ (Victory over Japan) night with a large bonfire in the back street outside our house. The atmosphere was more celebratory than I can ever remember before or since, with normally taciturn people laughing, singing, dancing at the end of a terrible war. Furniture was brought out of houses to keep the blaze going. The fire became so high the telephone wires were burned down. The paint on our back gate blistered and peeled off. It went on all night, and in the morning I helped to douse the fire and shovel the ashes into tea chests to be taken away. When the space was cleared, the celebratory bonfire had left a black circle of scorched cobbles with thick scars of tar.

Forty-five years later, the circle is still there. Looking into that circle I once thought of it as the night-sky globe totally devoid of stars, an annihilated universe. It was something like Byron's vision in 'Darkness':

> I had a dream, which was not all a dream.
> The bright sun was extinguished, and the stars
> Did wander darkling in the eternal space . . .

It looked like this when my imagination couldn't cope with the twentieth century. It was in this starless shape, even before I became a poet, that I learned to relate our celebratory fire, with the white-hot coils from domestic sofas, to that terrible form of fire that brought about the 'VJ' when unleashed on Hiroshima and Nagasaki in August 1945. One element for celebration and terror. One space for the celebrant and the sufferer.

I began to learn to people that scorched orchestra only after an immersion in the drama of the ancient Greeks. Things just as 'dark' occurred in this orchestra of Dionysus, but it was lit by the sun and was surrounded by a community as bonded in their watching as we had been by our celebratory blaze. It was a drama open-eyed about suffering but with a heart still open to celebration and physical affirmation. In the late twentieth century, what clues to existential survival could be found in an ancient drama which managed to face up to the worst things it could imagine and yet not banish the celebratory? What style permitted the sufferer and the celebrant to share the same space? What were the ways and means?

Though the texts of ancient drama are constantly annotated and re-annotated, some of the factors I have found essential to the drama's affirmation are often overlooked.

The first thing to observe about Greek drama is that it was staged in the common light of day. A shared space and a shared light. Our word 'theatre' is derived from the Greek word '*theatron*', 'a place of seeing'. Not only did the audience (*hoi theatai*, 'those who see' in Greek) *see* the action of tragedy, not only did the audience *see* the actors and chorus, but the actors and chorus *saw* the audience. They were all equally illuminated by the light of the sun. The lighting grid was the great globe itself. In Athens of the fifth century BC that 'obvious reciprocity' that Harbage found between actors and audience in Shakespeare's theatre was created from the beginning of the experience by the shared space and shared light. When Bertolt Brecht writes in one of his theatre poems, 'The Lighting',

> Give us some light on the stage, electrician. How
> can we
> Playwrights and actors put forward
> Our images of the world in half-darkness? The dim
> twilight
> Induces sleep. But we need the audience's
> Wakeful-, even watchfulness. Let them
> Do their dreaming in the light.

and when Yeats writes that in the theatre 'the essential thing is always full or almost full light because the actor comes first', and how he would like to compel a theatrical producer to 'produce some Shakespearian play with all the stage lights in every scene', applying that principle even to the storm scene in *King Lear*, when Peter Brook brought the house lights up at the end of the first act of *King Lear*, before the blinding of Gloucester; when Poel looked for a lighting which 'evoked the open air'; and when Granville Barker's plans for an 'exemplary theatre' included 'provisions for performing in daylight', a suggestion his biographer calls 'wonderfully radical' – when all these men of the theatre made these statements and gestures, they were expressing, in their various ways, a deep nostalgia for the theatre of daylight.

The Greeks had no need of a lighting system to 'evoke the open air'. They had such a system in the sun, which linked audience and performers in a common light. There was no atmospheric darkening of the stage for illusionary effect, nor to conceal such a spectacle as the Oedipus with gouged eye sockets. Voltaire's suggestion, in his note to Corneille's preface to *Oedipe*, that dim lighting might make that terrible image tolerable would make no sense to Sophocles, who has the blinded king described as a 'spectacle', something to be looked at, a *theama*, from the same root of the verb 'to see' that gives us 'theatre'. It is also as a 'spectacle', in the same Greek word, that Prometheus in *Prometheus Bound* draws attention to himself and the injustice he 'suffers at the hands of Zeus'. His final cry is to the 'common light' that unites actor and audience, theatrical space and outside world, the imaginary and the real.

This 'light common to all' ('*pantōn koinon phaos*', *Prometheus Bound*, 1091–2) is the first essential of ancient drama.

The light is the first thing to be addressed by Prometheus or Alcestis or Ion, and it is not only the illumination in the sense of the lighting that unites audience and performer in a shared experience, but also in the sense of spiritual under-standing. Things are brought, as Oedipus says, '*eis to phōs*', 'to the light', or as we might say, 'to the light of day'. Shared space and shared light. How different from the darkened auditoria of our day.

A Greek theatrical mask is part of the existential survival gear. It gives the bearing of survival to the actor wearing it. It represents a commitment to seeing everything through the eyes that never close. It represents a commitment to going on speaking when the always-open eyes have wit-nessed something unspeakable. The masks must witness the unendurable. That is why they are created with their eyes open. The mouth must continue to speak in situations where the human being would be speechless or screaming and unable to articulate its agony. The shared space and light allow this seeing and this speaking. The shared light begs a common language. The mask is always 'presented'. It sees the audience looking at it. It seems to see more people than a human eye. A chorus of masks patrols the attention of the audience. If you know you are seen, you know you are being addressed, and you attend.

The space and light and the mask are created for a com-munal act of attention, a deep concentration in which the spellbinding metrical language also plays a primary part. Performability is not something injected afterwards into a text. Greek texts are created with the performability for that known space in the conditions of shared light, and created to be spoken in masks to an audience that is *seen* and never cut off in darkened seats. Above all, since the expression 'to see the light' in Greek means 'to live', the final sense is that of shared *life*. And it is to that life that the masked upright figure of Hecuba commits herself and us at the very end of *The Trojan Women* of Euripides, and not to the 'total nihilism' that Sartre found in the play.

But even that commitment to life was not the end of the drama. The broken Trojan refugees were not the final image. After every third play in a group of three tragedies, as *The Trojan Women* was, would come a satyr play written by the same author, with a chorus of what we can see as men in their animal condition, represented as half or three-quarters man with horse or goat attributes and an erect phallus. The unease that is felt and has long been felt at the idea of the bloated celebrant following hard on the heels of the sufferer has been responsible, along with natural oblivion, for the loss of these plays, which amount to a quarter of the whole large output of the great dramatists, Aeschylus, Sophocles and Euripides.

With the loss of these plays we are lacking important clues to the wholeness of the Greek imagination and its ability to absorb and yet not be defeated by the tragic. In the satyr play, that spirit of celebration, held in the dark solution of tragedy, is precipitated into release, and a release into the worship of the Dionysus who presided over the whole dramatic festival. In the one complete surviving satyr play, the *Cyclops* of Euripides, the very last line allows the chorus the prospect of being liberated finally from the dark shadow of the Cyclops Polyphemus and spending the rest of the time in the service of Bacchus. This journey back into the service of the presiding god seems to be paralleled by the release of the spirit back to the life of the senses at the end of the tragic journey. It is unlikely that the quaffing promised to the Dionysian band was one in which a drop was taken from the cup for the sufferers of the preceding tragedy, as at Passover one drop of wine is removed from the cup of joy for each of the ten plagues which befell Egypt at the time of the exodus, but the sensual relish for life and its affirmation must have been the spirit of the conclusion of the four plays. The satyrs are included in the wholeness of the tragic vision. They are not forgotten or forced out by pseudo-'refinement'.

Without the satyr play we cannot know enough about the way in which the Greek spirit coped with catastrophe. The residue of a few tragedies might give us the illusion of something resolutely high-minded, but it is a distortion, with which post-Christian culture has been more comfortable than with the whole picture. The thought of tragedy and satyrs co-existing has not been easy even for the most comprehensive of scholars. Sir Arthur Pickard-Cambridge, to whom we are all indebted for the description of the material environment of Greek drama, has a problem characteristic of the scholarship on it:

> The problem which is baffling to modern and Christian readers – how it was possible for the same audience, possibly even on the same day, to be absorbed in the noblest tragedy and pass immediately to the grossness, which . . . comedy displayed for at least a century

and a half – would not have been appreciated by the Athenians of the fifth century, and it is one which will never be completely solved.

The stress on Christian and *readers* helps us to understand the problem. Christianity, with what D. H. Lawrence called its 'lust . . . for the end of the world', certainly drove a wedge into human nature and subverted the wholeness of an earlier imagination. The shrivelled private scope of readership rather than presence in shared light and space made both parts of the Greek spirit harder to accommodate. The essential catholicity of Greek drama, the unity of tragedy and satyr play, has been betrayed into divided and divisive categories, 'high' and 'low'. The Byzantine compilers helped to initiate this process by choosing only a few representative tragedies for study. Discoveries outside of this ancient selection include those plays that help to undermine the view of drama as uniformly high-minded, even, given its early period of history, straining for an acceptable monotheistic maturity! The so-called 'alphabet' plays of Euripides included not only the one surviving satyr play, but also the category-disturbing *Alcestis*, often termed 'proto-satyric' because Euripides offered it in place of the satyr play as the fourth play of his competition entry. In this play Euripides introduced his 'satyr', in the shape of Herakles, into the very body of the tragedy: the celebrant admitted before the tragic section had come to an end. The playwright thus showed both elements intertwined, doing what Johnson said of Shakespeare, depicting neither 'tragedy' nor 'comedy' but the real state of 'sublunary nature' in which '*at the same time* the reveller is hasting to his wine and the mourner is burying his friend', or, in the case of Herakles in *Alcestis*, getting drunk while Admetus is burying his wife. It is, of course, precisely this quality in Shakespeare that has given those who want their genius more 'refined' the same problems that classicists have had with Greek drama. One such characteristic voice was that of Robert Bridges, Poet Laureate from 1913 to 1930:

> Shakespeare should not be put into the hands of the young without the warning that the foolish things in his plays were written to please the foolish, the filthy for the filthy, and the brutal for the brutal; and that if out of our veneration for his genius we are led to admire or even tolerate such things, we may be thereby not conforming ourselves to him, but only degrading ourselves to the level of his audience, and learning contamination from those wretched beings who can never be forgiven their share in preventing the greatest poet and dramatist of the world from being the best artist.

How far we already are from that shared space and light of the Greeks. The divided art is perpetuating divided audiences, divided societies. This audience of Shakespeare's time, so despised and patronised by the Poet Laureate, is exactly the same as that which Alfred Harbage thought should take some of the credit for the greatness of Shakespeare's plays. It was due in part to that 'obvious reciprocity' which also existed abundantly in ancient Athens. Harbage's account of the audience in Shakespeare's theatre immediately shows up all that is thoroughly undemocratic in the view of Bridges:

> Mere coincidence will not explain why every Elizabethan play addressed to a *sector* of the people, high or low, learned or unlearned, is inferior in quality; why neither university nor law school, nor guild hall, nor princely banquet house begat dramatic poetry comparable to what came from the public theatres; or why Blackfriars failed to sustain the level achieved at the Globe. The drama reached its peak when the audience formed *a great amalgam*, and it began its decline when the amalgam was split in two.

If we stress the 'free' and the 'men' of 'freemen of Athens', we have a similar 'great amalgam' in ancient Athens, despite the fact it seems highly likely that slaves and even women were not at the theatres. A recent survey has shown that modern theatre audiences are composed of elite and privileged *sectors* of our society. For two of the greatest moments in world drama it seems to have been otherwise. W. B. Stanford has shown that the Athenian audiences were not simply intellectuals and sophisticated citizens, but 'farmers, craftsmen, shopkeepers, manual labourers, in far greater numbers than the priests, poets, philosophers and sophists'. He tells us that we should do well to remember that when it came to voting for the groups of four plays submitted in the competition, the vote of a shoemaker was as good as a vote from a philosopher. The social composition of the audience in that shared space and shared light was not only a 'great amalgam' but could see that it was. Those gathered together had that kind of recognition of each other as belonging to the same society, but would only gather together on these important festival occasions; the uniqueness of the event also united them. We might say that TV reaches such an amalgam, but it is not present in the same space: TV viewers are not aware of each other attending, and therefore sharing not only the space and the light, but the illumination in the spiritual sense. When drama lost those conditions, it became less able to bear and digest the worst things it could imagine. Dramas became texts divided into 'high' and 'low' art. The loss of satyr plays is both a symptom and a consequence of this division. What is lost is a clue to the wholeness of the Greek imagination and its deep compulsion to unite sufferer and celebrant in the same space and light. In the end those who feel excluded from 'high' art and relegated to 'low' will sooner or later want to destroy what they are not allowed to inhabit.

If we have a nostalgia for the theatre of daylight, it is a sign of regret for a culture where the celebrant is born out of tragedy before our eyes. With us the masque and the anti-masque are as divided as they were when Shelley saw that division as both the 'sign and the thing signified' in his regrettably uncompleted drama *Charles I* of 1819:

> Ay, there they are –
> Nobles, and sons of nobles, patentees,
> Monopolists, and stewards of this poor farm,
> On whose lean sheep sit the prophetic crows,

Here is the pomp that strips the houseless orphan,
Here is the pride that breaks the desolate heart.
These are not the lilies glorious as Solomon
Who toil not, neither do they spin, – unless
It be the webs they catch poor rogues withal.
Here is the surfeit which to them who earn
The niggard wages of the earth, scarce leaves
The tithe that will support them till they crawl
Back to her cold hard bosom. Here is health
Followed by grim disease, glory by shame,
Waste by lame famine, wealth by squalid want,
And England's sin by England's punishment.
And, as the effect pursues the cause foregone,
Lo, giving substance to my words, behold
At once the sign and the thing signified –
A troop of cripples, beggars, and lean outcasts,
Horsed upon stumbling jades, carted with dung,
Dragged for a day from cellars and low cabins
And rotten hiding-holes, to point the moral
Of this presentiment, and bring up the rear
Of painted pomp with misery!

THE YOUTH

                                        'Tis but
The anti-masque, and serves as discords do
In sweeter music. Who would love May flowers
If they succeeded not to Winter's flaw;
Or day unchanged by night; or joy itself
Without the touch of sorrow?

SECOND CITIZEN

I and thou –

A MARSHALSMAN

Place, give place!

And the Marshalsmen of division go on crying, 'Place, give place!' in all our palaces of culture still.

II

In 1907, Grenfell and Hunt, the Holmes and Watson of Oxford papyrology, discovered the tattered remains of a lost satyr play of Sophocles, the *Ichneutae* ('The Trackers'). The discovery of the papyrus with some four hundred incomplete lines was announced at the Annual General Meeting of the Egypt Exploration Society by Dr Hunt, in the following words:

> . . . Three years ago we were indebted to Oxyrhynchus for some extensive remains of a lost tragedy of Euripides, the *Hypsipyle*. It is now the turn of Sophocles: and most fortunately the discovery to which I refer represents a side of the poet concerning which we have been very much in the dark. As you know, it was customary to produce tragedies in trilogies, or sets of three, which were followed by a Satyric drama, a lighter piece in which the chorus consisted of Satyrs, and the high tension of the preceding tragedies was relaxed. Only one specimen of such a Satyric drama has come down to us, the *Cyclops* of Euripides. Of the work of Sophocles, as of

Aeschylus, in this line there exist only short disjointed fragments preserved in citations by grammarians and others. I am glad to say that for Sophocles what may be considered a fair sample is now recovered.

When found, the papyrus in question was, as usual, much broken up; in fact, the various fragments were not even all obtained in the same year. But they have fitted together remarkably well, and as now arranged make up the first sixteen columns of the play, accounting for over 400 lines, of which about one half are complete or easily completed, and many more sufficiently well preserved to be intelligible. Since the length of a Satyric drama seems to have been considerably less than that of the ordinary tragedy, the amount recovered may well represent as much as half of the original whole. The play is the *Ichneutae*, or 'The Trackers', of which practically nothing beyond the title was previously known. It is based upon the familiar myth of the exploits of the infant god Hermes – his theft of Apollo's cattle and his invention of the lyre. Apollo, in an opening speech, announces the loss of the cattle, for which he has vainly sought, and offers rewards to the finder. Silenus then appears with his attendant Satyrs, and proposes to join in the search. Encouraged by Silenus, the chorus start out on the quest – they are the 'Trackers' from whom the play is named. They soon discover traces of the cattle, leading to the entrance of a cave; but here they are alarmed by curious sounds which they do not understand – the notes of the newly-invented lyre with which Hermes is amusing himself down below. Silenus upbraids them for their timidity, and at length himself knocks at the barrier, and a nymph emerges. In answer to their questions, she explains that she is the nurse of the child who has been lately born to Zeus, and whose abnormal growth is so startling, and tells them of his invention of the lyre. But she stoutly defends him against the imputation of being concerned in the theft. They remain unconvinced; some cowhide admittedly has been used in making the lyre, and there are tell-tale tracks on the ground. While the dispute is in progress Apollo returns, and accepts the evidence offered by Silenus and the Satyrs as entitling them to the promised reward. Here the papyrus breaks off; no doubt in the sequel Hermes appeared on the scene and appeased Apollo by the gift of the lyre, as narrated in the Homeric hymn.

The piece was thus slight enough. Like the *Cyclops* of Euripides, it is a short and simple dramatisation of a well-known story, to which a Satyric setting was appropriate. An element of comedy was supplied by the grotesque figures of Silenus and the chorus, whose imitation of dogs upon the scent lends itself to some rather broad humour. While bearing the unmistakable Sophoclean stamp, this play thus differs entirely in theme and treatment from the other plays of Sophocles which we possess; and it fills up to some extent a gap in our knowledge of the dramatist's art.

III

As Dr Hunt says, we can probably assume that in the gaps of the papyrus Hermes appeared and appeased Apollo by the gift of the lyre, and certainly in the Homeric *Hymn to Hermes* the infant inventor makes a mollifying benefaction to the god. The story goes as follows in Shelley's version of the hymn:

LXXXI

'Thou canst seek out and compass all that wit
    Can find or teach; – yet since thou wilt, come take
The lyre – be mine the glory giving it –
    Strike the sweet chords, and sing aloud, and wake
The joyous pleasure out of many a fit
    Of tranced sound – and with fleet fingers make
Thy liquid-voiced comrade talk with thee, –
It can talk measured music eloquently.

LXXXII

'Then bear it boldly to the revel loud,
    Love-wakening dance, or feast of solemn state,
A joy by night or day – for those endowed
    With art and wisdom who interrogate
It teaches, babbling in delightful mood
    All things which make the spirit most elate,
Soothing the mind with sweet familiar play,
Chasing the heavy shadows of dismay.

LXXXIII

'To those who are unskilled in its sweet tongue,
    Though they should question most impetuously
Its hidden soul, it gossips something wrong –
    Some senseless and impertinent reply.

But thou who art as wise as thou art strong
    Canst compass all that thou desirest. I
Present thee with this music-flowing shell,
Knowing thou canst interrogate it well.

LXXXIV
'And let us two henceforth together feed
    On this green mountain slope and pastoral plain,
The herds in litigation – they will breed
    Quickly enough to recompense our pain,
If to the bulls and cows we take good heed; –
    And thou, though somewhat over fond of gain,
Grudge me not half the profit.' Having spoke
The shell he proffered, and Apollo took.

But there is an alternative version to this story of the tranquil takeover of the lyre, just as there is an alternative version of the story of the peaceful transition of the shrine of Delphi from Gaia to Apollo as told, for example, in the *Oresteia*. In some stories Apollo bludgeoned his way into possessing what was once a female shrine. 'And Apollo took'! In the Valley of the Muses, near Askra, the birthplace of Hesiod, in Euboea, which I visited in 1987, and again after the premiere of *The Trackers of Oxyrhynchus*, there was once, according to Pausanias, who saw it, a bronze of Apollo and Hermes *fighting* for the lyre.

In these thorn-strewn slopes leading up to the summit of Helicon there were not only statues to the Muses, looted by Constantine, and the one mentioned by Pausanias representing the struggle of Apollo and Hermes for the lyre. There were also other cautionary bronzes. There was a statue of Thamyris shown blind, with his lyre shattered at his feet. He was blinded for his presumption in offering competition on the lyre. Near by was a statue of Linus, killed by Apollo for offering him rivalry in singing. Pausanias doesn't mention that there was a bronze of Marsyas, the satyr flayed alive for competing on the flute against Apollo's lyre. For the divine patron of music and poetry, the Parnassian supremo, this is appalling savagery, but this pugnacity and paranoid possessiveness are characteristic of Apollo's early transition from macho cowpoke to cultural impresario. Rival lyre players, singers, upstart satyr flautists, flayed, butchered, blinded, were set up as deterrents in the Valley of the Muses and elsewhere. Herodotus says that the skin of Marsyas was pegged out in a public square in Celaenae (in what is now Turkey), and though it vibrated sympathetically to any Phrygian air, remained stubbornly silent when hymns in praise of Apollo were played in its vicinity. We are told that Apollo had the flute of Marsyas hung up as a trophy in his temple at Sicyon in the Peloponnese. Apollo was only reconciled to the flute he always abhorred after his competition with Marsyas, when it was used by the flute player Sakadas to play a hymn to the god in Delphi. Flute players are admitted if they play the Paean to Apollo. It seems that the flute of Marsyas did not show the same loyalty to its first animator as 'the auld Orange Flute' or indeed the skin flayed from the flautist himself.

The Roman emperors Augustus and Nero both loved to dress up as Apollo, and it was probably the lyre of Apollo that Nero 'fiddled' on while Rome went up in flames, a cool behaviour long endorsed by Apollo himself. A few months ago in Nicosia I saw a sign saying 'APOLLO: quality underwear', and I suppose the Y-front endorsement is appropriate, as the male ego has had aeons of Apollonian support. His contemporary endorsements include an answering machine and a particularly repellent form of torture used in the prisons of Iran. In some manifestations Apollo would not have shied away from the vast statue that Hitler had planned for him in Berlin. And yet, everywhere, his image is at the apex of the pediment of our palaces of art.

IV

It was in Delphi, so powerfully presided over by Apollo, that *The Trackers of Oxyrhynchus* had its unique one-performance world premiere on 12 July 1988 in the ancient stadium. It was a joint production between the National Theatre Studio and the European Cultural Centre of Delphi. I have always wanted to prepare a piece for *one* performance. This was what the ancient dramatists did. In the theatre I most admire, poets, and I stress poets, wrote for actors they knew and for a space they knew.

From the beginning, this text was created for two actors, both Yorkshiremen, who had worked with me before in *The Oresteia* and *The Mysteries*. I created the part of Grenfell/Apollo for Jack Shepherd and the part of Hunt/ Silenus for Barrie Rutter. It is more than half the battle of creation to know the instruments you are writing for. The space too was important. The International Meeting of Ancient Drama, which takes place in Delphi every year, was inspired by the first festival at Delphi, set up by the Greek poet Angelos Sikelianos and his American wife, Eva Palmer, in 1927. For their dramatic performances they used the ancient theatre, lower down the slope and closer to the Temple of Apollo. Nowadays the ancient stadium is used, but with a wooden platform at one end of the racetrack, as if that differently structured curve at one end were the seating of an ancient theatrical space. I resolved to dispense with the platform and use the entire stadium space. This helped to dramatise a contemporary division in our culture between sport and art. In the Pythian Games, with its athletics and flute contests, poetry and drama, held on this site, such a division would have been incomprehensible. As would the division between tragedy and satyr play, 'high' art and 'low' art. And in honour of that ancient wholeness we performed our piece, and we became *Ichneutae*, 'Trackers', seeking in fragments of our past and present a common wholeness, a common illumination, a common commitment to survival.

V

Our 'technical' rehearsals lasted throughout the night of the 11th until after dawn on the 12th. The night had had unusually wild weather and the rocks of the Phaedriades surrounding the stadium concentrated and confined the winds there. The expedition tent of Grenfell and Hunt was blown away. Our papyrus flapped and struggled to be free and fly off to join the eagles that hung over Delphi. We never finished our rehearsal. I had to cover the possibility that the same thing might happen on the 12th. The relay race I had planned, to define the space of the stadium and give us ghosts of its ancient function to awaken the roars of the thousands who once sat at the Pythian Games, had unfortunately dwindled down to one solitary runner, who ran like an ancient Marathon runner bearing an Olympic, or should we say Pythian, torch.

Three hours before our premiere, I wrote and gave the following lines to Barrie Rutter to cover both for the expectation of new destructive gusts and to accommodate the solitary, message-bearing runner:

> Everything we've searched for, everything we found
> goes in Grenfell's mania, round and round.
> Grenfell's recurrent nightmare recreates
> careering caravans of Oxyrhynchus crates,
> crates of papyri in a never-ending train,
> and fragments like a hurricane hurtling through his
>   brain
> and voices, thousands, from the ancient past
> exhorting him to find the 'Ichneftes' FAST!
> That's Grenfell's nightmare and I could add
> another like it that could make everybody mad.
> That the play in the papyrus should reach the light
> in the Stadium of Delphi on a very windy night.
> Last night the wind blew and it stripped
> the stage of everything but actors and a script.
> Let's concentrate, and despite the gusty weather,
> reconstruct the 'Ichneftes' *mazi* 'together'.
> Memory runs a marathon, a human mind relay

from century to century to recreate our play.
Memory, mother of the Muses, frees
from oblivion the 'Ichneftes' of Sophocles.

[Newcastle-upon-Tyne]

Hecuba to Us

1991

The one performance, the unique occasion of an ancient Greek play may strike us now as an almost reckless encounter with the inexorability of transience, yet in its very uniqueness lies the secret of the glory of the continuously passing present of performance. We know, in proscenium terms, that once the curtain has risen it has to fall. The current obsession with televising and videoing stage performances almost inevitably undermines the true nature of the theatrical. But the play published here, conceived as it was for the National Theatre's Olivier stage, entered oblivion rather as unlucky players of Monopoly enter jail without passing GO. It entered the stream of oblivion without ever having been buoyed on it for even the brief unique performance that most Greek tragedies and comedies were designed to have.

My previous piece, *The Trackers of Oxyrhynchus*, although it later found a brief life on the same NT stage, had been originally conceived in this spirit, for one unique performance in the ancient stadium high up the slope of Delphi, a site considered by the ancients as the centre of the world. How differently the energies of performer and audience are concentrated if they know there is only one chance to give or receive the occasion. It was in this spirit too that the papyrus of the ancient play was in that version literally destroyed by fire, and it was in this spirit that the company prevented three rather peeved TV crews from filming what we all thought then would be the first and final performance, so that everything was committed to the care of memory, that last resort in the ruins of time. As Spenser wrote in 'The Ruins of Time':

> For deedes doe die, how ever noblie donne
> And thoughts of men do as themselves decay,
> But wise wordes, taught in numbers for to runne,
> Recorded by the Muses, live for ay . . .

And elsewhere,

> For not to have been dipt in Lethe Lake
> Could save the sonne of Thetis for to die:
> But that blinde bard did him immortal make
> With verses, dipt in deaw of Castalie.

All of us in the *Trackers of Oxyrhynchus* company drank literally the 'deaw of Castalie' before the performance, at the sacred spring beneath the towering, red-hued Phaedriades at the beginning of the Sacred Way in Delphi. It was to give inspiration for that one occasion. But then surprisingly the play, although in a form altered for the specifics of the South Bank, was given more performances, and what was intended to have been the last took place, again with local textual additions, in Carnuntum, near Vienna, Austria, on 19 May 1990. Carnuntum was a former frontier post of the Roman

Empire and the military base of three emperors, as commemorated on the label of the local Grüner Veltliner, wine
grown by Josef Köck, the *Dreikaiserwein*, emblazoned with
the heads of Marcus Aurelius (161–80), Septimius Severus
(193–211) and Diocletian (284–305). Marcus Aurelius, when
he was in Carnuntum in AD 173, during his campaign to keep
the marauding Marcomanni and Quadi respectful of the
imperial border and stay on their side of the Danube, wrote,
in his quieter moments, what became Chapter Three of his
Meditations in Greek. My original intention for the one performance in Delphi had been extended to Carnuntum, and
on both sites there were associations of transience, in the
spirit of which I had originally conceived the unique performance. At Carnuntum, Marcus Aurelius was thinking
about the inexorability of time and he wrote:

> Hippocrates, after curing many sicknesses, himself fell
> sick and died. The Chaldean astrologers foretold the
> death of many persons, then the hour of fate overtook
> them also. Alexander, Pompeius and Julius Caesar, after
> so often utterly destroying whole towns and slaying
> in the field myriads of horse and foot, themselves also
> one day departed from life. Heraclitus, after many
> speculations about the fire which should consume the
> Universe, was waterlogged by dropsy, poulticed himself
> with cow-dung and died. Vermin killed Democritus;
> another kind of vermin Socrates.

Around that same time, Pausanias, the physician from
Asia Minor who wrote a guide to Greece in the second

century AD, saw the ancient stadium of Delphi, where we had played our first performance. It must then have just been refurbished with marble from Mount Pentelicus by Herodes Atticus, who died around the same time as Marcus Aurelius. All that is left of that marble refurbishment is the chisel marks in the quarry from which the marble was taken. When Sir James Frazer, who edited Pausanias and checked on his descriptions at the end of the nineteenth century, stood on the site of the stadium he reflected that the marble had 'probably gone in the way of so many other ancient marbles in Greece, into the lime kiln'.

Whenever I work at the National Theatre I usually walk to the South Bank, and every morning as I walk along the Thames from Vauxhall I pass groups of Japanese tourists doing the same thing, taking pictures of each other from a position that gives them a shot of Big Ben in the background. The succession of clicks like an orchestra of clave-wielders tuning up always makes me go forward to rehearsals committed to the essential transience of theatre. Theatre can only celebrate its presented moments by embracing its own ephemerality. In that is the glory of performance. Theatre has to be given and received at the moment of delivery. This is its essence. The mythologies of fame are mere yellowing calling cards. When the world-famous conductor Herbert von Karajan died in 1989, his fellow conductor Sir George Solti observed: 'This year everyone talks about him. Next year it'll be 50 per cent less. The third year no one will say anything. This is the human fate, to be forgotten.' Heinrich Heine was appalled by the vision that he had of his *Book of Songs* being used by the grocer for packets into which to pour tobacco and snuff, rather as Ragueneau's wife, Lise, uses the manuscripts of her husband's poetic friends to wrap pastries and tarts in, in Act Two of *Cyrano de Bergerac*. Addison, reviewing a show at Drury Lane for the *Spectator* in 1714, wrote of 'a dozen showers of snow which, I am informed, are the plays of many unsuccessful poets artificially cut and shredded for that use'. At the National Theatre stage door I came across a rehearsal draft of *The Trackers of Oxyrhynchus*, torn into three-inch squares, being used to write telephone messages on. And Jack Shepherd, who played Grenfell/ Apollo in the production, told me that when he had been filming a legal drama, the brief that his lawyer character carried was made up of old pages of a script of mine for a film poem about death in Naples called *Mimmo Perrella non è piu*. None of these fates is quite the indignity that Lord Chesterfield mentions in his letters of 1747, where, advising his son not to waste time, he cites the good example of a gentleman who purchased 'a common Horace, of which he tore off gradually a couple of pages, carried them with him to that necessary place, read them first, and then sent them down as a sacrifice to Cloacina'. The Egyptian *fellaheen* employed by Grenfell and Hunt in the excavations in *Trackers* used the papyri of Plato and Euripides as compost for their greens, and in the final version for the NT in 1991 the rubbish tips of the South Bank contained the poster, programme and text of the play being performed. The play contained the rubbished version of itself. Sometimes, walking from rehearsals, either via Covent Garden or via Waterloo, I came across other emblems of the ephemerality of theatrical endeavours I had been associated with. Walking past the now padlocked, dilapidated Lyceum I look up and take wry note of a piece of flapping poster saying 'The Best Show in Britain, no less' of the National's *Mysteries* that transferred there in 1985. Or walking through Cardboard City to catch the Underground at Waterloo I see the now scarcely recognisable features of Edward Petherbridge and Sian Thomas and the fragmentary letters 'ON . . . IS' of my own name on what was once a poster for my version of *The Misanthrope*, revived at the NT in 1989. On a concrete pillar in front of the crates and cartons that are the refuge of the homeless is the already disintegrating papyrus of a *Trackers* poster: '. . . CKERS', it says. It is also heavily graffitied, and in one place in smaller writing, to accommodate the message to the medium, the phallus of the leaping Silenus has been pencilled 'Mrs Thatcher' – who has herself now entered the stream of oblivion meditated upon by Marcus Aurelius.

This contemplation of the ruins of time is a common theme in all literature and thought. As the philosopher George Santayana wrote:

> The spectacle of inexorable change, the triumph of time, or whatever we may call it, has always been a favourite theme for lyric and tragic poetry, and for religious meditation. To perceive universal mutation, to feel the vanity of life, has always been the beginning of seriousness. It is the condition of any beautiful, measured, or tender philosophy.

It is to find the meaning of suffering in such a context that Greek tragedy exists. And out of the same source comes the laughter of comedy and the celebration of the satyr play. Closer to our own precarious days the theme of transience was taken up by one who certainly helped us to become more fearfully aware of it. The 'father' of the atom bomb, J. Robert Oppenheimer, was thinking perhaps of a vista longer than the one his own invention shortened when he wrote:

> Transience is the backdrop for the play of human
> progress, for the improvement of man, the growth of
> his knowledge, the increase of his power, his corruption
> and partial redemption. Our civilizations perish; the
> carved stone, the written word, the heroic act fade into
> a memory of memory and in the end are gone; this
> house, this earth in which we live will one day be unfit
> for human habitation as the sun ages and alters.

Certainly Oppenheimer's invention, unleashed upon the world in 1945, made a great many people feel that we did not have to wait for the ageing of the sun for the earth to become unfit for human habitation. The American psychologist Robert Jay Lifton, who studied the survivors of Hiroshima, showed that when our sense of 'symbolic immortality' is undermined and threatened, as it was in the cold war after 1945, then our 'confidence in the overall continuity of life gives way to widespread death imagery'.

It was into this new context of the old idea of transience experienced in the worst times of the cold war nuclear confrontation that I chose to put the *Lysistrata* of Aristophanes and *The Trojan Women* of Euripides together as *The Common Chorus*. I imagined them played and performed by the women of the peace camp at Greenham Common for the benefit of the guards behind the wire who were defending the silos where the weapons of our ultimate extinction were stored. Nuclear weapons gave mankind what Hannah Arendt called a 'negative solidarity, based on the fear of global destruction'. Their presence also made us stare into the face of oblivion in a way unlikely to be redeemed in the memory of those whom Hecuba addresses as 'later mortals', and into whose hearts and songs she commits the suffering of her women at the end of *The Trojan Women*. As my Lysistrata is made to say, in the text published here:

In the Third World War we'll destroy
not only modern cities but the memory of Troy,
stories that shaped the spirit of our race
are held in the balance in this missile base.
Remember, if you can, that with man goes the mind
that might have made sense of the Hist'ry of Mankind.
It's a simple thing to grasp: when we're all dead
there'll be no further pages to be read,
not even leaflets, and no peace plays like these,
no post-holocaust Aristophanes.

And no post-holocaust Euripides either! No Hecuba entrusting her story to the future. That moment in *The Trojan Women* was central to my understanding of how the tragedy and comedy produced within four years of each other might be played together. When everything has been taken away from the women of Troy, with their city in flames, the death of all their menfolk, the execution of the child Astyanax, it is left to the one who could be said to have lost most to seek for one last redeeming idea. Hecuba says (1242–5):

εἰ δὲ μὴ θεὸς
ἔστρεψε τἄνω περιβαλὼν κάτω χθονός,
ἀφανεῖς ἂν ὄντες οὐκ ἂν ὑμνήθημεν ἂν
μούσαις ἀοιδὰς δόντες ὑστέρων βροτῶν.

But if God had not surrounded us and hurled
us headlong beneath the earth, we would have
disappeared and never been hymned by Muses,
providing themes for the songs of later mortals.

If we hadn't suffered, we wouldn't be songs for 'later mortals'. The song for later mortals is the tragedy being performed. Hecuba addresses the Athenian audience of 415 BC across time from an already mythical and long-ruined Troy. They are the very 'later mortals' whose songs are Hecuba's redemption. Every time the play is played through history in all its versions the 'mortals' become 'later'. And we are the latest mortals now. We are in that long line of 'later mortals' first addressed in 415 BC as if from the present suffering of the Trojan Women of centuries before. We are the latest mortals who guarantee that the suffering was not in vain, and that the chain of commemorative empathy is unbroken.

The Trojan women exit into the imagination and memory of each audience whenever the play is played. Hecuba leads her women into theatricality and into the only redemptive meaning known to the pre-Christian world and, I might add, to our *post*-Christian world. The pathos of her address to us in our lateness in mortal history is all the more precariously and transiently poised when it is made outside the base where a destructive force is housed that will undermine history and human memorialisation permanently. It becomes an appeal for the past not to be betrayed along with the present and the future. As Lysistrata says:

> Since 1945 past and present are the same.
> And it doesn't matter if it's 'real' or a play –
> imagination and reality both go the same way.
> So don't say it's just a bunch of ancient Greeks.
> It's their tears that will be flowing down your cheeks.

In order to place the tragedy in this context I had to use the contemporaneity of comedy to first establish the parallels and allow the play to pass from Greenham to Greece and back in a fluid way.

If I am a serious witness of mutability and the ruins of time, I have to confess that I believe that versions of ancient plays have to be redone for each new production. There exists the basic culturally deciduous network of stems and branches of the original, which itself changes shape through growth and atrophy, and there is also the foliage for each new season's versions. I live on yet another border of the Roman Empire, and often walk on the wall built by

the Emperor Hadrian to divide the Romans from the bar-
barians. It has survived, or not, in various ways, ways that
affect all monuments whether physical or spiritual. There
are portions that have survived pretty well and can give a
reasonable idea of the scale of the original enterprise. Then
there are the bits of it – stones, milestones, altars, columns –
from the wall and adjoining camps that have been recycled
to become barns, farmhouses, pig troughs, gateposts, even
church fonts and church pillars as at Chollerton. And there
are sections – like the marble hewn from Mount Pentelicus
to make the stadium seats in Delphi – which have gone into
the lime kilns, some of which you can still see, to become
mortar for building new structures in a modern style, or
fertiliser for depleted fields. Representing an ancient play
uses all these processes. Sections can be revealed intact.
Some are cannibalised as elements of modern structures,
some transformed into bonding or fertilising matter, gen-
erating new growth here and now.

Twenty years before I embarked on *The Common Chorus*,
I had done another version of the *Lysistrata* of Aristophanes
for a group of student actors and village musicians in
northern Nigeria in collaboration with the Irish poet
James Simmons (see p. 85). The text is unperformable outside Nigeria and was responsive to the tensions that later
erupted into a devastating civil war. Contemporaneity is
essential to the serious comedy of Aristophanes. The political situation has to be mortally serious. His play was written in the twenty-first year of the Peloponnesian War that
eventually destroyed Athens. And neither his play nor that
of Euripides prevented it happening.

A women's peace magazine produced from Brighton in the 1980s called itself *Lysistrata*, and there was in its pages a reaching backwards to the suffering of the past, meeting, if you like, the hands held out by Hecuba to the 'later mortals' from the ruined city of Troy. There was a sense expressed by these women and the women of Greenham that 'we are all interdependent, we are all responsible for each other, how delicate the strands, how strong the web'. Their historical empathy with the suffering of the past and their concern for the very existence of mortals later than themselves gave me the essential spirit to allow the play to move between Greenham and Athens in 411 BC. If the tragedy I had wanted to perform with the comedy declared that remembrance was the one human redemption, then the comedy, in the spirit of the peace women's banners at the Cenotaph, declared that remembrance is not enough, and all their effort in the play is to prevent that dark, soul-rending effort of remembrance from becoming necessary once again in human history – if remembrance itself could survive the ruins of time in any Third World War. In that spectacular photograph of Greenham women dancing hand in hand in a circle on top of a missile silo I like to imagine both Lysistrata and Hecuba.

As Jeffrey Henderson tells us in his study of Aristophanic sexual imagery, 'of several words used to indicate the cunt whose basic notion is that of an opening or passageway, θύρα [= gate] is the most popular'. And it is outside the gate into the missile base that the Greenham women pitched their bender tents. On one notorious occasion the women padlocked the main gate. The hilarious sequence of soldiers and police trying to reopen the gate can be seen in the film *Carry Greenham Home*. I use the action to represent the occupation of the Acropolis in the ancient original and symbolically to represent the women closing the entrances to their bodies. As Henderson also points out, the most notable use of θύρα is in the *Lysistrata*, where it is used to mean the gate of the Acropolis and the gates of love.

Leaflets inviting women to come and demonstrate at Greenham by linking arms and forming a chain around the perimeter fence declared that 'we will turn our backs on it. Turn our backs on all the violence and destructive power it represents . . .'. In theatrical terms, by turning their backs on the base the women turn themselves towards the audience. Thus they are continually 'presented', as they would have been in the masks worn in the original ancient production. Also, the Greenham women faced forwards in order to scrutinise those who passed by the base on foot or in cars for signs of support. In this way I could find a ready motivation for the actors to face outwards and play out to the audience. The cruise-missile bunkers had three metal shuttered openings, like the back of the Olivier stage. I had intended these to be raised at the end of the second play, *The Trojan Women*, to let out the headlights of the convoy bearing the missiles, blinding the audience before the final blackout.

I imagine the first play, the comedy, the *Lysistrata*, played with all its robust Aristophanic language as a direct response to the sexually abusive language that was continually directed at the women, especially when trying to sleep, by the guards at the wire. I spoke to Greenham women about this, and it is recorded by Caroline Blackwood in her book on Greenham, *On the Perimeter* (1984):

> 'I am so tired,' Pat said. 'We had such an awful night with the soldiers. They abused us all night. They just wouldn't stop. It was sexual, of course. It's always sexual.'

Apparently, many of the soldiers were under the impression that all the peace women were only camping round the base because they wanted to sleep with them. This was such a vain and deluded assumption it was comic. Never had any group of men seemed less sexually desirable than the defenders of the cruise missile when seen from the peace camps.

What is the matter with these soldiers, I wondered when I later heard them bellowing their horrible obscenities. Presumably they didn't carry on like dirty-minded schoolboys at home. Yet the peace women brought out everything that was sadistic and infantile in these men. The sex war that was raging on the perimeter was a very ugly and cruel one.

And, of course, behind these British guards, in the heart of the base, were the USAF personnel, recreating the comforts of the USA and singing the kind of songs that appeared for sale in a publication from the USAF 77th Tactical Fighter Squadron at Upper Heyford. The following are typical fare:

> I fucked a dead whore by the roadside
> I knew right away she was dead

The skin was all gone from her tummy
The hair was all gone from her head.

And as I lay down there beside her,
I knew right away I had sinned.
So I pressed my lips to her pussy
And sucked out the wad I'd shot in.

Sucked out, sucked out.
I sucked out the wad I'd shot in, shot in,
Sucked out, sucked out,
I sucked out the wad I'd shot in.

Or:

I love my wife, yes I do, yes I do, I love her truly.
I love the hole she pisses through,
I love her ruby lips and her lily white tits,
And the hair around her asshole.
I'd eat her shit gobble, gobble, chomp, chomp,
With a rusty spoon, with a rusty spoon.

Not all the songs are of masculine sexuality. There are battle
cries also:

Phantom flyers in the sky
Persian pukes prepare to die,
Rolling in with snake and nape.
Allah creates but we cremate.

North of Tehran, we did go
When FAC said from below,
'Hit my smoke and you will find
The Arabs there are in a bind.'

I rolled in at a thousand feet,
I saw those bastards, beating feet,
No more they'll pillage, kill and rape
'Cause we fried them with our nape.

I imagined such songs spluttering through the walkie-talkies of the British guards at the wire, songs with a Budweiser slur, coming from close to the silos where all the mod cons of Milwaukee were available, so that the Americans didn't have to feel they were actually abroad. We shall be glad to be rid of such songsters and the weapons they brought with them.

Unfortunately, the Quick Reaction Alert – which involved at least one flight of nuclear-armed missiles being permanently in readiness – is not a common category in the world of theatre, as opposed to the theatre of war. There is no QRA at the RNT! By the time various managements had lingered over this text, the tension of a topical present and a tragic past had leached away into oblivion. Thankfully, the cold war has ended and my play has been marooned in its moment. The 'text', as Tarkovsky said of the film script, gets 'smelted' into performance. This text never went through that essential smelting process. If I wanted to do *Lysistrata* now, I might have to begin again with a third and totally different version. To recognise that a performance text has to be done again and again is to acknowledge the transience, the flow, the ephemerality of all theatrical realisation. And it is in that spirit that I have to acknowledge also that the time for this particular version of the *Lysistrata* of Aristophanes has passed, with the thankful ending of the fearful cold war that produced it. However, in July I received from friends in Dubrovnik *An Appeal for Peace in Croatia*. It was written on the opening night of a play: 'In these times of deafness in which the word that cries for peace and understanding has become inaudible, our company is playing *Hekuba* by Marin Džić – the tragedy of a mother at the end of an absurd war.' Hecuba is once more committing herself to later mortals, aware of their imminent mortality. And where Hecuba is, then Lysistrata isn't far behind.

Honorary Doctorate, Athens:
Acceptance Speech

1998

I started learning ancient Greek exactly fifty years ago almost to the day, at the age of eleven, three years after the end of the Second World War.

And I am celebrating that half a century of involvement with the drama of Greece in two ways: by the opening of my new film for the cinema, *Prometheus*, on 9 November at the London Film Festival; and four days later, here in this hall receiving the honour you so generously bestow on me today. It is the first such honour I have accepted, although many have been proposed to me. It may seem strange to you that I have never accepted an honorary degree before. I will try to tell you why. When I began learning ancient Greek I came from a family who had no knowledge of literature and culture, and in fact considered themselves uneducated and inarticulate. It was this awareness of that background that gave me a hunger for articulation, for all forms of eloquence, and gave me a passionate taste for the supreme poetry of ancient Greek, and also with the same passion made me into a poet. It is a famous and much-anthologised poem of mine, which is almost considered my signature tune, that expresses this:

'Heredity'

'How you became a poet's a mystery.
Wherever did you get your talent from?'
I say: 'I had two uncles, Joe and Harry,
one was a stammerer, the other dumb!'

My awareness of the wound of inarticulacy, of dumbness
and stammering made me grasp at Greek and grasp at the
growing identity of poet, so that an awareness of inarticulacy and ancient Greek eloquence were the double helix
of my inspiration. In retrospect, I see that I was hoping to
express things my parents and uncles had never been able
to express, and I was taking as my model the greatest body
of literature and drama known to Europe. For the great
hunger there was the greatest food.

One of the ways I taught myself to be a poet, at this very
early stage, was through translation, and I translated a great
deal of ancient Greek as a way of finding a style of my own,
never for mere philological or archaeological purposes.

I worked hard at both, and my parents, whose lives had
always been insecure, wanted me to become something like
a teacher and were thrilled when I began to do research for
a doctorate. On the point of submitting my thesis I decided
to burn my boats, abandon any aspiration towards academic life, and though I knew it was bitterly disappointing
to my mother, I ventured everything on becoming a poet
first and foremost, and that is what I have always been. I
had conceived of a deeply serious role for the poet from
my reading of ancient Greek, and it had to be my whole

life, and as much of a job as my father's, who worked long hours in a bakery. My mother later learned to have pride in my work for the National Theatre, but she always regretted that she would never be able to call me 'doctor'. It was the same instinct for freedom that made me decline honorary doctorates from a number of British universities. I worried about being weighed down with honours as I grew older, when it was the time when I hoped to be freest in my art.

And my mother had died and was not there to be proud of me. The two things that puzzled her – my love of Greek and my absolute commitment to the art of poetry – have come together in a way today, as it is those two obsessions of mine which I assume you are honouring me for today. And I know now that my mother will understand why I had to take that journey and can now be proud of me, and call me 'doctor'. It makes me very proud that my one and only doctorate should come from Athens, the source of both our drama and our democracy.

Today and tomorrow and every day that I have spent or will spend in Athens I go for a few hours when the sun is shining and sit in the Theatre of Dionysus, and inspired by that sunlit orchestra I have dreamed up some of my projects: a language for masks in the *Oresteia*, which I did with Peter Hall for the National Theatre; and my play which incorporated the *Ichneutae* fragments of Sophocles, *The Trackers of Oxyrhynchus*, which had its world premiere in the ancient stadium of Delphi in 1988, and then played at the National Theatre in London, all over Europe, and is, as I speak, now on the stage of the West Yorkshire Playhouse in Leeds, the city of my birth. These and many other plays and also poems were sketched out in that ancient theatre, not far from here, which I use as an al fresco study whenever I am in Athens, much as Shelley, the poet who said 'we are all Greeks' made use of the Baths of Caracalla in Rome to compose his *Prometheus Unbound*. My route to the theatre usually goes via the, for me, very auspicious route, Odos Shelley and Odos Byronos. Shelley and Byron, who have been my guides in my love of Greece, its history, its culture and its freedom.

I have tried to understand how this habit has been so productive for me. I said that I started my acquaintance with ancient Greek three years after the end of the Second World War. The end of that war, what was called VE Day and VJ Day were respectively commemorated by bonfires in the back street. Even at the age of eight I connected our celebratory fire with the fires that had devastated Dresden and the atomic bombs that destroyed Hiroshima and Nagasaki. To this day, on the cobbles in that street there is a scorched black circle which became for me a kind of 'orchestra', a blackened theatrical space where art could not measure up to the barbarities of European history. Over that intimidating darkness was gradually superimposed another space, not a scorched orchestra but an illuminated one, and that was the space of ancient tragedy. I began very early to look for clues to how to express the tragedy of our century in the drama of ancient Athens.

But I mustn't make myself seem so wholly serious. At the same time as I was studying, say, the *Alcestis* of Euripides and appearing as the Shelley Cyclops in the one known extant satyr play at school, I was going to the theatre and seeing more music-hall comedians and pan-tomimes than so-called serious theatre. The important thing about this kind of theatre is that it is all out front, it continually acknowledges the presence of the audience. In the pantomimes men played women and women played men. When I saw my first proscenium play in a drawing room I was horrified that no one on stage seemed aware of me and the rest of the audience. This early experience of popular theatre helped me, I think, to unlock Greek drama in my translations and productions. As I was working on the *Oresteia*, in the early days of the ten years I took to prepare the text, I had a dream. There was a queue of old men outside my house wanting to be in the chorus of the *Agamemnon*. I asked them to sign their names in a book. When I looked at the names, they were all the comedians I had seen as a child – Norman Evans, Nat Jackley, Albert Modley, Frank Randle, Robb Wilton, etc. I think they were urging me to bring all the experience I had had with them even into my confrontation of tragedy. And somewhere to bring about an end to that grating division in our culture between so-called 'high' art and 'low' art.

Prometheus: Fire and Poetry

1998

I

As a child I learned to dream awake before the coal fire in our living room. Staring into the fire, with its ever-changing flames, shifting coals, falling ash and what were called 'strangers' – skins of soot flapping on the grate – evoked in me my first poetry. My first meditations were induced by the domestic hearth. I have always associated staring into flames with the freedom of poetic meditation. It has been proposed by Gaston Bachelard that it is from brooding before flames that early man developed his interior life. It was also my job to light the fire, and to fetch the coal up from the cellar. With a bucket from the dark dank cellar that had been our shelter from German air raids and incendiary bombs, I brought the black coal that fuelled my dreaming. I later learned that the Latin for hearth is *focus*. And fire is what I focus on in *Prometheus*. And I remembered my Latin when, filming *Prometheus* on the roads of Romania, I saw on a forest-fire sign the word *foc*: 'fire'.

II

The myth of Prometheus, who brought fire to mankind, keeps entering history at significant moments. One of the sources of my film is the *Prometheus Bound* of Aeschylus

(525–456 BC). Most Greek tragedy shifts its timescale from immediate suffering to some long-term redemption through memorial ritual or social amelioration, or simply through the very play being performed. The performed suffering was old, the redemption contemporary. The appeal to futurity is not simply that 'time heals' because it brings forgetfulness and oblivion, but because creative memory is at work, giving the suffering new form, a form to allow the suffering to be shared and made bearable across great gaps of time. And who continually cries out across millennia to present himself to 'later mortals' as a *theama* (something to be looked at), especially in his final words, more than Prometheus? Who calls from a remoter past than the bound Prometheus, and yet who still manifests himself when history moves in directions where defiance and unfreedom cry for help? It is a myth because of its timescale that encompasses many generations of mortals, which continually makes us reassess our history. It might give the disappointed utopian a refuge from despair. And maybe these days the socialist.

No play in the ancient repertoire works over a longer timescale than *Prometheus Bound*. Or deals with more unbroken suffering. Its span is not, as in the *Oresteia*, the ten fateful years of the Trojan War, but thirty millennia: thirty millennia of tyrannical torture, thirty millennia of defiance. And so it is not surprising that at times of the collapse of ideas that might have created liberty and equality the figure of the chained Titan, Prometheus, is remembered. Nor is it surprising that for those who dramatise history as dialectical struggle Prometheus has come to embody the tyrannically restrained champion of the downtrodden and oppressed. When men feel themselves in chains, the myth of the Titan re-enters history. Out of hopelessness comes a new need for the chained martyr's undiminished hope, though every day Zeus' eagle tears the liver from his body:

> To suffer woes which Hope thinks infinite;
> To forgive wrongs darker than death or night;
> To defy Power, which seems omnipotent;
> To love and bear; to hope till Hope creates
> From its own wreck the thing it contemplates;
> Neither to change, nor falter, nor repent;
> This, like thy glory, Titan, is to be
> Good, great and joyous, beautiful and free;
> This is alone Life, Joy, Empire, and Victory.

So Shelley concludes his own *Prometheus Unbound* (1820), when the wreck that Hope had to contemplate was the failure of the French Revolution to deliver liberty, equality and fraternity. But hope is also created out of the contemplation of the wreck of tyrannies, earlier despotisms demolished over a long period of time, not overthrown by revolution, with Nature running riot over ruined imperial stones. It was precisely this spectacle that Shelley had all around him as he composed his *Prometheus Unbound* in Rome in 1819. Shelley found this everywhere in the ruins of the imperial city:

> Rome has fallen, ye see it lying
> Heaped in undistinguished ruin:
> Nature is alone undying.
> ('Fragment: Rome and Nature')

THE INKY DIGIT OF DEFIANCE

And specifically in the Baths of Caracalla, which he chose as his al fresco study in which to write his play. These grandiose baths, built by the Emperor Caracalla (211–17) on the Aventine hill of Rome and enlarged by Elagabalus (218–22) and Alexander Severus (222–35), were in use until AD 537, when the Goths of Vitgis cut the aqueducts of Rome. The famous Farnese Hercules, the hero who finally killed the tormenting eagle of Zeus and freed Prometheus, stood in the colonnaded passage between the *frigidarium* and the *tepidarium*. The ruins of the ideals of the French Revolution turned Shelley to the myth, and the famous posthumous painting by Joseph Severn, now in the Keats–Shelley House in Rome, shows him working on his *Prometheus Unbound* in 1818/19 in the ruins of the Baths of Caracalla. Such ruins revealed to Shelley the proof that even the greatest of powers come to an end, a suitable ambience in which to compose his *Prometheus Unbound*. And the Baths of Caracalla is still an appropriate place in which to contemplate the ruins of time and the collapse of empire, with their braced brick molars, thirds of arches, seagulls on the jagged rims fenced off with hazard tape, or with a red-and-white warning hurdle. The bricks abraded back to rock and dust. Signs which give you a clue to the vast ruins: '*apodyterium*'; '*natatio*'. The whole vast collection of fragmentary walls braced and netted, sometimes held together, by the roots of briar and blackberry, laurel, yew, fig. And fennel – perhaps the most appropriate plant to preside over this preface as it was in a stalk of fennel that Prometheus hid the fire he stole for mankind. This preface to my *Prometheus* film was sketched there, as Shelley's *Prometheus Unbound* was a hundred and eighty years ago, in the Terme di Caracalla, Rome. The whole of Shelley's great poem, which I had in my pocket, seems to end back in the Baths of Caracalla, when, as Richard Holmes writes, 'the vision has dissolved and Shelley is sitting within the blossoming labyrinths of the Baths of Caracalla'. These ruins helped Shelley to give the struggle between Zeus and the chained Titan a millennial scale. Zeus or a Roman emperor, or a regime intended for all time, could also be like Ozymandias:

> 'My name is Ozymandias, king of kings:
> Look on my works, ye Mighty, and despair!'
> Nothing beside remains. Round the decay
> Of that colossal wreck, boundless and bare,
> The lone and level sands stretch far away.
>
> ('Ozymandias', 1817)

It is the time that dealt, again in Shelley's words, with Bonaparte:

> A frail and bloody pomp which Time has swept
> In fragments towards Oblivion.
>
> ('Feelings of a Republican on the
> Fall of Bonaparte', 1816)

Everything toppling into the 'dust of creeds outworn' (*Prometheus Unbound*, 1.697). The 'vast and trunkless legs of stone' of the ruin of Ozymandias could well refer in 1989 to the dismantled and toppled statues of Lenin and various eastern European communist leaders in bronze or stone all over the Eastern bloc. Ozymandias and the ruins of the Baths of Caracalla for Shelley, as the toppled Berlin Wall for us, were evidence of time overturning the tyrannies, an assurance that Prometheus would not suffer for ever.

Byron has similar reactions to Rome and the triumph of time:

> Oh Rome! my country! city of the soul!
> The orphans of the heart must turn to thee,
> Lone mother of dead empires! and control
> In their shut breasts their petty misery.
> What are our woes and sufferance? Come and see
> The cypress, hear the owl, and plod your way
> O'er steps of broken thrones and temples, Yea!
> Whose agonies are evils of a day –
> A world is at our feet as fragile as our clay.
> 　　(*Childe Harold's Pilgrimage*, Canto iv, lxxviii)

> Cypress and ivy, weed and wallflower grown
> Matted and mass'd together, hillocks heap'd
> On what were chambers, arch crush'd, column strown
> In fragments, choked up vaults, and frescos steep'd
> In subterranean damps, where the owl peep'd,
> Deeming it midnight: – Temples, baths or halls?
> Pronounce who can; for all that Learning reap'd
> From her research hath been, that these are walls –
> Behold the Imperial Mount! 'tis thus the mighty falls.
> 　　(*Childe Harold's Pilgrimage*, Canto iv, cvii)

Byron's statue by the Danish sculptor Bertel Thorvaldsen (1831) in the garden of the Villa Borghese has a thoughtful poet seated on a fallen fragment of column and beside it a human skull, imperial might and fragile clay made one in time's momentum. The momentum that crushed hope, and Prometheus who kept it burning like a torch of liberty. The Titan has been described as 'a primordial figure in the history of hope'. In Shelley and Byron's time the 'history of hope' had met its obstacles, and if Prometheus was, as he was for Shelley, 'the saviour and the strength of suffering man' (*Prometheus Unbound*, i.817) and the patron saint of the overthrow of tyrannical power, then he too was tormented by that shrivelling of hope in man. One of the things that Prometheus is tortured by, apart from the eagle eating his liver, is the vision sent to him of what is in fact Shelley's own anguish, the failure of the French Revolution:

> Names are there, Nature's sacred watchwords, they
> Were borne aloft in bright emblazonry;
> The nations thronged around, and cried aloud,
> As with one voice, Truth, liberty, and love!
> Suddenly fierce confusion fell from heaven
> Among them: there was strife, deceit, and fear:
> Tyrants rushed in, and did divide the spoil.
> This was the shadow of the truth I saw.
> (*Prometheus Unbound*, i.648–55)

Byron also writes with Shelley's bitterness about the effect of the failed French Revolution on Europe's struggle for freedom:

But France got drunk with blood to vomit crime,
And fatal have her Saturnalia been
To Freedom's cause, in every age and clime;
Because the deadly days which we have seen,
And vile Ambition, that built up between
Man and his hopes an adamantine wall,
And the base pageant last upon the scene,
Are grown the pretext for the eternal thrall
Which nips life's tree, and dooms man's worst –
  his second fall.

(*Childe Harold's Pilgrimage*, Canto iv, xcvii)

Both Byron and Shelley call on Prometheus and his commitment to man's future to help them weather what Shelley calls in his Preface to *The Revolt of Islam* (1818) 'the age of despair' that, for intellectuals like him, followed on from what he had to call, in the lines above, the 'strife, deceit and fear' of the French Revolution. What is needed for the creation of a just, independent society after this setback, writes Shelley, is 'resolute perseverance and indefatigable hope, and long-suffering and long-believing courage'. Such perseverance and indefatigable hope are symbolically pre-eminent in the apparently hopelessly chained Prometheus. Shelley writes:

The revulsion occasioned by the atrocities of the demagogues, and the re-establishment of successive tyrannies in France, was terrible, and felt in the remotest corner of the civilised world . . . This influence has tainted the literature of the age with the hopelessness of the minds from which it flows.

Metaphysics, and inquiries into moral and political
science, have become little else than vain attempts to
revive exploded superstitions, or sophisms like those
of Mr Malthus, calculated to lull the oppressors of
mankind into a security of everlasting triumph.

The 'oppressors of Mankind' are gathered together as 'the
Oppressor of Mankind', as Shelley called Zeus/Jove when,
in the same spirit as *The Revolt of Islam*, he wrote *Prometheus
Unbound* in the following year.

III

Shelley considered *Prometheus Unbound* his finest piece of
work. It sold less than a score of copies, and is still never
given a theatrical presentation or even thought of as a
play. H. S. Mitford's is a typical attitude. He edited *The
Oxford Book of English Romantic Verse 1798–1837* (Oxford:
OUP, 1935), and like so many editors of dreary antholo-
gies, excluded the poetry from dramatic works, giving a
very narrowed view of the range of verse. Songs from plays
were admitted as they fitted the lyrical cliché. And he also
made an exception of a passage from Shelley's *Prometheus
Unbound*, on the grounds that 'no one would call that a play'.
Shelley's *play* (and indeed most of the dramatic efforts of the
Romantic poets) is considered untheatrical and unplayable,
and judged by the theatrical clichés of today it may seem
irredeemable as a dramatic text. But George Bernard Shaw
had the musical and Wagnerian insight to see in Shelley's
Prometheus Unbound 'an English attempt at a Ring', and
Wagner's ideas were deeply inspired by Aeschylus. Later

critics, like Timothy Webb, have also sought to justify and incorporate Shelley's attempts into the theatrical canon by stressing operatic models: 'Prometheus Unbound in particular seems to owe a considerable debt to operatic models as well as to masque and, more obviously, to its Aeschylean prototype. Its exploration of musical analogies and its use of strategies and structures from opera and ballet extend the boundaries of dramatic form.' Isabel Quigly makes similar operatic parallels in her introduction to Shelley's selected poetry in the Penguin Poetry Library:

> . . . *Prometheus Unbound,* a drama on so heroic a scale
> that his lack of dramatic competence does not matter,
> for this is not theatre but huge/metaphysical grand-
> opera, where the scenery can creak if the singing is
> good enough.

The preponderant cliché of naturalism in contemporary British theatre makes anything even a little different unwelcome, but there are salutory reminders from an Indian scholar whose traditions of non-European drama give him a sympathy for Shelley's play greater than any expressed in Shelley's native land:

> It clearly represents a rejection of the literary theatre
> as known to the Western World. But all theatre is not
> the property of the relatively small continent of Europe.
> Shelley's thought and art in his singular iridescent
> poem seem in luminous fashion to look beyond the
> confines of Western usage and tradition to the more

imaginative dramas of other civilisations, to the theatre
of the dance, with its accompanying music, or to the
theatre of the dancing shadow puppets of the Far East.
His imagination deliberately and resoundingly defies
our more temporal stages as developed for our human
actors in flesh and blood. Curiously enough, on the
contrary, it even invites Indian play of shadows, or
puppet shows based on the epics.

And H. H. Anniah Gowda, the Professor of English at the
University of Mysore, goes on to say something that con-
firms my despair of most contemporary theatre and that
gave me, in what I've italicised, a nudge in the direction of
my own *Prometheus*:

> It is easy to conceive Shelley's infinite choreographic
> work as a chant for a dance not as yet created, a
> libretto for a musical drama not as yet composed,
> a poetic companion to some *future revelation in the
> imaginative film* . . . *Prometheus Unbound* can be a
> dramatic reality only when the theatre itself is unbound
> from innumerable restrictions now confining it so
> firmly that this liberation remains for the less daring
> and imaginative minds an unthinkable change . . . The
> student of practicable drama at the present does ill to
> overlook even so apparently anti-theatrical a text as
> Shelley's drama-poem. In such unlikely sources may
> lie concealed the seeds of a future burgeoning. Now
> that the winter has come to the theatre, even a new
> *Prometheus Unbound* may not be far behind.

I have always thought that Shelley's *Prometheus Unbound* had 'seeds of a future burgeoning', though the snow still lies deep on most of our stages and the footsteps poets have made on them have disappeared under new chill flurries. I can only echo Ibsen when, in the face of hostility to his *Peer Gynt*, he asserted that 'My book *is* poetry; and if it isn't, it will become such'. Shelley's play, unfortunately, is still in the process of becoming. And I have to say that my *Prometheus is* a film; and if it isn't, it will become such!

IV

Shelley's reaction to the idea of writing a parallel trilogy to that of Aeschylus, with détente finally achieved between the punisher and the punished, was that he wanted absolutely no reconciliation. 'I was averse', Shelley writes in his Preface to *Prometheus Unbound*, 'from a catastrophe so feeble as that of reconciling the Champion with the Oppressor of mankind.' No détente. As we do not possess the other two plays of the *Prometheia*, Aeschylus' Promethean trilogy, then we are left with undiluted defiance and enduring tyranny.

Karl Marx is said to have observed that he regretted that Shelley died at the age of twenty-nine, 'for Shelley was a thorough revolutionary and would have remained in the van of socialism all his life'. Marx's disputed remark was at the expense of Byron, who Marx is said to have prophesied would have become a 'reactionary bourgeois'. Paul Foot takes up this speculation in his *Red Shelley* (1984) and imagines Byron supporting the Reform Bill of 1832, which enfranchised only property owners, and Shelley supporting the extension of the bill and the Chartist movement. These speculations are, according to the former leader of the Labour Party, Michael Foot, extremely unfair on Byron (*The Politics of Paradise: A Vindication of Byron*, 1988). After Byron's death in Greece, Michael Foot points out that Heinrich Heine (1797–1856) actually identifies Byron with Prometheus himself: 'He defied miserable men and still more miserable gods like Prometheus.' And the same identification was made all over Europe. Adam Mickiewicz (1798–1855), Poland's national bard, wrote that Byron 'had cursed and fumed like Prometheus, the Titan, whose shade he loved to evoke so often'. And in Italy, Giuseppe Mazzini (1805–72), the great soul of the Risorgimento, honoured the dead poet in these words: 'never did the "eternal spirit of the chainless mind" make a brighter apparition amongst us. He seems at times a transformation of that immortal Prometheus, of whom he has written so nobly, whose cry of agony, yet of futurity, sounded above the cradle of the European world.'

After Shelley and Byron, Prometheus' 'cry of agony, yet of futurity' gradually began to be identified with the struggle for socialism. Eight years after the death of Byron, Thomas Kibble Hervey (1799–1859) published an eighty-three-line poem, 'Prometheus' (1832), which places the chained Titan, with contemporary geographical accuracy, in the frozen plains of Russia, with its oppressed serfs taking inspiration from their manacled champion:

> Amid this land of frozen plains and souls
> Are beating hearts that wake long weary nights,

Unseen, to listen to thy far-off sigh;
And stealthily the serf, amid his toils,
Looks up to see thy form against the sky.

He writes of kings as 'the petty Joves of earth' and has a
vision of freedom and deliverance, with the masses, inspired
by the American example of monarchless democracy, coming to liberate Prometheus:

And thou shalt rise – the vulture and the chain
Shall both be conquered by thine own stern will!
Hark! o'er the far Atlantic comes a sound
Of falling fetters, and a wild, glad cry
Of myriad voices in a hymn to thee!
Hail to that music! To its tune sublime
Shall march the legions of the world of mind,
On to thy rescue, o'er each land and sea.

John Goodwyn Barmby (1820–81), a Christian Socialist who
is credited with the invention of the word 'communism',
published a monthly magazine in the 1840s called *The
Promethean or Communist Apostle*. The second step towards
Prometheus becoming a patron saint of socialism was probably the association of the Titan Fire-Giver with the heavy
industries and technologies dependent on fire in one form
or another. 'Thanks to fire . . . man has attained domination over the world,' writes Paul Ginestier in *The Poet and
the Machine* (1961). In the heartland of German industry in
the nineteenth century, the title of the magazine that kept
its readers abreast with new industrial technology seemed

almost inevitable: *Prometheus: Illustrierte Wochenschrift über die Fortschritte in Gewerbe, Industrie und Wissenschaft* (*Illustrated Weekly on Developments in Trade, Industry and Science*, Leipzig, 1899–1921). Prometheus becomes the patron of technology and the smokestacks of the industry of the Rhine, the Ruhr and the north of England, where I myself grew up, inhaling the sulphurous fumes of the Promethean gift: 'The Iron Kingdom where his Majesty Fire reigns', as Guy de Maupassant puts it. This identification with industry transformed Prometheus from being, in the words of Timothy Richard Wutrich, in his study on *Prometheus and Faust* (1995), the 'primordial figure in the history of the concept of hope', to being what the Marxist classical scholar George Thomson, making the concept of hope more specifically political, calls Prometheus in *Aeschylus and Athens* (1941): 'the patron saint of the proletariat'. Karl Marx himself, who referred to Prometheus as 'the first saint and martyr of the philosopher's calendar', was, during his editorship of the *Rhineland Gazette*, depicted in cartoons as Prometheus bound to a printing press, with the Prussian eagle gnawing his liver. At his feet, like the chorus of the Oceanides, the Daughters of Ocean represented the cities of the Rhineland pleading for freedom.

When the English poet and magazine editor John Lehmann wrote a book on the Caucasus in 1937, he called it *Prometheus and the Bolsheviks* – 'because Prometheus is the oldest symbol of the Caucasus, and can at the same time be considered as the oldest symbol of what the Bolsheviks have had as their aim: the deliverance of man from tyranny and barbarism by the seizure of material power'. On a *Sovtorgflot* boat on the Black Sea, heading for Sukhum in Georgia, Lehmann has a dream of meeting Prometheus, who says to him: 'I find myself passionately on the side of the Bolsheviks when I hear accounts of the Civil War struggles. *It reminds me of my own struggles with Jove over the fire business* [my italics].' Prometheus then announces that he has made a momentous decision: 'I have decided', says Prometheus, 'to join the Party!' Then Lehmann wakes from his dream, and the boat docks in Sukhum.

But as Prometheus gathers his supporters, so does the tyrant Zeus, whose parallel manifestations take on historically terrifying forms. As Shelley wrote, humanity is 'heaven-oppressed' (*Prometheus Unbound*, 1.674). The ministers of Jupiter trample down the 'beloved race' of Prometheus. These ministers are 'thought-executing'. The brain of Jove is 'all-miscreative' (1.448). All monolithic ideologies, religious and political, are 'miscreative'. Zeus (or Jupiter, or Jove) is the image of recurrent tyranny and he wants to destroy mankind through human agents like Hitler and Stalin; and though Prometheus foiled his destruction of mankind once by stealing fire, perhaps he now plays into the tyrant's hands by giving men the freedom to use fire as they will. And because Prometheus, in his socialist avatar, is the champion of the industrial worker, the miner, the steel-worker, Zeus particularly glories in fiery destruction and smoky pollution, and mankind's slower death by poisoning the earth with factories fuelled by Promethean power.

The hasty and massive industrialisation of the social-ist countries in the 1950s took little heed of the ecological consequences, and guidebooks to places like Romania glorified the industrial sites in a way that suggests they were conducting Prometheans around the sacred temples of their Titanic champion. 'The town of Bicaz is already an important tourist centre,' we read in *Romania: A Guide Book* (Bucharest, 1967). And why? 'In this region beside the hydro-power station of Stejarul we find . . . the new mines of non-ferrous metals at Lesul Ursului and of barites at Obcina Voronetului, the cement mill at Bicaz, the timber-processing factory at Vaduri, the refinery at Darmesti – all of them industrial units built by socialism in its forward march.' The prose is straining to become a Promethean poetry, and the cumulative roll call with its chemical and geographical names could in the hands of an Aeschylus or a Milton have epic scale. The writer is always relieved to leave natural scenic surroundings for the lyrical nomenclature of the chemical industries:

> Presently, however, this charming natural scenery will have to give way to a monumental achievement of man's hand. We are nearing the big industrial aggregate of Gheorghiu Georghiu-Dej Town [with its] huge tanks, cylindrical towers, silvery pipes, black pipes, white pipes curling gracefully . . . It supplies coke for electrodes, propane propylene for phenol, and butane-butylene for synthetic rubber.

Copşa Mică, once the most polluted town in Romania and maybe the world, whose carbon-black factory that blackened everything around it – houses, hills, people, sheep

– and which is now derelict and its workers jobless and hopeless, gets this Promethean puff:

> We continue to travel along the Tirnava Valley
> and after ten km we reach Copşa Mică, one of the
> important centres of the Romanian chemical industry,
> nicknamed the 'retort' town. We shall be struck by the
> bizarre outline of the carbon-black works looking like
> a dark castle – and our attention will be arrested by the
> installations of the sulphuric acid works and of the first
> Romanian works for polyvinyl chloride . . .

In my film, Hermes takes the golden statue of Prometheus to have it daubed and desecrated with carbon black thrown by the redundant workers of Copşa Mică. It took the whole crew days to get clean, and for weeks carbon black soiled everything we had. When we crossed the border into Bulgaria, the border guards asked our interpreter if British people were always so dirty.

The pattern of rapid Promethean industrialisation was replicated all over the former socialist world. The steel works of Nowa Huta, where I also filmed, were hurriedly constructed on a site where there was neither iron ore nor coal to create a proletarian workforce ten kilometres east of the ancient university town of Krakow, with its long-standing traditions of culture and religion. The idea of a bright future based on industrialisation and five-year plans created vast, technically out-of-date temples to Prometheus which are now, since 1989, rapidly becoming derelict 'rustbelts' with thousands out of work. The same fate has happened to the most 'Promethean' industries in Great Britain, coal and steel. Nick Danziger, in *Danziger's Britain*, uses the expression 'industrial genocide' to describe this end to heroic industry, and paints a frightening picture of its aftermath of unemployment, vandalised inner cities, children without hope turning to drugs and then to crime to maintain their habit.

One of the visions sent to torment Shelley's chained Prometheus is the beginning of the Industrial Revolution and urban industrialisation:

> Look! where round the wide horizon
> Many a million-peopled city
> Vomits smoke in the bright air.
> Hark the outcry of despair!

The Prometheus of a hundred and eighty years later has to hearken to cries of despair from the now smokeless dereliction.

V

'No doubt it has often been stated that the conquest of fire definitely separated man from the animal,' writes Gaston Bachelard in *La Psychoanalyse du Feu* (1938), 'but perhaps it has not been noticed that the mind in its primitive state, together with its poetry and knowledge, had been developed in meditation before a fire . . . the *dreaming man* seated before his fireplace is the man concerned with inner depths, a man in the process of development.' And Dennis Donoghue equates the theft of fire with 'the origin of consciousness':

> Fire enabled them to move from nature to culture,
> but it made culture a dangerous possession: *it*
> *made tragedy possible* . . . We have found the stolen
> fire identified with reason and knowledge, but it
> is probably better to identify it with the symbolic
> imagination . . . Above all, Prometheus made possible
> the imaginative enhancement of experience, the
> metaphorical distinction between what happens to us
> and what we make of the happening. That is to say,
> Prometheus provided men with consciousness and the
> transformational grammar of experience.

The fire that primitive man gazes into and that prompts him, in his flame-lit reverie, to become a poet is one thing; the fire we are forced to gaze into as we cross millennia at the end of the twentieth century is another. The poetry from this fire-gazing is hard though essential to achieve, and is almost the artist's greatest challenge. The fire we must gaze into burns in Dresden, Hamburg, in the ovens of Auschwitz, in Hiroshima, Nagasaki, in all those places where non-combatants were burned to death; in the looted and destroyed villages of the Balkans; in the millions of Greek manuscripts and books burned in the library of Alexandria by Muslim fanatics, in Jewish and so-called 'decadent' books in Germany burned by Nazi fanatics; in the bonfire of the books of dissidents, including the poetry of Yannis Ritsos, in front of the Temple of Zeus in Athens under the Metaxas dictatorship; in Muslim books in the Institute for Oriental Studies of Sarajevo destroyed by rockets on 17 May 1992, with the incineration of the entire library of documents and manuscripts of Ottoman Bosnia; in Salman Rushdie's *Satanic Verses* burned by affronted Muslims in Yorkshire, England. The fire in which man discovered his poetry is used to destroy poetic endeavour. Poetry will either be tempered in that burning history or disappear. The meditative hearth now contains the Holocaust and the H-bomb. 'The atom smashers may be regarded as the most Promethean of the Prometheans. By releasing the power latent in the nucleus of the atom they made the theft of Prometheus a very minor piece of effrontery.'

The flames that created reverie create nightmares. The flames that once created man's capacity for dreaming are now fuelled by tragedies, and the expression we seek from their contemplation has to imagine those worst things in the dancing fires that cast our shadows into the next millennium. And if I say that the fire offered by the Prometheus of Aeschylus had not yet acquired the accretions of our bestial and barbaric human history, I would have to add that I think that Aeschylus gazed into what, for him in the fifth century BC, was an equivalent historical destruction, the eradication of an entire civilisation in the razing of the city of Troy. The beacons that brought the news of the fall of Troy after ten years to Argos and the torches that accompanied the procession that honours the Furies at the end of the *Oresteia* were lit from the annihilation of Troy. The gift of fire was already ambiguous to Aeschylus. The destructive had to give birth to the celebratory fire, and the celebratory fire, like our own VJ street bonfires in 1945, can never be a different element from the destructive flame. The images of torches in procession, the destructive element as a redemptive symbol, is paralleled in the way Jewish pilgrims to Auschwitz place *Yohrzeit* (Remembrance) candles in the ovens where over a million were cremated, a candle into the heart of dark, destroying flame.

VI

The *Prometheus Bound* of Aeschylus ends with a great cry to the light that is common to all and that unites the audience with the surrounding universe and their suffering champion:

> ὦ πάντων
> αἰθὴρ κοινὸν φάος εἰλίσσων,
> ἐσορᾷς μ' ὡς ἔκδικα πάσχω. (1091–3)

> O you heavens who roll around the light
>   that is common to everything,
> you witness the injustices I suffer.

This common light is at the heart of the experience of Greek tragedy, as I have written in my introduction to my play *The Trackers of Oxyrhynchus* (see this volume, pp. 201–22). Why, you might ask, should I – who have often claimed that we cannot understand the essence of ancient tragedy unless we remember that the common light united audience and performer, and have refused all offers to have my theatrical presentations filmed – use the cinema for my *Prometheus*?

In fact, many years ago, I had wanted to stage the original play of Aeschylus in Yorkshire, as one of what have been called my 'kamikaze' performances, on a Caucasus of coal slack on some colliery spoil heap close to a power station. It became a cinema venture because of a feeling I had that my poetic reveries in front of our living-room coal fire and my earliest experiences of films were connected. Wolfgang Schivelbusch, a German historian of the industrialisation of light in the nineteenth century, articulates a parallel that I had always felt – between gazing into fire where our poetry began and looking at images in the cinema, which needs the surrounding darkness:

> In light-based media, light does not simply illuminate existing scenes, it creates them. The world of the diorama and the cinema is an illusory dream world that light opens up to the viewer . . . He can lose himself in it in the same way that he can submerge himself in contemplating the campfire or a candle. In this respect the film is closer to the fire than the theatre. An open-air performance in bright daylight is quite feasible, while a campfire in the light of day is as senseless, even invisible, as a film projected in daylight. The power of artificial light to create its own reality only reveals itself in darkness. In the dark, light is life.

The connection between my obsession with fire and my obsession with movies led me to make a film about fire and poetry. The other factor which led me to the cinema is the way the size of the cinema screen can give heroic stature to the most humble of faces, and this became an essential requirement in a film where the most unlikely wheezing ex-miner is slowly made to represent Prometheus himself. Men projected onto large screens could become Titans or gods.

In 1978, I worked at the Metropolitan Opera in New York with John Dexter, doing a new English libretto for Smetana's opera *Prodaná Nevěsta* (*The Bartered Bride*). The designer was the great Czech scenographer Josef Svoboda, with whom I spent time in Prague as I was researching my scenario in Bohemia. He gave me a book on his work by Jarka Burian, *The Scenography of Josef Svoboda* (Wesleyan University Press, 1971). I had lived and worked in Prague in the 1960s and had seen many of his truly innovative designs in the theatres there and his thrilling combinations of film and stage at the Laterna Magika, so I was very glad to have a book which documented these productions and gave me detailed information on those I hadn't seen. One in particular stayed in my mind: the Staatsoper Munich production by Everding of Carl Orff's opera *Prometheus*, in 1968. Svoboda tried to solve the problem of a man portraying a Titan by using simultaneous video to literally *project* the singing Prometheus onto the rock where he was bound so that the tenor sang from between his own projected Titan's eyes. Svoboda described his ingenious solution thus:

> . . . The main device was the use of live television to project an enlarged image of Prometheus' face onto the very surface of the rock to which he was nailed, in other words, we saw Prometheus 'in' the image of his face, thereby providing tremendous emphasis to his torment. We used the technique at special moments

only, for maximum impact. The ending, during which I used dozens of low-voltage units, had its own special effectiveness. I had the entire frame of the proscenium lined with low-voltage units aimed at the rock and Prometheus. During the ending of the opera, the intensity of these units was gradually increased at the same time that the rock was gradually being withdrawn. The intensity of the special lights increased to a painful, blinding glare in which the TV image faded and the rock began to function as a mirror. The audience was blinded for nearly a full minute, in the meantime the whole setting – the rock and the stairs – disappeared, leaving only a blank space. Prometheus was consumed in the fire of light.

VII

What remained to do was to put the poetry I had nurtured in the flames of the family hearth into the cinema. I happen to believe that film and poetry have a great deal in common. One of the first things I learned from the ten film poems I have made was that poetry could enter the inner world of people in documentary situations. Auden, probably the first poet to write verse specifically for a screen documentary, *Night Mail* (1936), is reported to have said in a lecture on 'Poetry and Film': 'Poetry can also be used to express the thoughts of characters, in rather the same way as Eugene O'Neill introduces "the interior voice" in *Strange Interlude*.'

I disagree wholeheartedly with Auden's opinion that 'the generally accepted metrical forms cannot be used in films, owing to the difficulty of cutting the film exactly according to the beat without distorting the visual content'. In my own film poems I have used the quatrain of Gray's *Elegy* and the quatrain of Fitzgerald's *Rubáiyát of Omar Khayyám*, as well as octosyllabic couplets. Auden's remark, of course, only applies to the kind of task Auden was set – that is, to compose verse to an already edited picture, as a film composer usually produces his score. Although I sometimes work in this way, when the editor has come up with an exciting sequence, I usually begin drafting even before the editor has done his first rough assembly. In fact, when I wasn't on the shoot itself (and after my first collaboration with the BBC director Peter Symes, I always was present and sometimes composing on the spot) I would see all the rushes and begin sketching lines and sequences.

The person who wrote notes on Auden's lecture observes that 'Mr Auden even found it necessary to time his spoken verse with a stop-watch in order to fit it exactly to the shot on which it commented'. Auden was working before the video machine made it possible to have frame-accurate time codes and easily replayed sequences. And perhaps the new digital editing has made it possible to experiment much more with the relations between poetry and film. Whereas manual editing on the Steenbeck gives a run-up, albeit in fast forward, to the sequence being worked on, and therefore a quick reprise of the wider context, digital editing with its speed can allow you to try many different variations in much shorter time. It also allows the editor to call up clusters of related imagery from any part of the logged and telecined rushes. This can be the visual equivalent of laterally garnered clusters of poetic imagery, and my deep-rooted way of letting disparate images grow together has been fed by the Avid or Lightworks editing programmes.

Auden clearly wanted to learn more about the technicalities of film-making in the 1930s and to explore the possibilities of what he could do, not after the film was edited, but before and even during the shooting. He was to have been co-director on Grierson's planned sequel to *Night Mail*, to be called *Air Mail to Australia*. The endeavour was abandoned, but it shows that Auden was keen to extend his relationship with film. In 1935, Auden served as production manager and assistant director on another GPO Film Unit production, *Calendar of the Year*, in which he also played a small role as Father Christmas! Auden clearly saw the possibilities of film and poetry, and seems to have been willing to apprentice himself to all the processes, with a view to doing what I, in fact, have ended up doing in my own film poems – being there as a constant presence during the shoot with a very sympathetic colleague like Peter Symes, and then, following the logic of the organic process developed during our collaborations, directing the films myself.

Another great figure in British cinema, the documentary film-maker Humphrey Jennings, was also a poet both on the page and in his cinematic practice, and the perception of the affinity could also be found at the same time in the Soviet Union. Sergei Eisenstein began work on *Alexander Nevsky* in 1937, the year of my birth. When he began his shooting script he was inspired by Milton's *Paradise Lost*. Thus, 'Milton's imagery of the Battle of Heaven became the battle on the ice in *Alexander Nevsky*,' writes Marie Seton,

Eisenstein's biographer. He broke lines of Milton down into scenes 'to illustrate how *cinematic construction could be found in poetry* [my italics]'.

Pier Paolo Pasolini was a poet before he was a film director. Even towards the end of his career a film like *Teorema* (1968) began life in the form of a verse tragedy, and Pasolini used his own verse, as Eisenstein used Milton's, as a template for cinematic construction. Victor Erice, the Spanish director of *The Spirit of the Beehive* and *The Quince Tree Sun*, said, in an interview in the *Guardian* on 1 April 1993:

> As Pasolini used to say, there is the cinema of prose and the cinema of poetry, and I try for the latter kind . . . Nowadays, prose is triumphant. We are very frightened of poetry. Hollywood deals with prose and it is as powerful in Spain as everywhere else. I can't compete with it, still less beat it. All I would say is that there is another cinema and surely it should be allowed to exist.

There were earlier attempts before Pasolini to distinguish the cinema of prose from the cinema of poetry, and probably the first was by the Russian Victor Shklovsky, whose 'Poetry and Prose in the Cinema' was published in 1927. Maya Turovskaya, in her study of Tarkovsky, quotes Shklovsky's distinction:

> There is a cinema of prose and a cinema of poetry, two different genres; they differ not in their rhythm – or rather not only in their rhythm – but in the fact that in the cinema of poetry elements of form prevail over

elements of meaning and it is they, rather than the meaning, which determine the composition.

She then goes on to ask a very important question: 'Why is it that at some moments in history the cinema feels the need for a poetic treatment of its raw material?' She answers her question by saying that this need 'is particularly sharply felt during periods of historical change, when our "normal", accepted notions and perceptions become inadequate in the face of changing realities, and new perceptions have to be developed'. And in these changing realities the often forgotten captive champion, Prometheus, tends to be remembered. Of course, she includes the films of Tarkovsky as 'poetic', and though Tarkovsky himself grew irritated with the label, he admires and quotes his father's poetry in his films and in his 'Reflections on Cinema', *Sculpting in Time*, and himself applies the adjective to the cinema of Kurosawa. Tarkovsky, who confesses that his favourite art form is the three-line Japanese haiku, writes: 'I find poetic links, the logic of poetry in cinema, extraordinarily pleasing.' And among those he designates as creating 'great spiritual treasures and that special beauty which is subject only to poetry' he includes not only poets in the literary sense – Pushkin, Mandelstam and Pasternak – but also film-makers: Chaplin, the Russian Dovzhenko and the Japanese director Mizoguchi.

Pasolini also includes Chaplin and Mizoguchi, along with Bergman, as producers of 'great cinematic poems', but goes on to say that their films were not constructed according to the laws of what he calls 'the language of the cinema of poetry': 'This means that these films were not poetry, but narratives. Classic cinema was and is narrative, its language is that of prose. Its poetry is an inner poetry, as, for example, in the narratives of Chekhov or Melville.' For Pasolini the cinema of poetry means, among other things, making the spectator aware of the camera's presence, and 'a primarily formalist world-view of the author'. He speaks (in an article which, considering it is by a poet, is surprisingly bogged down with semiotic jargon) of an emergent 'prosody'.

Though much of this thinking comes from directors who are either poets themselves or have a close affinity with poetry, they are usually referring to a kind of cinema in which, as Pasolini defines it, we are aware of the camera and its movement and what he calls a 'free indirect subjective'. We are not talking about the actual use of verse, though again Tarkovsky uses his father's poetry to wonderful effect in *Mirror*. Nor are they talking about films which are cinematic versions of theatre – Shakespeare, say, or Rostand's *Cyrano* with Gérard Depardieu. My own *Prometheus* brings my experience of film verse and theatre verse together.

There is an underlying connection between verse, metrical poetry and film which my colleague Peter Symes draws attention to in his introduction to a volume of my film poems, *The Shadow of Hiroshima* (Faber, 1995). The twenty-four (or twenty-five) frames per second have what can be called a prosodic motion. In my first experiences of the cutting room of Jess Palmer at the BBC in 1981, I realised that my own rhythmic preoccupations had a parallel in what I now think of as the scansions of edited sequences. It is not merely the twenty-four frames per second, nor the metrical beats in a verse line, but how they succeed one another and build into gratifications or disappointments of expectation. Tarkovsky expresses a similar view: 'Feeling the rhythmicity of a shot is rather like feeling a truthful word in literature.' In poetry, of course, the truthful word is also the right metrical word, the word with its truth and its sound placed on the most telling grid of the metric. The cinematic construction in poetry that Eisenstein found in Milton is paralleled by the poetic construction of cinema. And, I have always thought, the two prosodies can be plaited, metrical beat and cinematic scansion.

VIII

At the very end of the film, when there is a kind of *Götterdämmerung* caused by the Old Man's flung cigarette, intended to destroy Hermes, the golden statue of Prometheus is consumed 'in his own concoction, bloody flames'. We see real red and yellow flames consuming the black-and-white projected flames on the Palace Cinema screen, as the whole collected cast of statues melt and scream like humans in a conflagration. We only had one chance to film it, and although the charred limbs fell apart and tumbled down the rocks in a quarry belonging to Titan Cement, Elefsina, nonetheless what remained was the chained but still defiantly clenched fist of the champion of mankind, burned off at the shoulder. And what remained of the silver statue of Hermes was a fist still grasping his *caduceus*, the symbol of his office. No détente!

There are times in all art when you accept what you are given, and this was one. However, as I often do, when everyone else had left for England I went back and looked round the quarry. At the foot of the towering rock was the charred head of Prometheus, matted blackened fibreglass still with the Titan's features, looking uncannily like the photograph of the Iraqi soldier burned in his truck on the road to Basra during the Gulf War, about whom I had written my poem 'A Cold Coming'. What was remarkable about this incinerated head was that in its eyes it retained the gold leaf it had been painstakingly gilded with. So that for all its having passed through holocaust it retained its golden visions. The vision seen by the golden eyes in the carbonised profile isn't diminished. They take their sheen and glitter from 'the fire of light', from the future, from the flicker of the screen whenever their journey is projected and witnessed by new eyes. As I held the head I remembered that wonderful poem of Yannis Ritsos on the Bulgarian poet Geo Milev (1895–1925), who had a glass eye, and when he was arrested and burned alive by the police, all that was left of him in the crematorium was the blue glass eye:

His eye is being kept in the Museum of Revolution
like a seeing stone of the struggle. I saw his eye.
In his pupil there was the full story of the Revolution,
blue scenes of blood-stained years,
blue scenes with red flags
with dead who carry in their raised hands a blue day.
His eye never closes,
this eye keeps vigil over Sofia.
This eye is a blue star in all the nights.
This eye sees and illuminates and judges.

Whoever looks at this eye wins back his eyes.
Whoever looks at this eye sees the world.

(trans. Ninetta Makrinikola)

Poetry rises out of its own ashes and continues its ancient dream in front of fire. Not only the animated flame but also smoking ash and cinders with their bits of bone, rings, a bluc glass eye, the golden pupils of the first champion of mankind, strike the aboriginal poetic spark. Whoever looks into the golden eyes of Prometheus set in the cremated sockets sees the early hope of the world and knows its late despair.

[Terme di Caracalla, Rome
Delphi, Greece]

The Tears and the Trumpets

2000

D. W. Blandford, in what he admits is a 'red-nosed' epilogue to his essay on the Virgil Society in *Pentekontaetia*,
wonders if the Society 'should . . . perhaps go for "street
cred" and appeal to YOOF. We could revamp the Society
as the Virgil Fan Club, issue lapel badges with the motto
AMO MARONEM', etc.

I have to confess to wondering if asking me to be your
president was part of the same fantasy, as I have, even in my
sixties and long past my YOOF, been recently styled in the
press as the 'Liam Gallagher of modern poetry'.

This tabloid branding presumably was for the outcries
in 1987 surrounding my poem *v.* At the same time as I was
being branded as a yob from the gas works I was also president of the Classical Association. Because of the huge controversy the *Independent* published the whole poem on its
news pages. On the very day that it appeared I was trying
to decipher the *Res Gestae* of Augustus on a temple wall in
Ankara, Turkey, where I'd been invited to give a reading of
my poetry.

v. is a poem which has the central place in the collection
of my poetry published in Italian translation by Einaudi
in 1996. Since its publication I've had many invitations to
Italy to read my poems: Rome, Venice, Bologna, Torino,

Genoa, Milan and Napoli, where I returned the year before last. My first visit to Napoli was in 1987, to make one of my film poems for the BBC called *Mimmo Perrella non è piu*, about the burial customs of the modern Neapolitans, showing how bodies are exhumed after a year in the volcanic soil of Naples and deposited in marble lockers in the vast Cemetery of Poggioreale. Each year the remains of the dried, disintegrating corpse are taken out, spoken to gently, dusted with DDT, given new cerements and put back again. I'm not suggesting that this *rifresco*, as the Neapolitans call it, is analogous to the ritual of this Presidential Address, but the theory behind the *rifresco* is that the more attention you give to the remains of a loved one, the more favours the 'refreshed' spirit will give back; the more disintegrated the leathery remains of skull or pelvis, the more tender the devotion. I believe you could say that the more deconstructed the *Aeneid*, the more potent and precious the fractured residues. And I have gone in search of Virgil's literal remains, as well as his remains in a literary sense. Each time I've been to Napoli I've made my pilgrimage to Mergellina and the Parco Virgiliano. After paying homage to Virgil, and Leopardi next to him, I would eat in the Piazza Sannazaro, where the descendants of the fisherman protagonists of the *Piscatory Eclogues*, inspired by Virgil's, of the square's eponymous poet still land baby octopuses deliciously dished up at Pasqualino's near the supposed *tomba di Virgilio* in Mergellina.

I am currently translating a poem by Sannazaro on Cumae. The last time I gave a reading of my poetry in Italy was in September last year, at a festival in Mantua.

One of the poems I read was 'Laureate's Block', another poem which got me hounded by the same ignorant *Daily Mail* journalists. 'Laureate's Block' is a poem I wrote for the *Guardian*, deliberately designed to ruin any chance I might have had of being made Poet Laureate and declaring my republican sentiments with as obvious, if versified, clarity as your first president's declaration that he was 'a Royalist in politics, an Anglo-Catholic in religion and a classicist in literature'. It's probably being a republican that also makes me, like Shelley, and unlike T. S. Eliot, a great admirer of the iconoclastic Lucan, notwithstanding his subversive vandalising of Virgil, and of that even greater republican poet, John Milton, whose epic probably owes more to Lucan's *Pharsalia* than to Virgil's *Aeneid*. I have a certain wariness or non-laureate's block when I think that Virgil was probably the first poet to set the style of laureate verse.

There were other poems I read in Mantua which might also identify me as an 'atheist in religion', and of course, this makes me unsympathetic to the posthumous press-ganging of Virgil into Christianity as *'anima naturaliter Christiana'*, something I also associate with your first president. It is amazing the lengths these posthumous proselytisers will go to, even with less malleable material than Virgil. Franz Werfel (1890–1945), the German dramatist and poet who translated Euripides' *Trojan Women* just before the outbreak of the First World War, could even see in Hecuba an anticipation of the passion of Jesus Christ. 'And thus we see', Werfel wrote, 'the notorious atheist Euripides as a harbinger, a prophet, an early dove of Christianity.'

But most of the poems I read last September in Mantua, republican or atheist as they may well be, all show at least one and one only congruence between your first and your latest poet-president, and that is that I'd also call myself, with some qualifications, 'a classicist in literature'. Perhaps a classicist who graffitis and vandalises his own carefully wrought edifices and structures. The vandal with the aerosol has to value highly what he desecrates with his daubing, no less than Lord Byron, who chiselled his name on columns at Sunion and Delphi, or Giuseppe Boba (1790), Casper Pinottem (1728), G. Mahiev (1735), CFFB (1737), clearly devotees of different nationalities, who chiselled their names or initials just beneath the lead inlaid laurels on the inscription on Virgil's tomb in Mergellina.

I also read one poem in Mantua, probably the only one I've written in which the influence of Virgil is clear. I will read it at the end of my talk. I didn't go directly to Mantua from England. I was, coincidentally, on my way back from another long filming journey, after the eleven-week Odyssey across Europe making my film *Prometheus*. This new film followed the route of the severed head of Orpheus down the Maritsa river, as the Hebrus is now known in Bulgaria, down the Evros, as it's known in modern Greek, and across the sea to the resting place of the head and the lyre of the poet in Lesbos.

I had a complete Virgil with me, and whenever we could get close enough to the river, and it was not the militarised border zone between Greece and Turkey, from its banks or from a boat on its current I'd declaim:

tum quoque marmorea caput a cervice revulsum
gurgite cum medio portans Oeagrius Hebrus
volveret, Eurydicen vox ipsa et frigida lingua,
a miseram Eurydicen! anima fugiente vocabat,
Eurydicen toto referebant flumine ripae.

(*Georgics* 4.523–27)

And even then, when Oeagrian Hebrus spun that
head, torn from its marble neck, around in mid-
flow, the incorporeal voice and the tongue, now
cold, called on Eurydice – ah, poor Eurydice! – as
the spirit departed. 'Eurydice,' the banks re-echoed,
all the way down the stream.

When I tell you that the head that we floated down the
river from its cascading source high up in the Rhodopes
through Plovdiv, past Didimoticho and Soufli and all the
way to Lesbos was modelled from my own head, you will
understand the degree of empathy I brought to the project
and to what I might say today about Orpheus.

After the poetry reading of last September in the tranquil walled garden of a Mantuan *palazzo*, I was given dinner by the festival directors in a *trattoria* which served the
local culinary delicacy, which you could translate as 'ass cas-
serole' or 'donkey stew'. As I ate I found myself quoting,
though I know it is not by Virgil, from the *Copa*:

delicium est asinus (26)

In some ways I'd like to think that Virgil *had* written the

Copa, but although it has been described as 'an elegy bubbling over with the joy of life', the writer (P. J. Enk) goes on to say that it is 'too cheerful, however, to allow ascription to Virgil'. It would be good to think that his life was not all poetry and *'lacrimae rerum'*, and that he got out to the taverna now and then. I've eaten in La Taverna di Virgilio in Brindisi, near the Scalinata Virgilio, which was a cheerful enough place, even though it is in the town of the poet's death.

> *pone merum et talos*

the *Copa* ends;

> *pereat, qui crastina curat!*
> *mors aurem vellens 'vivite' ait, 'venio'.*

'Live,' says Death, 'I'm on my way.'

I'm not much of a gambler, but after the reading I had a taste for Mantuan *merum*. (I think it was Bianco di Custoza from the hills of Cremona.)

The next morning (or perhaps I should say the morning after, since the day brought me some sobering thoughts), as I'd never been to Mantua before I spent the first of a few days looking round. Because Orpheus was still on my mind after my three-week journey along the Hebrus, I started with the Palazzo Ducale, where the first purely secular Italian drama, the *Orfeo* of Angelo Poliziano, was played in 1480, and later what is often regarded as the first opera, the *Orfeo* of Monteverdi, in 1607. Both *Orfeo*s derived from the same Virgilian text I'd carried with me and declaimed along the Hebrus through Bulgaria and Greece. The lament and echo of the Orphic voice lead to the heart of opera; the very metrical repetition of grief and loss is the direct source of plaintive aria.

Around the same time as Poliziano's *Orfeo*, the Gonzaga Bridal Room, the *Camera degli Sposi*, was decorated by Mantegna (1431–1506), and I went, with my binoculars, to examine the ceiling spandrels, which depict Arion of Lesbos astride a dolphin, Orpheus charming a lion, Orpheus charming Cerberos and a Fury, *and*, finally, a fallen Orpheus, his hand lolling over the spandrel's border, being brutally clubbed to death by three women. It is this last shocking decoration which inspired Albrecht Dürer, who was in Italy in the 1490s. In Dürer's etching of the same murder, above the scene of Orpheus being clubbed and battered, there is a banderole looped decoratively in the branches of a tree which reads:

Orfeus der erst Puseran

which can only be translated in its crude hostility as 'Orpheus the first faggot'. Like the fragments of Phanocles before him (who was known and used by the brilliant Poliziano), Ovid, though not quite so butchly belligerent as Albrecht, has this version of the poet's murder in *Metamorphoses* 10:

> *ille etiam Thracum populis fuit auctor amorem*
> *in teneros transferre mares citraque iuventam*
> *etatis breve ver et primos carpere flores.* (83–5)

> Indeed, he was the first amongst the people of Thrace
> to transfer his love to tender youths, and revel in the
> fruit of their brief springtime, and early flowering, this
> side of manhood.

The implication behind the savage dismemberment of
Orpheus was that he was 'unmanly' in some way, *mollis*, not
durus ('soft', not 'hard'). It may well be the first story that
suggests that the practice of poetry is not really a manly
activity. At least not this kind of poetry.

Orpheus is the first non-sword-wielding hero in the
myths, who either turned to the love of boys or was killed
because his grief was excessive, just as the nightingale in the
simile in the *Georgics* sings its grief, and gives us a sense of
the art of lamentation considered obsessive in contrast to
the world where the *durus arator*, the 'harsh ploughman',
gets on with the business of cultivation. And the empire-
builder with conquest, killing, spoils and triumphs!

The Thrace where Orpheus was born was also the birthplace of Ares, god of war. And for the Greeks the mountains
of Thrace always resounded, writes the Bulgarian archaeologist Ivan Mazarov, 'either with the clash of weapons or the
song of the lyre'. Either/or! 'There is . . . something about
Orpheus that sets him apart from all the other great figures
of Greek myth [which] is pre-eminently heroic myth that
enshrines martial values: courage, killing, blood-lust . . .' All
the other great figures of Greek myth, whatever else they
may be, are great killers; Orpheus carries with him that
essentially powerless power of poetry, as it detaches itself
from the heroic mode and in its very detachment becomes

dangerously undermining of the martial ideal, as it gives scope for frailty, tenderness, doubt, tears and sorrow. This poetry is not like that of Cretheus, the Trojan bard, killed by Turnus in *Aeneid* Book 9:

> *semper equos atque arma virum pugnasque*
> *canebat.* (777)

> He always sang of horses and men at arms
> and battles.

The *arma virum* reminds us too much of the opening of the *Aeneid* itself not to make us wonder why Virgil has his fellow heroic poet die.

The lyre of Orpheus, thrown in the same river as its dismembered player, came with the head to Lesbos, where a non-heroic poetry prospered for the first time into the personal lyric: Terpander, Sappho, Alcaeus, a poetry that liberates itself from the metrical military morale-boosting and tunes itself to something more tender than laureate triumph. The torment of Orpheus bloomed into a tenderness unknown in the heroic world, and impossible to maintain for more than a moment among martial clamour. We shouldn't forget how brass, the *aerea cornua*, and percussion drown out the magic lyre of Orpheus in *Metamorphoses* 11:

> *Sed ingens*
> *clamor et infracto Berecyntia tibia cornu*
> *tympanaque.* (15–17)

But the vast clamour of the Berecyntian flutes of
broken horn and the drums.

How can the lyre make itself heard above the din of clash-
ing steel, the killing and screaming?

After the story of Orpheus, Virgil's *Georgics* end with a
kind of epilogue in which Virgil, you could say, allows us to
hear the lyre and the clash of weapons, and seems to give
all the glory to the martial sound and fury, casting himself
dismissively as '*studiis florentem ignobilis oti*', 'flourishing in
the pursuits of obscure retirement', in contrast to Octavian,
Caesar magnus, thundering in war and, as victor, giving laws
to 'willing' nations (though the willingness of the nations
might be the first whiff of the laureate spin that colours the
Aeneid). The *fulminat* ('hurls lightning') inevitably drowns
out the *carmina*. Art is cast as inglorious compared with triumph and conquest, or, indeed, with the agricultural labour
of the *durus arator*. The final lines you might almost call
Virgil's valediction to the Orphic voice. How does a spirit
probably more inclined towards the grief of the nightingale
or the sorrow of Orpheus fare among the clash of weapons?
Can an Orpheus become a Cretheus? How does this *mol-
lities* (*morbidezza*, as Mackail translates it), this tenderness,
which carries with it the brand of weakness or effeminacy
among the braying trumpets, fare in an imperialist mission where the solemnised advice from the Underworld for
future Romans begins:

> *excudent alii spirantia mollius aera*
> (*Aeneid* 6.847)

others will hammer out bronze that breathes with
more refinement than ours

though, of course, the Romans would make their own *aerea
cornua* against whose bellicose, rasping notes even the lyre
of Orpheus is helpless. The Orphic voice which is *mollis*,
refined, is certainly not a creator of epics. Verse that cel-
ebrates Caesar is *durus*, as Propertius writes to Augustus'
'arts czar' Maecenas, who asks why his poetry is *mollis*:

> *nec mea conveniunt duro praecordia versu*
> *Caesaris in Phrygios condere nomen avos.* (2.1.41–2)

Nor do I have the stomach to trace Caesar's name
back to Phrygian ancestors in hard enough verse.

What happens to *versus* when it has to become *durus*, especially when it is composed by one whose spirit seems to
be more essentially *mollis*? What compromises have to be
made if the lyre enters that world willingly and tries to
serve both power and the empathetic, tragic, compassionate heart of poetry? It seems the dilemma of the Virgilian
imagination in his imperial epic.

On the same day in Mantua after the Palazzo Ducale,
with the spirit of the grieving, inconsolable, then battered
Orpheus and these thoughts much in my head and with my
Virgil in my pocket, I went to look for the statue of the poet
this Society is devoted to, in a park off the Piazza Virgiliana.
The statue seemed to me, I have to say, a monument more
appropriate to a conqueror than to a poet, or to a poet who

had to raise a naturally more gentle voice to measure up to the clash of weapons, or be heard above the din of *aerea cornua*:

aereaque adsensu conspirant cornua rauco. (7.615)

and bronze horns breathe in hoarse assent.

Part of the explanation is that the statue was erected in anticipation of the bimillennial celebrations of Virgil's birth in 1930, during the dictatorship of Mussolini (1922–43). The statue is raised many metres above the ground, and I had to use my binoculars to have a decent view of the face I was forced to gaze up at in compulsory awe and reverence. The statue is in a declamatory pose, and certainly not reading his work on the same plane as his audience, as I had done in the *palazzo* the night before. At ground level, beneath the belittling bard, are the coronets of the limescaled sprinklers of two dried-up fountains, not an appropriate symbol for a poet whose *Aeneid* has been on the curricula of Europe since Caecilius Epirota put him on the syllabus soon after the epic's publication. There were two used hypodermics in the fountains, a condom and discarded juice cartons.

It is easier to associate the poetry of empire with this imposing figure than the poetry of loss and doubt, and that is probably the point of this particular sculpture, as the rest of the monument makes clearer. Beneath the raised right arm of the declaiming bard is another statue of two men, one, the Roman, with his foot planted triumphantly on the stomach of the other, and on the pedestal, along with more recent red and blue graffiti of gang vendetta and vengeance, is the text from the *Aeneid* the sculpture is meant to illustrate, and the lines I have no doubt the statue of the bard above was meant to be declaiming:

> *Tu regere imperio populos, Romane, memento*
> *(hae tibi erunt artes) pacisque imponere morem,*
> *parcere subiectis et debellare superbos.* (6.851–3)

> But you, Roman, learn to rule peoples with your
> imperial power, for this shall be your skill – to
> impose the rule of peace, to spare the conquered
> and subdue the arrogant.

'*Superbi* were simply those who', in the words of de Ste. Croix, 'refused to submit to Roman domination, and beaten down they were.'

The verb '*debellare*', 'subdue', is, interestingly enough, not used before the Augustan period. The ghost of Anchises is militantly fond of '*debellare*', as he also uses it when he appears to Aeneas in Book 5 (730 f.), when he tells his son that there is a *gens debellanda*, a 'people which must be subdued', in Latium.

Titus, son of Vespasian, who sacked Jerusalem in AD 70 with appalling carnage, was called *Vespasianus Iudaeorum debellator*, 'subduer of Jews' (Tertullian, *Apologeticum* 5), and the Vulgate has the word '*debellator*' coupled, appropriately, with '*durus*', for which the Authorised Version has 'fierce man of war' (Wisdom of Solomon, 18.15). These lines on the pedestal are, said Robert Graves, in one of the most virulently hostile diatribes against Virgil outside the Whigs of the eighteenth century, '. . . a favourite declamation of imperialists who consider themselves heirs of Augustan Rome'.

Certainly prominent among those who considered themselves the heirs of Augustan Rome in more recent times was Mussolini, under whose dictatorship the declaiming bard was erected. 'Five years from now,' Mussolini declared on 31 December 1925, 'Rome must appear in all its splendour: immense, ordered, and as powerful as it was at the time of the first empire, that of Augustus.' Mussolini was called 'a second Augustus' by his foreign minister, Dino Grandi, who, as Mussolini's spin doctor, spoke of his invasion of Ethiopia as Italy's 'mission to civilise the black continent'; Mussolini, of course, also heeding the Elysian advice of Anchises inscribed on the monument I was sitting in front of, practised his brand of 'civilised' *debellare* against black *superbi* in Ethiopia with mustard gas. By 1937, the bimillennial anniversary of the birth of Augustus (63 BC–AD 14), Mussolini's archaeologists and architects had created the Piazza Augusto Imperatore, with the reconstructed mausoleum of the emperor and the Ara Pacis enclosed in a building by the Tiber where today it is *Chiuso per Lavori*.

When I last saw it recently, a fig tree with small green fruit was growing out of a fissure in the *Res Gestae*. Mussolini subsidised editions of the *Aeneid* to help promote his new 'Augustan' imperialism. It is, unfortunately, inescapably true that it is all too easy to co-opt Virgil into these enterprises. Especially a Virgil like this statue I was trying to crane my neck to look at declaiming *Aeneid* 6.851–3 to the air way above my head. Definitely declaiming those very lines. The pose says it all.

It was a beautiful September day in Mantua, and I had some hours spare before my next appointment with donkey stew, so I sat on a bench in the park and, dwarfed by the monument, alternately looked at the commemorative image of the declaiming, elevated bard and read his *Aeneid* 6 for the context for the three lines on the pedestal of the triumphant Roman. The sculpted victor with his sandalled foot on his defeated foe has not a shred of *parcere subiectis* in it. Rather the victor (whose visage, coincidentally or not, bears a close resemblance to Mussolini himself) with his sandal on the guts of the defeated looks out towards the camera or the sculptor like a hunter from the British Raj snapped with his boot on a dead tiger. Scanning the pair from my bench with my binoculars I noticed that the conquered foe beneath the Roman had a Greek meander pattern on his kilt. Was this, I began to wonder, a conflation of Lucius Mummius, the conqueror of Corinth in 146 BC, and the Italian invader of Corfu in 1923, the first example of the dictator's violence on an international scale, which Dino Grandi, who became Mussolini's ambassador to Britain and whom *Il Duce* would always detest for making him back down over Corfu, called 'a real contribution to European peace'? That sort of 'spin' was typical of the first Augustus too!

'Sparing the defeated', which I don't think was on the mind of the sculpted Mussolini lookalike, is a central proud entry on the marmoreal CV of the crumbling *Res Gestae* housing the now closed Ara Pacis, which the second Augustus restored in honour of the first. The words are a chiselled sentence I first read in Turkey:

Bella terra et mari civilia externaque toto in orbe
terrarum
suscepi, victorque omnibus superstitibus civibus
peperci.

I often waged wars on land and sea, civil and
foreign, throughout the whole world, and
although victorious, I spared all citizens who
asked for pardon.

The necessity of sparing is put even more passionately and
urgently by Anchises earlier, in the crucial matter of civil
conflict rather than foreign domination. At the end of civil
war and vendetta someone has to start the process of reconciliation and disarming. It becomes the victor to throw
away his sword:

ne, pueri, ne tanta animis adsuescite bella,
neu patriae validas in viscera vertite viris;
tuque prior, tu parce, genus qui ducis Olympo;
proice tela manu, sanguis meus!
(Aeneid 6.832–5)

My sons, don't allow your souls to become
accustomed to such wars, never turn the mighty
powers of your fatherland against itself. You be the
first to spare others, you, who trace your ancestry
to Olympus; cast the weapons from your hand,
you who share my blood!

The vehement alliteration of the 'v's and 'p's is followed by the choking into silence on the broken line, which seems to show Anchises choked and silenced at the sorrow of the Roman Civil War and being unable to continue. I don't want to get sidetracked into the question of half-lines. We might say that, if it was deliberate, it is a brilliant dramatic device. If it wasn't, then it shows that Virgil was having trouble with the transition, and it was his own shocked silence, not Anchises', over what was coming next.

Under the dominating fascistic statue I felt again one of my greatest moments of unease in the *Aeneid.* Something has always appalled me at how Anchises recovers his didactic composure after his moment of silence by reaching for the inspiring and gloriously triumphant figure of Lucius Mummius, destroyer of Corinth, famous for the Greeks he has butchered. Not one of my heroes! We 'pass again to triumph', says R. D. Williams:

> *Ille triumphata Capitolia ad alta Corintho*
> *victor aget currum, caesis insignis Achivis.* (6.836–7)

Dryden has:

> Another comes, who shall in triumph ride,
> And to the Capitol his chariot guide,
> From conquered Corinth, rich with Grecian spoils.

Lucius Mummius Achaicus destroyed Corinth in 146 B.C. If we quote the simple sentences of Pausanias on this great Roman triumph, it is to measure the poeticising against a more prosaic and disturbing reality, and to realise all that is suppressed in the *durus versus* glorification of triumphant Rome's vengeance for Troy:

> Most of the people found in [Corinth] were massacred by the Romans, and Mummius sold the women and children . . . The most admired monuments of piety and art he carried off . . . (7.16)

Not much *parcere subiectis* here, though I'll mention the one recorded incident of compassion later.

The myths of Roman clemency have to be maintained for Lucius Mummius as well as for Augustus Caesar, and to compensate at least for the sequestration of these monuments of piety and art something presumably far more inspiring and publicly educative was set up, if the inscription found on a pedestal of what had been an imposing equestrian statue in Olympia is anything to go by:

> The city of Elis erected this statue of Lucius Mummius . . . commander-in-chief of the Romans, on account of his virtue and the kindness which he continues to show to it and to the rest of the Greeks.

The conflation of Lucius Mummius and the Mussolini look-alike, which was hard to ignore as long as I sat in the park, put me in mind of the Italian newspapers that reported how, after Mussolini's invasion of Greece in 1940, which was a complete flop, 'the Greeks were welcoming the Italian troops and gratefully accepting the imitation bronze busts of the *Duce*'.

Not only was the sacked city re-embellished with equestrian statues of its sacker, but, according to Dio Chrysostom, Corinth was the first Greek city to be blessed with that most Roman of institutions, gladiatorial games. Dio goes on to note with horror and disgust that these barbarities then went to Athens itself, where a still visible marble barrier round the orchestra of the theatre of Dionysus shows 'too plainly the bloody nature of the exhibitions to which that splendid palace of art was degraded', as Mahaffy puts it.

Brutal and even blasphemous fact in the holy place of spellbinding poetry, but it is, though, an inevitable consequence of the choices made by the *durus debellator* dramatised by Virgil in the *Aeneid*. All roads lead to the Colosseum, and to the blood-curdling charade of the death of Orpheus, literally and fatally enacted before 50,000 Romans. In Martial's *De Spectaculis* (AD 80) there is an epigram that tells us of Orpheus being literally torn to pieces by a bear in the Colosseum. It is a shocking emblem and blasphemous enactment of where the triumph of *durus* over *mollis* (I think inevitably) leads. I have always read it as an elegy for the death of the imagination, and with the imagination the death of compassion:

> *Quicquid in Orpheo Rhodope spectasse theatro*
> *dicitur, exhibuit, Caesar, arena tibi.*
> *repserunt scopuli, mirandaque silva cucurrit,*
> *quale fuisse nemus creditur Hesperidum.*
> *adfuit immixtum pecori genus omne ferarum*
> *et supra vatem multa pependit avis,*

ipse sed ingrato iacuit laceratus ab urso.
haec tamen ut res est facta, ita ficta alia est.
(*Epigramma 21 – De Orpheo*)

Whatever scene it is said that Mount Rhodope
witnessed, that same scene was displayed to you
on the arena's Orphic stage. Rocks crawled and
a marvellous wood rushed onwards, like the
reputed grove of the Hesperides. Every type of
wild animal was there, mingling in the herd, and
myriad birds, hovering over the bard. But he fell,
gored by an ungrateful bear. This deed was done
in fact which elsewhere is done in fiction.

I used the *ficta/facta* contrast also in a play I staged in
a Roman amphitheatre in Carnuntum, on the Danube,
between Vienna and Bratislava. I have Commodus say:

Greek bloodshed is all *ficta*, ours is *facta*
we Romans really kill the fucking actor.

The road from Lucius Mummius to a mangled Orpheus
in the Colosseum is a straight Roman one. How the truly
poetic shrivels in triumphalism.

Do the conscience and compassion of Virgil here fall
lamentably short in not giving Corinth the poetic equivalent of the temple mural in Carthage that made Aeneas
stand and weep? Surely it suppresses the poet's own sensibility, nurtured as it undoubtedly was on Greek culture and
art. What did it cost Virgil personally to suppress those

feelings to create the *durus versus* of Roman triumphalism?

Oddly enough, there is a pertinent anecdote about Lucius Mummius, the destroyer of Corinth and looter of its art. There is, as with Aeneas and the murals of Carthage, a moment of tears. Perhaps here we can find a momentary flash of *parcere subiectis*. The story is told by Plutarch (*Quaestiones Convivales* 737a):

At the point of destroying Corinth Mummius collected all children of free birth and asked those who knew their letters to write down a line of poetry in front of him. One of them wrote:

τρὶς μάκαρες Δαναοὶ καὶ τετράκις, οἳ τότ᾽ ὄλοντο

Thrice and even four times blessed were the Danaans who perished then.

(*Odyssey* 5.306)

Mummius is moved, weeps at the child's written line from the *Odyssey*, and spares the family of the child, though all the others, who couldn't write or couldn't remember an apposite quotation, are sold into slavery. The *durus debellator* can't afford to be *mollis* for more than a moment. Though capable at times of such feelings, the Roman's capacity for fierce *debellare* might be impaired, and the imperial mission jeopardised, if he surrendered to them. The *parcere subiectis* of Lucius Mummius is a blip in the belligerence. The tears are dried, the city levelled. Aeneas at the very end of the epic is also shown almost surrendering to the kind of compassion he had sensed in the murals of an alien city. By making the helpless Turnus invoke Anchises, Virgil makes us remember what Anchises told Aeneas: *parcere subiectis*. Aeneas ignores the advice, and the compassion which had made him weep in Carthage is suppressed in him, but awakened in the reader. The ending shows the cost of not learning *parcere subiectis*. It is a moment when the *aerea cornua*, the drums and trumpets of empire, are too loud to hear the lyre of compassion, though after the sound and fury of Aeneas killing Turnus we hear the lyre note send the complaining soul off to the shadows.

The unheard or unheeded lyre is the one thrust into the hands of the criminal, who had to enact Orpheus by showing the futility of his lyrical art and being torn to pieces.

Though we cannot expect Virgil to have had Sibylline foresight of Nero and Caligula and Commodus, even though he is credited by some with prophetic insight into the coming of Christ, he would have been aware of what are the momentous consequences of 146 BC, when both Carthage and Corinth were razed to the ground.

In the conflagration of Corinth, like a Titanic forge, such metals as had not been or could not be looted, gold, silver, copper fused together into a new, and highly valued, alloy, which was known from that time on as *Corinthium aes*. Can we take *Corinthium aes* as a metaphor for the alloy out of which the *durus versus* of the Roman epic is made, as something of value from Greece metamorphosed by Roman destruction? Whatever was *mollius* in the art resmelted in conflagration is only apparent when reworked in flashes, flecks and fragments in the refashioned metal. Instead of giving a quality to the whole work, its melted residues are hammered into a glint or glimpse of something tenderer that once gave a coherence to the whole.

Though Scipio Africanus was a more restrained looter than Mummius, I wonder if it is legitimate to ask if the fresco or set of panels depicting the Trojan wars before which Aeneas stood and wept was carried off to Rome, where its 'compassion', as Gavin Douglas has it in his translation of the passage, or its *'commiseratio calamitatum'*, as Ruaeus paraphrases in the edition of *Aeneid* that John Dryden relied on, might trouble the *durus debellator*'s conscience for decades to come. Or did it lose all detail in the fierce heat, and did Priam and the suffering Trojans become fused into a new molten alloy, a Carthaginian brass, out of which less compassionate images could be forged and over which no tears need be shed?

What makes the mural in Carthage a different art from almost anything else in the whole *Aeneid* is that it represents the compassion for the suffering of people who are not kith or kin:

> *sunt hic etiam sua praemia laudi,*
> *sunt lacrimae rerum et mentem mortalia tangunt.*
>   (1.461–2)

> Here too renown brings its own rewards,
> There are tears for events and mortal matters touch
>   the heart.

The second line has always been detached from its context to give Virgil a universality that has been used to counter the unease we feel about his propagandist purpose, and to create an Orphic voice singing in descant to the clash of arms. And although I have long believed, like Nicholas Horsfall, that 'only rank bad Latin can make of these lines a general reflection on the human condition', it goes on being used in the way it was used last year in the *Daily Telegraph* by Harry Eyres, who, under a headline saying that Virgil was a 'writer whose verse can be read as an elegy for the pain of Kosovo', said that 'though Virgil does not minimise the blood and sweat needed to complete the huge task of founding the imperial city, what interests him most are the tears . . . Tears seem to flow on every page . . .'

> *sunt lacrimae rerum et mentem mortalia tangunt.*

Mr Eyres ought to be careful, as it is also possible to find a parallel in the justification of the domination of Greece as revenge for the Trojan War, almost a millennium before, and Slobodan Milošević's use of the medieval battle of Kosovo to justify his atrocities.

The much-misused line (*'sunt lacrimae rerum et mentem mortalia tangunt'*) is even more profound when considered back in its proper context. The murals which move Aeneas to tears are recent and show compassion for the suffering of people unrelated to the artists and the Carthaginians. *Hic etiam*, 'even here', far from Troy, art shows compassion and empathy, *commiseratio calamitatum*. That it is *Tyrian* pity for *Trojan* woes (as Dryden translates) is an essential part of

the effect of the work of art on Aeneas and on us. That the
sufferer and the sympathiser are distinctly unrelated is the
very essence of the idea of shared humanity and mortality.
There are certainly other tears in the *Aeneid*, but they almost
all involve kinship. There are no Roman equivalents of the
Carthaginian murals. Such art could induce the *debellator*
perhaps [to] *parcere superbis*. Official Augustan art is like
the Shield of Aeneas or that temple imagined in *Georgics* 3,
with Caesar, as usual, in its centre:

> *in medio mihi Caesar erit templumque tenebit*
> (*Georgics* 3.16)

Caesar will hold central place in my temple

and with the (no doubt looted)

> *Parii lapides, spirantia signa.* (3.34)

Breathing statues made of Parian marble.

None of it is art of which could be said:

> *sunt lacrimae rerum et mentem mortalia tangunt.*

The drama of the *Aeneid*'s ending is precisely that struggle
between *mollis* and *durus* which I had found that morning
in Mantegna's Orpheus. Are we to look at that end like
Aeneas looking at the fresco in Carthage, or like Aeneas
looking at the moulded figures on his shield? There is a

world of difference. You weep at one and carry the other into the clash of weapons, to the sound of the drums and trumpets that drown out the lyre of Orpheus, which I swear I heard softly in my ear as I walked away from the declaiming statue in the Mantuan Park. Was someone at ground level, I wondered, strumming the coronet of the dried-up fountain as I walked along the banks of the Mincio to the place of donkey stew (*delicium est asinus*)? If the bronze bard heard it too, it might well crumble.

I began by telling you about the poems I read in the Mantuan *palazzo* singing for my first supper of donkey stew. Another poem I read is probably the only poem I've written that I am conscious of being influenced by Virgil. As president of the Classical Association, on 3 November 1987 I wrote my one and only letter to *The Times*. The correspondence columns had been full of two subjects while I'd been away in Ankara: the future of Latin studies, and the merit and scandal of my poem *v*. I wrote in my letter that without the years I'd spent studying Latin and Greek, I would never have been able to write *v*. I can say now that without the years I've spent reading Virgil, I could never have written the following poem that I read in Mantua in September and will be reading in Norway tomorrow. It was reprinted recently in *The Faber Book of War Poetry* (London, 1996), edited by the former Home Secretary, Kenneth Baker. I'm pleased to say that it appears with extracts from Books 1 and 2 of the *Aeneid*.

It is called 'The Cycles of Donji Vakuf'. And it's about my taking my lyre into the clash of weapons in Bosnia. Somewhere in it you will recognise Virgilian images and

also, perhaps, the contrast of *mollis* and *durus*, and something in the consoling mandolin lost to its player that might
remind you briefly of the Orpheus who came with me that
September morning in Mantua to look at the statue of Virgil:

We take *Emerald* to Bugojno, then the *Opal* route
to Donji Vakuf where Kalashnikovs still shoot
at retreating Serbs or at the sky
to drum up the leaden beat of victory.
Once more, though this time Serbian, homes
get pounded to facades like honeycombs.
This time it's the Bosnian Muslims' turn
to 'cleanse' a taken town, to loot, and burn.
Donji Vakuf fell last night at 11,
Victory's signalled by firing rounds to Heaven
and for the god to whom their victory's owed.
We see some victors cycling down the road
on bikes that they're too big for. They feel so tall
as victors, all conveyances seem small,
but one, whose knees keep bumping on his chin,
rides a kid's cycle, with a mandolin,
also childish size, strapped to the saddle,
jogging against him as he tries to pedal.
His machine gun and the mandolin impede
his furious pedalling, and slow down the speed
appropriate to victors, huge-limbed and big-booted,
and he's defeated by the small bike that he's looted.

The luckiest looters come down dragging cattle,
two and three apiece they've won in battle.

A goat whose udder seems about to burst
squirts her milk to quench a victor's thirst
which others quench with a shared beer, as a cow,
who's no idea she's a Muslim's now,
sprays a triumphal arch of piss across
the path of her new happy Bosnian boss.
Another struggles with stuffed rucksack, gun, and
   bike,
small and red, he knows his kid will like,
and he hands me his Kalashnikov to hold
to free his hands. Rain makes it wet and cold.
When he's balanced his booty, he makes off,
for a moment forgetting his Kalashnikov,
which he slings with all his looted load
on to his shoulder, and trudges down the road
where a solitary reaper passes by,
scythe on his shoulder, wanting fields to dry,
hoping, listening to the thunder, that the day
will brighten up enough to cut his hay.

And tonight some small boy will be glad
he's got the present of a bike from soldier dad,
who braved the Serb artillery and fire
to bring back a scuffed red bike with one flat tyre.
And among the thousands fleeing north, another
with all his gladness gutted, with his mother,
knowing the nightmare they are cycling in,
will miss the music of his mandolin.

The Fanatic Pillager

2001

Harrison, fanatique pillard.
Victor Hugo, Preface to
Cromwell (1827)

I

Rigoletto was the first grand opera I ever saw, when I'd hitch-hiked to Paris in my teens and queued for the gods at the Paris Opéra, the Palais Garnier, topped by a gilt Apollo brandishing his lyre like a winning team captain in the FA Cup. Somewhere on that day the seeds of both *The Trackers of Oxyrhynchus* and *The Prince's Play* were sown without my knowing it. I've never forgotten the experience, though I have seen countless productions since. The impression that the final scene made was profound. The storm, the stabbing of Rigoletto's daughter Gilda, the jester exulting over the sack he thinks contains the Duke of Mantua:

> *Quest' e un buffone, ed un potente e questo!*
> *Ei sta sotto i miei piedi! E desso! oh gioia!*

> Here is a buffoon, and a powerful buffoon!
> And standing under my foot! It is him! Oh joy!

The lightning flash, the thunder machine that Verdi spec-
ifies in the score, affected me more than any theatre I'd
seen since the comedians, magicians, verse pantomimes
and 1940s and '50s variety in Leeds which first made me
love and want to create theatre. The success of Verdi's opera
(1851) eclipsed Hugo's play (which was banned after only
one performance in 1832), and is often used to belittle the
original drama by critics like George Steiner, for example,
who wrote that 'Victor Hugo's *Le Roi s'amuse* is an insuffer-
able piece of *guignol*; as *Rigoletto*, it is enthralling'. It seems
to me enthralling before it was ever set to music. Verdi had
better dramatic instincts and thought *Le Roi s'amuse* 'perhaps the greatest drama of modern times', and Triboulet
'a creation worthy of Shakespeare' and, in another letter,
'a character that is one of the greatest creations that the
theatre can boast of, in any country and in all history' (23
April 1850). He writes to his librettist Piave of his flash of
inspiration:

> Oh, *Le Roi s'amuse* is the greatest subject and perhaps
> the greatest drama of modern times. Triboulet is a
> creation worthy of Shakespeare . . . I was going over
> several subjects again when *Le Roi s'amuse* came into
> my mind like a flash of lightning, an inspiration . . .
> Yes, by God, that would be a winner.
>
> (8 May 1850)

When, years later, I read Hugo's play from a copy I'd
come across on the stalls of a *bouquiniste* on the Seine, it
had the same effect on me, but instead of being created

by the music, it was induced by the unadorned verse of Hugo, who, for the same scene, where Verdi draws on the resources of a huge orchestra, and a distillation of Triboulet's speech, has a much longer magnificent tirade in his own brand of the alexandrine. It was the Hugo version of the alexandrine I'd always wanted to explore since my earlier immersion in those of the comic Molière and the tragic Racine for the Old Vic, using the same metre for different ends, and in need of radical renewal by the Romantics. The cumulative venom of the verse is redistributed in the opera to horns and strings, with the baritone Rigoletto left with only a simplified Italian couplet or two from Triboulet's French *tirade*. The unaccompanied verse works by the venomous accretions of crowing vengeance. The Jester drags the sack in which he believes he has the dead King down to the Seine:

TRIBOULET
Il est là! – Mort! Pourtant je voudrais bien le voir.

Here, according to Hugo's stage directions, Triboulet touches the sack:

C'est égal, c'est bien lui – Je le sens sous ce voile
Voici ses éperons qui traversent la toile. –

Now Triboulet puts a triumphant foot on the sack.

Maintenant, monde, regarde-moi.
Ceci, c'est un bouffon, et ceci, c'est un roi! –

Et quel roi! Le premier de tous! Le roi suprême!
Le voilà sous mes pieds, je le tiens. C'est lui-même.
La Seine pour sépulcre, et ce sac pour linceul.
Qui donc a fait cela?

(Croisant les bras.)
Hé bien! oui, c'est moi seul. –

Hugo makes the alexandrine perfectly conversational, stopping and starting to accommodate action, and then comes up with a beautifully balanced line like:

La Seine pour sépulcre, et ce sac pour linceul

and at once completes the couplet with prosaic address.

His plays represent a total reworking of the neoclassical alexandrine. It was this speech that I went to when I wanted to persuade Richard Eyre that it should be done at the National Theatre. I offered him the choice of two plays by Victor Hugo: *Le Roi s'amuse* or *Torquemada*, another powerful play on the dangers of ideology, with the Inquisitor swearing he'll burn everyone to save them from Hell, lighting bonfires from here to the stars. Both plays are well worth the resources of the National Theatre. Richard Eyre went for *Le Roi s'amuse* probably because I already had an idea for a London setting for the play.

II

The Comédie-Française actor Ligier, who was to play Triboulet, wept through the whole of Act V, which contains the speech I quoted from above, when Hugo read *Le Roi s'amuse* to the company. Hugo records what Ligier said to him afterwards: '*Ligier me disait hier à la répétition que je reconstruisais le théâtre français.*' What sort of reconstruction of French theatre was it exactly? How did Hugo and the Romantics throw off the restraints of neoclassical verse drama? Central to the endeavour was the example of Shakespeare, who combined high and low, sublime and grotesque, poetic and prosaic. Shakespeare's example stultified subsequent English drama but helped to reanimate both the German and French stages. In some ways the ghost of Shakespeare prevented English Romantic poets being quite as radical as Hugo, who was inspired by his dramaturgy but was not obliged to imitate his language. The English failure to do this is mocked by Coleridge:

> As the ingenious gentleman under the influence of the Tragic Muse contrived to dislocate 'I wish you a good morning, sir! Thank you, sir, and I wish you the same,' into blank verse heroics:

> > 'To you a morning good, good sir! I wish.
> > You, sir! I thank: to you the same wish I.'

As Hopkins wrote to Robert Bridges in 1885: 'The example of Shakespeare . . . has done ever so much harm by his very genius, for poets reproduce the diction which in him was modern and in them is obsolete.'

It was a great loss to English theatre when the great, all-accommodating flexible blank verse of Shakespeare lost its theatrical energy and poetry adopted neoclassical 'rules'. What Thomas Nashe could call the 'drumming decasillabon' in 1589 would become in the hands of Shakespeare and the Jacobeans one of the most flexible and varied metres in any language and richer than almost any other dramatic medium. That it encompassed a greater scale of language than anything else also depends on the heterogeneous audience, and audiences became more restricted after the age of the Globe. The blank verse eventually became the style parodied above by Coleridge, and we can see the process in its earlier stages in the work of Sir John Denham as early as 1642, with his play *The Sophy*, which shows, according to the Rev. Gilfillan, 'here and there an appreciation of Shakespeare – shown in generous though hopeless rivalry of his manner'. The year 1642 saw not only the closing of the theatres, but also the publication of Denham's *Cooper's Hill*, with the beginning of the monotonously regular couplet, losing the blank verse of the drama, where dramatic situations create the variety of invention in the verse, scansion being as much a question of dramatic character as metronome. Half a century later, John Dennis is regretting what has been lost and what he calls 'the Harmony of Blank Verse', whose

> Diversity distinguishes it from Heroick Harmony, and bringing it nearer to common Use, makes it more proper to gain Attention, and more fit for Action and Dialogue. *Such Verses we make when we are writing prose; we make such Verse in common Conversation.*

It was dramatic sensitivity that gave immense variety to what could be monotonous dramatic blank verse.

Verse always needs to return itself to 'prose and common conversation'. Returning verse to the realities of prose is also to acknowledge the truth of dramatic situations. When they drift apart, we tend to have our culture falling into the mutually exclusive categories of 'high' and 'low'. Verse and prose. Sublime and grotesque. As the constantly perceptive Granville Barker says, the lines of Shakespeare and the Jacobeans 'are to be scanned – and can only be scanned – *dramatically and characteristically*'. Perhaps it is even better expressed by Coleridge in *Biographia Literaria*: 'Every passion has its proper pulse, so it will likewise have its characteristic modes of expression.'

I remember having a conversation about this with Richard Eyre, who was to direct *The Prince's Play*, during a rehearsal of *The Changeling*, which he was directing at the National Theatre. He had invited me to talk to the actors about verse, as it is a sad truth that even experienced actors often have little familiarity with verse – even Shakespeare – as their careers (and mortgages) are dependent on the intimate techniques of TV and film. To illustrate the truth of Granville Barker's observation, we could look at examples from the play they were rehearsing:

> ALSEMERO
> Even now I observ'd
> The temple's vane turn full in my face,
> I know 'tis against me.

JASPERINO

> Against you?

The servant completes the five-stress line with an utter disbelief prosodically expressed in the three equally stressed syllables: 'Against you?' His surprise and mocking disbelief are part of the metre. His bunched stresses question his master's sanity. There is something similarly simple at the end of the play, when De Flores is confronted:

> TOMAZO
> Ha! my brother's murderer?

> DE FLORES
> Yes, and her honour's prize
> Was my reward; I thank life for nothing
> But that pleasure; it was so sweet to me
> That I have drunk up all, left none behind
> For any man to pledge me.

The defiant sexual relish of De Flores before Alsemero, the husband of Beatrice Joanna, and Vermandero is metrically flourished in 'was so sweet . . .'. It's a similar dramatic stress to what we find in Wyatt's line from his sonnet 'They flee from me that sometime did me seek', so misunderstood by his editor, Tottel:

> It was no dream; I lay broad waking.

Tottel, who edited the poem, didn't understand the dramatic stress of 'I lay broad waking' and printed the line as:

It was no dream, for I lay broad awaking.

Almost all critics and academics who review poetry or the theatre are afflicted with a bad case of Tottel's ear. In one of the very few good scholarly books on theatre poetry, *The Poetics of Jacobean Drama*, Coburn Freer condemns most of his colleagues when he says:

As far as the bulk of published criticism on English Renaissance drama is concerned, including criticism of Shakespeare, the plays might as well have been written in prose . . . when the verse is noted at all, it is made to sound like a background Muzak.

What the rare perceptive critic could see in Jacobean verse could also be applied to Molière:

The opinion, still often encountered, that Molière wrote 'carelessly' or 'awkwardly' usually overlooks the fact that he was a *dramatic* poet, and that alexandrines that are criticised for their ungainly style may, in their dramatic context, be the apt expression of a character's evasiveness, embarrassment, anger or pedantic self-importance, as the case may be.

We can see in *The Misanthrope* the headlong angry impetus of Alceste and that of the mollifying Philinte trying to apply the brake, and the insinuation of Arsinoe. The variations on the basically similar metrical base both distinguish the characters by a bespoke tempo and also bind them in a united fate emblemised by the shared metrical code. No one understood this fact better than Victor Hugo himself, and as he himself puts it in the great gauntlet-throwing preface to *Cromwell* (1827): '*Molière est dramatique.*'

III

So while the influence of Shakespeare stifled English theatre, because it came removed from its English, it vivified German and French theatre in different ways. In Germany, the example of Shakespeare, whom they also adapted for Weimar, helped Goethe and Schiller to create a new German drama. Goethe's *Götz von Berlichingen* (1773) 'used . . . for the first time since Shakespeare . . . a dramatic language which ranged from the coarse expressions of the soldiers' camp to the heights of poetic rhetoric'. A contemporary review termed the work 'the most beautiful, the most captivating monstrosity'. It was monstrous, of course, because it shattered every rule of French classical dramaturgy. It was in fact 'Shakespearean', and to those who cleaved to the ideals of neoclassical French, that was repellent. Frederick the Great of Prussia was one such, and even in 1780 called it '*une imitation détestable de ces mauvaises pièces anglaises*'.

Significantly, this early stage work of Goethe was written in *prose* which could pass from high to low with greater facility than the neoclassical verse derived from Corneille,

Racine and Voltaire. The increasingly classicising world of Weimar found itself less able to accommodate the Shakespeare who encompassed both low and high. Goethe's later practice was to convert a first prose version into blank verse, creating blank verse derived from Shakespeare by the rules of French neoclassical drama. As Michael Hamburger observes, 'At their most Shakespearean, Goethe and Schiller wrote their plays in prose.' As Goethe and Schiller became more self-consciously 'classical', they tried to omit from Shakespeare those aspects – the low characters and language – which were the very things that inspired the French Romantics to throw off the restraints of Racine. Both Goethe and Schiller adapted Shakespeare more to the taste of Weimar. The porter in *Macbeth* was an obvious casualty in Schiller's version. So was Mercutio in Goethe's *Romeo and Juliet*. By 1815, Goethe had come to the opinion that Shakespeare was better read than performed.

The French had their own neoclassical verse drama, with its Aristotelian unities of time and place and rarefied language and in the regular alexandrine, which a renewed acquaintance with Shakespeare helped to overthrow. Shakespeare was rediscovered by the French Romantics during the visit to Paris of Charles Kemble's company in 1827, with Harriet Smithson (1800–54), who played Ophelia and Juliet and later married Hector Berlioz in 1833, a member of the appreciative audience, which also included Gautier, Dumas *père*, Delacroix and Victor Hugo, for whom Shakespeare became the inspiration to overthrow the restrictions of neoclassical drama in France, with its unities and its diction that excluded everything prosaic. For

Hugo Shakespeare was 'the deity of the theatre, in whom the three characteristic geniuses of our own stage, Corneille, Molière, and Beaumarchais, seem united, three persons in one' (Preface to *Cromwell*).

Hugo was not, like Goethe and Schiller, anxious to delete or devulgarise the porter in *Macbeth* or exclude the Fool from *Lear*. Far from it! In his groundbreaking but rarely performed *Cromwell*, Hugo gives the Protector no less than four fools: Trick, Giraff, Gramadoch and Elespuru! It is in the great Preface to this huge play that Hugo sets out his credo for the theatre of his time. Again we find verse being renewed by plunging it into the constant flow of conversational prose, the language of real situations.

What Hugo says in his Preface to *Cromwell* is that, like Shakespeare, he wanted to run the whole poetic gamut from the high to the low, from the most elevated ideas to the most vulgar, from the most comic to the most serious, without ever leaving the confines of the spoken scene. This is the sort of poetry a man would write if a spirit had endowed him with the soul of Corneille and the head of Molière. '*Il nous semble que ce vers – là serait bien aussi beau que de la prose*' (Hugo's emphasis). 'I have flung classical verse to the black dogs of prose!' he writes in a wonderfully combatant manifesto poem which can be set beside the Preface to *Cromwell* as a central French Romantic text. Both Preface and poem bristle with Hugo's phenomenal energy:

> *Je fis souffler un vent révolutionnaire,*
> *Je mis un bonnet rouge au vieux dictionnaire.*
> *Plus de mot sénateur! plus de mot roturier!*

Je fis un tempête au fond de l'encrier,
Et je mêlai, parmi les ombres débordées,
Au peuple noir des mots l'essaim blanc des idées . . .
Je massacrai l'albâtre, et la neige, et l'ivoire;
Je retirai le jais de la prunelle noire,
Et j'osai dire au bras: Sois blanc, tout simplement.
Je violai du vers le cadavre fumant;
J'y fis entrer le chiffre; O terreur! Mithridate
Du siège de Cyzique eut pu citer la date . . .
J'ai dite aux mots: Soyez république! Soyez
La fourmilière immense, et travaillez! croyez,
Aimez, vivez! – J'ai mis tout en branle, et, morose
J'ai jeté le vers noble aux chiens noirs de la prose.

I caused a revolutionary wind to blow,
I put a red bonnet on the old lexicon.
No more senator words! No more plebeian words!
I revelled in the tempest of ink I had stirred
And blended, among all the shadows spilling out,
Swarms of white ideas with the black words of the
    crowd . . .
I massacred ivory, alabaster, and snow;
I said to arms: 'You're white, plain white, as children
    know.'
I removed all the jade from the pupils of the eyes.
I exhumed all the reeking carcasses from lines.
I used numbers. Terror! Mithridates referred
To the date on which the siege of Cyzicus
    occurred . . .
I said to all the words: 'Be democratic, give

And work with others like an anthill. Trust and live
And love!' – I started things, then mixed others with
   those:
I threw the noble line to the black dogs of prose.

The old dictionary flaunts the red liberty cap of the revolutionary. (I have one of Jocelyn Herbert's Fury masks from
the *Oresteia* on my *OED*!) Arms are simply white, not 'alabaster' or 'ivory'. He will use prosaic calendar dates, as he
did when he flung down the gauntlet in the very first line
of *Cromwell*:

> *Demain, vingt-cinq juin mil six cent cinquante-sept . . .*

Tomorrow, 25 June 1657 . . .

Words will be republican and *work*. The distinctions
between high and low are abolished. This is not a theatrical
sensibility that would shy away from *le mouchoir* as translation for Desdemona's handkerchief of Vigny's *Othello*, even
if the grand actress Mlle Mars would find it utterly objec-
tionable and ask for the genteel circumlocutions of neoclassical verse at its worst – Mlle Mars (1779–1847), past whose
somewhat stern and disapproving bust I walk when I go
to see anything at the Comédie-Française, or even when I
just pass by. Her stare looks through the glass doors of the
Comédie-Française whenever I walk from my favourite little hotel, next to the statue of Molière, to any of my favourite
brasseries. She was not hospitable to assaults like Hugo's on
'*le vers noble*', being renowned for rejecting Vigny's *mouchoir*

from his *Le More de Venise* (1829). She would have accepted the periphrastic euphemism of *'fatal tissu'* or *'lin leger'*. Snot rag was still a century away. The handkerchief became the kitchen sink of French Romantic drama. Oscar Wilde, in *The Truth of Masks*, talks about the French Shakespearean translator Jean François Ducis (1733–1816), who had to adapt the plays so that they conformed to the 'unities' of French neoclassical taste. He had great difficulty also with the handkerchief and tried 'to soften its grossness by having the Moor reiterate *"Le bandeau! Le bandeau!"'*. And a sack with a king's body in it? Unthinkable!

In 1829, a production of Hugo's earlier verse drama *Marion de Lorme* was planned, with Mlle Mars as Marion. But the Ministry of the Interior refused to authorise its performance, on the grounds of its suspected allusions to Charles X. So Hugo turned from the Comédie-Française to the boulevard theatre. The actress Marie Dorval (1798–1849), unlike Mlle Mars, came from boulevard theatre and was unused to the grand verse style and found the alexandrine uncongenial. She played at the Théâtre de la Porte-Saint-Martin, which was not subsidised by the state and less hassled by censorship. Its staple was melodrama, its audience more mixed than that of the Comédie-Française. One reason for this was that its prices were a good deal cheaper, and the writer who wrote most plays for it was Pixérécourt (1773–1844), 'the Corneille of Melodrama', who always claimed that he 'wrote for those who cannot read'.

A year before *Le Roi s'amuse*, Hugo had given his *Marion de Lorme* to this theatre, and Marie Dorval had played the title role. Romantic drama shocked this public less than the elite at the Comédie-Française. What is interesting about this experience for Hugo, who wanted to bring her to the Comédie-Française for *Le Roi s'amuse*, is that a study of the emendations he made during the rehearsals for *Marion de Lorme* reveal the influence of the boulevard actress pushing Hugo further along the road of his manifesto aims in the Preface to *Cromwell*. The manuscript as studied by the scholar M. Descotes shows that the actress was frequently inducing Hugo towards making his verse more broken up, more jagged, in short more *prosaic*. This is the kind of change that I am also used to making in rehearsals. Hugo clearly valued the experience, as the manuscript contract with the Théâtre Français for *Le Roi s'amuse* makes clear in the controversial point that it was Hugo himself and not Alfred de Vigny, her lover, who insisted on the engagement of Marie Dorval, '*sur l'expresse demande de M. Hugo*'. Hugo even threatened to take the play elsewhere if she could not be hired. She was unavailable on this occasion. Mlle Mars refused. Marie Dorval wasn't to appear at the Comédie-Française until 1834, in the role of Kitty Bell in *Chatterton*, by Alfred de Vigny (1797–1863), her lover, with whom she turned up for the première of *Le Roi s'amuse*. Mlle Mars turned up too, who had refused a role in the play and whose jealousy eventually was to drive Marie Dorval from the Comédie-Française back to the boulevards.

IV

This impulse to bring the energy of natural prose into verse is a constantly renewing strategy, as natural colloquial speech which changes rapidly can leave successive poetic styles marooned, and when poetry reconnects with prose it reanimates itself. Sometimes it means that the inherited form struggles to accommodate itself to the freedom of conversation, and sometimes, as in the case of Ibsen, it means an abandonment of poetic drama entirely. To consider the case of Ibsen is crucial for anyone who wants to write poetry for the theatre. Ibsen, who was a great dramatic poet, did not re-energise his verse by tempering it in douches of prose, but deserted the medium entirely for prose because, as he wrote to Lucie Wolf in 1883:

> The stage is for dramatic art alone, and declamation is not dramatic art . . . Verse has done immense injury to the art of the theatre . . . It is most unlikely that the verse form will be employed to any extent worth mentioning in the drama of the immediate future; for the dramatic aims of the future will pretty certainly be incompatible with it. It is therefore doomed to extinction. For art forms die out, just as the preposterous animal forms of prehistoric times died out when their day was over . . . I myself, for the last seven or eight years, have hardly written a single verse, but have cultivated exclusively the incomparably more difficult art of poetic creation in the plain unvarnished speech of reality.

This is a daunting text for the dramatic poet of our day, though I comfort myself by noting he refers to the *immediate* future. It is also some comfort to know that Ibsen told C. H. Herford, who translated *Brand* into English, that he would probably write his last play in verse, 'if only one knew which play would be the last'. *When We Dead Awaken* was his last, but I can imagine Ibsen not wanting to fulfil his promise to Herford because he would never want to face the fact that anything he was writing could be his last. But his English translator and biographer Michael Meyer wrote that he thought that *When We Dead Awaken* 'would have been a much greater play if he had written it in poetry – as he nearly did'.

V

Hugo's *Le Roi s'amuse* had its first and *last* performance on 22 November 1832. It was 'suspended' by the Ministry of the Interior. Contemporary accounts speak of the tumult in the house following Triboulet's

> *vos mères aux laquais se sont prostituées.*

Your mothers have been prostitutes to lackeys.

A review which history has dragged out of its timid anonymity, and shown to be by Lucca, described *Le Roi s'amuse* as one of the 'most grotesque abortions of French dramatic literature'. A supercilious critic said that the much-vaunted revolution in drama had met its Waterloo:

> *La révolution dramatique a été battue avant-hier à*
> *la Comédie-Française, elle est en pleine déroute: c'est le*
> *Waterloo du Romantisme.*

It wasn't played again until 1882, and a witness noted that

the respectful silence was a hundred times more cruel than the hostile cries of 1832. The actor Got, who played Triboulet fifty years after Ligier, noted in his journal that there was above all *'froideur'* and *'ennui'* in the audience. Edmond Bire: *'Le grand poète offre au peuple, au mauvais peuple, un tableau jacobin.'* He condemns not only *Le Roi s'amuse*, but also *Lucrèce Borgia* as belonging to the 'prolonged revolution'.

Lucrèce Borgia (1833) was Hugo's next play after the disappointment of the banned *Le Roi s'amuse*. He speaks in the Preface of the two plays as a 'bilogy' conceived at the same time, but with the important difference that he wrote *Lucrèce Borgia* in *prose* for the boulevard theatre, the Porte-Saint-Martin. Graham Robb, in his wonderfully full, engrossing and often funny biography of Hugo, records how the old claque of Romantics, who came as vociferous supporters to both *Hernani* and *Le Roi s'amuse*, were horrified to know that the characters of the new play would speak prose and demanded an explanation of Hugo. He convinced them that 'it was the duty of Romanticism to renovate prose just as it had smashed the old alexandrine mould'. And that in itself, if he had done nothing else, was a great achievement, even for this nineteenth-century giant.

VI

How could I bring the 'Waterloo of Romanticism' to Waterloo? As with the Paris of de Gaulle in *The Misanthrope*, with street unrest and disturbance round the corner in 1968, or with the Indian Mutiny hovering over *Phaedra Britannica*, I was looking for a way of setting *Le Roi s'amuse* in a more

familiar period that would re-energise the social tensions and clarify the corruption and anti-royal tirades of
Triboulet. I wanted to bring it a little nearer home, and
came up finally with the mid-1880s, the London of Jack the
Ripper, with its answering *guignol*, and constant rumours of
royal scandal round Eddie, the Duke of Clarence. It was the
world of that earlier Bloody Sunday of 13 November 1887,
when an estimated 20,000 unemployed demonstrated in
Trafalgar Square. Sir Charles Warren opposed them with
4,000 constables, plus Life Guards and Grenadier Guards.
And it was a time of royal affiliations with actresses, chorus
girls and comedians like Dan Leno, known universally as
'the King's Jester'. The King's Jester in my version eventually became a Glaswegian music-hall comic. I didn't begin
to finalise the comic's speeches, even though they were the
ones I was first naturally drawn to, until I knew who we
would find to play him. I would always seek to use the natural first accent of the actor, so had not decided whether
the comic was a Cockney or a northerner, a Lancashire Ian
McKellen or a Geordie, like Alun Armstrong, or, as it finally
turned out, a Scot, when Richard Eyre cast Ken Stott. I
made him a working-class Glasgow comic who found success in London and was patronised by His Royal Highness.
Ken Stott, who proved utterly brilliant in the role, bridging
the comedy and tragedy with an ease that would have glad-
dened the soul of Hugo, became Scotty Scott, with a tartan
hump made to look like the bag of a bagpipe bristling with
chanters. He became like a bitter version of Harry Lauder,
with no chance whatever of being dubbed a knight. The
way he has to ingratiate himself on stage and off to the

set that hangs around HRH eats like a canker in his soul. On the other hand, the Poet Laureate, whom I made the equivalent of Hugo's Clement Marot, poet to the court of Francis I, although like Scotty Scott also of humble origin, had totally transformed himself, modelling his accent and behaviour on the gang of witless aristocrats hanging round HRH. He becomes a genteel version of the Jester, writing the romantic chat-up lines for a prince who can't think them up himself. Verdi and Piave don't bring the Poet into *Rigoletto*. But, unbelievably, we still have a Poet Laureate, and a monarchy! It should be pointed out that I created this character out of the Marot of Hugo, and it was some five years before I wrote my poem 'Laureate's Block'!

The period we chose to set the play in was also a time when, as now, the Prince of Wales was a great asset to republican propagandists. Ramsay MacDonald, looking back on the period, writes in the journal *Democracy* for 23 February 1901, 'the throne seemed to be tottering . . . the Queen and the Prince of Wales had no hold on the popular mind; there was a spirit of democratic independence abroad; the common man believed in the common man', but is forced to add: 'That has gone.' Even Queen Victoria wrote to the Lord Chancellor when the behaviour of the Prince of Wales was increasing that democratic independence 'of these days when the higher classes, in their frivolous, selfish and pleasure-seeking lives, do more to increase the spirit of democracy than anything else'. 'Democracy' is, of course, a dirty word. It's no surprise that when the Queen saw Tom Taylor's adaptation of Hugo's play *The Fool's Revenge*, she was not amused: 'a dreadful play', she notes in her journal, 'adapted from Victor Hugo's *Le Roi s'amuse*, and the same subject as *Rigoletto*, only altered. It is a most immoral, improper piece . . .'

My aim was to bring that immorality and impropriety the unamused monarch saw underneath the play out into the open. In *Cromwell* Hugo gives Harrison, the fanatic pillager, the following lines:

Il ne reste plus rien des biens de la couronne.
Hampton-Court est vendue au profit du trésor;
On a détruit Woodstock, et démeublé Windsor.

Nothing remains of all the Crown Estates.
Hampton Court is sold to profit Cromwell's
treasury; Woodstock is destroyed and Windsor
dismantled.
(Victor Hugo, *Cromwell*, Act I, scene ix)

Egil and Eagle-Bark

2001

Aischulos' bronze-throat eagle-bark at blood
Has somehow spoiled my taste for twitterings!
Robert Browning, *Aristophanes' Apology* (1875)

I

The date on page one of the first of what became over a dozen
thick notebooks devoted to my workings and reworkings
of the *Oresteia* is 8 March 1973, about two weeks after the
opening of my *Misanthrope* at the Old Vic, which was the
home of the National Theatre before the new building on
the Thames was completed. The trilogy of Aeschylus finally
opened in the Olivier Theatre on 28 November 1981, after
a false start aborted owing to industrial disputes at the NT
in 1979. So the style of it had a long gestation, owing partly
to a protracted grappling with the Greek and partly to the
Gargantuan birth pang of a newly opened 'theatre industry' complex on the South Bank. I have written pieces for
all three auditoria of this complex, but most have appeared
in my favourite of the three, the Olivier – inspired, said
the architect Denys Lasdun, by the ancient Greek theatre
of Epidaurus, where to my great gratification the National
Theatre's *Oresteia* became, in 1982, the first foreign production ever to be presented in its two-thousand-year-old

space. One of the things that attracted me to the Olivier space was that it was inhospitable to the clichés of naturalistic drama that have become the norm on TV and in most theatrically anaemic modern drama. It seemed a space ready for poetry, a verse drama that was public and presentational and owed nothing to that of T. S. Eliot, who, perhaps apart from *Murder in the Cathedral*, forced verse theatre into anorexia in order to squeeze it into the proscenium drawing room, and made it so discreet and well bred in its metrical gentility you wondered why it bothered to go public at all. The kind of theatre I was most exposed to as a child, the last days of music hall and pantomime, introduced me to verse in the theatre in both the comic monologue and the panto, in rhymed couplets which, though often crude, clumsy and gauche, had a vernacular energy to crackle across the footlights and engage an audience. The language and the style of playing, the butch male 'dame', the glamorous leggy girl 'principal boy', have always been in my mind as something which could, given a serious context, suggest clues for a kind of theatricality I was looking for as a poet, and which made me use the languages I'd learned and the earlier poet/ dramatists to clear a space for a new verse drama.

Once I had agreed to work with Peter Hall on the *Oresteia*, I had a vivid dream – unusual because I dream very rarely. I've always supposed it's because I spend most of the waking hours of my days dreaming. But on this occasion I dreamed that there was in my hallway in Newcastle a large, rather ornately bound visitors' book, but its engraved cover read '*Oresteia*', or, to be precise, 'ΟΡΕΣΤΕΙΑ', as it was embossed in Greek script. I think it was meant as a

kind of audition roster for the chorus of Aeschylus' trilogy. In my garden at dawn, or even before dawn, there was
assembled a long queue of men, all old men. They all wrote
their names in the book and left without a word. Each of
them seemed to have no trouble with the Greek script on
the cover, and they each ran a finger over the gilded Greek
and then opened the book, ran the same finger down the
list of previous signatories and then signed themselves,
then closed it again for the man behind to read and trail
his finger on the ancient Greek. Strangely, though it was a
repeated action, each signatory brought to the occasion his
own definite individual style. When the last one had left, I
picked up the book and read the names. They were all the
names of the comedians I had seen in panto as the dame
or as a solo act, at the Leeds Empire or Grand Theatre:
Norman Evans, Frank Randall, Nat Jackley, Robb Wilton,
Arthur Lucan ('Old Mother Riley', but for some reason
without Kitty), Jewell and Warriss, etc. . . . the list went on
for pages. The kind of theatricality that they had, though
still defiantly alive in the last days of vaudeville, had more
or less disappeared from so-called 'serious' theatre, and I
carried their presences with me as a sometimes grinning
and gurning, but always supportive, chorus, paradoxically,
into the quest for an Aeschylean *gravitas*. One of the essential secrets of that theatricality, still preserved in the popular
forms, is that the audience is there to be addressed, entertained, moved, accosted, not to be eavesdroppers on some
private happening. This simple fact is behind almost all the
pieces I created for the Olivier, but perhaps most obviously
in *The Trackers of Oxyrhynchus* (1990) and *Square Rounds*

(1992), both of which I also directed, in order to allow the old men who signed my *Oresteia* visitors' book to be there at every stage of the productions. In the unashamed coupling of 'high' and 'low' the theatrical poet finds his most persuasive voice.

Leading into our collaboration on the *Oresteia*, I also felt that Peter Hall was looking in his own way for an equivalent theatricality to fill the Olivier, and very early in the history of that auditorium he made discoveries in it that, though they have to go on being rediscovered, made him ripe for our *Oresteia*. His production of Marlowe's *Tamburlaine* in 1976 was the first in the Olivier space to show its exciting potential. Harley Granville Barker had likened the relation of actor to character in *Tamburlaine* to that of the black-clad handler to his puppet in Japanese Bunraku. 'Marlowe', he wrote in one of his marvellous *Prefaces to Shakespeare*, here to *Hamlet*, 'had made the character something rather to be *exhibited* than acted.' Peter Hall was evidently of a similar opinion, and one of the ways he found of reaching this was by playing on the NT terraces to anyone who happened to be passing. He notes in his *Diaries*:

> An actor cannot speak thirty lines of blank verse to another actor's eyeballs. It must be shared with the audience – told like a story-teller.

Full daylight, the conditions in which most of the great verse dramas were played and where the actor can see the audience as clearly as they see him, is a great way to discover the nature of this kind of theatre, and clearly the cast of *Tamburlaine* learned to fill the Olivier by being in the open-air makeshift spaces of the NT terraces. On the Easter Saturday the following year, we also played *The Passion*, which I had adapted from the northern mystery cycles, outside on the NT terraces, and the experience similarly helped to unlock the public style of the drama, which was then fed into the Cottesloe performances indoors. In another note in his *Diaries*, Peter Hall observes of Albert Finney, who was to be a wonderful Tamburlaine, that he was 'in terrific form: one feels all those years of his youth in Manchester studying stand-up comics' (9 July 1976). In a similar way, I felt that chorus of old comics cheering me on to the serious business of Greek tragedy. I believe that when we started the sadly aborted first rehearsals in 1979, both Peter Hall and I agreed on the points he records in his *Diaries* for that day, 27 February:

> I started the *Oresteia* . . . Three main factors – the use of masks, the use of percussion, and the whole text being spoken by the actors to the audience, not to each other – were understood from the start.

We never got to play or rehearse on the terraces a drama that was created for the light of day. Granville Barker also wrote of Greek drama, and indeed of open-air full daylight theatre in general, that it suffered in the transition 'from sunlight to limelight. The mere transference from outdoors in will prove deadening.' All through our workshops and rehearsals we kept the original conditions in mind – large open-air theatre, masks, all-male company – not in the spirit of pedantic archaeology but in order to discover a theatricality the Olivier space cried out for and, sadly, even now, rarely gets. We weren't to know then that we would eventually take the *Oresteia* to Epidaurus, though, alas, and perhaps tragically ironic after what I have said about the theatre of daylight, the Greeks hold their festival performances at night, in lighting conditions more suitable for the football pitch than to the dark tragedy, originally flooded with spring sunshine illuminating equally actors and some 15,000 in the audience.

Looking at the theatre of Epidaurus we were to play in seven years later, Peter Hall wrote in his diary for 19 May 1975:

> I long to do a play here: with nothing, and with
> daylight, with the hillside pouring into the auditorium.
> But, say the Greeks, it is too hot. Well too hot in July
> and August, when they have the festival, but originally
> Greek theatres were built to operate in the spring, in
> March and April.

II

I brooded over my much-annotated Greek text, with its alliterative clusters underlined in red, for years, though in the period I also worked on other theatrical projects for the National Theatre, like *Phaedra Britannica* 'after Racine' in 1976; and *Bow Down*, a music-theatre piece with Harrison Birtwistle, who was to contribute the music to our *Oresteia*; and *The Passion*, from the alliterative medieval northern cycle of mystery plays, both in 1977 — all of which fed into what became the obsessive quest for the right form of English for Aeschylus.

The style I eventually came up with for the National Theatre's *Oresteia* (1981), after a great deal of experimentation in workshops with masks and music, was characterised by alliterative metrics and compound words which I invented for reasons I will explain below. Two of my Anglo-Saxon-style neologising inventions – or what I'd thought of as my own inventions – namely 'yokestrap' and 'hackblock', I recalled suddenly, at a later stage, I had lifted from Robert Browning's much maligned *Agamemnon* of 1877, though I never felt tempted to lift the more archaising, chivalric 'troth-plight', which, unlike the former examples, sounded too 'poetic' for me to want to plagiarise. I think it might be true to say that the seeds of my principal choices were lurking there in Browning from the beginning without my fully realising it.

John Keats, to whom the melody of vowels was the principal essence of verse music, spoke of the ancient Greek tongue as 'vowelled Greek'; but Robert Browning, in his probably unplayable, unperformable and even, to many, unreadable but, to me, constantly fascinating version of the *Agamemnon*, corrects Keats in his Preface and uses the phrase '*consonanted* Greek'. Though clearly both modes of articulation are necessary to speech, immoderate affiliation to or affection for one or the other can polarise poetics. Dr Johnson called English a language 'overstocked with consonants'. Henry Lawes, the composer who collaborated with Milton, envying the vowels of Italian for sung text said in 1651 that 'our English seems a little over-clogg'd with consonants'. It is only 'overstocked' or 'over-clogg'd' if you have a distaste for them or want to use vowels and their capacity for sustained drone as a sort of operatic helium. The repeated consonants of medieval northern drama helped the words to carry directly over the unstructured hubbub and bustle of a Corpus Christi crowd in the York streets.

Aristotle thought vowels were of the spirit and consonants of the body. The poetic seeks first to inhabit flesh. 'Consonants are secular,' wrote Mandelstam, 'vowels are monastic.' My poetics are grounded in the flesh and the secular. Since I was a child I have loved the consonantal play at the heart of Yorkshire idiom and was delighted, when I worked in Prague and began to learn Czech, to come across a tongue-twister, '*strč prst skrz krk*', which has not one vowel in it. So my affiliation, no doubt conditioned by my Yorkshire accent, was heavily consonantal, and my instinct was to go with the clogging but to search for a metrical current that had enough force to carry the consonantal crag-splinters with it. It is certainly Browning's feel for the consonantal, potentially clogging energy of Aeschylus' verse, his awareness of the oral physicality and what George Steiner calls the 'aural density' of the original language, that distinguishes Browning's *Agamemnon* translation. It may clog but it never cloys like so much inferior Victorian poetry. Somewhere, though, almost more than in any other English-speaking poet who has tackled Aeschylus, I have always felt, even before I began to think of translating him myself, there were clues to the way Aeschylus might sound in English in the Browning version. Already using a kind of poetic compounding, and happily combining 'grind' or 'grate' and 'strident' in the Miltonic 'griding' (*Paradise Lost*, VI, 329), both resources he would use liberally to match Aeschylus almost forty years later, Browning talks of the Greek tragedian in *Sordello* (1840) thus:

> The thunder-phrase of the Athenian, grown
> Up out of memories of Marathon,
> Would echo like his own sword's griding screech
> Braying a Persian shield –

I also took to the word 'braying', as I'd used 'bray' even as a toddler in Leeds to mean 'give somebody a beating', and to the subdued alliteration that enacts the striker and the struck in the voiced and voiceless counterparts of 'b' and 'p' in 'Braying a Persian shield'. There is also a similar pairing of voiced and voiceless consonantal counterparts in the previous line's 'sword's *g*riding *scr*eech'. The following are examples of Browning listening to that 'griding screech', that 'bronze-throat eagle-bark':

> And – so upsoaring as to stride seas over,
> The strong lamp-voyager, and all for joyance –
> Did the gold-glorious splendour, any sun like,
> Pass on – the pine tree – to Makistos' watchplace.

Or:

> The old men, from a throat that's free no longer,
> Shriekingly wail the death-doom of their dearest.

Or:

> And when a messenger with gloomy visage
> To a city bears a fall'n host's woes – God ward off! –
> One popular wound that happens to the city,
> And many sacrificed from many households –
> Men, scourged by that two-thonged whip Ares
>   loves so,
> Double spear-headed curse, bloody yoke couple –
> Of woes like these, doubtless, who'er comes weighted,
> Him does it suit to sing the Erinues' paian.

Or:

> But blood of man to earth once falling – deadly, black
> In times ere these –
> Who may, by singing spells, call back?

Or:

> And blowing forth a brisk blood-spatter, strikes me
> With a dark drop of slaughterous dew – rejoicing
> No less than, at the god-given dewy-comfort,
> The sown-stuff in its birth-throes from the calyx.

Or in Clytemnestra's dominating response to the chorus after she has killed Agamemnon and Cassandra:

> Now, indeed, thou adjudgest exile to me,
> And citizens' hate, and to have popular curses:

Nothing of this against the man here bringing,
Who, no more awe-checked than as 'twere a beast's
    fate –
With sheep abundant in the well-fleeced graze-
    flocks –
Sacrificed *his* child – dearest fruit of travail
To me – as song-spell against Threkian blowings.
Not *him* did it behove thee hence to banish
Pollution's penalty?

Browning's devices, his dragging parentheses weighted
between hyphens (no poet uses more hyphens than
Browning!) that he uses in his own poetry but on a more
colloquial base than in his Aeschylus, his crabbed word
order, his compounds, all seeking to give weight to the line,
once familiarity and fluency have mastered them, have an
indisputable force and a power uncharacteristic of English
outside its earliest forms, Milton or Browning's contemporary, Gerard Manley Hopkins. Mostly, however, sequential
meaning struggles with word order and coinage.

Browning called his version a 'transcription' rather than
a translation. This is not only aptly applicable to the deliberately non-Latinate transliteration of Greek names like
Klutaimnestra, Kalchas, Skamandros, Kokutos or Threkian,
etc. – a habit Browning bequeathed to Ezra Pound, along
with much else – but also to the way he tries to reproduce
word order and grammar. 'He picks you out the English
for the Greek word by word, and now and again sticks two
or three words together with hyphens . . .' wrote Carlyle,
who came to regret that he had personally encouraged

Browning to translate Greek tragedy, once he was faced with the virtually unintelligible text of the *Agamemnon*. The kindest contemporary judgement was that of Sir Frederic Kenyon, who called the work a 'perverse *tour de force*'. But somewhere, I think, those very perversities point the way to a means of making the text massive and megalithic, doing honour to the daunting *Dunkelheit* of Aeschylus but without renouncing the intelligibility at the heart of all theatrical communication. The sense of the weighted net of Aeschylean verse is in the Browning version sporadically, but the movement of the metric and the narrative clarity become clogged, not so much by the compounds (which are a characteristic of his original), but because of Browning's commitment to a Greek, or at least a highly Hellenised and un-English, grammatical word order. In his Preface he says he is translating 'in as Greek a fashion as the English will bear'. John Aldington Symonds, in his diary for 1 November 1888, noted:

> Browning's theory of translation. Ought to be absolutely literal, with exact rendering of words, and words placed in the order of the original.

He comes up, he concludes, with something 'neither English nor Greek'. 'Browning's translation is the nightmarish product of the nineteenth-century dream of reproducing the past "as it actually was",' agreed the more contemporary translation theorist Reuben A. Brower.

Browning's *Sordello* (1840), another of his notoriously 'obscure' productions, and long regarded as the least comprehensible poem in English, was understood by so few readers that the poet offered to publish a more reader-friendly edition in which, though he would change nothing, he would write in 'the unwritten *every-other-line* which I stupidly left as an amusement for the reader to do'. In Browning's *Agamemnon*, there is a written '*every-other-line*' which can only be the original Greek of Aeschylus. You feel you are reading one of those interlinear texts of the Bible I used to use in school chapel services so that the act of worship I always thought ridiculous would not go to waste, and I would use the occasion to learn some Greek or Latin, or sometimes Lutheran German. A contemporary reviewer of Browning's *Agamemnon* claimed that the poet, who had always 'tortured' the English language, 'now tortures it even more fiercely'. Browning's rare apologists, like his contemporary Dr Edward Berdoe, thought that it was the very ruggedness of Browning's verse that was required 'to interpret correctly the ruggedness of Aeschylus'. Browning certainly constructs a hurdle course, daunting at first sight, but once the reader learns to clear these apparent obstacles to smooth forward progress, the motion is by no means sporadic, lamed, hobbled, hamstrung or encumbered, but each leap increases the forward, even at times stylish, momentum. Browning's 'semantic stutter' can reach a weighty eloquence. What G. K. Chesterton called Browning's 'staccato music', except when it is laboured and deliberately self-retarding or struggling vainly to ignite its dragging 'lumberingness', can rise to Aeschylean marmoreal grandeur. The 'lumberingness' of Browning undermines the dramatic need for momentum. Metrical verse serves as the guarantor of momentum. 'Metre', said Coleridge, is 'a stimulant to the attention'.

The momentum should appear unstoppable and keep the spectator spellbound and therefore never able to interrupt or intervene to relieve the sufferer or prevent an enacted consequence. In this respect the audience shares something of the condition of the Greek chorus, which is drawn into performance but never intervention through action. This sets up a kind of halfway house that ensures the basic decorum of theatricality. The speech of Clytemnestra as Agamemnon walks up the blood-coloured carpet strewn for him prevents the audience, by its spellbinding rhetoric, from behaving like kids at the panto and yelling, '*Don't go inside!*'

Actors need to be encouraged not to provide chinks in the momentum when the play runs down and the dramatic propellant leaks through the overlong 'psychological' pause, or the naturalistic prosifying of rhythmical verse used, in most cases, for its very quality of unstoppability and relentless, inexorable, though not boring, momentum. Yeats was probably feeling the same when he wrote:

> But actors lacking music
> Do most excite my spleen,
> They say it is more human
> To shuffle, grunt and groan . . .
> 'The Old Stone Cross' (1938)

In the aborted *Oresteia* workshops of 1979, I listened to actors reading Browning's version aloud with some

difficulty. We also read a dozen others. As Peter Hall wrote
in his *Diaries* for 5 March 1979: 'All were totally unspeakable and undramatic.' I have always thought that one of the
ways to make it both speakable and dramatic was to find an
English verse which would have maximum *weight*, of the
kind that Browning recognised in the Greek of Aeschylus
and was aiming for in his English, *but* with a maximum
momentum.

The weight, the ruggedness of Aeschylus consists partly
of craggy alliteration and compounding. A few random
samples suffice:

τὸ μὴ βεβαίως βλέφαρα συμβαλεῖν ὕπνῳ.
(*Agamemnon*, 15)

(Transliteration: *to mē bebaiōs blephara sumbalein
hupnōi.*)

πῶς φής; πέφευγε τοὔπος ἐξ ἀπιστίας.
(*Agamemnon*, 268)

(Transliteration: *pōs phēs? pepheuge toupos ex
apistias.*)

And Agamemnon's contemptuous reference to the ashes of
Troy, with his contempt for the effeminate sighing smoke
carried by repeated 'p's:

σποδὸς προπέμπει πίονας πλούτου πνοάς.
(*Agamemnon*, 820)

(Transliteration: *spodos propempei pionas ploutou pnoas.*)

This appears in my version as:

the ashes of surfeited Asia still sighing
the sickly cachou breath of soft living and riches.

στείχει γυναικῶν φάρεσιν μελαγχίμοις
πρέπουσα; ποίᾳ ξυμφορᾷ προσεικάσω;
                    (*Choephori*, 11–12)

(Transliteration: *steichei gunaikōn pharesin melagchimois prepousa? poai xumphorai proseikasō?*)

πρὸς ἔρυμα τόδε κακῶν, κεδνῶν τ᾽
ἀπότροπον ἄγος ἀπεύχετον.
                    (*Choephori*, 154–5)

(Transliteration: *pros eruma tode kakōn, kednōn t' apotropon agos apeucheton.*
Prose translation: 'for this protection against evil, this talisman to repel loathsome pollution'.)

θεῶν τις οὐδ᾽ ἄνθρωπος οὐδὲ θήρ ποτε.
                    (*Eumenides*, 70)

(Transliteration: *theōn tis oud' anthrōpos oude thēr pote.*
Prose translation: 'not one of the gods, nor a human nor an animal ever . . .')

Or over several lines binding the grief of Electra in strangled knots:

δμωαὶ γυναῖκες, δωμάτων εὐθήμονες,
ἐπεὶ πάρεστε τῆσδε προστροπῆς ἐμοὶ
πομποί, γένεσθε τῶνδε σύμβουλοι πέρι:
τί φῶ χέουσα τάσδε κηδείους χοάς;
πῶς εὔφρον᾽ εἴπω, πῶς κατεύξομαι πατρί;
πότερα λέγουσα παρὰ φίλης φίλῳ φέρειν
(*Choephori*, 84–9)

(Transliteration: *dmōai gunaikes, dōmatōn*
    euthēmones,
epei pareste tēsde prostropēs emoi
pompoi, genesthe tōnde sumbouloi peri.
ti phō cheousa tasde kēdeious chaos?
pōs euphron' eipō, pōs kateuxomai patri?
potera legousa para philēs philōi pherein?
Prose translation: 'Slave women, you keep good
order in our house, since you are present here as
my escorts at my ritual of supplication, please
advise me about this matter: what should I say as
I pour these funeral offerings? How shall I speak
graciously, how shall I entreat my father? Shall I
say that I'm bringing these offerings to a beloved
husband from his loving wife?')

That ruggedness, that weight, that craggy mass of the verse
which Dionysius of Halicarnassus likened to those vast
piles of Cyclopean masonry we associate with the citadel

of Mycenae, and which John Cowper Powys called 'mega-lithic', was certainly given, intermittently, an English coun-terpart in Browning, who, in a letter written in 1876, a year before his *Agamemnon*, proposes publishing it along with photographs of Schliemann's recent excavations at Mycenae in 1874, where the notorious fantasist gazed on the face of a wizened anonymous mummy and called it Agamemnon.

His mistake, I always felt, even long before I undertook the *Oresteia* trilogy myself, was to dam the natural flow and current of English syntax and word order, which would have the necessary strength and clarity to move the boulders of massed meaning and craggy lexical invention, so that the dramatic momentum was remorselessly maintained, for in the unstoppable ongoing momentum, the forward drive, the inevitability of rhythmical progression lies as much in the meaning, especially of the *Oresteia*, as in any local crux deemed to deserve infinite glossing in any *apparatus crit-icus*. No one had programmes or copies of the libretto to consult at the performance of the *Oresteia* in 458 BC. There was no 'rewind' mode in the inexorable one-off of Athenian performance. Meaning was delivered moment by moment. 'No Attic dramatist', writes Bernard Knox in the *New York Review of Books*, 'could afford to leave his audience puzzled.'

A style that deliberately compels *re-reading* is not one that will communicate on one *hearing*. Weightiness in verse was a Victorian preoccupation, except, perhaps, in Swinburne, who recklessly jettisons poetic cargo to swing along with untrammelled momentum. But in Browning, though the vessel groans, it carries valuable cargo, not ballast.

On my way back from Prague in May 1976, after

researching the geographical and economic background for Karel Sabina's scenario for Smetana's *The Bartered Bride* in Bohemia, I took the train to Vienna and saw the Ronconi production of the *Oresteia* at the Burgtheater, a building presided over by an Apollo with his lyre, and directly opposite the parliament building presided over by a giant statue of Athena. I would use a projected slide of the Burgtheater Apollo in a sequence of the dictator deity on almost all the opera houses and national theatres in Europe. I filed all this away for future use in *Trackers*, and though I took notes on my reactions to Ronconi's production, I remember sitting after the show in the Café Landtmann looking at my Greek text covered with notes in different colours, but primarily I recall still hearing in my head what was a Germanic echo of my text in its stocky compounds like *Blut-Klumpfen* and *Mutterblut*. Hearing such as these, which are as natural to modern German as they were in the Old English of my models, I went back to Britain confirmed in my choices. And I delivered the first draft of *Agamemnon* on 27 July 1976, almost exactly a century after Robert Browning's.

III

Some, including the Greek scholar W. B. Stanford, see in another Victorian poet Francis Thompson's poem 'The Hound of Heaven' 'one of the most Aeschylean in English'. Thompson's favourite poets were Aeschylus and Blake, and he carried the Athenian tragedian in one pocket and the English visionary in the other when he left Preston, Lancs., for London and lived as a destitute match-seller round Charing Cross. Certainly some of his lines could be said to be inspired either by Aeschylus or, for hostile critics, by the addict poet's 'morphomania', which finally helped to kill him. Professor Stanford's citation is from 'The Hound of Heaven':

> To all swift things for swiftness did I sue;
> Clung to the whistling mane of every wind.
> But whether they swept, smoothly fleet,
> The long savannahs of the blue;
> Or whether Thunder-driven,
> They clanged his chariot 'thwart a heaven
> Plashy with flying lightnings round the spurn
>   o' their feet . . .

And characteristic of Aeschylus is this synaesthetic image:

> The long laburnum drips
> Its honey of wild flame, its jocund spilth of fire.

'Its jocund spilth of fire' is on the way to being authentically 'Aeschylean', though I find his poem 'A Corymbus for Autumn' more like Aeschylus, even if it is only because its surface paganism throws off Thompson's encrustations of Catholic guilt:

> Hearken my chant, 'tis
>   As a Bacchante's,
> A grape-spurt, a vine-splash, a tossed tree,
>   flown vaunt 'tis!

Suffer my singing
Gipsy of Seasons ere thou go winging;
    Ere Winter throws
    His slaking snows
In thy feasting-flagon's impurpurate glows!

Tanned maiden! with cheeks like apples-russet,
    And breast a brown agaric faint-flushing at tip,
And a mouth too red for the moon to buss it
    But her cheek unvow its vestalship;
        Thy mists enclip
Her steel-clear circuit illuminous,
        Until it crust
        Rubiginous
With the glorious gules of a glowing rust.

None of this is anything like as grounded as Aeschylus
or even Browning, or, as in another style contemporary
with Browning's which achieved both the weight *and* the
momentum I was searching for in my own *Oresteia* drafts,
that of Gerard Manley Hopkins, also a Professor of Greek,
who achieves both the sweep and grandeur I have always
found in Aeschylus, and which Hopkins called his 'swell
and pomp', as in these lines, for example:

Wiry and white-fiery and whirlwind swivelled
    snow
Spins to the widow-making unchilding unfathering
    deep.

'Does this not read like an inspired translation of some unknown fragment of Aeschylus?' asks D. S. Carne-Ross. Indeed it does, an inspired *Victorian* translation, and I had always felt that Hopkins, with his clotted but never clogged or cumbersome line, and his thorough knowledge of Greek, had everything necessary to render a great translation of Aeschylus, except, perhaps, like most of his contemporaries, a feeling for theatre; and if a translation is not an *acting* translation, and cannot be *played*, it seems to me to fall far short of being a translation of Aeschylus at all. If one turns, however, to an actual, though admittedly extremely youthful, piece of Aeschylean translation from Hopkins (in this case *Prometheus Bound*), the cumulative vehemence of Hopkins's own alliteratively forged verse, with its anglicised versions of Welsh metrical effects from *cynghanedd*, becomes indistinguishable from the lines any Victorian gentleman might have turned out in response to the Greek:

> Sith I loved and lov'd too well
> The race of man; and hence I fell.
> Woe is me, what do I hear?
> Fledgèd things do rustle near.

Very disappointing stuff from the poet who could come up with English lines like:

> The sour scythe cringe and the blear share come,

or as Aeschylean a sequence of lines as the following:

O then weary then why should we tread? O why
    are we so haggard at the heart, so care-coiled, care-
    killed, so fagged, so fashed, so cogged, so cumbered?

or the packed line from 'Spelt from the Sibyl's Leaves':

Where, selfwrung, selfstrung, sheathe-and-shelterless,
    thoughts against thoughts in groans grind.

or could himself write a Greek verse with qualities quite
recognisably Aeschylean:

στροφή
λόγος Ὀρφέως λύραν καὶ δένδρεσιν
καὶ νεφοκτύπων ὄρεων κορυφαῖσιν θαμά, δαμείσας
    πόθῳ,
κελαδοῦντι δ' εὐθὺς ἀνθῆσαι ῥοδοισίν θ' ἁλίου τε
    γᾶν καὶ
ψακάδος οὐρανοῦ βλαστήμσιν καλλικάρποις

ἀντιστροφή
χιόνος κρύος μεσούσας. πόντιον δὲ κῦμα
τῶν τ' ἐριβρόμιον ἀίοντ' ἀνέμων πνεύματα γαλάνᾳ
    πέσεν.
κιθάρᾳ δὲ ταῖς τε Μούσαις ὡς ἔνεστ' εἰπεῖν τὸ
    παυσίλυπον
ἀδύνατον· κατεκοίμασ' αὐτίκα πάντα λάθα.

which is a version in Greek of the song from Act III, scene
i of *King Henry VIII*:

Orpheus with his lute made trees
And the mountain tops that freeze,
    Bow themselves when he did sing:
To his music plants and flowers
Ever sprung; as sun and showers
    There had made a lasting spring.

Everything that heard him play
Even the billows of the sea,
    Hung their heads and then lay by.
In sweet music is such art.
Killing care and grief of heart
    Fall asleep, or hearing, die.

Hopkins also manages to make another light Shakespearean
air gravid with compounds we might also find in Aeschylus,
'Tell me where is Fancy bred' (*Merchant of Venice*, III,
ii). What Hopkins is doing in these Greek versions of
Shakespearean songs is making them weightier, making
them dance, but dance in Greek clogs rather than ballet slippers. It is somehow the opposite of what Gilbert
Murray does to Aeschylus. He relieves him of the heavyish
clogs in which he is brilliantly agile and gives him the comfort of slippers in which, paradoxically, he feels awkward
and gauche. It's not the light fantastic the translation needs
to trip but the gravidly grounded. Browning and Hopkins
give a modern poet *some* feeling for what Aeschylus might
sound like in English, and certainly give more clues than
the melodiously Swinburnian versions of a scholar like
Gilbert Murray. Louis MacNeice, while translating the

Agamemnon, wrote in *The Spectator* (1935) that 'a touch of Gerard Manley Hopkins might have helped Professor Murray'. He gives an example:

Thus if for

'Hark! in the gates the bronzen targes groan'

we substitute

'Hark! in the gates the bronze shields groan'

we improve both rhythm and diction and so make the whole more real.

Murray's verse always comes too trippingly off the tongue and the need to keep metrically light-footed makes him opt for what is, even for his own time, a dated poetic diction. Murray nevertheless, in his use of pronounced rhythms, rhymes and energetic, if balletic, metric, at least gives us an inkling of the momentum I find essential to deliver the dramatic meaning, though much valuable con-sonantal cargo is thrown overboard to lighten and stream-line the skiff. His versions have more feeling for the pace of the drama, even when wallowing in 'melody' and religi-ose musicality, than Browning.

When I began work on my version for the National Theatre in 1973, I had in mind two basic things: weight and mass on the one hand, and rhythmical energy on the other; the weight never quite so ponderous that the rhythm became clogged or ground to a halt, nor the rhythm so jaunty that the words escaped on the wing. In addition to this, when we take into account at an early stage the masked nature of these plays, which so many scholars, it seems to me, treat only as a by-the-way, a masked nature which makes speeches one block of solid colour rather than the lurches and subtextual twists we associate with Stanislavskian readings of more modern texts, or intimate screen acting, the sense of necessary weight and momentum is linked to a world of primary emotional colours which complicate their palate by accretion and cumulative effects rather than by a prismatic surface.

The early emphasis I'd placed on consonants rather than vowels made me keen to use the kind of actors I'd been working with in *The Passion* – the first part of *The Mysteries*, an adaptation of the northern, heavily alliterative mystery play cycles which came to complete epic fruition at the National in 1985. The work on this northern classic often betrayed by churchified gentility was also a deliberate reclamation for northern voices, part of my long, slow-burning revenge on the teacher who taught me English at Leeds Grammar School and wouldn't let me read poetry aloud because of my 'common' south Leeds accent. It was an accent that honours consonants and shortens vowels, ideal for the poetry of *The Mysteries*, written for earlier versions of that accent and, tentatively at this stage, right for the style I was looking for in the *Oresteia*. So the actors I eventually kept trying to insist on were those with accents somewhat like my own, with short vowels and a sensuous consonantal quality in their speech. Something also of the style of the medieval plays, written like Greek drama for the open air, influenced my early use of alliteration, which sends dramatic speech like a speeding arrow across large stage spaces, or across the Corpus Christi Day hubbub of crowded medieval streets. Very early in our workshop experiments the instinct for the northern alliterative style seemed to be right in one important and extremely practical respect: the clarity of language in masks depended more on the consonants than on the vowels, and when vowels were lengthened it caused a vibration in the masks that fogged the language and seriously disturbed the actors' concentration.

The concern for consonantal mass led me to alliteration with its repeated consonants, and its aid to al fresco clarity. This concern led me to invent a ghostly alliterative metre that owed something to the earliest metrics of northern poetry, and something to the earliest and most democratic drama in English. The echo of *Beowulf* seemed appropriate enough when we think of the plays of Aeschylus being described as 'slices from the banquet of Homer' and of the parallels often drawn between the heroic world of the *Iliad* and *Odyssey* and *Beowulf*, as in, for example, J. Wight Duff, *Homer and* Beowulf: *A Literary Parallel* (London: Viking Club, 1906). W. P. Ker, in his *Epic and Romance*, says of the epic clan life of early Britain: 'there is no question that the life depicted has many things in common with Homeric life'; and 'how much the matter of the Northern heroic literature resembles the Homeric, may be felt and recognised at every turn . . .' Everywhere Ker finds 'the affinities and correspondences between the Homeric and the Northern heroic world', and describes *Beowulf* as a 'Northern *Odyssey*'.

You can see the translator C. D. Locock in the 1920s making similar connections when he not only offers thirty-two passages from both the *Iliad* and the *Odyssey*, but also *Fritiof's Saga*, a nineteenth-century romantic recasting of the Norse saga *Fritiof the Bold*, by the Swedish poet Esaias Tegnér (1782–1846), who was also a Professor of Greek at Lund University.

What I felt emerging as we experimented was a language that suited the full classical mask, that had an echo of our own 'heroic' clan world and the northern energy of our earliest drama, but that would give me the resources I also needed as a modern poet.

One aspect of the style of Aeschylus that Browning tried to reproduce was his compound words and coinages. In *Clouds* (line 1,367) Aristophanes mocks Aeschylus as στόμφαξ, 'one who speaks mouthfilling words', and κρημνοποιός, which could be translated as 'precipice-spouting' or 'crag-composing', and it is an aspect of his style that has always drawn me to his poetry. W. B. Stanford likens the stylistic device of compounding in Aeschylus to 'kenning', a word derived from medieval Icelandic treatises on poetics to denote those periphrastic, circumlocutory expressions characteristic of Old English and early Teutonic poetry, Old Norse and Icelandic, with typical examples like *oar-steed* for 'ship' and *sword-storm* for 'battle', or more adventurous and far-fetched ones like *wound-leek* for 'sword'.

That great compendium of 'The Poetry of the Old Northern Tongue', the *Corpus Poeticum Boreale* (1883) of Vigfússon and Powell, singles out Egil Skalla-Grimsson, the tenth-century Icelandic poet, who lived also in Norway

and England, as a great creator of 'kennings'. Egil wrote
one of his best-known poems, 'Hofud-Lausn' ('The Head
Ransom'), an end-rhymed *drapa* of twenty staves, composed overnight, with kennings like 'wound-mews' lips' for
arrow barbs and 'woundbees' for arrows, to save himself
from execution by King Eric Bloodaxe in York in about
948. Speaking of Egil's kennings, Vigfússon and Powell say:

> In Egil's vigorous and concise figures we have the
> noblest examples of this kind [of kenning], often as
> deeply thought out and as ruggedly true and bold as the
> tropes of *Aeschylus himself*.

Perhaps my Yorkshire Aeschylus is a descendant of Egil,
a skald-kin at least! Egil's style helped the eagle to bark
in modern English. And York was also the city where the
drama I had in mind and was influenced by was created.
The spirit of Egil led me back to Aeschylus, and the 'kennings' of Aeschylus back to the saga skald.

> The Greek language permitted great freedom in coining
> words. Aeschylus made the most of this. Neologisms
> are used by him with great frequency.

Stanford quotes compounds such as ἀταύρωτος (*Agamemnon*, 245, 'unbulled'), used of Iphigenia, and the marvellous Ἀρειθύσανος ('tassel of Ares', epithet of a warrior,
Aeschylus fragment 51), and comments that they sound 'so
grotesque in a literal English version that they are usually
mitigated in translation'. Browning looked for the opposite

of such linguistic mitigation in his version, and I also took to compounding with great relish, happy to associate the 'eagle-bark' of Aeschylus with Egil the Icelander coining his kennings under the threat of King Eric's axe.

One of my favourite Aeschylean neologisms is from *Prometheus Bound*:

ναρθηκοπλήρωτον . . . πυρὸς πηγὴν (109–10)

fennel-filling fountain of fire

Old English has a facility for compounding which is characteristic of its poetic style, and I tried to use it not necessarily to match an Aeschylean compound exactly, but wherever I could as a means of also dramatising the tensions and antagonisms of the drama. There was no intention of chauvinistic Saxonising in my echoes, and echoes only, of our 'heroic' world. I wasn't intending to be like Sir John Cheke, the first Regius Professor of Greek at Cambridge, who in Milton's time 'taught Cambridge and King Edward Greek' but whose version of the gospels goes for Anglo-Saxon neologising like *hundreder*, for 'centurion'. Nor was it going as far as William Barnes, who influenced Hopkins with his *An Outline of English Speechcraft* (London: C. Kegan Paul, 1878), which comes up with Saxonising beauties like *push-wainling* for the Latinate 'perambulator', *matter-might* for 'mechanics', while 'laxative' becomes *loosensome*, 'horizon' *sky-sill*, 'embrasure' *gun-gap*, 'emporium' *warestore*, 'forceps' *tonglings*, 'genealogy' *kin-fore*, 'meteor' *welkin-fire*, 'telegram' *wirespell*. But there is something basic to English and its poetics in such 'kennings'.

In a letter to Robert Bridges, Gerard Manley Hopkins called Barnes's work 'a brave attempt to restore English to a sort of modern Anglo-Saxon, a vastly superior thing to what we have now'. Both Cheke and Barnes, and, of course, Hopkins, were in the back of my mind when I was looking for new compounds, not only to evoke the ghosts of Anglo-Saxon epic and saga, but to help lay bare tensions at the heart of the drama. And those tensions are those of the 'sex-war'. As two eminent scholars have remarked of the *Oresteia*, there is 'continual emphasis . . . on the sexual antithesis' (R. P. Winnington Ingram), and 'the clash between man and woman' forms one of the trilogy's pervading themes (Hugh Lloyd-Jones). Into that clash entered my coined compounds ready to engage.

IV

In April 1979, we had mask workshops and improvisations, and as I had done in the music-theatre piece *Bow Down*, another collaboration with Harrison Birtwistle, I made little poems out of the attitudes of the actor to his part of the story, giving to the actor's sometimes strong emotional outbursts a similar rhythmical energy, with my own improvisatory coinings groping towards the style they were helping me to find. As these early workshops included women, the sexual polarisation of the trilogy's matter was made brutally clear. Out of the actor/singer Michael Heath's Apollo, dramatically interrupted by a lightning flash that ran down a pipe into the rehearsal room, and the Clytemnestra of Yvonne Bryceland, Tony Robinson's Cassandra, Jack Shepherd's Orestes, came the frank brutality behind the sex war of the *Oresteia*. I called them 'gloss songs'. They were my way of putting myself into the same vulnerable improvisatory situation as was expected of the even more intrepid actors. These are five examples of gloss songs that survive in my notebooks, though there were many on scraps of paper that I binned as readily as the actors were ready to trash earlier improvisations for something better. I kept a few to register the vehemence and often crude responses the material of the myth seemed to elicit from the actors.

1. ZEUS

Godchamp thought himself so strong
he challenged come-who-may

Godchamp wasn't godchamp long
the son who threw him soon got thrown

Chronos Ouranos the same way
godchamps first and then unknown

so it went on: father/son
father/son again
till zeus himself's the champion

zeus the stayer sing his praise
zeus champion for evermore
Godchamp zeus the one who stays

raise the paean zeus will reign
with laws for mortals like the law:

awareness comes from pain.

2. FURIES

Son of Earth-she-god GAIA
and sky-he-god OURANOS, he,
CHRONOS castrated his own sire
and flung his sperm-bag in the sea.

From Sky-he-god's sack of sperm
oozing blood into the brine
came the FURIES whose locks squirm
venomous and serpentine.

Out of Sky's kin-mangled gender
a god now neither she nor he
sprang to hound the gore-offender
punish bloodguilt ruthlessly.

Crone-kinder never knowing childhood
she-things with one task to do
snouts pressed to the spoor of shed blood
till the killer gets killed too.

3. APOLLO

Only seven months in the womb!
Couldn't get out fast enough!
Got fattened up on nectar and am-

brosia not papmilk stuff!

Loathed that warm blood-padded cell
that grounded blimp of blood
that gorge of pulsing pinkish gel
that slime of motherhood.

Look at this lot at my feet
all tits and purple clitoris
old vulva-face, foul bitch on heat
not even scorpions would kiss.

That cunt Cassandra got the gift
of APOLLO's prophecy
but when I yanked up her silken shift
she crossed her legs on me!

The gangbang god of muscled air
I rape my crazy Trojan screw
and when she screams out: *Look he's there!*
no one believes it's true.

4. CLYT'S TITS
My suckled he-child made me sore.
He needed just more tits than two
always mewing more more more
and more he got but still not through!

I fed him first with bursting tit
my milk was warm and sweet

ORESTES grew too fond of it
tugged four years at the teat.

I gave him my own breast a queen,
my breasts were ripe and wet
I gave him to a nurse to wean
or he'd be suckling yet!

He stands before me mouth agape
as though he'd suck me if he could,
each breast throbs no no escape
both nipples ooze their motherblood.

V

'Patriarchy means all that is depersonalised, alienated, it
means multinational industry, nuclear war, urban isolation, capitalism, as well as rape, the stifling of women's
creativity and sexuality. It is a very bad word indeed,' wrote
Liz Forgan in *Women's Guardian* (20 March 1979), in an
article entitled 'Beware the Bloodthirsty Matriarchs', an
account of a Matriarchy Study Group. I was intrigued,
and as there were often days when Peter Hall was forced
to abandon rehearsals for industrial diplomacy, I invited
these 'bloodthirsty matriarchs' to come into a workshop
day to talk and debate sexual politics with the company,
and especially what they considered to be the defeat of
the Furies at the end of the trilogy. The debate was very
polarised.

The *Oresteia* is a sexual battleground. In 1886, just before
he started work on *The Father*, Strindberg, whose dramas

of the sex war are almost unbearably raw, had come across an article by Paul Lafargue, the son-in-law of Karl Marx, in *La Nouvelle Revue* (1886), entitled '*Le Matriarcat: étude sur les origines de la famille*'. This view of the trilogy sees Orestes as an almost revolutionary initiator of the patriarchal era: '*Oreste est le personnage symbolique qui doit fouler aux pieds toutes les coutumes de la famille maternelle.*' Not only did Orestes kill his mother, destroying the mystique of motherhood, but later married Hermione, the daughter of Helen, sister of Clytemnestra. This would have been incest in early societies. After Hermione he married Erigone, the daughter of his own mother, Clytemnestra, and Aegisthus.

Lafargue was, of course, echoing Bachofen. The rediscovery of Bachofen's *Mutterrecht* by US academic feminists in the 1960s and 1970s had spawned a great deal of pseudo-scholarship about the existence of matriarchal societies before their forceful appropriation by patriarchy. Perverse as much of this was, and unproven as was the historical basis, it had long roots, and most certainly gave a mythological focus to the heated discussions that we also engaged in.

Engels had written in *The Origin of the Family, Private Property and the State* that the defeat of Mother-Right, which he derived from the *Mutterrecht* of Bachofen, which he found dramatised in the *Oresteia*, represented 'the world historical defeat of the female sex'. Freud also found 'still audible in the *Oresteia*' the idea of the matriarchal social order being succeeded by the patriarchal one, but he found the transition

an advance in civilisation, since maternity is proved
by the evidence of the senses while paternity is a
hypothesis, based on an inference and a premise. Taking
sides in this way with a thought process in preference to
a sense perception has proved to be a momentous step.

For Hegel, the distinction between what I was to call *bed-bond* and *bloodbond* in the *Oresteia* was the basis of the creation of the State:

> The notion, in short, and the knowledge of the
> substantiality of marital life is something later
> and more profound than the more purely natural
> connection between mother and son, and constitutes
> the beginning of the State as the realisation of the free
> and rational will.

But the beginning of the State initiated patriarchy and all its repressions. The 'bloodthirsty matriarchs' – who were, in fact, mild but militant feminists whom I had invited into rehearsals to make the polarisations of the play palpably clear – reversed the dictum of Apollo, which I gave its stark brutality:

> the womb of the woman's a convenient transit.

This blunt judgement, though it made women in the audience at the National audibly gasp at the affront, has the support of contemporary Athenian science. Aristotle's work links biology and politics:

the female provides the material, the male provides
that which fashions the material into shape . . . Thus
the physical part, the body, comes from the female and
the soul from the male since the soul is the essence of a
particular body.

And in the *Politics* we find:

. . . by nature the male is superior, the female inferior,
the one rules, the other is ruled.

The women who came to condemn patriarchy reversed the
dictum of Apollo with quotations from Elizabeth Gould
Davis, who wrote: 'In nature's plan the male is but a glorified gonad.' Athena, who gives the casting vote to the male,
was regarded by radical feminists as a masculine fifth col-
umnist, a status confirmed by her birth (or rebirth) out of
the head of her father, Zeus. She is called by Mary Daly,
in *Gyn/Ecology: The Metaethic of Radical Feminism* (1978), 'a
puppet of Papa', 'a fembot'.

Not all the new feminists were as mildly reproving as
those we debated with. There are works which revisit the
violence of the world of Aeschylus and relish in a way
that does deserve the epithet 'bloodthirsty' the fate of
Agamemnon at the hands of Clytemnestra. In Nancy
Bogen's novel, for example:

This is what: take his phallus and put the knife to it,
and then as I watch the pain spread across his face
when he realises what is going to be, say – 'This is what

you made the child with, this is what you hurt me with again and again, and it is because of this that the people all follow and serve you right and wrong.' And with this draw the blade over it and – 'Now look at it' – fling it in his face.

Reading this we have to remember that Aeschylus uses the word 'ἐμασχαλίσθη' (*Choephori*, 439) for what Clytemnestra does to Agamemnon and I translate as 'hacked off his cock'.

Interestingly, the actor who became angriest at the feminist revisions of history was eventually cast as Apollo, who is described by Philip Slater in his *The Glory of Hera* as 'the personification of anti-matriarchy'.

One of the results of these discussions and my research and the developing process of rehearsal was that I used the facility for compounding I had allowed myself as a way of linking the clan world of Aeschylus with the Anglo-Saxon, a compounding that helped me clarify these sexual polarities, and underscoring what the aspect of Greek gender can do and English cannot. The choice of a muscular narrative energy of the alliterative line haunted by Anglo-Saxon was then able to carry on it such compounds as *bloodbond* for the claim of kinship, and *bedbond* for the claims of the marriage tie, which sound in this formation like equally matched contestants, and in the court of Athena the final choice of importance has to be made between two other words of equal weight: *bloodright* and *bondright*. So my choices began to throw up words which carried the whole tension of the trilogy. In the same way, it enabled me to underline the sexual polarities of, for example, θεός ('god') and θεά ('goddess'), which the Greek gender denotations allow to sound of equal status, whereas the '-ess' suffix of English makes the female form sound diminutive. In the same way, I used pairs like *he-child* and *she-child*.

Once I had established the principle, in the course of the trilogy I came up with compounds and coinages like the following:

bloodkin bloodclan blood-due bloodright bloodbond preybirds nest-theft childloss clanchief star-clans thronestones godstones chief-stave he-god she-god he-child she-child lust-lode man-hive sky-curse guestright godgrudge mangrudge manlord life-lot god-sop god-plea god-seer yokestrap (after Browning) godkin godstone bondright bloodright bond-true bond-proof bride-snatch love-gall spearclash shieldclang wavegrave stormflash waveforce galesqualls blood-price spoil-spouse gut-truth warcar blood-dew gore-lust grudgehound blood-quag hackblock (after Browning) dirgeclothes ghostsop godsop blood-glut grave-cups gift-glut gore-shots shrinestool ooze-clots grave-garb brute-clan netmesh blood-smog spearspoil croprot griefstrings.

Though I was overruled by the management, I had the feeling that though we shouldn't make the trilogy 'holy', we could, by segregating the audience into male and female (like a Greek Orthodox church), electrify the auditorium, and make those sex-war stichomythia go from the male or female mask to the divided banks of sexual supporters.

Ironically, the copies of my *Oresteia* text rushed from the printers for sale at the premiere came wrapped in old sheets of a textbook called *Placental Physiology*. On one page there was the sentence: 'The existence of the mammalian ovum was not proved until 1812.' And on another: 'The placenta is the fetal exchange station.'

VI

As there are three auditoria on the South Bank, it means that there are actors from three plays meeting and mingling. There was some resentment expressed by actresses about men taking over what seem like brilliant female roles in Greek drama. I half promised that I would construct a satyr play to follow the *Oresteia* and let the women play the half-men/half-goats and wear the phalluses as a mode of comment and redress. It was another enterprise that floundered because of the industrial disputes at the NT. But I never lost my determination to write about satyrs, as we cannot understand the whole experience of Greek tragedy without them, though they have perished as the divisions between high and low art hardened. I eventually created *The Trackers of Oxyrhynchus*, first in the ancient stadium of Delphi in July 1988, then in a revised version for the Olivier in March 1990. But I didn't get to see women wearing the piano-wire-stiffened foam rubber cocks until girls at the University of Durham did a production some years after.

It also led me to conceive an ill-fated trilogy, *The Common Chorus*, for a large cast of women. I also planned it for the Olivier. It was to be the *Lysistrata* of Aristophanes and the

Trojan Women of Euripides, as performed by the women's peace camp at the Greenham Common US missile base for the education of the guards behind the wire. The third play was to be a new piece by me about the origins of the machine gun, and the inventors, Hiram and Hudson Maxim. For various reasons the trilogy never happened, and history rather marooned the play once the missile base had gone from Greenham.

The Common Chorus, Part One had an energetic performance at Leeds University, but *Part Two* has never been performed and therefore lacks all the kinds of detail and radical revision I always do in rehearsals. All my pieces for the theatre are fundamentally altered and defined in rehearsals and previews. However, the third play became *Square Rounds* (1992), which I wrote and directed for the Olivier, for a group of women who played all the male parts, except for two. Only now in retrospect can I see the unity in my theatrical ventures. With its magic, transformations, song and women munitionettes transformed into top-hat-wearing males like Vesta Tilley, *Square Rounds* drew on the same early experiences of theatre that had led me to my dream of unlocking the energy of 'high' art with the more obviously demonstrable energy of 'low', which launched me into the *Oresteia*.

Square Rounds

2004

I

The date on the first of twelve notebooks devoted to the research notes, doodles, drawings and drafts of *Square Rounds* is 14 September 1975, and the play didn't see the light of day until 1 October 1992. Seventeen years of brooding! It started brewing as an idea that came from other work I'd been doing at the National Theatre: the *Oresteia*, which I'd begun working on in 1973, and *The Mysteries*, which involved years of work and months of practical workshop experiment, followed by long rehearsals. In each case, what frustrated me was that having got together a group of actors to explore a theatrical style that was not the usual inert naturalism, they were then disbanded. As these large-scale events were happening, I had hoped to evolve with the companies created a modern piece that I would write making use of the verse and acting techniques discovered during the extended rehearsals.

This never happened, although my urge to evolve a satyr play performed by *women* wearing the phalluses as an epilogue to the *Oresteia* led to my play about the discovery in the Egyptian desert in 1907 of fragments of a lost satyr play by Sophocles, the *Ichneutae*. This became *The Trackers of Oxyrhynchus*, though it was not played by women. I'd partly come up with that idea in the sometimes fierce arguments I'd had with actresses at the National about men playing great roles for women in the *Oresteia*. I had promised them and myself that I would reverse that cross-gender casting in a play one day. In my earliest experiences of theatre, men played women and women played men, and I'd always searched for ways of using these verse pantomime conventions in serious pieces of theatre. The play that started in 1975 became what was intended as the third in a trilogy about war for the Olivier, in which I would also use two contemporaneous ancient Greek plays, a comedy and a tragedy. The comedy was the *Lysistrata* of Aristophanes and the tragedy *The Trojan Women* of Euripides. The trilogy was to be called *The Common Chorus*, as it was to be the group of women encamped at Greenham Common outside the US missile base performing the ancient plays for the benefit of the guards on the other side of the wire.

The third play was to be about the invention of the machine gun, and about weapons developing as far as the nuclear. *Part Three*, on Notebook 1's first page, has a title which reads: *Maxims (or Tongues of Fire) or The American Contribution to Civilisation*. I have the names of three Maxim brothers next to the title: Hiram Maxim (1840–1916), the inventor of the machine gun; his brother Hudson Maxim (1853–1927), who developed a smokeless explosive powder called Maximite; and the final brother Leander, who died in the American Civil War at the Battle of Spottsylvania Court House in 1864. His ghost had a number of speeches, but he never emerged from the notebooks. *The Common Chorus* never reached the Olivier, and the end of the cold war rather marooned the idea of the Greenham Common setting. The versions of the ancient Greek plays are only now being given performances, and *Part One*, the *Lysistrata*, became the basis of a demonstration outside the Houses of Parliament against the war in Iraq in 2003. The third play, *Maxims*, eventually became *Square Rounds*. When conceiving the original trilogy it was obvious that Aristophanes and Euripides were verse plays and that my version would honour that fact, as indeed it had been through translation of dramas whose poetic qualities could not be avoided that I first cleared a space for my own poetic plays. But, defensive as even I am about 'verse drama', I had to find a reason for the verse of the third play.

The first justification came from my early research on the Maxim brothers with which the early notebooks are filled. I discovered that Hudson Maxim, the explosives inventor, had not only written a book called *Defenseless America* (1915), in which he describes his brother's invention, the machine gun, as 'the greatest life-saving instrument ever invented' and claims that it is 'a matter of solemn certainty that the quick-firing gun is the most beneficent implement of mercy that has ever been invented', but also a book called *The Science of Poetry* (1910), which he tells us that he spent ten years writing, in between bouts of invention and the development of explosives. The book 'scientifically' reveals the engineering of poetic form and offers many examples, all invented by himself, embedded in his appendix between Shakespeare, Milton, Keats, Shelley and other poets, in the expectation that by not attributing the quotations, his readers would mistake his work for theirs. There is a braggadocio arrogance about the whole book. He seems to place poets, whom he despises for their lack of science, in the same category that he places the pacifist or 'peace-sophist' in *Defenseless America* (1915): 'Their delicatessen natures shrink from contact with the stern, man-making realities of life. They are disciples of soft stuff. The mush and moonshine of maudlin sentimentalism are their element.' In *The Science of Poetry* he writes: 'Modern verse has degenerated largely into twaddle . . . The present-day bard goes daffodillying in the flower garden. A great part of modern verse is based on sentimental mooning and spooning, while ruby lips, limpid eyes and sunsets and moonlight are the bricks and mortar of the poet's building.'

He had written poems himself from the age of fifteen, as we learn from *Hudson Maxim: Reminiscences and Comments* (1924). He seems to believe that his smokeless powder, Maximite, and poetry have some kind of affinity, and reminds us that 'poetry and gunpowder were born about the same time – some fifteen hundred years before Christ'. Often he uses the power of the explosive to debunk the poetic. In Hudson Maxim's collection of stories about dynamite accidents, there is no more relished explosive fate than that of the poor unfortunate poet:

> It is perfectly safe for the poets to live and move and
> have their being in error, but it does not do even for
> a poet, when working with explosive materials, to
> eliminate scientific procedure, for in that case he is
> likely to get an uplift that will sprinkle the feet of
> the angels with his filamented fragments. This very

thing actually once happened in the Pennsylvania oil region when the poet laureate of his community was blessed by the discovery of petroleum on his otherwise worthless farm. One well sunk by the oil company gushed a large quantity of both oil and natural gas. The royalty received by the poet was immense. One day he conceived the idea of climbing to the top of the oil-derrick and writing a poem to vent his pent-up fervour. He had engaged the services of a photographer to catch his beatitudinations . . . The poet loosed his divine afflatus and set his fine frenzy to doing things. The following science-confounding doggerel is what he effused:

> Poetry is a divine art
> And I am a poet to the heart,
> And am writing these lovely lines
> Right where the setting sun shines,
> Just at the close of a beautiful day,
> Under the milk-like Milky Way,
> But which cannot be seen just yet though
> Because of the sunset's brighter glow.
> Yet I know it is there, and poesy may
> Raise me nearer the Milky Way.

And it did, for at this point the poet struck a match to light a cigarette, and the explosive mixture of natural gas and air about him fired first. When last seen the poet was headed for the Milky Way.

The flavour of the endorsements Hudson proudly appends to the book also enjoy playing with the idea of the explosives expert taking poetry apart:

> Your daring as a chemist in high explosives, your originality in contributing to the destructability of war as the shortest way to international peace . . . have all been outdone by your book on *The Science of Poetry*. Poetry has never been sciented before. You analyse and classify the whole mysterious compound, you label its constituents and even give receipts for remixing them to produce any kind of poetry desired as a cook would make a cake.
>
> Rev. Dr James Clarence Jones, poet and preacher

> It will give many long haired poets a shock.
>
> Newton Harrison (no relation!), noted electrical expert

> You have probably won more undying fame by your epoch-making book, reducing poetry to science, than you have achieved by making that dread *Maximite*.
>
> J. H. P. Kenyon, writer

> Your big, breezy book blew in upon us like a 'splosion of *Maximite*.
>
> Dr David Todd, Professor of Astronomy

There are two illustrations in *The Science of Poetry*, by William Oberhardt, of Hudson Maxim riding Pegasus like a bronco-buster, with Maxim's cloak flying and Pegasus trying to buck him off, the creator of Helicon's wings in frantic motion. It is titled 'Breaking Pegasus', and its sequel shows a relaxed Maxim, one hand on his hip, mounted on the docile mythical stallion, its wings trailing on the ground. This is called 'Pegasus Broken'. Mounted on the now broken-in Pegasus, Hudson has the temerity to 'improve' Milton's *Paradise Lost* and Hamlet's 'To be or not to be' soliloquy by his superior paraphrase.

They don't come much brasher than Hudson Maxim. Hudson's contemptuous hostility to and undoubted facility in the art of verse were seminal in the early doodles that became *Square Rounds*. The discovery of Hudson Maxim's debunking *Science of Poetry* gave me the licence to conceive the whole enterprise in verse. His bragging insensitivity combined with a certain poetical facility seemed to lift into the kind of theatrical bluff I needed to command the Olivier space. Inventive genius in chemistry or mechanics could manifest itself just as well in verbal creativity. Hudson has no doubts about his own exuberant talent in science and poetry. It is also interesting to note that the Swedish dynamite tycoon Alfred Nobel has gone down to posterity as an inventor and philanthropist, but it is not fully realised that the famous chemist and explosives expert was at heart a poet, and there was some doubt which path he would choose, that of invention or poetry. In March 1896, when he was, in fact, dying, Nobel wrote to Bertha von Suttnert: 'Not having been able to engage in more serious work during my recent illness, I have written a tragedy.' It was a tragedy about Beatrice Cenci called *Nemesis*.

The brothers Hiram and Hudson were very competitive

and both claimed the invention of the smokeless powder Hudson had patented. Hiram Maxim claimed that he was 'the only American that was found to have done anything whatsoever in the early invention of smokeless powder'. But Hudson contradicts his brother and says: 'In truth, not a single feature of the powder originated with him, and he himself was never able to invent or produce a powder of sufficient merit to compel its use.' With this contention fuelling their lifelong rivalry, it was easy to imagine Hiram not wanting to be outdone in versifying invention by his younger brother. What discoveries I made I put into verse, without much thought for the final context of the lines, and I have an early draft of the beginning of the poetic rivalry between the brother inventors:

HUDSON
Just to show you that versified speech
is within every competent man's reach
I shall address the audience, impromptu,
in poetry the entire night through.

HIRAM
Well, if brother Hudson can spout in verse
I don't want anyone thinking I'm worse.
If Hudson can do it then so can I.
The rest of the evening's in poetry.

HUDSON
You'll have to do better than that, brother.
That last couplet's awful. Try another.

HIRAM
I was the greater inventor of the two
and so will write a better poetry than you.

And as with Hudson's explosive, there seems to have been some kind of ambiguous attraction between rhythm and Hiram's invention, the machine gun, as was clear in the next discovery in my research: James Puckle (1667–1724), the Englishman who patented a gun with a revolving chamber in 1718 and advertised his invention in rhyming verse. I also found out that the Russian Mikhail Kalashnikov, who invented the Kalashnikov automatic rifle, the AK-47 and its successor the AK-74, wrote many lyrical poems about his invention. Metre, rhythm and ballistics seemed ineluctably bonded. And the great Italian tenor Luciano Pavarotti told the *New York Post* of 18 March 1981 that he owed his sense of rhythm to listening as a kid to the sound of gunfire between local fascists and the Germans, claiming, 'If I have a good sense of rhythm it's from having that beat of the automatic weapons drilled into my head as a child.' The headline to the interview said, 'First Taste of Rhythm: The Rat-a-Tat-Tat of the Guns'.

All these discoveries were further encouragement towards the central rhythmical energy I was searching for, but the invention of the Englishman James Puckle became even more important by the time the production reached the Olivier in 1992, during the Gulf War, because the singular peculiarity of Puckle's ammunition chamber was that it contained two forms of bullets: round ones to kill fellow Christians and square ones to kill Muslims. Hence finally my paradoxical title *Square Rounds*. Had it been the more recent Gulf War and not the first, prompted by Saddam Hussein's invasion of Kuwait, I could have extended the irony of my chosen title up to the minute. The cluster bombs which were used illegally by the so-called coalition in bombing Baghdad and elsewhere once contained bomblets full of round metal ball bearings. These were then 'improved' by substituting cubical for spherical rounds to make them, as with Puckle's square rounds, more painful. The ingenious inventor then made these cubes plastic so as not to be detectable by X-ray.

The passion for rhyming in two of my scientific protagonists in their recorded lives was sufficient to get me started on the play. At the time I was scanning the poetic credentials of my weapon inventors to give an authentic base to their bragging self-approval and advertisement for self, explosive or innovative ballistics, I was unaware that Fritz Haber, the pioneer first of nitrogen fixation, for which he later won the Nobel Prize, then of chlorine gas as the invention to break the deadlock of the First World War created by the Maxim gun, was accustomed to penning verses and also even ordering apparatus in his lab in rhyming couplets, provoking his colleagues to respond in kind. Discovering this made me sure that the verse forms I had chosen were on the right lines and launched me into early drafts.

II

Serendipity and omens are important to me in the early stages of searching for the shape of a theatrical piece. On page 9 of Notebook 1, I have copied from Hudson's book what he writes on Hiram: '. . . and at the end of his days suffering from bronchitis he invented an inhaler, hailed by Harley Street, and inhaled by grateful asthmatics everywhere. It eased the pain of those whose lungs had been destroyed by gases invented by the equally ingenious. Remembering the Indians of his boyhood in Maine, he called his invention, his inhaler, the Pipe of Peace.' This led on the same page to my doodling the following verse quatrain:

> He invented an inhaler *hailed* (pun! pun!)
> though never quite as much as was his gun,
> by Harley Street, and inhaled by those who'd been
> gassed at Ypres by lung-ravishing chlorine.

– and scribbled after the glued-in typescript is 'by that inventor, Haber'. Not long after, I found an intact 'Pipe of Peace' in a Newcastle junk shop, which I took as a favourable omen. It had the delicate glass inhaler, the chemicals and the instructions. In my imagination the two inventions of Sir Hiram Maxim were related, and the cough that racked him in his final years became the sound of his machine gun, complete with eerie ricochet. This bronchial onomatopoeia was extended also to the Chorus of Munitionettes, as the women who worked in the munitions factories filling shells with trinitrotoluene (TNT) were racked with coughing. According to an article, 'Observations on the Effects of Tri-Nitro-Toluene on Women Workers', in *The Lancet* 2 (12 August 1916), by two women doctors who itemise the coughing, another effect on the Munitionettes was that their skin turned yellow. They were called 'canaries'. This fact I stored away, and it helped to bring about my finale transformation into China.

I spent time researching the consequences of gas attack other than Hiram Maxim's invention of an inhaler which soothed the lungs of those exposed to gas on the French front, or trinitrotoluene on the home front. I played a good deal with an account of one gas victim at the front, whose experience had global consequences:

> The piercing pain in my eye sockets was diminishing; slowly I succeeded in distinguishing the broad outlines of the things about me. I was given grounds for hoping that I should recover my eyesight, at least well enough to pursue some profession later. To be sure I could no longer hope that I would ever be able to draw again . . . I decided to go into politics.

This victim's account of being gassed was by Adolf Hitler. I even doodled with a song for Hitler. There was first a chorus of what I called the 'reassembled men', for which I was going to use the conjuror's device of the 'sphinx box' invented by Thomas Tobin in 1865. I even worked out, with Ali Bongo, my magic consultant, a way of bringing on a chorus of blown-off heads which sang! The sphinx boxes contained various heads of those blown apart by explosives. Fritz Haber conducted their song.

Having caught a bomb and been beheaded
the head blown several yards from all the rest
with never any chance of reuniting
I'd say explosives are the weapon to be dreaded
and death Professor Haber's way is best
and I'd prefer it any day to Maximiting.
I'd sooner live but if it's fated then I pray
Lord send me death Professor Haber's way, *etc., etc.*

Then there was a kind of counter-chorus of gassed men, their bodies intact, but like the line of men with bandaged eyes in the painting by Sargent in the Imperial War Museum. One of these reveals himself as Adolf Hitler, who reprises the lines of the first chorus:

I'll rule my country and one day I'll slay
millions Professor Haber's way.

Then the ghost of Clara Haber, the scientist wife of Fritz, who killed herself through shame at his actions, sang:

Fritz never lived to see his fellow Germans use
his form of killing on his fellow Jews.

A song by Adolf Hitler reminded me too much of 'Springtime for Hitler', in the film *The Producers*, and it was soon stifled, though I believe many round me were thinking that *Square Rounds* would be the perfect sure-fire vehicle for the Zero Mostel/Gene Wilder theatrical investment scam where all the investors lose their money! Only Clara's song survived.

Another victim of mustard gas in the Battle of the Marne in 1918 was the father of General H. Norman Schwarzkopf, 'Stormin' Norman', in charge of Operation Desert Storm in the Gulf War. I was particularly interested in this, as not only did his father's experience greatly influence the son's rigorous anti-chemical weapon drills, but also because General Schwarzkopf was a keen amateur magician whose speciality was pulling flags or multicoloured silk napkins out of his mouth!

III

It was a photograph of Sir Hiram Maxim standing above the then Prince of Wales, the future King Edward VII, who is trying out the Maxim machine gun, that first made me think of magicians. They are both wearing the top hat and tails of the traditional conjuror. Top hats were an early addition to the emblems with which I was juggling. The image of the inventor (in Fritz Haber's case, the successful fixation of nitrogen from the atmosphere was likened to plucking bread from the skies) was close to that of the conjuror bringing novelties from his top hat. And from the top hat came silks, as from the mouth of General Schwarzkopf. It so happens that the dyes that created the most colourful silks, like violet, could be used as the base of phosgene gas, which was more poisonous than chlorine. And as William Moore tells us in his book *Gas Attack! Chemical Warfare 1915–1918* (1987), 'In the First World War the German chemists switched from making dyes to mustard gas and back with extraordinary rapidity.' It is true that most First World War gases could be manufactured in bulk using the same methods and machinery that were normally used in making dyestuffs, and as Robert Harris and Jeremy Paxman point out in *A Higher Form of Killing: The Secret Story of Chemical and Biological Warfare* (1982), 'the chlorine that poisoned our grandfathers at Ypres [was] available thanks to our grandmothers' desire for brightly coloured dresses'. At the start of the war, Germany produced 75 per cent of the world's dyes. From these facts it was an easy step to imagine silks of various colours representing poisonous gases produced from the top hat of their inventor. Silk and top hats became a basic metaphor of the piece.

A chemist who had learned much in dye factories was Fritz Haber, though he left the job as soon as he could and only took it in order to escape another job where Justus von Liebig's process of making fertiliser from dissolving bones in sulphuric acid made what Haber called 'a little known town in Galicia', Poland, pungent and repellent. Although in another early draft I allow Fritz Haber to mention that he learned his chemistry at his father's dyeworks, in the final draft I do not allow this Jewish inventor of poison gas to unearth the dreadful irony of the place of his previous employment. I did write it, though:

FRITZ HABER
After leaving university it was hard to get a start.
I think that anti-Semitism played a major part.
My first job was in a distillery in Budapest
making *Schnapps* from apricots, a drink that I detest.
Then more appropriate work but in a place much too
     remote

in Galicia, called Auschwitz, a town of little note
except that it possessed, ever since von Liebig's time,
a factory for synthesising phosphates of lime
by the fertiliser process he was first to pioneer.
The work was menial. I left Auschwitz in a year.
The work was not what men with doctorates do
and I quit Auschwitz in 1892.
Most chemistry, I do admit, is likely to offend
the nostrils but Auschwitz was the end.
Bones in sulphuric acid being rendered down
sent out a stinking pall that choked the town.
Both jobs were so frustrating I ended trying
to work with my father in merchandising dyeing.

I think this was one of those cuts, and there were many, that occurred when I would see out of the corner of my eye my assistant and stage manager Trish Montemuro making vigorous scissor movements with her fingers. She was usually right, but if the composer Dominic Muldowney ever writes the full-blown opera of *Square Rounds* he keeps promising, I think the almost too terrible irony of Haber's early employment will have to be reinstated, as maybe the aria for the blinded Hitler, and the square rounds of coalition cluster bombs.

IV

Fritz Haber claimed that he created the nitrogen-fixation process to make the world greener, more fertile, and it was others who used the nitrates to manufacture deadly explosives:

HABER

NH_4NO_3 and $(NH_4)_2SO_4$
fertilisers, Clara, not materials of war.

Duality reigns. It wasn't my decision
to have my ammonia turned into ammunition.

Think of fire, you fire pots with it, you bake
a crusty loaf with it, a Christmas cake.
You keep warm with it in winter, cheer the night
with the controlled glow of candlelight,
but when a building or a city goes up in flame
the destructive element is chemically the same.
Did Prometheus think he was giving man the means
for blowing the world up into smithereens?

And it was probably budget that forced me to jettison a notion and its speeches involving another use for nitrates, apart from fertiliser and explosives: namely as film. Hudson Maxim also made a film, called *The Battle Cry of Peace*, based on his book *Defenseless America* (1915), to encourage the USA to arm. Film is another nitrate composition, and can as it decomposes be explosively volatile. It was another element I had wanted to use, to recreate the film with my women actors. So I wrote a song for Hudson Maxim boasting of the effect of his film on the USA and its showing in London, but regretting that the cellulose in it was now too volatile to use. Only the first three stanzas of the following survive in the final draft.

HUDSON MAXIM

What Fritz Haber's done, that ingenious Hun,
Europe's first ammonia synthesiser,
is to create a supply of nitrate
for the bullets and shells of the Kaiser.

The German supplies are now on the rise
when they'd almost dwindled to zero
when the Brits' naval forces blocked Chilean sources
conjuring nitrates made Haber a hero.

Because his side got a boost from the nitrates produced
from the endless supply in the air
it's the year that I say to the USA
wake up, get armed and prepare.

My eloquence on the theme of defence
soon got my countrymen scared.
I made them aware that they should prepare
and, after my book and my film, they prepared.

If nitrates from the skies both fertilise
and make TRINITROTOLUENE
the stuff also goes into cellulose
and puts movies that warn on a screen.

And just down the road your Government showed
the film that first terrified the USA
in the open air in Trafalgar Square
and when they saw it they joined up right away.

When the Germans invade us it shows that the raiders
would kill all the menfolk first
then after that slaughter every mom, wife and daughter
would be subjected by Huns to the worst.

Once they'd had a good gander at my propaganda
they soon wanted to arm for the fight.
I couldn't have been prouder of my smokeless powder
when they stocked up with my *Maximite*.

And I must mention my brother's invention
the greatest thing ever for saving of life.
You'll bless my brother when Huns lecher your mother
or turn lustful eyes on your wife.

I'd like to replay that old film today
that you used as recruitment aid
but what scared the US is a volatile mess
and the film it was made of's decayed.

Best not to get too close to that cellulose
or you might well end up blown apart.
But the US of A is so armed today
thanks to Hudson Maxim's eloquent art.

I don't wish to boast but I've done the most
of any to win you this war.
I was the one got the Yanks on the Hun
with a film fifty millions saw.

And my book did impress the entire US
just how grave the matter could be
and once properly prepared war was declared
and if anyone's to be thanked then it's me!

Maximite, Maxim gun, will demolish the Hun
when the full might of the States attacks him,
He won't stand a chance once the Yanks get to France
and they're coming to France thanks to Maxim.

V

Once I had entered into the imagery of conjuror and magician, I thought of a performer I greatly admired, and wanted him to bring his unique skills to the idea of transformation as a basic image of chemistry. He was Arturo Bracchetti, the Italian quick-change genius. In Italian the art of quick change is called *Fregolismo*, after its star practitioner, Fregolo, who used to do an act with an orchestra conductor's podium, and who would appear instantly transformed into, say, Beethoven or Wagner, whenever their music was playing. I have only found one example in English music hall, and that was a woman known as 'the Incomparable Vonetta', who flourished in the halls between 1906 and 1914. A poster of the period announcing 'Mademoiselle Vonetta, the Only Lady Illusionist, Protean and Quick Change Artiste' shows a long queue of male and female figures in various costumes and uniforms, all instant transmogrifications of the Incomparable Vonetta. Arturo Bracchetti had carried the art of quick-change to incomparably brilliant heights.

The piece was performed by a Chorus of Munitionettes who were 'transformed' by visiting the WC cabinet into the male scientists. It was meant as the kind of transformation that happened in the chemistry that was the core of the theme. But also behind it, apart from the fact I like cross-gender playing, was the idea that all the men had gone to the front, so that there were none left to play the male characters. The only men were the old, as with Sweeper Mawes, who opens the play, and those who had returned from the trenches seriously traumatised, as in the character I wanted Arturo to play. I wanted him to change from the shell-shocked man into the soldier he had been at the front, and then into a woman in the black clothes and veil of the widow. The shell-shocked man inhales laughing gas from the top hat left by Justus von Liebig, rushes behind a pile of crates and emerges immediately as a soldier, who then runs towards the audience, and as he does so, is metamorphosed into a widow. I got everything I'd asked for, except that Arturo added, for good measure, a lighted candle in the hand of the widow. When I saw the final result I could scarcely believe its brilliance. And for the finale he devised a spectacle of instant transformation of what were meant to be clouds of poisonous gas in the sky into Chinese silk costumes. I still think of it as one of the most beautifully theatrical things I have ever seen. He is an artist I humbly salute.

VI

And I can't write an introduction to *Square Rounds* without saluting my treasured collaborator of twenty years, the designer Jocelyn Herbert, who died on 6 May 2003. She was utterly essential and utterly supportive in our work on *Square Rounds*, as she had been on all ventures from the *Oresteia* (1981), *The Trackers of Oxyrhynchus* (1988), *The Kaisers of Carnuntum* (1995), *The Labourers of Herakles* (1995), the feature film *Prometheus* (1999) and *Fire and Poetry* (Theatre Olympics, Shizuoka, Japan, 2000), to my next work for the National Theatre, as yet uncompleted, which we were discussing up to an hour before she died.

I had been thinking about *Square Rounds* and collecting material for about twenty years, and as with any long and layered project, it needed a bold simplification to resolve its tensions and contradictions. There was no one better to talk to at this stage, before even the workshop text had been written, than Jocelyn. She had an ability to share a vision, and without making it conventional, to find physical images to earth the lightning. She was extraordinarily patient with my crude sketches and kindergarten collages. I bombarded her with images of men in top hats: the gentleman 'inventor' removed from the bloody action he contributes to; the conjurors producing silks from their top hats; the formal funeral director; Vesta Tilley; Burlington Bertie. What resulted was a beautifully formal black circle on a white floor, with three screens on which were projected images of blasted trees which could have been from the shell-shattered landscapes of the First World War or from the acid-rain-wasted landscapes of polluted Europe. I thought she made the Olivier look as beautiful as it had ever looked. Whatever else it was, I believe that *Square Rounds* produced one of the best designs Jocelyn had ever done.

After long periods of despair about finding a style, we had workshops which involved Jocelyn, the magician Ali Bongo and Arturo Bracchetti, the Italian quick-change genius. She warmed to their inventiveness and painstaking practicality, which she recognised as close to her own, and the style of *Square Rounds* emerged from the month in the NT studio and long subsequent sessions at her own studio before the beautiful model that she always made for a production. I loved these visits to Princedale Road, sitting for hours with a glass of her favourite Pouilly-Fumé or retsina, moving the cut-out figures stabilised with blobs of plasticine about the modelled Olivier stage. Even before the text was finalised, this process helped me to clarify the quite complicated things I wanted to explore. It was for me a deeply important process because behind it I detected, in both designer and poet, a need to make (or remake) the theatrical process more organic, to rescue the actor and text from the suffocation of naturalism or from being dwarfed by high tech. I felt in those sessions that it was possible to create a new poetic theatre that drew from the past, but which looked straight into the depths and disturbance of our own times.

There were two 'eureka' moments in *Square Rounds* that I celebrate. One was when we were poring over albums of photographs in the Imperial War Museum. We were looking at pictures of Munitionettes for costumes and factory routines, and we also looked at the sections on Gas. I was struck by the variously improvised gas alarms: a gas sentry striking a bell hung from three lashed poles in Fleurbaix in June 1916; another picture of three lashed poles, but with a dangling iron bar to be struck in the event of gas; a soldier using a frying pan as a gas alarm; a gas sentry with a large gas gong in Combies in March 1917; an improvised gas alarm made from a metal oil drum struck with a large stick; a giant metal triangle for gas alert; large metal tubes of various sizes hung in different ways; a gas-alarm horn; bells of various sizes, including church bells used as gas alarms; a bell hung from a structure like those I'd seen in Japanese temples. The Chinese invented, developed and perfected tuned bells in about 600 BC. I proposed to Dominic Muldowney, the composer, that we combine all these sounds into a chaotic crescendo of panic, which then gradually turns into Chinese music to introduce a Chinese finale in which all the inventions boasted of by Maxim and Haber had been thought of over a thousand years before in China. This gave my Italian quick-change genius Arturo Bracchetti his greatest opportunity.

The second 'eureka' moment was after a very long session in Jocelyn's studio with the model, going through scenes over and over, when she put up the scene where the invention of gas for use in mass destruction is represented by beautifully coloured silks falling from the flies over the black circle in succession. These suddenly beautiful silks produced from the 'top hat' were, paradoxically, the poisonously lethal gases from chlorine to Zyklon B, and they would hang there until Arturo Bracchetti, as the Chinese conjuror, would redeem them in the costumes he transformed them into for himself and the chorus of Chinese Dancers. It had the qualities I had hoped for, that I had seen in my mind's eye but couldn't see before my very eyes until Jocelyn's vision and practical patience had given it substance. I was very moved by what I saw because I also knew that it was inspired by the Matisse of the late collages, an artist we both adored.

I often suffered from self-doubt over the difficulties of this piece. The theatricality it demanded from the performers was mostly alien to their narrow naturalistic fixations, and although Jocelyn often disagreed with me over details to which she was vigorously opposed, she was never once unsupportive and I have never known her to be negative. If I had nothing else to be grateful to her for, and I have much more than I could ever give words to, then I will never forget her loyalty, both artistic and personal, during this very ambitious enterprise, when many people around us were losing faith. What was remarkable, I remember thinking once, though after all I have known of her I shouldn't have been surprised, was that the oldest member of the company was the most adventurous spirit in the room.

VII

There was a memorial for Jocelyn Herbert at the Royal Court Theatre on 12 October 2003, at which I recalled the last weekend of my dear friend and collaborator in, more or less, the following words:

'Your spirit lifts with the wonder of being there,'
Jocelyn once wrote about Delphi. She had a glorious
capacity for wonder. There were many times I saw
her spirit lift like that, and one was on the Sunday,

the day before she died. We were out at Andrew's
Farm, the cottage that Jocelyn had bought with
George Devine. On the Saturday night we had a
belated celebration of my birthday, which had been
the week before. Jocelyn surrounded a chocolate cake
with camellias. It had candles and I blew them out.
We were all laughing. Trish [Montemuro] cooked a
delicious roast lamb. Jocelyn had put cowslips on the
table and Sian [Thomas] had brought some bluebells
back from her walk to add to them. Yellow and blue,
the great affirmative colours. Sun and sky. Matisse and
Hockney. Sian described the wood, which had bluebells
as far as the eye could see. I suggested we should all
go on Sunday. As she became a little frailer, Jocelyn
would normally let us go for even such a short walk
by ourselves, but this time she decided she wanted to
see the wood full of bluebells, and we all walked gently
there at Jocelyn's pace. When she saw the bluebells she
was so happy. She made us put our heads from side
to side so that we would see the flowers like a delicate
mist change from mauve to blue to purple. As we all
did this we noticed that in front of us two young deer
were watching. Then they flew over the blue clouds and
away. Jocelyn's face was lit with happiness. I saw that
her 'spirit lifted with the wonder of being there'. These
words of Jocelyn's I've used are from an account she
wrote of working with me in Delphi where we first did
The Trackers of Oxyrhynchus in 1988 and another piece
called *The Labourers of Herakles* in 1995:

When you find yourself in Delphi, drinking from the
Kastalian spring before walking up the Sacred Way to
the Temple of Apollo, up again to the ancient theatre
and further still till you come to the vast stadium and
you look up and see high above you the eagles wheeling
majestically round the mountain peaks as they did
centuries ago, then the isolation, fragmentation and the
sense of the futility of much of our modern way of life
falls away and you feel in touch and linked to those ghosts
of far-off times and your spirit lifts with the wonder of
being there.

I must have done that walk at least thirty times with
Jocelyn. There was never once when she didn't find it
thrilling. We did it for the last time in 1998 and she
felt triumphant that she'd still been able to make the
climb. I did it again myself three weeks ago and missed
Jocelyn every inch of the Sacred Way.

On Monday, the day Jocelyn died, we talked a lot
about Delphi, as we often did. Jocelyn insisted that
she would cook lunch and she made her delicious
scrambled eggs and smoked salmon and we drank
retsina outside at the table under the May tree. The
retsina always made us talk about Greece. And we
talked for hours. About Delphi. About the first time I'd
taken her there twenty years ago.

It was somewhere she had discovered with George
[Devine], and I always felt she included his spirit in the
work we did there. We talked about recces to Delphi,
our favourite part of the work process, with some free

time to swim and explore and to talk at a table outside into the night about the work. The recces to Delphi with Trish and Vicki [Hallam]. The recce with Sian for *Prometheus.*

We must have been about ten times to Delphi together, our spirits full of the wonder of being there. The last time was in 1998, and Jocelyn, Sian and I all went down every day for a swim in Galaxidi. And after to the same wonderful fish taverna, Tassos. There was no one else there swimming. There were pine trees to give shade. We were all treading water together in the sea and we looked up and above us was Delphi on the mountainside, where we did our work together, and above it Mount Parnassus, the home of the Muses. We floated, gazing, full of 'the wonder of being there'.

We remembered all these things about Greece in our sunny conversation on Monday under Jocelyn's May tree. In fact, we covered all the work we'd done together, our 'adventures', as she called them, with undiminished enthusiasm. The things we'd done in Delphi and at the National, and many projects we'd worked months, even years, on that were abandoned: an opera on Medea at the New York Met; a trilogy set at Greenham Common; a fragmentary piece of Euripides where we'd worked out how to fly a singing hang-gliding chorus from the Phaedriades into the Delphi stadium.

And we talked a lot about what was probably our greatest 'adventure', in Carnuntum, on the Danube between Vienna and Bratislava, about the lions and

tigers we had beneath the audience's seats in the
Roman amphitheatre, about the bears that got loose,
and about the speech I'd written for Sian, which Jocelyn
loved as much for the way it came about as for its
quality or content.

I'd been rehearsing a very incomplete text and we
were about to leave for Austria. Sian said, 'I wish I
could come and see it.' I said, 'You can if you are in
the play.' 'As what?' she said. I said, 'As the Empress
Faustina, the wife of Marcus Aurelius, the philosopher
of tranquillity, and the mother of Commodus, one of
the most violent of all Roman emperors.'

I went home to Newcastle, wrote a speech for
Faustina, faxed it to Sian. She went with the fax to
Jocelyn in Princedale Road. They read the speech
together and they went off to the Portobello Market.
Jocelyn found a long red drape in an Indian shop. On
the way out they noticed a dummy in the window
with grey velvet and jewellery. Jocelyn said, 'That's
her,' and bought the velvet, the necklace and bangles.
And the very next day we all flew to Vienna, drove to
Carnuntum and started rehearsing.

And we talked about our epic journey for our film
Prometheus, when at the age of eighty-one she rode
on a truck with me through Germany, Slovakia, the
Czech Republic, Hungary, Romania, Bulgaria, and back
to the Greece we loved. And on the day she died she
reminded me how I filled my straw hat with mulberries
I'd picked from a tree while setting up a shot in
Bulgaria and brought them for her. There are not many

people who would inspire a man to fill his straw hat with mulberries. But Jocelyn was the sort of Muse you made those kinds of offerings to. They were received with her unique joy.

As well as all our many adventures we also talked about death, as we often did, under the May tree, sitting in the sun. She said how she wanted to be – 'sprinkled' was the word she used – she wanted to be sprinkled at Andrew's Farm to be with George. I said how most people in my family had been doing something one minute and the next were dead: my mother, my father, my grandfather, who got a pint of beer from the bar, sat down, took a sip, put his glass on the table and died. 'How wonderful!' she said. Then she said, 'Do you remember in Delphi how you used to read those beautiful poems you wrote about your mother and father's deaths, as we sat on the balcony overlooking the sea of olives and our swimming place in Galaxidi?' I did remember. I was sitting on that same balcony three weeks ago missing Jocelyn and remembering her final day. It was on our last trip to Delphi in 1998. Sian said, 'He's just written a new one that was published the other week in the *London Review of Books*.' Jocelyn said, 'Oh, read it to us, darling.' We were still sitting under the May tree and I read the poem. It's about a large clock over a jeweller's called Dyson's in Leeds, under which my mother and father used to meet when they were courting. But it is also about Time, that brings us all together in the end.

'Under the Clock'

Under Dyson's clock in Lower Briggate
was where my courting parents used to meet.
It had a Father Time and *Tempus Fugit*
sticking out sideways into the street
above barred windows full of wedding bands,
'eternities' to be inscribed with names,
like that I felt on Dad's when we held hands,
or on Mam's crumbling finger in cremation's flames.

Today back on Briggate I stopped and saw
the red hands on the Roman XII and V
those lovers won't meet under any more,
glad stooping Father Time and I survive.
I see the scythe, the hourglass, the wings,
the Latin you'd proudly ask me to construe
and think of the padded boxes with your rings,
under the clock to keep our rendezvous.

'Oh, that's beautiful,' Jocelyn said. 'Beautiful.'

'"Under the Clock",' she repeated the title. 'And here
we are,' she said. 'Under the May.' Then she said, 'The
May is all the more beautiful when you're also aware
of Father Time.' It was as if she were saying that the
wonder of being there or anywhere was enhanced by
the awareness that one day you wouldn't be.

'We're here under the May and we're blessed,' said
Sian.

'Yes, we are,' Jocelyn said. 'Blessed that we know one

another, blessed that we are here together in the sun on this beautiful day.' And we all sat quietly absorbing that feeling of being blessed by the place, the day and the bond of our deep friendship and our work. Then Jocelyn went to have a sleep and we washed up.

And if we'd reminisced in the sun about our glorious adventures of the past, in the evening over supper we had a wonderful conversation about the new play of mine she was going to design. She was very focused and kept challenging me to make what I was after clearer and clearer. And she helped me over a real block. I said I was sorry that on the recce for this we wouldn't be able to swim or drink retsina in Delphi, but may need to go to the Arctic Circle to view the Aurora Borealis.

'But that would be wonderful,' she said. 'I can't wait!' A few minutes later she went upstairs, sat on the bed, and died.

Her bedroom window was open to the night, the moon and the scent of the May tree we'd sat under talking and drinking half the day.

Recces were our favourite part of work, though we loved the work too.

Over our sunny lunch we'd talked about our work and recces to Delphi, to Carnuntum, to Elefsina, to Japan, and only last year to Los Angeles.

I think of her now on a recce I can't join her on just yet.

I think again of her climbing the stairs after we had had our wonderful conversation and think now again of how she wrote about Delphi:

When you find yourself in Delphi, drinking from the
Kastalian spring before walking up the Sacred Way to
the Temple of Apollo, up again to the ancient theatre
and further still till you come to the vast stadium and
you look up and see high above you the eagles wheeling
majestically round the mountain peaks as they did
centuries ago, then the isolation, fragmentation and the
sense of the futility of much of our modern way of life
falls away and your spirit lifts with the wonder of being
there.

She had a beautiful capacity for wonder.

This time she climbed further still, and three weeks
ago I swam as I swam with her in Galaxidi as recently
as 1998, and I looked up and saw Delphi, and above
Delphi, Mount Parnassus, the home of the Muses,
where I know she has joined them and will be inspiring
me and all of us for the rest of our days.

All our spirits have been lifted by the wonder of
Jocelyn being here.

[Newcastle-upon-Tyne]

Weeping for Hecuba

2005

> What's Hecuba to him, or he to Hecuba,
> That he should weep for her?
> *Hamlet*, Act II, scene ii

Though no doubt the original Athenian audiences wept for Hecuba in the two plays of Euripides in which she is the principal figure – *Hecuba* of about 423 BC and *The Trojan Women* of 415 BC – the first named person we know who wept for Hecuba was a notoriously cruel tyrant, Alexander of Pherae, in the fourth century BC, and he was ashamed of it. Plutarch tells his story in two versions, and in one it seems that the monster shed tears at a performance of *The Trojan Women*, and in the other at a performance of *Hecuba*. The tyrant was so moved to pity by the spectacle of the Queen of Troy, without husband, sons or city, reduced to slavery, that he jumped up and ran from the theatre as fast as he could. He said it would be terrible if when he was killing so many of his own subjects he should be seen to be shedding tears over the sufferings of Hecuba and Andromache. Alexander the tyrant almost had the actor who played Hecuba severely punished for having softened his heart 'like iron in the furnace'.

What the man of iron had been surprised by was that bond of empathy and compassion that can cross centuries, and which, along with the imagination that needs to be primed to experience both, was dangerously undermining for the tyranny and oppression that upheld Alexander's power. Oppression and empathy can't co-exist.

In these two plays of Euripides, set in the immediate aftermath of the Trojan War, the poet creates one of the great archetypes of suffering. For an actress it is a role of the tragic grandeur of Lear, except that for the Queen of Troy the play begins by cutting straight to Shakespeare's Act III, the storm and the heath – and the sense of total deprivation. Hecuba enters deprived of everything she had – husband, sons, city, wealth, status – reduced to ending her days as a Greek slave scrubbing Agamemnon's latrines.

This reversal of fortune was the theme that appealed to the earliest appreciators of *Hecuba* in the sixteenth century, when it was translated from Greek into the more accessible Latin by Erasmus and Philip Melanchthon, who put on his version acted by students of his university at Wittenberg, where Hamlet was said to have studied.

The other theme was revenge, though it is a strange play about revenge that begins with the ghost of a murdered Trojan boy asking simply for burial and a last embrace from his mother, Hecuba. But he also tells us of another, angrier, unresigned ghost: that of Achilles, who can't rest without the shedding of more innocent blood. We are encouraged to cheer Hecuba on to her revenge against Polymestor, who has murdered her son Polydorus for gold, though we are chilled by the action when it happens. Euripides never makes it easy for us, tears or no tears.

It took the twentieth century's horrors and the rediscovery of *The Trojan Women* to turn the moralist of fate and the vicissitudes of fortune into an almost modern political playwright. Once discovered, it revealed that *Hecuba* was about the corruption of both power and powerlessness. The range of compromised violence it covers, even from a distance of twenty-five centuries, is from computerised aerial bombardment to the suicide bomber.

Three months after Franz Werfel, the Austrian poet and dramatist, translated *The Trojan Women* in 1914, the Serbian nationalist Princip assassinated Franz Ferdinand in Sarajevo. Werfel had written prophetically in his preface to his version of Euripides: 'Tragedy and hapless Hecuba may now return; their time has come.' In fact, Hecuba's time had already come at the beginning of the century, since when her glaring spotlight has never been dimmed. Gilbert Murray, the great humanist, early idealist of the League of Nations and (despite the later rejection of his Swinburnian poetic ear) the great populariser of Greek drama, did a version of the same *Trojan Women*, which Harley Granville Barker, who was responsible for groundbreaking productions of Greek tragedy, directed at the Royal Court Theatre in 1905.

The production was seen as 'pro-Boer'. Murray was outspoken in his opposition to the Boer War. He saw inevitable parallels between the suffering of Hecuba and the women of Troy and the Boer women and children whose homesteads were burnt to the ground and who were interned by Lord

Kitchener in concentration camps – a phrase coined then to describe this British invention. The Edwardians were made to squirm uncomfortably with guilt at the obvious similarities between Greek and British imperialism. Euripides no doubt deliberately made his own audience squirm when, in an almost blasphemous parody of a democratic process, he shows the assembled coalition army debating whether to sacrifice Polyxena, the daughter of Hecuba. The principal proposers of the motion are the two sons of Theseus, Athenians. He also allows Odysseus, the 'molasses-mouth' master of spin, to win over the coalition vote for sacrificing an innocent girl.

The girl, Polyxena, is to be sacrificed to the ghost of Achilles by Achilles' son, the notoriously psychotic, Arkan-like Neoptolemus. Neoptolemus' notoriety is given graphic detail on some extant vases. On a red-figure vase in the Archaeological Museum of Naples, Neoptolemus is shown savagely hacking at the old King Priam, the husband of Hecuba, who has their grandson on his knees, also hacked to death. There are numerous slashes and gashes on the body of the child and on the old man's head, to show the fury of the assault. On a cup in the Louvre, Neoptolemus is shown braining Priam with the hacked body of his dead grandson. He is also shown, nearer home in the British Museum, sticking his sword into the gullet of Polyxena, who is held over the sacrificial tomb by three soldiers. It is one of the most brutal of amphorae. It makes us think of Nietzsche's description of the Greeks as 'civilised savages'.

Euripides knows the track record of Neoptolemus but he deliberately gives us another version, which shows him moved for a moment, like Alexander. Pity wells up in him and has to be suppressed. The coalition's messenger, Talthybius, who goes further and weeps for the daughter of Hecuba, in a great descriptive speech tells how Polyxena requests that no one should restrain her and that she will die 'free'. He describes her being lifted onto the tomb like a stage from which she makes her speech and then, of her own will, rips open her robe, baring her breast and throat to the executioner's sword-thrust. Even the compulsively vicious Neoptolemus is impressed by the bravery of the victim's performance and for an instant holds back his sword. But only for an instant. There are empathetic tears in the Greek coalition ranks and they throw tokens of regard on the body of the girl, though they'd roared assent at the decision to sacrifice an innocent. Behind it also lies Euripides' questioning of the use of tears, and by implication of tragic drama itself, at a time when Athens was in the process of a bloody and ultimately self-destructive war. Or at any time since for that matter.

In my notebooks, where I glue pictures among the drafts of translations from the Greek tragedies I've done, I have a recurring image of an old woman appealing to the camera that has captured her agony or the heavens that ignore it, in front of the utter devastation that had been her home, or before her murdered dead. They are all different women from many places on earth, with the same gesture of disbelief, despair and denunciation. They are in Sarajevo, Kosovo, Grozny, Gaza, Ramallah, Tblisi, Baghdad, Falluja: women in robes and men in hard metal helmets, as in the Trojan War. Under them all, over the years, I have scribbled

Hecuba. My notebooks are bursting with Hecubas. Hecuba walks out of Euripides from 2,500 years ago straight onto our daily front pages and into our nightly newscasts. She is never out of the news. To our shame she is news that stays news.

When Granville Barker took Gilbert Murray's version of *The Trojan Women* to New York in May 1915 and played in the Adolph Lewisohn Stadium, an effort was made to persuade President Woodrow Wilson to write a special preface to the published text, but he replied that he must 'detach himself from everything which seems to bear the character of an attempt to make opinion even in the interest of peace'. I wonder what President Bush would reply if the RSC asked him to write a preface to my version of *Hecuba* to coincide with its visit to the Kennedy Center in Washington. And would he weep for Vanessa Redgrave's Hecuba if he could be somehow tricked into attending a performance?

At the end of the First World War, in 1919, Sybil Thorndike played Hecuba at the Old Vic, in order to raise funds for the newly founded League of Nations (Gilbert Murray was the chairman of the League of Nations Union). She tells of a tough cockney barrow-woman saying to her, 'Well, dearie, we saw your play . . . and we all 'ad a good cry – you see, them Trojans was just like us, we've lost our boys in this war, 'aven't we, so no wonder we was all cryin' – that was a real play, that was, dearie.' Sybil Thorndike remembers a later performance at the Alhambra Theatre in Leicester Square as the most moving she could ever remember: 'All the misery and awfulness of the 1914 war was symbolised in that play, and we all felt here was the beginning of a new era of peace and brotherhood.'

Many had a good cry, but the League that Hecuba's tragic fate raised funds for didn't prevent the Second World War, and the four Doric columns used in this setting for the sufferings of Sybil Thorndike's Hecuba were destroyed in a German bombing raid on the RADA theatre in the London Blitz. Nor did the UN, the institution that succeeded the League, manage to prevent the 'coalition' invading Iraq. We may still be weeping for Hecuba, but we allow our politicians to flood the streets of Iraq with more and more Hecubas in the name of freedom and democracy. The audience might weep for Hecuba in Washington when the tragedy plays there, but will they squirm with regret for Iraq, or the re-election of George Bush, or pause a moment before going for the gullet of Iran?

[Newcastle-upon-Tyne]

Even Now

2004

It's almost fifty years since I came across *Black Marigolds*. From a much-frequented stall in Leeds Market, I picked up, for a pound, the wonderful *Anthology of World Poetry*, edited by Mark Van Doren (1929). Even now I always buy copies if I see them to give to others. Its over 1,200 pages include translations of poems from Chinese, Japanese, Sanskrit, Arabic, Persian, Hebrew, Egyptian, Greek, Latin, Italian, Spanish, French, German, Scandinavian, Russian, as well as English, Irish, American poems.

Among all these mostly unknown foreign treasures one discovery began to haunt me from the moment I first read it in the 1950s: *Black Marigolds*, a version of the Sanskrit *Chaura-panchasika* by Edward Powys Mathers. It seemed somewhere to chime with remembered complex childhood feelings of the pleasure of, say, biting into a beautiful apple in our bomb-shelter cellar as German bombers droned above; and then in the '50s with the teenage apprehension of individual death at the same time as the unfathomable well of sensuality. The epigraph attributed to Azeddin El Mocadecci, which I am now inclined to believe is a brilliant invention of Mathers, stayed so vividly in my mind for forty years that when I was making a film about three women with Alzheimer's and noticed that the floor of the psychiatric hospital was decorated with mosaics of black daisies and that all the women had photography of their by now forgotten weddings beside their hospital beds, remembering Mathers's epigraph to *Black Marigolds* I called the film *Black Daisies for the Bride*. I was looking for a way to dramatise a mode of affirmation in women whose capacity for recall was gone, and who were prisoners of oblivion. The *Even now* of *Black Marigolds* became my talisman, for the dark affirmation in that film, and in my life.

Whenever I came across any book with the name of Edward Powys Mathers on the spine I bought it, and now have a good many, including a first edition of *Black Marigolds* (1919), though as they were mostly the sort of mildly erotic Eastern literature published 'for subscribers' or from publishers of fine books like the Golden Cockerel Press, they have never been easy to come by, and too expensive when they could be found. I wanted to know more about the poet/translator, but there were only the most tantalising clues, which seems appropriate enough for Edward Powys Mathers, who, as well as being a translator of Eastern poetry, had more fame and repute as Torquemada, the setter of crossword puzzles for the *Observer*. Torquemada is even now setting us puzzles. Some of his crosswords have clues which make up a poem that rhymes from clue to clue, and many of his 'original' poems are hidden behind cyphers. The autobiographical clues are as hard to solve as Torquemada's. But his wife Rosamond, in a memoir prefaced to a collection of his best crossword puzzles, gives us a few facts.

Edward Powys Mathers was born in Forest Hill on 26 August 1892 and died on 3 February 1939. He was at Trinity

College, Oxford, from 1910 to the outbreak of the First
World War. Although everyone remembers him as suffering from an unspecified 'illness', he had himself finally
accepted as a private in the 24th Middlesex Regiment,
though he was after some months given his discharge. He
seems, characteristically, to have been extremely quick and
efficient at decoding cyphers, which earned the budding
Torquemada, generally known to close friends as 'Bill', the
nickname of 'Willy the Cypher King'. At one of the camps
where he was billeted as assistant to the medical officer (either Woldingham, Halton or Northampton), Cecil
French, a fellow private with literary tastes, remembers that
'*Black Marigolds* his first translation was in progress'. And
Mathers himself tells us that 'my rendering was finished in
1915, in two or three sessions on a box by the stove in hutments'. Since Mathers admits to having only 'a very small
smattering of Sanskrit' and, indeed, that all his Eastern
poetry was 'translated at second-hand', he probably had to
make use of a previous translation of the *Chaura-panchasika*
by Sir Edwin Arnold, who did know Sanskrit and published in 1896 the Sanskrit text and his verse rendition in
his own handwriting with his watercolours of tropical flowers and Indian scenes. Mathers points out almost in the
same words as Arnold that each stanza in the original starts
with *adyapi*, 'a word of reminiscence'. Arnold writes that
this repeated Sanskrit word gives to the stanzas 'a melodious and ingenious monotony of fanciful passion', and
Mathers that it gives to the poem 'a recurring monotone
of retrospection, which I hope my unchanging *Even now*
also suggests'. Arnold varies his response to the recurrent

word, as in 'I die, but I remember!'; 'Dying I recall'; 'I die, yet well I mind . . .'; 'Ah, dying – dying – I remember'; 'Yet I will die remembering'; and then finally in stanza 27 comes up with the phrase that Mathers lifted to make the heart of the captive condemned lover affirm his celebration in the shadow of death:

> And, even now, when any dawn may bring
> Such as shall slay me to the prison-gate . . .

It is also possible that he lifted the phrase 'Even now' from Arthur A. Macdonell's *A History of Sanskrit Literature* (1900), which speaks of the fifty stanzas of the *Chaurapanchasika* 'each beginning with the phrase "Even now I remember"'.

Whatever the source, EPM had the dramatic instinct to use the repeated 'Even now' with the effect of both passing bell and the beat of the condemned but affirmative and death-defying heart. In the pause before each second line comes in we hear the bell toll, which opens the condemned captive's mind and heart to his sensual memories. They remain in the celebratory kaleidoscope in his soul until the last brilliant line, which is pure Mathers:

> The heavy knife. As to a gala day.

The darkness and the colours make each other more profound. All the 'Even now's tolling with certain mortality nonetheless fill the heart so full of sensual recall that it goes out to execution with the gaiety of a gala.

The phrase 'Even now' reverberates beyond the poem to the time and place of its translation, affirming the sensual at the time of the 1914–18 war in the hutments of an army camp where we know Mathers composed it. 'Even now' asserts the sensual fullness of all the translations in this book which were done in the same period. Even now in times of darkness and extinction the passions of the heart and the pleasures of the sensual body have to be remembered. Even now the child slowly relishes his apple, with unfriendly Fokkers growling overhead. In a time of war the idea of death tomorrow for a young man of twenty-three, as Mathers was, would have been extremely common, though not for the offence of loving a Kashmiri princess. Bearing in mind that they were written in the First World War, they have something of the sensual tonic of the silk-clad odalisques of Matisse in the Second World War, and of my childhood apple!

Charles Tomlinson, in his *Oxford Book of Verse in Translation*, which surprisingly does not include Mathers, claims that Ezra Pound's *Cathay*, with its Chinese poems of parting or frontier service, had an implicit link to the campaigns in France of the First World War and quotes Hugh Kenner as saying, '*Cathay* is largely a war-book.' One can say something similar about *Black Marigolds*, in which Mathers's 'Even now' allows us to hear the passing bells of the First World War tolling behind a passionate sensual recall. But to achieve that celebratory note it has to have an exotic location. It couldn't come from the front, even though men under the shadow of death dreamed of their women at home. The darkness of the same shadow enhances the delicate sensualities of *Coloured Stars*, published in the same year as *Black Marigolds*, 1919, the title taken from a line in 'Song' (p. 29):

> If our clear blue night full of white stars
> Turned to a night of coloured stars

This poem, along with 'English Girl' (p. 40), the one poem by which Mathers is represented in W. B. Yeats's *Oxford Book of Modern Verse* (Oxford: Clarendon Press, 1936), and 'Being Together at Night' (p. 34), is attributed by Mathers in his note to an American-born Chinese, a valet by profession. He names him as J. Wing (1870–1923) – 'or Julius Wing as he hated to be called!' E. Allen Ashwin, in a memoir prefixed to a collection of Torquemada's puzzles, says that J. Wing and John Duncan, the 'lowland Scot' responsible for the Arabic poem 'Climbing Up to You' (p. 47), 'represent one of their author's most successful flights in imaginative fiction'. They are both without a doubt among EPM's Pessoan *personae*.

He gives much longer sequences to both in later books, and much more elaborate and suspicious biography. J. Wing's 'The Green Paper Lanterns' appears in Volume XI of *The Eastern Anthology*, and Mathers elaborates on his life: 'He might have inherited a great charcuterie business' but he became 'a sort of chasseur at hotels in San Francisco and Saint Louis, and a gentleman's gentleman in New York and Boston. Later he shook cocktails, and contributed verse in English to three or four American journals. As a valet he visited England, France, Spain and Italy. He perished of consumption in lodgings by the harbour at Vigo in 1925, just as the boat on which I had come to visit him was mooring under a green dawn cloudy with gulls.' He claims to have spent six months in the island of Teneriffe with Wing in 1921. It is interesting to note that they were, supposedly, in Oratava, the place where Sir Edwin Arnold wrote his version of the *Chaura-panchasika*. Torquemada clues?

He tells us that in the poems of J. Wing, 'opium and wine speak for themselves'. It seems that Mathers used both the translations of genuine poems from Eastern poets and those from the invented *personae* as a safer context for what are hinted at in the meagre reminiscences as 'alcoholism' and drug addiction and bisexuality, which Mathers needed to place in an exotic Eastern location to address. He certainly found the sexual reticence of the English poetic tradition frustrating, and he praises the Islamic poet who 'takes his veneration and description from the navel to the knee without altering his key of worship. Few English poets have been able to do this.' He complains in an essay on Arabic prose and verse that from Chaucer to the great Victorians, poets could not mention the female pudenda without waiting, as it were, for the laugh to follow. 'Breasts they could manage and remain the devout lover; but the rest was a matter for mirth.'

Christopher Sandford, who took over the Golden Cockerel Press from Robert Gibbings in 1933, described EPM in a 1980 letter to Michael Dawson, another would-be solver of the puzzle of Mathers, as an 'alcoholic', 'bearded, wide and squat', but adds that he was the most benevolent man he'd ever met, though he implies that the beaming benevolence owed much to the amount he'd imbibed and the level of his inebriation. He also said that EPM was 'very loving – maybe too loving – with women and men', and describes how Mathers made a dead set at seducing him.

Just as in the invented poems of the Chinese American Julius Wing 'opium and wine speak for themselves', so in EPM's short scenarios, what he calls 'the squibs' of *Red Wise*, on the life of the real Abu Nowas, with invented incidents and poems, there is much wine drinking and a chapter on experiments with chewing *bhang* that only a genuine devotee could imagine. There is one poem attributed to Abu Nowas in which the beauty of the whole world turns into wine and becomes quaffable:

> If He made all beauty out of wine
> He'd get no worship to compare with mine:
> For, when my purse were flat and credit far,
> I'd suck the golden nipple of a star
> Or that blue grape He dangles up on high,
> The infinite first vintage of the sky . . .

He further elaborates on John Duncan (1877–1919), the supposed author of 'Climbing Up to You' (p. 47), in the next book he published, *The Garden of Bright Waters: One Hundred and Twenty Asiatic Love Poems* (Oxford: Blackwell, 1920). He makes him a lowland Scot who lived in Edinburgh until he was between twenty and twenty-five and, after a disastrous love affair, left Scotland, and in two years was an established member of a small tribe of nomadic Arabs, travelling up and down the whole line of the south-west coast of the Persian Gulf with them. He married an Arab, and all his forty-odd poems are addressed to her. Like this one, 'Sand', with another metamorphosis of the world into first milk, then the always welcome wine!

> The sand is like acres of wet milk
> Poured out under the moonlight;
> It crawls up about your brown feet
> Like wine trodden from white stars.

Once alerted to the pseudonymous *personae*, you begin to suspect them everywhere. In the twelve volumes of *The Eastern Anthology*, EPM claims as one of the real 'discoveries' of the whole series – which covers Cambodian, Japanese, Arabic, Bengali, Sanskrit, Chinese, Turkish poetry and stories, all translated from the French – a poem called 'A Love Song', where 'there is a reaction under wine and a letting go . . . [where] the poet swings back to the old severe intricacies of versification and, with them, to the homosexual ideal':

> Surely the faces of women are pleasant, but the taste of cheeks that have been newly shaved is better.

This 'discovery' is attributed to a Turkish poet Jenab Shehabuddin. In his note EPM writes: 'I have been able to find out no more about this very real poet than that he was born in 1870 and studied medicine and wrote much of his verse in Paris.'

'He [EPM] had a scholar's knowledge of French . . . but he was not a good linguist,' wrote E. Allen Ashwin. Mathers's sources for all the Eastern poems were collections in French translation. As, I think, a smokescreen for his own pseudonymous activities, he explains how he abandoned one already advertised part of *The Eastern Anthology* when he discovered that it was 'a clever and entertaining French forgery'. I think if assiduous search were made in those French collections he cites, many other poems would be found to be by an EPM alias. Especially those for which he provides notes.

His wife Rosamond observes sadly that his health prevented his fulfilment as an author. 'A melancholy and self-distrustful temperament undermined his faith in his conceptions before they had attained full maturity', and 'the pile of work brilliantly begun and laid aside mounted out of all proportion to that brought to completion'. But many, especially the translations represented here, were also brilliantly completed. It seems that translation and pseudonyms were safer for his depressed and diffident talent, though he qualifies his invented Abu Nowas poems in *Red Wise* by saying, 'I have not forgotten that my hero was a lyric poet of the first excellence. We must suppose that the examples ascribed to him were each written on an "off day".'

The apologia and the pseudonymous gloss protect what is a sensitive real talent looking to the sensuality and sexual tenderness of the East for its poetic release. Rosamond also writes that the fame as Torquemada 'in no way compensated for his disappointment as a creative artist'. I feel that Mathers is placing himself with accustomed diffidence when he writes about the Chinese American Julius Wing that 'if I had had nothing to do with these poems . . . I would say that Wing was a true poet, if only a true minor'.

And Mathers, erotic aesthete, cocktail-shaking Chinese American, honorary Arab nomad, *bhang*-chewer, Turkish bisexual, tormenting puzzler-setter, was a true, if minor, poet whose assimilation of Eastern modes should rank with Arthur Waley or Ezra Pound, and who should be much better known than he is. And *Black Marigolds* is a masterpiece that still affects me in the same way even now after almost fifty years. Perhaps even more with the 'gala day' ever nearer. Even now!

[Newcastle-upon-Tyne]

Flicks and this Fleeting Life

2006

I was an early and avid film devotee. My street in Beeston, Leeds, was within walking distance of a number of cinemas. The Pavilion in Dewsbury Road, where I went to Saturday-morning showings of serials and cartoons, Laurel and Hardy, Abbott and Costello, the Three Stooges, the Marx Brothers, Tarzan with Johnny Weissmuller, costume flicks with Errol Flynn. There was the Crescent, also in Dewsbury Road, and the Rex, at the end of the same road, near Middleton. On the Beeston Hill side there was the Malvern, near to where my dad was born and to his dad's former pub, The Harrisons. Further on, a slightly longer walk or a two-stop tram ride took me to the Beeston Picture House. I remember my mother taking me to *Bambi* and *Snow White and the Seven Dwarfs* at the Malvern, and later going with my father to see gangster films, especially James Cagney. I'll never forget *White Heat* and Cagney's 'Top o' the world, Ma!' as he goes down in a hail of gunfire on the top of a globe-shaped gasometer. I saw it with my dad when I was twelve. I wrote one of my *School of Eloquence* sonnets, 'Continuous', about this experience:

James Cagney was the one up both our streets.
His was the only art we ever shared.

A gangster film and choc ice were the treats
that showed about as much love as he dared.

He'd be my own age now in '49!
The hand that glinted with the ring he wore,
his father's, tipped the cold bar into mine
just as the organist dropped through the floor.

He's on the platform lowered out of sight
to organ music, this time on looped tape,
into a furnace with a blinding light
where only his father's ring will keep its shape.

I wear it now to Cagneys on my own
and sense my father's hands cupped round my treat –

they feel as though they've been chilled to the bone
from holding my ice cream all through *White Heat*.

Flicks were classified as U films and A films. U films you
could go alone to as a kid, but you had to be accompanied by
an adult to go into an A. Sometimes by myself and sometimes with my friends I would wait outside the Pavilion
and accost people to take us into the A film. 'Will yer tek
us in, mister [or missus]?' I saw as many flicks as I could.

Calling it 't'flicks' associated the filmic process with flick
books, which had successive drawings on each following
page that when flicked by the thumb made a continuous
movement. I often drew and made my own. I drew them on
the corners of school exercise books and Latin grammars,

and it made me grasp early that combination of stillness and momentum that is the heart of film creation: so many 'frames per second'. It was a cheap movie version of Pollock's Toy Theatre. But I made cut-out theatrical figures too, which I coloured and arranged on the biggest dinner plate from the set my parents had been given as their main wedding present, a great oval one which I still serve my Christmas goose on.

So I made 'flicks' and theatre, not in a Pollock's proscenium but 'in the round', or more accurately, 'in the oval', more like the ancient spaces in Greece or the Roman amphitheatre on the Danube that I was much later to do some of my pieces for. After I'd seen ice shows in Blackpool, where we went for our holidays, I made figures that I blew gently on so that they skated across the surface of the same plate. That I did these more or less simultaneously gave me, I think, a simple but early understanding of the difference between cinema and theatre. The kind of theatre I saw most often was late music hall, or 'variety', and panto, and though it was in proscenium theatres like the Empire, the fourth wall was broken down by the direct address of the comics I saw there: Norman Evans, Frank Randle, Old Mother Riley, Albert Modley, Robb Wilton and even Laurel and Hardy live on stage.

When I first saw a play in a proscenium theatre like the old Theatre Royal in Leeds, with actors only addressing each other and pouring drinks and smoking cigarettes, I felt bored and excluded. But I could enter into the realism of cinema because it was not a live exchange. The actors didn't know I was there. I grew up loving both cinema and theatre, but because I've felt so conscious of how different they really are, I have always hated any video recording of my theatrical works, and when I have deliberately embraced the ancient ephemerality of the one performance of a theatre piece, as with *The Trackers of Oxyrhynchus* in the stadium of Delphi or *The Kaisers of Carnuntum* in the Roman amphitheatre of Petronell-Carnuntum, I have forbidden any filming of it.

A tram ride into town took me to the big cinemas: the Odeon and the Majestic, where the blockbuster Hollywood films were shown. There was also a small cinema, the News Theatre, now the Bondi Beach Bar, next to the city station and the Queen's Hotel in City Square. It was there, just after the Second World War ended, that I saw the newsreel footage of the Nazi concentration camps. I don't remember who took me – I think maybe my grandfather, the retired Hunslet signalman who lived with us – but there was something overwhelming in seeing such terrible images on a large screen, much bigger than life-size. I think my reaction was almost on the scale of those early viewers of the Lumière brothers' film of the train arriving in a station in 1895. It wasn't that I tried to escape from the heaped corpses moving towards me, but I felt that jumbling cascade of bulldozed, emaciated Belsen bodies were being dumped onto the art deco carpet of the cinema and into my consciousness for ever. It almost blighted my life, it had such a powerful effect on me, and made me draw a line between what I knew in my heart was 'pretend', the films that entertained me and made me laugh, and what was news: real dead bodies bulldozed into pits at Bergen-Belsen. I have never forgotten that introduction to the filming of real life, or in this case, real and terrifying death. Nor how jarring the voice-over narrations were! What narrator could find the right tone for such terror? This newsreel changed my attitude to life and film for ever.

When poetry became my chief obsession, it didn't diminish my interest either in theatre or film, and I saw all the great classics at the Leeds University Film Society showings, from Eisenstein to the GPO Film Unit and *Night Mail*, with the famous verse sequence by W. H. Auden and music by Benjamin Britten. At the other side of City Square was another small cinema that showed new foreign films as they came out – Bergman, Antonioni, Visconti, etc. – something it's hard enough to find now even in London. I didn't know how I could ever commit to both poetry and film, and never imagined I'd find a way eventually.

As I believed that some of the greatest poetry was in the greatest drama, I also wanted to write poetic plays, though Eliot and Fry were to dry up the taste for them, and I only began to clear a space for myself as a poet in the theatre by translating, from the languages I'd learned, plays from that two-thousand-year-old tradition, starting with the great Greek tragedians, of drama by poets. My first translation was a version of the *Lysistrata* of Aristophanes I did in Zaria, northern Nigeria, in March 1964 for a group of students, in which I incorporated local village drummers and dancers. It was called *Aikin Mata* (Hausa for 'Woman's Work') and was written in collaboration with my old friend, the Irish poet James Simmons. We had collaborated at Leeds University on writing and performing revues with, among others, Barry Cryer and Wole Soyinka. We also directed *Aikin Mata*, and it began with a montage from newsreels and documentaries projected onto the back wall of the theatre – suggesting, by visiting US audio-visual specialist Paul Robinson's editing, instead of innocent Hausa horsemen honouring the Emir of Zaria more aggressive cavalry charges and battle preparation. Magajiya, the Lysistrata of the original, flung a large water pot at the back wall to put an end to the warlike images. That was my first brief glimpse into the practicalities of the editing process and how you could make a shot mean many different things by changing what it was juxtaposed with, and how something seemingly quite innocent could be made sinister by editing in a terrified reaction. There is something also in the process of translation, in this case of an ancient Greek play into a modern Nigerian setting, that trains the mind in searching for equivalents, attempting to stay open to all local impressions but having to remain within the confines of an original drama. A combination of fixed form and fleeting content.

My hesitations about the creative co-existence of poetry and film were deepened when my first book of poems, *The Loiners*, won the Geoffrey Faber Memorial Prize in 1972 and because of that was given some minutes on a TV arts programme. I read some poems on camera, and someone went out and shot some images to go with the reading that were so clumsily and clunkily cut into the text that I had to switch the programme off. It was as if the 'director' had only read the nouns in the poems and decided that we wouldn't understand them without a show-and-tell picture. Over thirty years later, that kind of clumsy illustration can still be seen accompanying poetry. It is everything a film poem shouldn't be. That experience made me wary of entrusting poems not specifically written for it to TV, until Richard Eyre directed my reading of my long poem *v.* in 1987 for Channel 4, with a great sensitivity to the poetic text.

Sadly, after my *Lysistrata* in northern Nigeria it was ten years before I did another work for the stage, *The Misanthrope* of Molière for the National Theatre at the Old Vic in 1973. One of the results of this venture's success in London, Washington DC and on Broadway was that I was asked to work on more than one film, though producers soon lost interest when I innocently enquired what metre they imagined the text would be in! But there was one director who saw the play and thought he wanted the kind of verse he'd heard on the Old Vic stage. George Cukor, who had recently directed Alec McCowen with Maggie Smith in the film *Travels with My Aunt* (1973), came to see him playing Alceste and felt that he wanted some of those 'couplays', as he always called my rhyming couplets, for his new film, *The Blue Bird*.

So the first film I ever worked on was *The Blue Bird*, based on the play by the Belgian poet and dramatist Maurice Maeterlinck (1862–1949), who won the Nobel Prize for Literature in 1911. Although I have been frequently mocked for this sentimental skeleton in my closet, I have some fond memories of being involved in it. Despite the fact that it became one of Hollywood's greatest disasters, I learned a great deal on the project, which I didn't realise I would draw on when I finally started to make film poems. *The*

Blue Bird had its very first production in Moscow, directed by Stanislavsky, in 1908. I saw a production at the Moscow Art Theatre in 1967, when I had been invited over to read my poetry at Moscow University, and the programme I'd kept and later pasted into my *Blue Bird* notebook still credited the director as Konstantin Stanislavsky. It was translated into English by Alexander Teixera de Mattos and was produced at the Haymarket Theatre in London by Herbert Trench in 1909. In a souvenir programme for the production I found in a junk shop, Herbert Trench called *The Blue Bird* 'a transcendental pantomime'. Although I was thrilled by scenic transformation and metamorphoses in panto as a kid, I wasn't so keen on them straining for transcendence, and I wasn't, I fear, naturally suited to the material of *The Blue Bird*. There had been a film version in 1940, intended as 20th Century Fox's rival children's fantasy to MGM's *The Wizard of Oz*. It was denounced as 'hideous kitsch' and was a great flop even with Shirley Temple as the little girl Mytyl. But Hollywood likes to repeat its mistakes.

My brief was to write lyrics for the songs that the Russian composer Andrei Petrov was going to write for the film. The music arranger was Irwin Kostal, who had done the same job on Leonard Bernstein's *West Side Story*. The composer and arranger fell out very early on, and I found myself working in separate rooms with them both, trying to mediate. It didn't make for an atmosphere of détente, and the shuttling back and forth didn't help my creativity much. Even when I was away I would get a letter from Kostal warning if he sent a telegram or phoned me saying, 'All is well with Kostal and Petrov,' it meant the opposite!

Their squabbles over credits were deeply boring. Kostal was quoted in *Newsweek* as saying: 'This is a ship of fools. I've got a fight with Andrei Petrov every day. It's a matter of national pride. He wants me completely off the picture one moment and the next we're great buddies. The problem is he wants to write American jazz, and I want Volga boatmen music. But it will all work out.' But it never did! Our interpreter, Sasha, was doing a doctoral thesis with the title 'Creative and Sociopsychological Interaction during the Shooting of the First Soviet-American Co-Production, *The Blue Bird*'. The interaction he witnessed and sometimes had to find wounding words for in both English and Russian was often turbulent!

Petrov had the premiere of his opera *Peter the Great* at the Kirov while I was there in June 1975. I was invited. Old women tutted at the length of my hair. Young men tried to buy my denims. I think Petrov felt he was too grand for Hollywood. And I thought that I just wasn't right for Hollywood, miscast as a musical lyricist for such potentially mawkish themes. I often felt in jaundiced mood when I came face to face with great art, as in my trips to the Hermitage when I wasn't required on set. I came across an old notebook marked 'Leningrad 1975', with a note about going to see Rembrandt's *Descent from the Cross* (1645). I jotted down details of the hyena-like dog's head with green eyes glaring through a clump of thistles, the pincers pulling out the nail that held Christ's left hand to the cross. I wrote, 'How much more human than the fucking *Blue Bird*! . . . I find myself trapped in a film where the categories of approval are "charm" and "prettiness".'

Charm and prettiness! Not my most outstanding qualities as a poet! And certainly not the qualities a poet would
need to give a voice to the Rembrandt or the terrifying
corpses dumped onto the carpet of the News Theatre in
City Square.

Although *The Blue Bird* ended up in a book called *The
Hollywood Hall of Shame: The Most Expensive Flops in Movie
History* (1984), it had given me the opportunity to get to
know a legendary director, and to involve myself every
day on the set, getting used to how things were done both
behind and in front of the camera. Behind the camera
was the great British cinematographer Freddie Young, of
Lawrence of Arabia and *Dr Zhivago.* The second camera was
operated by Jonas Gritsius, who had been director of photography on Kozintsev's *Hamlet* and *King Lear.* I watched
them at work and stored what I could for the distant day
when I might have need of it. And with them behind
the camera was the Hollywood veteran George Cukor,
renowned as a great director of women, though when anybody said that, he retorted what about Clark Gable, Cary
Grant, James Stewart, Spencer Tracy . . .? Because he was
directing another band of renowned women, all the press
on *The Blue Bird* listed his previous 'temperamental women'
credentials. Cukor had directed Garbo, Joan Crawford,
Katharine Hepburn, Judy Garland, Judy Holliday, Marilyn
Monroe, Vivien Leigh, Ingrid Bergman, Sophia Loren, etc.
In front of the camera in Leningrad were Elizabeth Taylor,
Ava Gardner, Jane Fonda, Cicely Tyson. There was also a
young Russian actress, Margarita Terekhova, playing the
role of Milk, who one day asked me if I would like to go

with her to see a film, in which she had the starring role, that had just been made and released grudgingly and in a limited way in the Soviet Union in 1975. ('Not a single poster, not a single advertisement,' noted the director in his diary entry for 8 April 1975.) The film was *Mirror*, directed by Andrei Tarkovsky, which I thought was brilliant and a very welcome relief from the film I was writing my lyrics and couplets for. According to the Russian critic Maya Turovskaya, '*Mirror* is the most documentary, and the most poetic' of Tarkovsky's films. The stark documentary and the poetic were interdependent. The film moved from colour to black and white, from lyrical fields to newsreels of the Spanish Civil War and more extended footage of the Red Army crossing Lake Sivash during the Soviet advance of 1943. Tarkovsky explains in his *Sculpting in Time*, which I bought and read when it came out in 1986, what drew him to the sequence:

> The film affected you with a piercing, aching poignancy, because in the shots were simply people. People dragging themselves, knee deep in wet mud, through an endless swamp that stretched out beyond the horizon, beneath a whitish, flat sky. Hardly anyone survived. The boundless perspective of these recorded moments created an effect close to catharsis.

It was not simply the power of the images captured by an army cameraman who was killed the day it was filmed. Over the sequence was the voice of the director's father, the poet Arseniy Tarkovsky, reciting a poem called 'Life, Life', which was, the son wrote later, 'the consummation of the episode' because it 'gave voice to its ultimate meaning'.

> On earth there is no death.
> All are immortal. All is immortal. No need
> To be afraid of death at seventeen
> Nor yet at seventy. Reality and light
> Exist, but neither death nor darkness.
> All of us are on the seashore now,
> And I am one of those who haul the nets
> When a shoal of immortality comes in . . .
> I only need my immortality
> For my blood to go on flowing from age to age.
> I would readily pay with my life
> For a safe place with constant warmth
> Were it not that life's flying needle
> Leads me on through the world like a thread.
>
> Arseniy Tarkovsky
> (trans. Kitty Hunter-Blair)

Although I knew little Russian, and though I got some whispered translations from my companion, there were no English subtitles as the cinema was in Leningrad, but I could hear the strong metre and the rhymes of the poem, and the combination went deep into my heart. A clue perhaps to dealing with those terrible images I saw at the News Theatre in Leeds thirty years before. As that other Russian poet, Joseph Brodsky, wrote: 'At certain periods of history it is only poetry that is capable of dealing with reality by condensing it into something graspable, something that otherwise couldn't be contained in the mind.' Was the poem the fittest narration for terrifying newsreel screen images? *Mirror* first compelled me to ask that question.

There was another poem of director Tarkovsky's father over an extended shot in black and white of Margarita Terekhova walking down a very long corridor in the printing works where the mother she was playing worked. It made you both watch and listen to the poem. It also stayed deep in my memory, and was still there when Peter Symes and I were filming *Black Daisies for the Bride* (1993) in High Royds Hospital in Menston, Yorkshire, and found a similar but more sloping corridor for our brides to walk down, singing. I think the idea of a snowstorm made out of wedding confetti was also somehow influenced by that Russian film I saw in a welcome break from *The Blue Bird*.

So that, though involved in the kitsch of *The Blue Bird*, I had had my eyes opened to a modern cinema which was unashamedly poetic, which had poems read by the poet himself, which made the images you saw, even from newsreel reality, mean a great deal more. One depended on the other. It sowed seeds I was only partially aware of then, though I longed more for the world of *Mirror* than that of *The Blue Bird*.

The other seeds were sown in a more jocular but, in retrospect, equally significant way. In 1974–5, I was in Leningrad four times, in the Lenfilm studio in the winter and on location in the park of Pavlovsk in June 1975, doing some of my writing in a room overlooking the battleship *Aurora*, which fired the first shot in the October Revolution, moored on the river Neva. I was rather impressed that the Lenfilm studio was where one of my great heroes, Eisenstein, had made *Battleship Potemkin* in 1925. The British actor Richard Pearson, who played Bread, made a speech on his arrival at the studios saying how honoured he felt that he was to be working in the studio where Eisenstein had made his great film fifty years ago. The Russian cameraman, Jonas Gritsius, smiled and said, 'You won't feel half so honoured when you realise we're using the same equipment!'

When I had to be away from *The Blue Bird* with the National Theatre and *The Misanthrope* in the United States, I would receive cables from George Cukor in Leningrad, the teasing tone of them scarcely concealing their desperation. The first when I was in Washington staying at the infamous Watergate Hotel and working in the Kennedy Center:

TONY OH MY POET TONY WHERE ARE
THEM COMIC COUPLETS WITH THE TOUCH
OF ASPERITY FOR LIGHT AFTER SHE HAS
CREATED FIRE WATER AND A CHARMING BUT
BRIEF VERSE AS THEY ALL ARE OFF TO CATCH
THE BLUEBIRD STOP MY TONGUE IS HANGING
OUT STOP COULD YOU FIND IT IN YOUR
HEART TO WIRE THEM STOP SHAKESPEARE
AND MILTON ALWAYS SENT THEIR SONNETS
BY WIRE SO WHY CAN'T TONY HARRISON?

YOUR DESPERATE ADMIRER GEORGE

Then, a few weeks later, when we opened on Broadway at the St James's Theater, I got another cable at the stage door:

DEAR TONY I KNOW YOU WILL TAKE NEW
YORK BY STORM BUT DON'T ABANDON YOUR
POOR FRIEND IN RUSSIA STOP HOW ABOUT A
COUPLE OF COUPLETS KID.

LOVING REGARDS GEORGE

Although I was used to writing and rewriting in rehearsals
from work with the director John Dexter on the National
Theatre *Misanthrope*, I hadn't yet liberated myself from the
practice of having to retire to a room on my own to write. It
was some years later, when I started to direct my own plays,
that I developed the ability simply to change a text verbally
and have the stage management write it down, so the idea
of wiring poetry by Western Union was not then what I
felt I could take to naturally, but with George Cukor's gentle goading I began to wean myself off being only able to
create after long hours of brooding. This developed in me
and stood me in great stead when I began to make film
poems, or write political squibs for the newspapers or write
from a battle in Bosnia and send the poem via satellite to
the *Guardian* in London. But the gently mocking cables of
George Cukor somehow began the process, though I wasn't
aware of it then.

When I'd cabled my couplets I would get a teasing, cour-
teous picture postcard of Lenin from George: 'Grateful
thanks to my favourite Long Distance poet!' Then another
sentence begging me to make another trip to Leningrad,
though the added caution of 'only if a working harmony
is established between Petrov and Kostal' hinted that the

strained relations between composer and arranger were little better. Then he concluded: 'The white nights will be upon us, what an opportunity for Britain's greatest poet (Newcastle Division). Huge thanks, Anthony, and affectionate regards, George.'

He also sent me contact strips from photographs in the studio or on location taken by Henry Wynberg, the used-car salesman who was Elizabeth Taylor's beau between her first and second marriage to Richard Burton. One of them shows Cukor in his black beret gesturing to someone. That someone had been me when we were discussing some of my couplets on location in Pavlovsk. He had inscribed the one of himself as 'a character'. This was joined to two of me listening to Cukor. He had captioned them as 'the brooding poet'. I heard of his death on 24 January 1983, on the one o'clock news, and then the obituary in *The Times* used the same photo as he had sent to me, the contact print that he was addressing me from. I wrote the following poem:

'Losing Touch'
In memoriam George Cukor, died 24 January 1983

I watch a siskin swinging back and forth
on the nut net, enjoying lunchtime sun –
unusual this time of year up north
and listening to the news at five past one.

As people not in constant contact do,
we'd lost touch, but I thought of you, old friend,
and sent a postcard now and then. I knew

the sentence starting with your name would end:
'the Hollywood director, died today.'

You're leaning forward in your black beret
from *The Times* obituary, and I'd add
the background of Pavlovsk near Leningrad
bathed in summer and good shooting light
where it was taken that July, as I'm
the one you're leaning forward to address.
I had a black pen poised about to write
and have one now and think back to that time
and feel you lean towards me out of Nothingness.

I rummage for the contacts you sent then:
the one of you that's leaning from *The Times*
and below it one of me with my black pen
listening to you criticise my rhymes,
and, between a millimetre of black band
that now could be ten billion times as much
and none that show the contact of your hand.
The distance needs adjusting; just a touch!

You were about to tap my knee for emphasis.
It's me who's leaning forward now with this!

I grew very fond of Cukor during our work in Leningrad
and my two visits to his house in Hollywood, and I only
wish we could have worked on something more congenial
to my own talent and more worthy of his. But I learned
a little of how to collaborate, happily with him and less

so with the warring musical factions. Their quarrels made me aware that it was important to find other artists who were truly open to collaboration and not scrabbling to buff up their own egos or squeeze a more prominent credit. It made me very choosy about composers, and the wariness created by this early film experience made me grateful to discover composers I could collaborate with in theatre and film, such as Harrison Birtwistle, Dominic Muldowney and Richard Blackford.

In my *Blue Bird* notebook there are some 'couplets' that I wrote but which were never used where I can see myself trying to match image and word in a way I found myself doing later in the film poems I had a fuller and more creative involvement in. Some are for a scene where the children of the poor woodcutter, Tyltyl and Mytyl (played by the seven-year-old Patsy Kensit), watch as the rich children skate on the lake, eat and watch fireworks. The word 'rich' is associated with the hiss of skates on ice, the spray of shaved ice as a skater stops a glide, foaming champagne, the sharpening of knives to cut a roasted joint, the whoosh of sky rockets, the swish of skirts, the drawing of curtains, servants sweeping the crumbs up off the floor of the banquet:

> Six white horses pull a sleigh
> of laughing children who can say
>
> we're rich, rich!
>
> The fireworks cascade, each spark
> that swooshes through the dark

says rich, rich!

Look, the ice skates as they glide
hiss and hiss, self-satisfied

rich rich!

Look at all the children skating,
what's everybody celebrating?

being rich!

The champagne bubbles effervesce
in surfeits of rich happiness . . .

rich, rich!

The happy boy who only eats
one or two from heaps of sweets

is rich, rich!

The happy girl who'll only taste
her cake and leave the rest to waste

is rich, rich!

The swish of silken crinolines
swirling as the lady spins

says rich, rich!

The knives being sharpened for the meat
for all the well-fed guests to eat

say rich, rich!

The velvet curtains that are drawn
by servants in the chilly dawn

say rich, rich!

The brushes that sweep up the mess
of other children's happiness

say rich, rich . . .!

This was a kind of song/montage that might have used some of the later techniques of my film poems had it ever got any further than my notebook. I seem to remember it was considered to have tipped a degree too far towards the 'Soviet' half of the co-production! As was a duet I wrote between the Dog (George Cole) and Cat (Cicely Tyson), the one inciting the forest trees into revolution and the other suggesting appeasement:

CAT
I sing to you this day of days
the forest kingdom's Marseillaise.
The time has come, you forest glades,

to use your boughs as barricades.
Be chopped no more to logs and sticks,
you servile trees, turn Bolsheviks.
The end's in sight to saw and axe
the tyranny of lumberjacks.
O sycamore, O elm, O beech
Liberty's within your reach.

DOG
Don't listen to those servile lies
there's always room for compromise.
O little shrubs and trees think twice
compromise can be rather nice.
I beg you all to reassess
Man's power and your powerlessness.
You humble trees were never meant
to question the Establishment.
You vegetables learn your place
to live and serve the human race.

etc., etc.

Admittedly uninspired, but it helped to teach me to write quickly when needed and also to bin lines almost immediately. It was good training for my later film poems, when I was trying to articulate things closer to my heart, or a greater burden on my spirit, but with something of the same pressures to produce the poetry.

I went over to Hollywood to see Cukor after the film had been almost universally savaged, except by a loyal Cukor fan on the *Los Angeles Times*. The reactions depressed him, but he showed it only fleetingly. It fared so badly it was never released in the UK, so I went to see it at a cinema in LA, and was horrified. I couldn't tell George Cukor that the critics were wrong and I tried to make him feel better by saying that I felt that I had let him down. It seemed to me he was thinking that *The Blue Bird* that had turned into a turkey had finished him in Hollywood. It finished me before I got started, though I'd always known it wasn't the place for me and didn't care. Seeing Tarkovsky's *Mirror* in the middle of the making of *The Blue Bird* stamped my poetic film priorities for the rest of my career. I felt sorry for George, but he wasn't so depressed that he couldn't go on making fun of me, of both what he called my 'humble origins' and my much-mocked 'elevated status' as a translator of 'highbrow' classics, with a hit on Broadway. 'I thought', he said, 'that someone of your humble origins might like to be picked up in a green Rolls-Royce.' And that's what he sent, and I rode in it down Sunset Boulevard. I'd given him some of my books of poems and theatre texts, and he said that he'd put me in his library with other authors who had been his friends and had inscribed books to him. He wasn't sure, he mocked, quite where I belonged, and pointed out my tomes wedged between Thomas Mann and Irving Berlin. Katharine Hepburn, who lived next door, dropped in for tea. He showed me the place in the garden where Laurence Olivier and Vivien Leigh had a blazing row.

When I was next in Hollywood I took my son Max with me. I had been asked to meet with John Williams, the film composer most famous for *Jaws* and *Star Wars*, to discuss the possibility of working together on a musical based on

Bernard Shaw's early novel, *Cashel Byron's Profession* (1882). Max, though still very young, had also been inspired by the great cinematographer Freddie Young when I'd taken him with me to Leningrad on one of my *Blue Bird* trips. He had by this time an 8 mm cine camera and was filming in George Cukor's garden, where I was talking with George and another person, who told Max not to intrude. Cukor threw a fit and berated his other guest for discouraging the boy. Then he went through the motions of setting up the scene for Max and calling 'Action!' Max wasn't discouraged. We also went to the studios to watch John Williams conduct the recording of his soundtrack to John Frankenheimer's film *Black Sunday*. John Williams and I came to a mutual decision that we weren't really suited to each other, and my Hollywood career ended for ever.

These were seminal experiences also for Max. It was my son Max who was to teach me many of the technicalities of film and deepen my understanding of the process. From an early age he had a brilliant grasp of the medium. I remember him coming with me to Cinecittà, the great film studios in Rome, where Franco Zeffirelli was shooting *La Traviata*, with my then wife, Teresa Stratas, singing the role of Violetta. Zeffirelli gave Max a giant wheel of Dolcelatte cheese as a reward for spotting that in the sets for *Traviata* at Cinecittà you would see the camera and crew reflected in the highly polished and gilded antique furniture. We watched films together, and he would provide a fascinating commentary on how the shots were set up. He came with me when we were filming *The Blasphemers' Banquet* in Bradford and in London. Before his cruel illness he became a camera assistant and worked in that capacity on Peter Greenaway's *The Cook, the Thief, His Wife and Her Lover.* My son taught me a great deal about film, passed on as he learned it with passionate commitment himself.

Certain seeds had been sown in these early experiences which meant that the tentative first verse commentary I made for *Arctic Paradise* in 1981 was not a venture into totally unknown territory, though it was my first experience of the cutting room, which by degrees became the place I did more of my work, rather than in a secluded room or study. For this film, produced by Andrée Molyneux, I used the metres of Robert Service, the Scots-born Yukon Balladeer. This story for a *World About Us* slot was of a young man, Roger Mendelsohn, who'd left his job in the city to go and live as a trapper with his wife and family in the Yukon. The first thing that struck me in trying to write verse for already cut film was that I often needed a longer hold on the beginning or end of shots. Even later I've found cameramen, even those who've worked with me on more than one film, using their free eye to raise an eyebrow at the length of time elapsing before being asked to cut. In a second shoot in the new Yukon gold rush, Andrée Molyneux brought back longer shots and it helped the verse to develop a story in a different, more concentrated way than in coinciding with a continuous, quickly intercut sequence. Later, working with my great collaborator, Peter Symes, we developed an understanding of the length of holds on close-ups and the pace and momentum of tracking and crane shots.

Arctic Paradise was a tentative beginning, but it led to another work for television produced by Andrée Molyneux,

The Big H (1984), not strictly a film poem of the kind Peter Symes and I pioneered, but again another step on the way to understanding the processes that made verse work or not on the screen. It was also the beginning of a screen collaboration with the composer Dominic Muldowney, who later worked with me on *The Blasphemers' Banquet* (1989) and *Black Daisies for the Bride* (1993), as well as the ambitious theatre piece for the National Theatre, *Square Rounds* (1992). *The Big H* (1984) was important too in that poet and composer collaborated from the beginning, even before the text was finished. All stages towards the fluid collaborations of the later film poems.

What I really needed, I thought, was an involvment in the entire process, so that I could join up all my fragmentary film experiences. And this is exactly what began to happen when I started to work with Peter Symes, first on *Loving Memory* (1987), then *The Blasphemers' Banquet*, *Gaze of the Gorgon* and *Black Daisies for the Bride*, a collaboration with a brilliant and patient colleague with whom I shared locations and cutting room in an increasingly creative partnership. We began from scratch with no ideas of models and slowly evolved a way of working that became increasingly organic, open and fluid.

In enterprises as collaborative as theatre or film I like to work with the same people, and go from one project to another, taking the discoveries made from project to project. In theatre it was the twenty-year relationship with the great designer Jocelyn Herbert, who also designed my feature film, *Prometheus*, which grew out of both my verse for the theatre and my TV film poems. With films it has meant rich, fruitful collaborations on eight films with the director Peter Symes, on five films with the cameraman Alistair Cameron, with the Bristol editor Peter Simpson and the composer Richard Blackford, who has worked on *A Maybe Day in Kazakhstan* (1994), *The Shadow of Hiroshima* (1995), *Prometheus* (1998), *Metamorpheus* (2000) and *Crossings* (2003), as well as plays like *The Kaisers of Carnuntum* (1995), *The Labourers of Herakles* (1995) and *The Prince's Play* (1996), and who will be working on my new play, *Fram*, for the National Theatre early in 2008.

The irony is that now I have found a brilliant team to work with, no one seems to want me to make any more films. The ranks of producers swell up with the stupid, the timorous and the mercenary. Few people, except those that were a part of it, understand how these film poems were made. Neither film people nor the sad poetry world. This volume, *Collected Film Poetry*, could well have been called *Complete Film Poetry*, as I don't think it's likely that I'll ever get funding for another film poem, though I am fuller of ideas than ever. There is much more for me to discover in the film poem.

The most apparently prosaic can be poetic. The camera's eye can make the most familiar or unregarded object or person worthy of new attention and regard. It was a feeling of this kind that I had when I wrote one of my 'couplays', solicited by a Cukor cable for Elizabeth Taylor in her role as Light in the 'transcendental pantomime' of Maeterlinck:

> I am the Light that helps men see
> the radiance in reality.

Sadly, this 'couplay' is still in the film, but I had taken the idea from the main theme of the original play. Even Maeterlinck was saying that the trail of the transcendent leads back to the illuminated, transformed ordinariness of home. When the two children in *The Blue Bird*, Tyltyl and Mytyl, return from their adventures in the Land of Memory, the Palace of Night, the Forest, the Palace of Happiness, the Kingdom of the Future, they have in Act VI, scene ii, 'The Awakening'. Maeterlinck's stage directions read: 'The same setting as in Act I, but the objects, the walls and the atmosphere all appear incomparably and magically fresher, happy, more smiling.' Tyltyl looks at his turtle dove in its cage: 'Hello, why he's blue . . . But it's my turtle dove! . . . But he's much bluer than when I went away! Why that's the blue bird we were looking for! . . . We went so far and he was here all the time!'

It is here and now all the time, not in any hereafter. It is the nature of the combined prosodies of film and poetry to keep on making this simple discovery. It is not in the hereafter, it is here and now all the time in both its ghastly agony and its glories.

When I did my *Lysistrata* of Aristophanes in the predominantly Muslim northern Nigeria in 1964, I put an epigraph in the programme and the published text from a translation of a sentence in the Koran about the Greeks: 'They care for this fleeting life but of the life to come they are heedless.' Which also describes my own feelings about this life and the hereafter, and I went back to the phrase when searching for something to be sung by a life-affirming voice against the ugliness of fundamentalist rant that we filmed in the controversial film Peter Symes and I made defending Salman Rushdie and blasphemy in *The Blasphemers' Banquet*:

Oh, I love this fleeting life!

The recognition of the fleeting nature of this life is certainly the most fruitful condition for the loving of it. The flickering momentum of the flicks is a condition for the framing and focus of the camera lens, and the metrical beat of poetry makes the mind both aware of the inbuilt transience of temporal motion and also relishingly sensible of the sensual sounds of combined vowels and consonants carried by that unstoppable beat. Metrical ictus and screen scansion reflect what is fleeting and can keep up alongside savouring the detail each passes through. 'Prosody', wrote Joseph Brodsky, 'is simply a repository of time within language.' Committing to metre is to emphasise the time that ticks away as our lives get shorter. It opens itself without panic to the time that is counting down to our ends. Again, as Joseph Brodsky has written in the same wonderful essay on Akhmatova, 'prosody absorbs death'. It was no accident, I think, that I began to realise these connections in a really organic way when Peter Symes and I made our first four films of the *Loving Memory* sequence. *Loving Memory* revealed this structure to me more clearly than ever before, partly because it involved so many graveyards and cemeteries. What I dramatised in the films was the struggle between memory that resists time and oblivion that lets time have its way. The scansions of the screen and the prosodies of poetry co-exist to create a third kind of mutually illuminating momentum, which is the film poem, whose potential range and depth have not been fully explored. These texts only partially represent my own various attempts at the form. They will always require the films they are an organic part of to be fully understood.

[Newcastle-upon-Tyne]

The Inky Digit of Defiance

2009

Harold Pinter said in the speech he made in 1970 on receiving the German Shakespeare Prize in Hamburg: 'If I find
writing difficult, I find giving a public address doubly so.'
I could double that again! Or quadruple it. I'm the most
reluctant of speech-makers.

But because this prize bears Harold Pinter's name, I am
touched and honoured to be thought worthy of it, and I
can feel it as a continuation of that warm encouragement
and support I had from Harold during his life. I would like
to humbly acknowledge the kinship I felt with him during
his life and that I feel now in accepting this prize in his
name. Harold Pinter not only was an inspiration through
all his own work, but also encouraged me in my work both
publicly and privately.

I feel that he is still sending those immensely generous
postcards I'd receive: for example, after the *Oresteia* opened
at the National Theatre in 1981, or my *Selected Poems* was
published, or a film poem went out on the BBC or Channel
Four. I have one that I will always treasure that I got after
The Shadow of Hiroshima, in 1995: 'Tony – Brilliant! In all
departments! Harold.'

When the full force of the *Daily Mail* and Tory rent-
a-quotes descended on me in November 1987 and there

were questions in Parliament about the broadcasting of my reading of my poem *v.* on Channel Four, Harold was a prominent public supporter. These were typical quotes from critics and MPs, etc., on my poem *v.*:

'a cascade of obscenities' (Teddy Taylor, MP)
'another probably Bolshie poet seeking to impose his
    frustrations on the rest of us' (Gerald Howarth, MP)
'the riff-raff takes over' (Sir Gilbert Longden, MP)

and:

'disgusting programme'
'surely nobody wants to hear this tripe'
'isn't there enough sadness in the world without
    showing this'
'totally disgusting'
'totally disgusting rubbish'
'unnecessary and obscene'
'a torrent of four-letter filth'
'Scargill poem is the pits'

What aggravated many even more than the language was that they thought I had dedicated the poem to Arthur Scargill, the leader of the miners' union. I hadn't dedicated the poem, but what I had done was to quote from an interview Scargill had given to the *Sunday Times* in 1982 and use it as an epigraph to the poem. Speaking of his father, Arthur Scargill said: 'My father still reads the dictionary every day. He says your life depends on your power to master words.'

Mastering words is an important struggle. It has been my struggle for over fifty years and I first witnessed it early in my two uncles that I celebrate in my poem 'Heredity':

> 'How you became a poet's a mystery.
> Wherever did you get your talent from?'
> I say: 'I had two uncles, Joe and Harry,
> one was a stammerer, the other dumb!'

My Uncle Joe, who lived with us when I was a child, had the worst stammer I have ever seen in anyone. Nonetheless, he worked in a printer's in Leeds and could set type brilliantly fast, without a single falter. His jaws would stick on a consonant for so long that the baulked energy would go through his whole body and make him stamp his feet, but as a compositor he was astonishingly fluent.

My Uncle Harry, deaf and dumb, was a window cleaner in Ilkley, and he wielded a thick Funk and Wagnalls dictionary in one hand, pointing to the word he wanted with the other, when I didn't have enough fluency in sign language. The boards of the dictionary were long ripped off. The pages were of tattered India paper. He licked his fingers frequently so as to be able to flick through the pages fast, and a little of the ink of the lexicon darkened his defiant digit. The defiance was always directed against what he called with two jabs at the brandished dictionary 'Tory error'.

I heard a phrase on a late BBC World Service programme about the recent election in Afghanistan. The reporter spoke of women coming from the polling booth proudly displaying fingers marked with indelible ink to show they had voted. 'The inky digit of defiance', the reporter called it. I thought that also described my Uncle Harry's finger, darkened by his manic lexical need. These early experiences of family inarticulacy were what drove me, I see now in retrospect, into a passion for language and languages, and for what is still for me the supreme articulacy and eloquence of poetry.

We poets acquire our inky digits, especially perhaps those like me who still use a fountain pen and notebooks in a digital age, through our own form of defiance.

The two inkiest digits are those of the V-sign (turned the wrong way round) or the 'Fuck you!' single middle digit. When Harold Pinter was awarded the Nobel Prize, a Steve Bell cartoon appeared in the *Guardian*, exactly four years ago today, showing Bush and Blair gloating over an award which was a mounted golden hand whose defiant middle digit had the head of Harold Pinter, and Bush saying, 'Great news! They've given us the Nobel Prize for World Statesmanship.' The golden hand with the Pinter-proud digit would make an appropriate trophy for this prize.

Richard Eyre, who directed my almost banned reading of *v.* on Channel Four, found film footage to include Mrs Thatcher giving the V-sign (no doubt directed at the British miners) the opposite way round from Churchill's V-sign in the war. But my choice of the quotation from Arthur Scargill was as much connected with my uncles as with mining, though the poem was written at the time of the miners' strike. My granddaughter, who wasn't even born when all the fuss about *v.* happened, has just received her A-level English reading list and it includes the poem heaped with condemnation twenty years ago. Harold was one of the writers who prominently defended the poem and the right to broadcast it.

His own poetry raised similar hostility.

I admired his laser-focused rage in those war poems, which I was proud and honoured to have read on his behalf at the Royal Court in October 2005. But, of course, it is that rage which makes the poetry world flutter, unable to understand that there is a necessary poetry to be made out of political fury. I had similar patronising responses: 'The fury of his polemic has been detrimental to his verse.' The poems of Harold's which raised the same literary hackles were such poems as 'Democracy':

> There's no escape.
> The big pricks are out.
> They'll fuck everything in sight.
> Watch your back.
>
> (March 2003)

or 'American Football (A Reflection Upon the Gulf War)':

> Hallelujah!
> It works.
> We blew the shit out of them.
>
> We blew the shit right back up their own ass
> And out their fucking ears.

It works.
We blew the shit out of them.
They suffocated in their own shit!

Hallelujah.
Praise the Lord for all good things.

We blew them into fucking shit.
They are eating it.

Praise the Lord for all good things.

We blew their balls into shards of dust,
Into shards of fucking dust.

We did it.

Now I want you to come over here and kiss me
    on the mouth.

(August 1991)

Harold had great problems getting this poem published, as
he recounts in 'Blowing Up the Media', in *Index on Censorship* (1992). The *London Review of Books*, the *Guardian*, the
Observer and the *Independent* declined to publish it.

I had a similar experience with one of my poems, though
it wasn't one of my anti-war poems. It was a republican
squib on what would be a laureate occasion: the second
marriage of Prince Charles.

'Legal Ruling'

Our future King *de jure* may be dunked
into his spouse's cunt no more his whore's.
O let Law make this monarch as defunct
as Camilla's tampon after menopause.

My own problems in this department include not only the
onslaught on *v.* and its broadcast on Channel Four, but also
letters from the Archbishop of Canterbury to the prime
minister recommending that my film poem in defence of
Salman Rushdie and blasphemy, *The Blasphemers' Banquet*,
in 1989, should not be broadcast. And on the twentieth
anniversary of the fatwa against Salman Rushdie – marked
by PEN at the National Theatre in February of this year
– the BBC chose not to repeat the programme for fear of
offending increasingly vociferous religious groups.

A poet's rage has as much place in his poetry as the
'emotion recollected in tranquillity'. We would all like to
concentrate on moments of beauty in our lives and poems,
maybe small haiku perceptions of wonder and joy and love.
There are such moments in Harold's poetry and in mine.
There are tender lines to Antonia in Harold's poetry, and
tender lines to Sian in mine. Harold called my poetry 'outrageous and abrasive', but added that my family poems
were 'immeasurably tender'.

And I sit at my desk and write and look at my apple
trees, my figs, my mulberries, and want so much to make
poems from them, but as Brecht wrote in 'Bad Time for
Poetry':

Inside me contend
Delight at the apple tree in blossom
And horror at the house-painter's speeches.
But only the second
Drives me to my desk.

The same tension between delight and horror, between blossoms and dangerous political bullshit, that Brecht talks about must exist in us all. At a time when my delight was in my apple trees, whose fruits I store and live on during the winter sliced into my porridge, many of the horrors came from Blair, Bush and their coalition cohorts, and the illegal occupation of Iraq.

But I do try to write about my apple trees, and in fact I was writing about one of my apple trees, and about love, in a poem which was called 'October 2006'. It tries to make a moment hang as if preserved in the amber of millennia:

This ladder creaks. Take that ring off
I bought for you in Gdansk,
first token of my growing love,
with the forty-million-year-old fly
embalmed in its amber,
resin oozed before Man,
not to bruise the apples I drop
for you to catch from the Bramley
I planted after that Polish trip.

I was tinkering with this poem when I heard Geoff Hoon saying on the radio that the mothers of mutilated children in Iraq would one day live to be grateful to the coalition cluster bombs. That drove me to my desk. I wrote four lines full of fury which I faxed to the *Guardian* immediately, and it appeared next day with a photo of a smug Geoff Hoon beneath an enormous tank. It was called 'Baghdad Lullaby':

Shhh! Shhh! Though now shrapnel makes you shriek
and deformity in future may brand you as a freak,
you'll see one day disablement's a blessing and a boon
sent in baby-seeking bomblets by benefactor Hoon.

But I have actually written many poems about trees, like 'Cypress and Cedar', and about fruit, for example, 'A Kumquat for John Keats' or 'Fig on the Tyne', and have coined a word for what is my basic existential philosophy – 'fruitility':

Meaningless our lives may be
but blessed with deep fruitility.

Again, thinking about a long poem I've been writing on and off about my compost heap, I was driven to my desk with the same ferocity when I saw the picture of the wide-eyed, beautiful Iraqi boy Ali Ismail Abbas, a victim of coalition cluster bombs, lying with no arms in his hospital bed. This was 'PM am':

Why is it, Lord, although I'm right,
I find it hard to sleep at night?
Sometimes I wake up in a sweat

> they've not found WMDs yet!
> The thought that preys most on my mind
> is the only arms they'll ever find
>
> (unless somehow I get MI6
> to plant them to be found by Blix
> that's *if* the UN sneaks back in)
>
> are Ali's in the surgeon's bin.

This went to the *London Review of Books*, but I later extended the poem into 'Holy Tony's Prayer', which features 'Holy Tony' imagining an Iraq victory photo op, with little Ali Ismail Abbas standing next to him making a 'V for victory' sign with his prosthetic arm, and ends with an injunction from Blair to the spin doctors to make sure they

> twist his wrist the right way round.

I cheered Harold's naming of our home-grown war criminal, Tony Blair, in his Nobel Prize acceptance speech. The contemplation of the apple blossom is continually broken by rage at political events. As Brecht says in another of his poems, 'To Posterity':

> Ah, what an age it is
> When to speak of trees is almost a crime
> For it is a kind of silence about injustice.

We must never forget that here in our own country there is a lust for censorship lurking in the undergrowth that could easily be inflamed. We need wide-eyed vigilance over our freedom of speech and must never be silent about injustice. But for the moment, while Myanmar (Burma), Iran, China and many other countries monitored by PEN put their poets in prison cells, we put ours in Poets' Corner! I sincerely hope to be spared both.

It's not that I shun monuments to, or busts and statues of, poets. In fact, I often make a point of seeking them out and have used them as mouthpieces in my film poetry, as with Heinrich Heine in *The Gaze of the Gorgon*.

Heine had one monument in a park outside the Frankfurt Opera which is used by heroin addicts to shoot up in. Heine's hair was covered in blood sprayed from the veins of junkies when the injections went wrong. The other Heine was in Corfu, in the palace of Sisi, Empress of Austria, who adored the poet. At her assassination the palace was bought by the German Kaiser, and his first act was to get rid of what he called 'that syphilitic Jew'.

Statues are one of the ways I try to test the traditions of European culture against the most modern destructive forces. I even have busts in my home. Before you enter my house you will see a brass classical lyre on my door. It is my door knocker. It marks the door into a poet's lair. What do you do with this lyre, the lyre that sets the key for 'lyrical' poetry, the lyre that accompanies the poetry of the trees you will walk through to the lyre on my door? What do you do with this lyre? You bang it hard against the door. You change it into percussion. When I hear the lyre banging on the door I will open it, and the first thing you will see in my hallway is a large eighteenth-century bust of Milton, who stares at me as I watch TV and reminds me of the grave and seriously committed role of the poet, and who, though he was blind, had one of the most unflinching and unswerving gazes of all English poets. He is one of my great heroes.

I have a mini-version of this bust looking at me as I type in my attic. I have small busts of Homer, Dante, Byron and Strindberg, and framed engravings of Molière, Shakespeare, Kipling, a photo and a manuscript of Yeats. There is also on my staircase a manuscript of Victor Hugo, along with a pressed flower from his spectacular funeral, at which, it was said, 'The prostitutes of Paris, as a mark of respect, draped their pudenda in black crêpe.' I made a republican version of his *Le Roi s'amuse*, with a libidinous Victorian Prince of Wales and an obsequious Poet Laureate in his rowdy retinue. I often find myself quoting from Victor Hugo after one of my many theatrical ventures. 'Now that my play is a failure,' he once said, 'I find I love it all the more.' I quoted that after *Square Rounds* at the Olivier in 1992. Fifteen years after, I re-directed *Square Rounds* in Russian translation at the Taganka Theatre in Moscow, where it is still in the repertoire. Every morning I walked into rehearsal up a staircase which had on every step on both sides a different statue of Pushkin.

From this venture I acquired another set of more portable writers' monuments: a Russian *matrioshka* doll, only this has a Turgenev inside a Pushkin inside a Tolstoy inside a Dostoevsky inside a Chekhov.

If the busts of John Milton and the others urge me on,

there is also watching me a bust of John Nicholson as a cautionary reminder of what happens to a poet who betrays his true voice for the praise of genteel admirers, money or fame. John Nicholson, known as 'the Airedale Bard', was a Yorkshire woolsorter who etched his poems in the grease left by the fleeces he worked with in the mill. He acquired the condescending appellation 'the woolsorter poet'.

He drowned in the River Aire, drunk, near Salts Mill, Saltaire, in 1843. He wrote about the exploited children in the factories of Leeds and Bradford, then was bribed by attention and money to become more pastoral and pleasing to his aristocratic patrons. I wrote a play about him for Salts Mill in 1993 which was revived in 2003. It was called *Poetry or Bust*. Nicholson swapped his integrity for a bust that meant fame, acceptance, compromise.

An old Yorkshire woman who saw the play at the Mill said she had the original bust of Nicholson, a plaster one, and that I could have it. She said, 'It's about as much use to me as a chocolate fireguard.' So I am urged on by the one John and served a warning by the other.

And my house is full of more important monuments to poets: their books. There are thousands of them in my house, from all ages and in many languages. There are ancient authors, especially the Greek tragedians, in hundreds of annotated editions; there are Czech poets, Polish poets, Russian poets, Italian, Spanish, Greek, South American, French, Sanskrit, Japanese, Chinese, etc., etc., etc. ... Poets who have been or are in prison, poets who have been murdered, poets whose books have been burned. There are signed copies by friends, like Wole Soyinka, with whom I did shows when we were both students at Leeds, whose crossing of the Nigerian junta resulted in his solitary confinement. Partly because of him, I spent four years in Nigeria.

After Africa, I spent a year and a half in Prague, and I got to know that wonderful poet and scientist Miroslav Holub, whose signed books I also have. He had long experience of surveillance and censorship. I dedicated a poem to him that I wrote in Cuba in August 1969, exactly a year after the Soviet Union invaded Czechoslovakia.

The Soviet fleet was making a very show-of-force visit to Havana. There was a torrential tropical downpour which brought all the celebratory posters down from the harbour lamp posts. I collected one, and the image was used on the cover of the *London Magazine* (April 1970), in which I wrote one of my rare pieces of prose, on Cuba (see 'Shango the Shaky Fairy', this volume, pp. 53–80). I framed the poster later to remind me. It is large and I've never put it up as the Soviet battleship's gun barrels are too central and too threatening. The poem I wrote for Miroslav Holub was called 'On the Spot':

> Watching the Soviet subs surface
> at the side of flagged battleships
> between Havana harbour and the USA
> I can't help thinking how the sword
> has developed immensely . . .
> while the pen is still only
> a point, a free ink-flow
> and the witness it has to keep bearing.

Miroslav, you must remember
there'd be no rumba now,
if the blacks who made Cuba
had not somehow evolved
either when shackled or pegged
or grouped for a whiplash harangue . . .

together, somehow, with slight spasms
of only the nipples or haunches,
a calf muscle tugging the chain taut,
the art of dancing on the spot
without ever being seen to be moving,
not a foot or a hand out of place.

I went back to Prague during the Soviet occupation and
saw Holub. I brought back with me, hidden in a child's
puppet theatre, many recent anti-occupation cartoons by
Jiří Jirásek. I arranged an exhibition of them. The front of
the catalogue had Jirásek's cartoon of a Soviet tank, with
its gun barrel belching forth smoke, that read in Cyrillic
capitals, 'PRAVDA!'

And among these busts and these thousands of books
in my house I have one of Jocelyn Herbert's masks for the
Oresteia I did with Peter Hall at the NT in 1981. The Greek
tragic mask is one of my main metaphors for the role of the
poet. The eyes of the tragic mask are always open to witness even the worst, and the mouth is always open to make
poetry from it. Neither ever close.

Along with all this, from my first film for the cinema I
have the burned head of my golden statue of Prometheus,

the great Titan who gave man fire and the inwardness and poetry that came from its contemplation. I keep it for its unflinching, unswerving, even still almost hopeful gaze, staring from the earliest times to our own. I had the twenty-odd-foot golden statue chained to a Caucasus I created in the appropriately named Titan cement works in Elefsina in Greece, next to the petrochemical works.

The film ends with a conflagration that consumes the golden statue except for the raised, still chained, though still defiant right hand, all its digits clenched. When the crew and actors had left, I found his burned head, which had fallen while it was blazing into the quarry. It was completely burned and black except for the two eyes, which remained golden, so though destroyed it still shone with its first glorious visions for mankind.

Like the tragic mask that I have with its always open eyes and the mouth always open for poetry, this charred head of mankind's first champion helps to remind me that the poetic gaze must keep unswerving and unflinching, as does the example of poets persecuted, silenced, killed in previous centuries and in our own.

Yiannis Ritsos, the great Greek poet whose books were burned before the temple of Zeus in Athens by the Greek colonels, has a poem about the eye of Geo Milev (1895–1925), the Bulgarian poet. Milev had a blue glass eye, and when he was arrested and burned alive by the police all that was left of him in the crematorium was the blue glass eye. This is from the poem of Ritsos:

His eye is being kept in the Museum of Revolution
like a seeing stone of the struggle. I saw his eye.
In his pupil there was the full story of the Revolution,
blue scenes of blood-stained years,
blue scenes with red flags
with dead who carry in their raised hands a blue day.
His eye never closes,
this eye keeps vigil over Sofia.
This eye is a blue star in all the nights.
This eye sees and illuminates and judges.
Whoever looks at this eye wins back his eyes.
Whoever looks at this eye sees the world.

(trans. Ninetta Makrinikola)

So I do not shun monuments to poets.

And though I have to confess I do not care for it, I even have visited the poets in Poets' Corner, late in my life, and more than once, for reasons that I will explain.

In my last play for the NT, *Fram*, the opening scene begins in Westminster Abbey, where light from the stained-glass Aeschylus in the rose window falls on the memorial to Gilbert Murray, one of his most renowned translators, and brings him back to life. Though I have a great resistance to making a Greek tragedian an honorary Christian, as T. S. Eliot also made of Virgil, this wonderful combination gave me the opening scene of my play. But I had gone to the Abbey on an entirely different, quite other quest. I went to the Abbey and to Poets' Corner to search for the monument of Thomas May, secretary to Cromwell's Parliament and the translator of the Roman republican poet Lucan, who committed suicide at twenty-six after being exposed as being part of a plot to remove the Emperor Nero, and whose epic, the *Pharsalia*, is regarded by Shelley for one as greater than the *Aeneid* of the Imperial Laureate, Virgil.

Though I came to share Shelley's preference for Lucan and knew May as one of his translators, I first came across him as a translator of the Roman epigrammatist Martial, some of whose satirical epigrams I used to make fun of New York when I lived there, in a pamphlet of poems called *US Martial*. But the poem that May had translated and which was my first experience of him wasn't satirical at all but a poem about Vesuvius, a volcano I had become obsessed with since the time when I made one of my film poems in Napoli called *Mimmo Perrella non è piu* in 1987. I have been often to Napoli since, most recently two days after I was told I would be given this prize. I also translated the same Martial poem myself and I have it in my notebook opposite a photograph of a wall painting from Pompeii showing Vesuvius before its great eruption in AD 79. It is verdantly green and covered with vines. My translation reads:

Vesuvius, green yesterday with shady vine,
     where the crushed grape gushed vast vats of wine,
ridges, Bacchus loved and put before
     his birthplace Nysa, Venus favoured more
than Lacedaemon, and where Satyrs stomped
     till now, and Herculaneum, all swamped,
engulfed by cinders in a flood of fire:
power like this not even gods desire.

(Martial IV, 44)

Thomas May translated the last line, 'The gods are grill'd that such great powers they had.' And I called the entire long poem *The Grilling* after his word, as it's a dialogue with the ghost of Goethe, who had climbed Vesuvius two hundred years before I did. I use Vesuvius as a metaphor for all the fiery devastation of our times, the power that not even gods desire grabbed blindly by men. This had also been prompted by my being told that officers in the Italian army were taught in the cold war that Napoli was the first target for Soviet nuclear weapons in the event of atomic warfare. And I had to advise Goethe that since his day the city of Würzburg, from where throughout his life he ordered his favourite wine, had been levelled by Allied bombing, and the special bottles associated with Würzburg wine, the *Bocksbeutel*, or 'goat's scrotum', exploded in the raid and all their glass fused together, and clouds of Riesling steam rose into the air.

I included my own translation of Martial's poem and Thomas May's together in *The Grilling*, set on the slopes of Vesuvius. And I had gone to Poets' Corner to look for my fellow poet and translator and, I should say, my fellow republican.

But Thomas May is no longer in the Abbey. As secretary to the Long Parliament and translator of the great republican epic the *Pharsalia* of Lucan, his remains were removed at the Restoration in 1660 and flung in a pit and the monument reused. Behind the present monument to a sub-dean, Thomas Triplet, there are the ghostly remnants of a larger monument. It had been that to Thomas May. It had an inscription from the republican Lucan. As David Norbrook says in his book *Writing the English Republic*: 'English literary culture has never entirely undone those expulsions.'

Opposite this space where Thomas May once had his resting place, and close to Gilbert Murray and either insensitively placed or put there maliciously, is Gilbert Murray's cruellest critic, T. S. Eliot. The Abbey geography of the Greek scholar and translator of Greek tragedy Murray set between the inspiring stained glass of his Aeschylus and his most vicious critic got me going on my play *Fram*, but it made me look at the qualifications needed to enter that sacred and exclusive club. The official guidebook to Poets' Corner (PC) says: 'Sometimes a poet's lifestyle or politics preclude him from being given a Poets' Corner honour (until a new generation has forgiven or forgotten).' For some the forgiveness takes a long time.

Shelley, who died in 1822, was refused a memorial 'because of his atheism', and didn't qualify till 1946 – 124 years! But he is still largely accepted for 'The Skylark' rather than:

> I met Murder on the way –
> He had a mask like Castlereagh
>
> *and when I got to Parliament Square*
> *the mask had changed to Tony Blair*

– at least that's what the pencilled addition reads in my copy of Shelley.

Byron, who died in 1824, was excluded till 1969 – 145 years. In 1924, on the centenary of his death, a petition for an Abbey memorial was turned down by Dean Herbert Ryle, who said that Byron, 'partly by his openly dissolute life and partly by the influence of his licentious verse, earned a world-wide reputation for immorality among English-speaking people'. It took Milton, who died in 1674, sixty-three years to pass muster.

T. S. Eliot, who is critically sniffy about Shelley and Milton and was a self-proclaimed 'Royalist in politics, Anglo-Catholic in religion, and classicist in literature', only had to wait two years to get into the Abbey after his death!

Robert Graves called Eliot 'the Senior Churchwarden to English Literature'. He was the first president of the Virgil Society, and I was president in 2000. It is interesting to compare our addresses. What will happen to T. S. Eliot when all his known, reputedly pornographic verses are published in the *Complete Poems* promised by Faber & Faber? Will he be removed like Thomas May?

It was my obsession with Vesuvius that led me to seek the now desecrated tomb of Thomas May, and just after I was informed that I would be the first recipient of the PEN/Pinter Prize I had to go to Napoli to read my poetry. The Italians have taken to my poetry far more readily than the British, if I am to be honest. I have three books of poems published by Einaudi, and that gets me many very welcome invitations to read there. And Napoli I especially love after I made one of my film poems there in 1987. I have been there many times since and know the city well. Sian and I always try to stay in the same little old-fashioned hotel. The rooms have a great view of Vesuvius. In the evenings we eat in the Piazza Sannazaro in Mergellina. There are, very close to the *trattoria* Da Pasqualino, the tombs and monuments to three poets whose presences have been important to me, one way or another. I visit them every time I am giving a reading or showing a film in Napoli.

Near the Mergellina station, in a small park, are the tombs of Virgil and of Leopardi. I lived long years with Virgil and almost completed a doctoral thesis on him before making a deliberate, defiant decision to abandon it. One reason was that I didn't want to be an academic and do poetry in my spare time. Poetry had to be the whole venture of my life. The other reason was that I began to have huge misgivings about Virgil's *Aeneid*. He was in a way the first laureate poet in history, and his epic reeks of the compromises he made. I began, like Shelley, to prefer Lucan and his lament for the Roman republic in the *Pharsalia*.

The Thomas May whose ejection from Westminster Abbey I mentioned earlier addresses Virgil and compares him to Lucan:

> Thou gott'st Augustus loue, he Nero's hate;
> But 'twas an act more great, and high to moue
> A Princes envy, then a Princes loue.

Robert Graves wrote: 'Few poets have brought such discredit as Virgil on their sacred calling.' Elsewhere he says why: 'Why Virgil's poems have for the last two thousand years exercised so great an influence on our Western culture is, paradoxically, because he was a renegade to the true Muse. His pliability; his subservience; his narrowness; his denial of that stubborn imaginative freedom which the

- 478 -

true poets who had preceded him had prized; his perfect lack of originality, courage, humour, or even animal spirits; these were the negative qualities which first commended him to government circles and have kept him in favour ever since.'

Next to Virgil is Leopardi, Italy's greatest Romantic poet, and I always read his poem 'La ginestra' (1836). I get myself a seat in a café in Mergellina, where I have a direct view of Vesuvius, and order a bottle of chilled volcanic wine, *Falanghina* or *Fino di Avellino* or *Greco di Tufo* or *Lacrima Christi*. I have already written a poem about walking to the summit of the volcano in *The Grilling*, where I use it to represent the unexpected and horrific, fiery, mostly man-made dangers of our times. What Leopardi's poem does is to focus not on the vines of the Martial poem that Thomas May and I translated, but on the bright yellow broom (*la ginestra*) that still now covers the slopes of Vesuvius, '*sterminator Vesevo*' (exterminator Vesuvius). *La ginestra* is bright yellow, and Leopardi insists it doesn't grovel to any superior power, man or god. It simply burns brightly. It's partly a metaphor for the poet. It is like Luther's apple tree planted on the eve of the Apocalypse. It doesn't have humanity's delusions of immortality. No religion makes it bow its head. Its defiance is its burning brightly, beautifully and conspicuously on the slopes of extinction.

On the other side of the Piazza Sannazaro, nearer to the sea, is the church, Santa Maria del Parto, in which if you go behind the altar you will find a bust and monument to Jacopo Sannazaro (1456/8–1530), after whom the square where we eat and drink our chilled volcanic wine is named.

You have a good view of the fishermen of Mergellina sell-
ing their clams and squid and all the ingredients you're
likely to taste in the dishes at Pasqualino's or Ciro's or any
of the nearby restaurants. I was intrigued by Sannazaro
long before I went to Napoli. He transferred the pastoral with the shepherds of Virgil and Theocritus to the
sixteenth-century fishermen of Mergellina. These were
Piscatorial Eclogues.

The monument almost hidden behind the altar has a
bust of Sannazaro which, if the altar and front of the church
were not there, would be directing its unswerving gaze at
Vesuvius. As if to confirm this association, there is behind
Sannazaro, above his marble head, a painting with Muses
bearing a laurel wreath to crown his bust with, and behind
them the winged Pegasus alighting not on Helicon to create Hippocrene, the fountain of inspiration from which
poets drink, but Vesuvius. Inspiration from your own locale
but from the most fearful source. Perhaps more a scalding
geyser than a fountain. The open eye of the poet has to keep
the volcano in his gaze. And even go nearer.

There is a great poem by Primo Levi, who went nearer
and deeper into the destructive fire of our times than most,
about the elder Pliny urging his boatmen to take him nearer
to the erupting Vesuvius in AD 79:

> Don't hold me back, friends, let me set out.
> I won't go far, just to the other shore.
> I want to observe at close hand that dark cloud,
> Shaped like a pine tree, rising above Vesuvius,
> And find the source of this strange light.

Nephew, you don't want to come along?
Fine, stay here and study.
Recopy the notes I gave you yesterday.
[. . .]
Sailors, obey me: launch the boat into the sea.

But many poets can make no journeys.

Some countries give their poets a corner of their own in a prison cell. One such poet in a Myanmar/Burmese poets' corner is Zargana, which is the pen name of Maung Thura, who has recently been condemned to thirty-five years in prison. When he was in solitary confinement he had to scratch his poems with a pot fragment on the floor of his cell, then commit them to memory. I would like in all humility and solidarity to offer the International PEN/ Pinter Prize to him, Maung Thura (Zargana). May all those poets I have summoned up today make him at this moment the centre of their gaze and honour the prisoner-poet for his still defiant poetic gift. He has a poem called 'Poetic Gift' which begins with an image of trees, but it is not 'silent about injustice'.

> From the tree of my feelings
> Sprang exquisite leaves,
> Tendrils, branches
> Which awoke my senses
> And entwined my thoughts.
> And from the lines
> Composed in mind,
> Came these verses

Written in blood,
On blank pages,
With invisible ink.
(trans. Vicky Bowman)

Once I had copied my notes for this reluctant address from my notebook, where I write with a fountain pen, into my laptop, I was aware that I needed to hurry to finish it and print it out. As each page came out of the printer, the big bold type still glisteningly wet, I realised that my shuffling through the pages was giving me the same inky digit I remember on my Uncle Harry's dictionary-raiding hand. This inky digit will always mean I have cast my vote in favour of the dumb or the silenced being given a voice, of totally free speech and the freedom of poetry and poets.

That said, I have also to add that these particular defiant digits become their most indelibly stained when I pick the ripe, juicy mulberries from the trees I'd like the peace and quiet to celebrate in poetry.

The Label Trail to Strasbourg

2011

All my writing life I have used the same notebooks, like this one. Old-fashioned they may appear now in our digital age, but for me poetry is still rooted in the physicality of writing with my hand, with a body in which the heart beats and the blood throbs, and whose rhythms help earth what I write, whose rhythms remind me I am still alive even though my mind wants often to confront the most despairing of events. This is probably why all my work is in verse, often the iambic metre of Shakespeare. '*Le coeur bat l'iambe*,' said the great French actor Jean-Louis Barrault, speaking of Racine. 'The heartbeat that journeys through tragedy.' All the work that is in these hundreds of notebooks is poetry. Poetry. For me the computer screen is too abstract to accommodate my poetry, although I make fair copies on mine and do final edits of long works like plays or film poems.

But when I cut and paste I use real scissors and real glue! There are scissors and glue in all my workrooms. But I have to make these fair copies on computer because after a day or two I can't read my own handwriting. I have a feeling that this illegibility is an almost conscious and deliberate strategy to make me rethink the scrawled and scribbled fountain-pen originals. I use Waterman fountain pens made in Paris. But scholars and researchers are beginning to study these many hundreds of notebooks all containing poetry.

Whether for the page, the stage, the opera house or the screen, it is all poetry, and all of it is written in this same kind of notebook that I have used for almost fifty years. These hundreds of notebooks contain drafts of poems, dramas, libretti, film verse, first in Waterman fountain-pen ink and then typed out, with each variation, sometimes many, glued over the last on the edge of the page so that all versions are quickly accessible. Sometimes the pages have up to ten layers of versions. The notebooks bulge with what is glued into them. They grow almost double or treble in thickness! The scholars who have studied various notebooks have also remarked that the poet has pasted into them newspaper cuttings, pictures, research notes, drawings and, what I think it is apposite to remark on here, wine labels detached from the bottle I'd quaffed and enjoyed and glued into the notebook opposite the page, stage or film poetry. There is a doctoral thesis waiting to be written on the wine labels glued into my hundreds of notebooks.

Although the archive of these hundreds of notebooks is either already placed in or destined for the Brotherton Library of the University of Leeds, the facts I will reveal may suggest that certain pages of them would be equally at home here in Strasbourg.

To give you an example: I recently picked up at random the fourth notebook of a set of four devoted to my translation of Sabina's Czech libretto for Smetana's *The Bartered Bride*, which I did for the Metropolitan Opera in New York in 1978 for the director John Dexter, with whom I'd collaborated at the National Theatre in London, in 1973, on *Le Misanthrope* of Molière, which we set in the Paris of de Gaulle, and, in 1976, on Racine's *Phèdre*, set in India in the early days of the British Raj. The wine labels in Notebook 4 of *The Bartered Bride*, dating from 1978, are on page 815. A set of notebooks devoted to a theatrical project may contain thousands of pages. The twelve notebooks for my most recent play, *Fram*, add up to 3,204 pages. So on page 815 of Notebook 4 for *The Bartered Bride* the scholar will find glued a Schlumberger Gewürztraminer 1974 from Guebwiller, Alsace. It was purchased, as a smaller label reveals, at the 67 Wine and Spirits' merchants on 67th and Columbus Avenue, diagonally across from the Lincoln Center. I must have enjoyed the bottle, as on page 817 of the notebook there is another Schlumberger Gewürztraminer 1974 label! On page 828 there is another label and yet another Alsatian Gewürztraminer 1974, but one produced by A. Willm at Barr, in the Vosges mountains of Alsace. After some drafts of part of a duet between Mařenka, the heroine, and the marriage broker Kecal, page 836 has another wine from A. Willm, a 1975 Cordon d'Alsace, Brut. Then after another hundred pages or so of operatic aria, duets and chorus drafts there is on page 948 the label of a Gewürztraminer, Kuehn from Ammerschwihr.

My work with John Dexter at the Metropolitan Opera led to the Met commissioning an original libretto for a collaboration with the New York composer Jacob Druckman. I finished the libretto. It was called *Medea: A Sex-War Opera*. Druckman sadly died before his score was completed and the opera was never performed, except as a theatre piece without music by a young radical theatre group, Volcano, and in that form it toured Europe. Though the opera had a sad conclusion, it had started auspiciously, as inside the front cover of a notebook, one of the six devoted to the opera, there is the label of a Schlumberger Gewürztraminer 1978 from Guebwiller. Page 1 of the *Medea* is dated September 1980. Composers and Alsatian wine seem to have been a constant in my poetic life.

The notebooks of 1986 are for many poems and a very ambitious theatrical project, *The Common Chorus*, which was intended to be a trilogy for the National Theatre in London consisting of the *Lysistrata* of Aristophanes and *The Trojan Women* of Euripides and, as the conclusion of the trilogy, a new play by myself about the origins of chemical weapons. It was to be imagined as if played by a group of women who were surrounding the US nuclear missile base at Greenham Common in Britain. I had conceived the project on one of my many visits to Delphi in Greece, where I have directed three of my theatre pieces, *The Trackers of Oxyrhynchus*, *The Labourers of Herakles* and *Hecuba* with Vanessa Redgrave. So, as you might expect, there are the occasional retsina and ouzo labels, but what do I find on page 486 of Volume 3 but a label for a Gewürztraminer from Martin Schaetzel, like M. Kuehn also of Ammerschwihr. I don't know if there was any connection between this particular Gewürztraminer from Ammerschwihr and these plays of war, but in the notebook 'Poems 1989–90' I find another Gewürztraminer Kuehn from Ammerschwihr in the pages next to my much-anthologised and translated poems on the first Iraq war, 'A Cold Coming' and 'Initial Illumination', both of which appeared in the news section of the *Guardian* in March 1991.

It was because of these poems that I was later sent by the *Guardian* with my helmet and flak jacket to write poems from Bosnia during the war and the siege of Sarajevo in 1995.

But sadly the project of the three war plays, after years of work, never saw the light of day, though the third play became *Square Rounds*, which I wrote and directed at the NT in 1992 and recently directed again in Russian translation at the Taganka Theatre in Moscow. The composer for *Square Rounds* was Dominic Muldowney, and opposite a programme for a world premiere of one of his compositions was the label from the bottle we shared when we met to discuss a joint project for BBC Television: one of my films called *The Big H*, about Herod's massacre of the innocents, set in a Leeds classroom. The wine which initiated this valued collaboration was a Gewürztraminer Hugel from Riquewihr.

I had first worked with Muldowney when he was a young assistant to the composer Harrison Birtwistle, when we collaborated on a piece of Meyerholdian music theatre called *Bow Down*. In the notebook for *Bow Down* on page 700 there is a label from another Gewürztraminer Hugel of Riquewihr 1974. A much more noted collaboration of mine with Harrison Birtwistle was on the *Oresteia* of Aeschylus exactly thirty years ago at the National Theatre. There are at least a dozen notebooks for this work, and to take a random example, *Oresteia*, Notebook 6, page 1,213 there is a label for a Cuvée des Comtes de Eguisheim Gewürztraminer 1975 from Leon Beyer of Eguisheim.

A wine merchant who was a friend of Harrison Birtwistle asked me, after the *Oresteia*, if there were some

THE INKY DIGIT OF DEFIANCE

good wine poems in ancient Greek which I could translate for his 1984 wine catalogue. I offered him versions
of Hermippus, Anacreon, Theognis, Antipater of Sidon,
Antipater of Thessalonika, Diodoros Zonas, Alcaeus and
Amphis. The page of this wine merchant's catalogue list-
ing wines from Charles Schleret of Turckheim, in Alsace,
is followed by one of the poems of Theognis, who flourished around 544 BC. My payment from the wine merchant
for these translations of ancient Greek was some bottles
of Muscat d'Alsace of Charles Schleret of Turckheim and
some Gewürztraminer from the same grower, as well as a
'Réserve Personnelle' Gewürztraminer from Louis Sipp of
Ribeauville 1976. The following page in the notebook that
has this wine label contains notes for a poem in my sonnet
sequence 'Art and Extinction'.

And in my notebook labelled 'Poems 1991–93' there is
yet another Gewürztraminer label, from Gustave Lorenz
of Bergheim, opposite drafts of my Republican poem
'Deathwatch Danceathon' (translated by Cécile Marshall
in the volume *FUK*).

In Notebook 3, page 727 for *The Mysteries*, my version of
the medieval biblical plays for the NT, which first played in
1977 and then in a complete cycle in the 1980s, and revived
in 2000, and about to be performed again at Shakespeare's
Globe this summer, and what I was working on now on
the train to Strasbourg, there is a label from a Louis Sipp
Gewürztraminer from Ribeauville. And also a note which
is the first idea for a play I wrote for Salts Mill in Saltaire,
Poetry or Bust, about John Nicholson, the Airedale poet.

I wanted to check on the locations of these various

Alsatian wine villages I found celebrated among my poetic manuscripts, which range over forty years from poems to plays to operas to films, and out of the map fell a price list of 1983 from the same Louis Sipp of Ribeauville. I had been in Alsace for the New Year and remember buying (though I haven't yet tracked the label in my notebooks!) a quite expensive bottle of *Eau-de-vie de baies de houx*. It was not simply that I had not heard of an eau-de-vie made from hollyberries, but – it is the poet in me – it was the sheer wonder of the sound: *Eau-de-vie de baies de houx! Eau-de-vie de baies de houx!* I couldn't stop saying it. It happens to me in Greece and I can never resist ordering rabbit with cinnamon (*kouneli me kanella!*) or have a dessert in the winter called *meela me meli ke kanella* (apples with honey and cinnamon). The taster of words and the taster of good things combine when I choose these dishes, and when I selected *Eau-de-vie de baies de houx* from the list of M. Sipp in Ribeauville in 1983. From the same Ribeauville there is on the final page of the three volumes of notebooks devoted to my republican version of Victor Hugo's *Le Roi s'amuse* – that is, page 965 – what must have been my reward for the completion of my version for the National Theatre, which opened on 18 April 1996. It is the golden label from a bottle of Gewürztraminer from Trimbach of Ribeauville, a Cuvée des Seigneurs de Ribeaupierre. Though to prove that my consumption was not entrirely alchoholic there along this wine label a label from an Eau d'Alsace Ribeauville! Also on page 98 of *US Martial*, a small collection I did of the Roman poet Martial which I translated while living in New York, is the label from a Marc d'Alsace de Gewürztraminer

from M. Gisselbrecht of Ribeauville. My splendid translator Cécile Marshall, when she came to Newcastle to talk
about the poems she was translating for this occasion,
brought a Marc de Gewürztraminer no doubt to put me
in a co-operative mood. She probably got her clue from
studying my notebooks when she did her doctoral dissertation on my work. Those scholars of the future who will
study the hundreds of notebooks will have continually to
associate my poems, plays, films and translations to the
labels of Alsatian wine, and work out the connection. I have
given you a random sample, but what they are to me are the
good omens of a trail which has led me here to Strasbourg
today to receive your generous award of the European Prize
for Literature, which I accept with great gratitude.

On page 102 of the same *US Martial* notebook there is
pasted in a photo of Ribeauville, dated December–January
1984, and on the very next page is the manuscript translation, scrawled almost illegibly with my Waterman pen,
of a very short poem by the fourth century BC Greek poet
Amphis, which will be my conclusion:

> One glass and no refill
> is life for men,
> so keep on pouring till
> Death says when.

[Strasbourg]

The David Cohen Prize
for Literature 2015

I wrote my first poems seventy years ago, and have literally spent my lifetime producing poetry for page, stage and screen. The unexpected recognition and enormous encouragement from this generous David Cohen Prize helps me to confirm my commitment to what I have always believed to be a united body of work, wherever the words were printed or performed. In this lifetime of writing I have tried to balance the isolation necessary for serious composition with the communal creation of producing poetry for actors or going on the road in my filming boots. This generous award for the body of my work is accepted with huge gratitude as I approach, with my energy renewed by it, my eighth and, I hope, most creative decade yet, with the poems, plays and films flowing till the end.

I have a short poem which has become a kind of signature tune. I wrote it in response to a woman I overheard talking about my work in the interval of the first night of *The Misanthrope* of Molière, for the National Theatre at the Old Vic in 1973. She was saying of me, 'He has such a command over language! But they say he comes from Sheffield.' It was Leeds actually, but it was all up north as far as she was concerned. I also wrote the poem because my mother around the same time would keep saying to me, 'Where does it come from, our Tony? There's never been anybody artistic in our family.'

The poem is called 'Heredity':

> 'How you became a poet's a mystery.
> Wherever did you get your talent from?'
> I say: 'I had two uncles, Joe and Harry,
> one was a stammerer, the other dumb!'

I feel very much the nephew of Joe and Harry when I have to speak in public like this. And I have always felt very much their nephew in my struggle for the ceremonious articulacy of poetry. From where I am now I can see quite clearly this family awareness of inarticulacy made me hunger for the gift of language. This deep appetite extended even to the dead languages of Latin and ancient Greek that I studied at Leeds Grammar School, to which I won one of the scholarships created by the 1944 Education Act, and later at university. This is a route now firmly closed to young people of the same background as me. From a very young age my head became full of rhythms and rhymes from those I learned on my mother's knee or at school in Beeston, or the Wesleyan hymns from Sunday school, to the ruder ones I learned on the street with other kids, like one that always accompanied the audible fart:

> 'ark! 'ark! T'sound o'thunder!
> Must be t'peas we 'ad on Sunda!
> Quick! Quick! t' closet door!
> Too late! too late! it's over t'floor.

I was drawn to the rhymed recitations of Cyril Fletcher's *Odd Odes* on the wireless and the rhyming of the pantomimes at the Leeds Empire, where I also saw the great northern comedians. Often when I went to the Empire I'd have my classics homework in my pocket, maybe a Greek text of the *Alcestis* of Euripides, and the direct address of the stage I used to unlock the tragic texts I had to study. Years later, when I was preparing the text for the masked NT *Oresteia* for Peter Hall, I had a dream. I dreamed that in my hallway in Newcastle there was something like a large, ornately bound volume embossed on the cover with golden Greek capitals saying '*Oresteia*'. It was intended as an audition roster for the chorus of the Aeschylus trilogy. At dawn there was a queue of old men in my garden. They all wrote their names in the book and disappeared. I picked up the book and read the names. They were all names of the comedians I'd seen as the panto dame or as a solo act at the Leeds Empire: Norman Evans, Frank Randall, Nat Jackley, Robb Wilton, Arthur Lucan ('Old Mother Riley') . . . The list went on for pages, and it was that ghostly chorus that was to enable me to unlock the *gravitas* of Aeschylus, using the so-called 'low' art to unlock the so-called 'high'.

As well as my devotion to the music hall I became a constant collector and reader of all the poetry books I could consume, though the two often found themselves mingling, as when I used to find myself singing Tennyson's 'The Lady of Shalott' to George Formby ukulele tunes:

> Four grey walls and four grey towers
> Overlook a space of flowers

And the silent isle embowers
The Lady of Shalott.

I was also drawn to the most serious poetry of the messenger in Greek tragedy. A messenger who comes on stage and says, 'I have seen things too terrible to speak about,' and then for two hundred lines speaks about the terrible things he'd seen. I became obsessed with the Greek mask, with its eyes that are always open to see everything and a mouth that is always open to speak or sing about it.

In my poem 'Them & [uz]' I recount how my English teacher stopped my reading of Keats in my Yorkshire accent. But I was allowed to play the drunken porter in *Macbeth*. And I was allowed to take part in a reading at the Classics Society of the *Cyclops* of Euripides, the only Greek satyr play that, so far, survives intact. It was in Shelley's translation.

It sowed a seed, and later I looked to the satyr play, where it seemed to me the great tragedians incorporated the low art into the high. Though most are missing or have been air-brushed out of classical literature, all the great tragedians wrote satyr plays. After the trilogy of tragedies on came the chorus of dancing satyrs, half man, half goat, with enormous phalluses. I couldn't resist trying to reclaim them, and I wrote a play about the discovery in 1907 in the deserts of Egypt at Oxyrhynchus the fragments of a lost satyr play by Sophocles, which became *The Trackers of Oxyrhynchus*. It had its world premiere in the ancient stadium of Delphi in Greece in 1988. Delphi has become important for me since then as I have been back scores of times to prepare and create a new work which was designed for the building site for a new classical-style, open-air theatre in 1995, and ten years after that taking Vanessa Redgrave in *Hecuba* to inaugurate the completed space. I have celebrated the importance of Delphi in my life in a new poem, 'Polygons', in the current issue of the *London Review of Books*. I'm indebted to the *LRB* as exactly thirty years ago they were also the first to publish another long poem of mine, *v.*, in 1985.

I want to read a speech from this play, *Trackers*, for a number of reasons. It's about the divisions of high and low art. And also because the play represents another enormous debt of gratitude to the John S. Cohen Foundation, without whose funding I could never have taken my clog-dancing satyrs to clatter under the Delphi cliffs. Or indeed take it back to the National Theatre, and from there to tour Britain and Europe. It was this tour that brought me into hugely creative contact with Jonathan Silver at Salts Mill in Saltaire, and Piero Bordin in Carnuntum, on the Danube between Vienna and Bratislava. For both of their special spaces I wrote and directed new works.

I write my poems for my own voice and don't often like to hear actors read them, but it is a great liberation to write for other voices in dramatic roles I couldn't do myself, and wouldn't try. The best thing for a dramatic poet is to write for actors he knows and loves. I've done this when I've written for Yorkshire actors like Barrie Rutter, Jack Shepherd or Mark Addy. I've also written roles for my partner, Sian Thomas, whom I met in the National Theatre revival of my version of Molière's *Misanthrope* in 1989. She then played the German chemist Justus von Liebig in my play *Square*

Rounds in 1992. I wrote her the role of Faustina in *The Kaisers of Carnuntum* in 1995, and then, and for me the best of the roles, that of Sybil Thorndike in *Fram* at the National Theatre in 2008, with Jasper Britton as the Norwegian explorer Fritdjof Nansen.

Having said all this, I'm going to dare myself to read this 'messenger' speech from *Trackers*.

Despite having in some ways 'occupied' Apollonian literature, I am still the nephew of my uncles Joe and Harry and still feel a brother to Marsyas, who picked up Athena's discarded flute and became a virtuoso, and got flayed by Apollo for his presumption. When I worked in Prague in the 1960s, Titian's painting of *The Flaying of Marsyas* was in a local castle I could visit. It went deep into my imagination. Though I have to confess the nearest I ever get to being flayed is the occasional scratching by literary or theatre critics, like the one who thought that the chorus in my *Oresteia* 'sounded like fifteen Arthur Scargills'.

SILENUS

That's Marsyas screaming! They ripped off his skin
and all he ever wanted was to join in.
Marsyas suffered his terrible flaying
for a bit of innocent aulos playing.
The aulos, Athene's flute. She flung it away
so why shouldn't Marsyas pick it up and play?
A few blows and the goddess gave the flute
she'd just invented the elegant boot.
She flung the thing aside. Do you know why?
Well, think of the aulos. Ever had a try?

You puff your cheeks out, like this, when you play
and she didn't like her face to look that way.
She thought it unattractive. Well, it's true
her cheeks looked like balloons when she blew.
And who should find the flung flute in the grass
but my brother satyr, Marsyas?
Questions of cosmetics scarcely matter
to one who has the ugly mug of a satyr.
It's not for good looks that us satyrs are noted
so Marsyas blew and let his cheeks get bloated.
He took himself off to a quiet bit of wood
and girned and puffed and grunted and got good.
That peeved Apollo. He'd crossed the bounds.
Half-brutes aren't allowed to make beautiful sounds.
And can't you just hear those Muses say:
'Who gave a common satyr licence to play?'
Music's an inner circle meant to exclude
from active participation a beast so crude.
'How can he be a virtuoso on the flute?
Look at the hooves on him. He's half a brute!'
His one and only flaw was to show that flutes
sound just as beautiful when breathed into by brutes.
It confounds their categories of high and low
when your Caliban outplays your Prospero.
[. . .]
They set up a contest, rigged from the start,
to determine the future of 'high' and 'low' art.
They had it all fixed that Apollo should win
and he ordered my brother to be flayed of his skin.
And the Phrygian skinner with his flaying blade

saw Apollo's pointing pinkie and obeyed.
While Marsyas suffered his terrible flaying
Apollo looked on with his 'doodah' playing.
While the Phrygian flenser slices and flays
Apollo plucks out a glib Polonaise.
And the skinners applauded Apollo's reprise
as my brother's flayed nipples flapped on to his knees.
The last thing Marsyas saw was his own skin
like a garment at his feet with no one in.
Wherever the losers and the tortured scream
the lyres will be playing the Marsyas theme.
You'll hear the lyres playing behind locked doors
where men flay their fellows for some abstract cause.
The kithara cadenza, the Muse's mezzo trill
cover the skinning and the screaming still.
Wherever in the world there is torture and pain
the powerful are playing the Marsyas refrain.
In every dark dungeon where blood has flowed
the lyre accompanies the Marsyas Ode.
Wherever the racked and the anguished cry
there's always a lyre-player standing by.
Some virtuoso of Apollo's ur-violin
plays for the skinners as they skin.

(*Silenus drinks from his wineskin as if to blot out the
memory of Marsyas.*)

So I don't make waves. I don't rock the boat.
I add up the pluses of being man/goat.
Unlike my poor flayed brother, Marsyas,

I've never yearned to move out of my class.
In short, I suppose, I'm not really averse
to being a satyr. I could do a lot worse.
I just have to find the best way to exist
and I've found, to be frank, I exist best pissed.

CLARISSA LUARD AWARD

I would like to bestow the Clarissa Luard Award on the Wordsworth Trust at Grasmere, to continue to support a young poet in residence. The great spirit behind the Wordsworth Trust was my friend and great encourager Robert Woof, who helped me when I moved to Newcastle some forty-five years ago. He believed the new poetry needed the old as the old needed the new. And I've always believed that too.

Now, to help you to concentrate on your drinks, a short ancient Greek poem from the fourth century BC poet Amphis:

One glass and no refill
is life for men,
so keep on pouring till
Death says when.

Notes

These notes were researched and compiled by Edith Hall. The assistance of John Kittmer, Hallie Marshall, Richard Poynder, Anna Reeve, Sarah Prescott and her team at the Brotherton Library, and especially Caroline Latham, proved indispensable.

FOREWORD

1 'over-mastered by some thoughts': *An Apologie for Poetrie, Written by the right noble, vertuous, and learned, Sir Phillip Sidney, Knight* (London: Henry Olney, 1595).

2 This learned Dr Agrippa: Dr Agrippa appears in Mary Shelley's short story 'The Mortal Immortal' (1833) and in Søren Kierkegaard's *Stages on Life's Way* (1845).

5 But it turns out that: these Leeds Grammar School chapel windows were unveiled in 1931, and there is a description of them in the *Yorkshire Post* for 21 September 1931, p. 6. I am very grateful to Dr Emma Stafford and especially Anna Reeve, a graduate student in the Classics Department at Leeds University, for helping me research these windows.

5 'bound in with shame': from John of Gaunt's speech in Shakespeare's *Richard II*, Act II, scene i.

6 There is a philanthropic 'charity': see the letter by Tom Phillips to the *Independent*, quoted in Christopher Butler, 'Culture and Debate', in Sandie Byrne, *Tony Harrison: Loiner* (Oxford: Clarendon Press, 1977), p. 114.

6 '*Vates* in the whole Import': *The Works of Mr John Cleveland, containing his poems, orations, epistles, collected into one volume, with the life of the author* (London: R. Holt, 1687), p. 3.

6 'With the possible exception of Louis MacNeice': E. R. Dodds, *Missing Persons: An Autobiography* (Oxford: Clarendon Press, 1977), p. 57.

8 'every Digit dictates': John Bulwer, praised in a poem by John Dickenson prefixed to Bulwer's *Chirologia: or the naturall language of the hand. Composed of the speaking motions, and discoursing gestures thereof* (London: Thomas Harper, 1644).

9 'the philosophy of nature': Strabo, *Geography*, Book 4, chapter 4, section 4.

10 In the 1960s, he published: T. W. Harrison, 'English Virgil: The Aeneid in the XVIII Century', *Philologica Pragensia*, vol. 10 (1967), pp. 1–11 and 80–91.

11 This in turn led to a flowering: see further Kevin J. Wetmore, *The Athenian Sun in an African Sky: Modern African Adaptations of Classical Greek Tragedy* (Jefferson, NC: MacFarland, 2002).

11 a development which has been traced: see the Introduction to E. Hall, F. Macintosh and A. Wrigley (Eds), *Dionysus Since 69: Greek Tragedy at the Dawn of the Third Millennium* (Oxford: OUP, 2004).

17 'a procession of arresting images': Edith Hall, 'Tony Harrison's *Prometheus*: A View from the Left', *Arion*, vol. 12 (2004), pp. 129–30.

19 He is intrigued by horticulture: see Edith Hall, 'Classics, Class and Cloaca: Tony Harrison's Humane Coprology', *Arion*, vol. 15 (2007), pp. 111–36.

20 'Tony wants the whole body': Richard Eyre, 'Tony Harrison the Playwright', in Byrne, *Tony Harrison: Loiner*, p. 45.

21 'ribald generic indeterminacy': Adrian Poole, 'Harrison and Marsyas', in Lorna Hardwick (Ed.), *Tony Harrison's Poetry, Drama and Film: The Classical Dimension* (Milton Keynes: Open University, 1999), p. 57.

21 'a diabolically gleeful grin': Joe Kelleher, *Tony Harrison* (Plymouth: Northcote House, 1996), pp. 20, 34, 64.

22 'the deft and opportunistic annexation': Patrick Deane, *At Home in Time: Forms of Neo-Augustanism in Modern English Poetry* (Montreal and Kingston, London and Buffalo: McGill-Queen's University Press, 1994), p. 30.

22 'profanation of holy and glorious antiquity': Jules Janin, in *Journal des Débats* (1859).

AIKIN MATA

This essay was first published in *The Lysistrata of Aristophanes*, translated and adapted by Tony Harrison and James Simmons (Ibadan: Oxford University Press, 1966).

41 'the greatest disturbance in Greek History': Thucydides, *History of the Peloponnesian War*, Book I chapter 1.

41–2 'The Greeks': Werner Jaeger, *Paideia* (New York: OUP, 1986, originally published in 1939), vol. 1, p. 359.

42 'It may well be': Erik H. Erikson, *Childhood and Society* (London: Random House, 2014, originally published in 1950), p. 370.

42 *Aikin Mata* was written: *Aikin Mata* was written and staged in collaboration with James Simmons (1933–2001), a poet and lecturer from Northern Ireland who had studied at Leeds alongside Wole Soyinka and Tony Harrison. At the time, he held a position as lecturer at Ahmadu Bello University in Northern Nigeria.

43 the Oshogbo *Agbegijo*: see Ulli Beier, 'The Agbegijo Masqueraders', *Nigeria Magazine*, no. 82 (September 1964).

43 *Gambari* (Hausa man): 'Hausa' means 'woman's work'.

45 'Power all their end': Alexander Pope, Epistle 2, 'To a Lady' (1735), line 226.

45 several neologisms: see A. H. M. Kirk-Greene, 'Neologisms in Hausa: A Sociological Approach', *Africa*, vol. 33.1 (January, 1963), p. 32.

FELLOWSHIP

This essay was first published in 1969. Tony Harrison lived in Africa from 1962 to 1966. He was awarded the UNESCO fellowship in poetry in 1969. He travelled to Cuba, Brazil, Senegal and the Gambia.

47 '*Hey, Ruso*' or '*Hey, Tovarich, dame chicle*': 'Hey, Russian' or 'Hey, comrade, give me chewing gum!' All the prose translations in this volume are by Edith Hall, unless otherwise indicated.

48 *Coca-Cola el refresco de la Amistad*: 'Coca-Cola is the drink of friendship.'

48 '*Checo?*' '*Sí*,' I lie: 'Czech?' 'Yes,' I lie.

51 a Wolof steward: the Wolof people are an ethnic group in western Africa.

SHANGO THE SHAKY FAIRY
This essay was first published in *London Magazine*, vol. 10 (April 1970), pp. 11–23.

53 Abioseh Nicol . . . in a poem called 'African Easter':
published in Langston Hughes (Ed.), *Poems from Black Africa*
(Bloomington, IA, and London: Indiana University Press,
1963), pp. 35–40.

53 Brâncuşi's *Le Phoque*: *Seal II*, a blue marble sculpture by
Constantin Brâncuşi (1943) in the Musée national d'art
moderne (Centre Georges-Pompidou, Paris).

54 'one of the finest African sculptures extant': William Fagg,
Nigerian Images (London: Lund Humphries, 1963), no. 87. The
staff is now in the Permanent Exhibition, National Museum
for African Art, Smithsonian Institution, Washington DC.

55 the film version of Lawrence's *Sons and Lovers*: directed by
Jack Cardiff (1960).

55 Olivier's Hamlet castigates Ophelia: in *Hamlet* (1948), directed
by and starring Laurence Olivier.

56 Nicolás Guillén: Nicolás Cristóbal Guillén Batista (1902–89)
was a Cuban poet, journalist, political activist and writer who
became the national poet of Cuba.

56 . . . *esta tierra mulata*: 'It is a mixed-race country, African and
Spanish (St Barbara on one side, and on the other side, Shango).'

57 *Schwarze Dekameron*: Leo Frobenius's *Black Decameron* (*Der
schwarze Dekameron: Belege und Aktenstücke über Liebe, Witz
und Heldentum in Innerafrika*) had first been published in
Berlin (1910) by Vita.

57 novel of Charles Williams: *Shadows of Ecstasy* (London: Victor
Gollancz, 1933), p. 40.

58 J. M. Cohen credits: *Writers in the New Cuba: An Anthology*
(Harmondsworth: Penguin, 1967), pp. 6-7, 9.

59 Jean Price-Mars: (1876–1969), a Haitian teacher, diplomat,
writer and ethnographer who supported the 'négritude'
movement.

60 Lydia Cabrera . . . study of the secret society *Abakuá*: *Anafor-
uana: ritual y símbolos de la iniciación en la sociedad secreta Abakuá*
(Spanish edition published in Madrid: Ediciones R, 1975).

60 of Efik origin: the Efik are an ethnic group in the west of the
Republic of Cameroon and southern Nigeria.

60–1 Caballero Calderón said: Eduardo Caballero
Calderón (1910–1993) was a Colombian journalist and writer.

61 Miguel Barnet . . . *El Cimarrón*: Miguel Angel Barnet Lanza's
Biografía de un cimarrón (Havana: Gente Nueva 1967) was
produced from transcripts of Barnet's interviews with Mesa
Montejo (1860–1965).

62 Oscar Lewis-type job: Oscar Lewis (1914–70),
an American anthropologist, whose portraits of life in the
slums of Mexico and Puerto Rico were notoriously colourful.

62 *Herald* correspondent James O'Kelly: James O'Kelly, *The
Mambi-Land; or, Adventures of a Herald Correspondent in Cuba*
(Philadelphia: James Lippincott & Co., 1874), p. 62.

70 famous and beautiful Shango figure: Fagg, *Nigerian Images*.

71 Manuel Mendive's drawing of Shango: Manuel Mendive
(b. 1944) is a leading Afro-Cuban artist who has returned to
Shango several times in his works.

73 Adrian Mitchell: (1932–2008), an English journalist, poet,
novelist, playwright and committed pacifist.

73 the trilogy on Cuban womanhood: *Lucía*, directed by
Humberto Solás, and written by Julio García Espinosa and
Nelson Rodríguez. It was the winner of the Golden Prize and
the Prix FIPRESCI at the 6th Moscow International Film
Festival in 1969.

77 Jan Hus's colour: Jan Hus (1372–1415) was a Czech priest and
Christian reformer burnt at the stake for heresy. Miroslav
Holub (1923–98) was a Czech poet.

79 Pai Apolinário: Father Apolinário Gomes da Mota, a notable
figure in the religious life of Brazil.

THE INKWELL OF DR AGRIPPA

This essay was first published as the Introduction in *Focus 4: Corgi
Modern Poets*, Ed. Jeremy Robson (London: Corgi Books, 1971).
The title is taken from 'The Story of the Inky Boys', in *The English
Struwwelpeter, or Pretty Stories and Funny Pictures for Little
Children* (first published Leipzig: Friedrich Volckmar, 1848). See
further Edith Hall's Foreword to this volume, pp. 1–3.

81 'To feel': the quotation is from Pablo Neruda's essay '*Infancia
e Poesía*', 'Childhood and Poetry', in Robert Bly, *Neruda and
Vallejo: Selected Poems* (Boston: Beacon Press, 1971), pp. 12–13.

82 a Livingstone's *Travels*: David Livingstone, *Missionary Travels and Researches in South Africa* (London: J. Murray, 1857).

83 'sedentary toil'. . . 'difficulty is our plough': the two quotations from W. B. Yeats are taken from his poem 'Ego Dominus Tuus', published respectively in the second part of *The Wild Swans at Coole* in 1919, and in a letter to Margot Ruddock of early April 1936.

84 Zárate's *History of Peru*: Augustin de Zárate, *Historia del descubrimiento y conquista del Perú* (Anvers: M. Nucio, 1555).

84 example of Rimbaud: Arthur Rimbaud (1854–1891) abandoned writing poetry altogether at the age of twenty-one and went to Africa.

84 Fracastorius: Girolamo Fracastoro, *Syphilis sive morbus gallicus*, a three-volume Latin hexameter poem (Verona: da Sabbio, 1530).

84 Edward Powys Mathers's masterly . . . 'And sometimes': *Black Marigolds: Being a Rendering into English of the 'Panchasika by Chauras' by E. Powys Mathers* (Oxford: B. H. Blackwell, 1919). On Mathers see the chapter 'Even Now' in this volume, p. 415ff.

85 a Nigerian version of the *Lysistrata*: *Aikin Mata*, on which see the first essay in this volume.

85 A. L. Moir . . . 'an attempt to represent': in *The World Map in Hereford Cathedral* (Hereford: Cathedral Press, 1955).

85 'There is all Africa': in Thomas Browne, *Religio Medici* (London: Andrew Crooke, 1643), Section 2, Chapter 15.

86 John Cleveland . . . 'Correct your maps': 'News from Newcastle; or, Newcastle Coal-Pits', in *J. Cleaveland Revived* (London: Nathaniel Brooks, 1668), p. 3.

THE MISANTHROPE

This essay is the Introduction to *The Misanthrope*, first published by Rex Collings Ltd (London, 1973), and reprinted in *Tony Harrison: Plays Two* (London: Faber & Faber, 2002).

87 series of articles that André Ribaud: collected in André Ribaud, *La Cour: chronique du royaume* (Paris: René Julliard, 1961).

88 the anonymous translator of 1819: *The Misanthrope, Translated from Molière* (Boulogne: Leroy-Berger, 1819).

88–9 a typical piece of ripe Virgilian translation: James Henry,

The Eneis, Books I and II. Rendered into English Blank Iambic (London: Taylor and Walton, 1845), p. 36.

89 Francis Galton . . . 'a Venus among Hottentots': *The Narrative of an Explorer in Tropical South Africa* (London: John Murray, 1853), pp. 53–4.

89 *rire dans l'âme*: 'laughter in the soul'. Jean Donneau de Visé, a French journalist and playwright, in a letter about Molière reproduced in *Oeuvres de Moliere*, Eds M. E. Despois and P. Mesnard (Paris: Librairie Hachette, 1907), vol. 5, p. 440.

91 'like a woman': Raymond Dexter Havens, *The Influence of Milton on English Poetry* (Cambridge, MA: Harvard University Press, 1922), p. 324.

94 'English isn't well equipped . . .': Anonymous, 'Commentary', *Times Literary Supplement*, Friday, March 16 (1973), issue 3,706, p. 97.

97 'Thou loving brothers': John Ogilby, *The Works of Publius Virgilius Maro* (London: John Crook, 1649); *Aeneid*, Book 7, p. 12.

98 'Unanimous Brothers thou canst': Ogilby, p. 362.

98 'the poem of force'. . . a 'contemporary': the references are to the Polish writer Jan Kott's *Shakespeare: Our Contemporary*, translated by Boleslaw Taborski (Garden City, NY: Doubleday, 1964), and the French writer Simone Weil's essay '"The Iliad", or The Poem of Force', first published in French in 1940 in *Les Cahiers du Sud*.

99 Charles Hockett . . . 'In an illiterate society': Charles Hockett (1916–2000) was an American linguist who published many books and articles. It has not been possible to identify the source of this quotation.

100 Walter Benjamin . . . 'the life of an original': in *Illuminations*, edited and with an introduction by H. Arendt and translated by H. Zohn (New York: Harcourt, Brace & World, 1968), p. 80.

101 André Ribaud's series of articles . . . collection by Juillard in 1961: Ribaud, *La Cour*.

102 *'La Cour . . . du despotisme'*: 'The Court was another tactic in the politics of despotism.' In the Duc de Saint-Simon's *Mémoires; ou, L'observateur véridique, sur le règne de Louis XIV, et sur les premières époques des règnes suivans* ('London' (i.e. Paris: Buisson, 1788)), vol. 13, p. 71.

102 *'Les fêtes fréquentes'*: ibid., vol. 1, p. 83.

103 'The frequent fetes . . .': translation by Bayle St John, in *The Memoirs of the Duke of Saint-Simon on the Reign of Louis XIV and the Regency* (London: Chapman & Hall, 1857).

104 'he was so narcissistically self-absorbed': on de Gaulle's narcissism see Stanley Hoffmann and Inge Hoffmann, 'The Will to Grandeur: De Gaulle as Political Artist', *Daedalus* 97 (1968) pp. 829–87.

104–5 Gérard de Nerval's comment . . . '. . . with the sense of': in *Sylvie* (1853), translated by Lucie Page (Portland, ME: Mosher, 1886), pp. 6–7.

106 Martin Turnell . . . 'His mania': in *The Classical Moment: Studies in Corneille, Molière and Racine* (New York: New Directions, 1946), p. 96, n. 1.

107 Erich Auerbach . . . 'meaningless': *Scenes from the Drama of European Literature* (Manchester: Manchester University Press, 1984), p. 166.

107 Gossman . . . 'Chekhov': *Men and Masks: A Study of Molière* (Baltimore, MD: Johns Hopkins University Press, 1963), p. 266.

112–13 Lucretius' *De rerum Natura*: the passage from Lucretius' *On the Nature of Things* reads, in the translation by Cyril Bailey (Oxford: Clarendon Press, 1910): 'A black love is called "honey-dark", the foul and filthy "unadorned", the green-eyed "Athena's image", the wiry and wooden "a gazelle", the squat and dwarfish "one of the graces", "all pure delight", the lumpy and ungainly "a wonder", and "full of majesty". She stammers and cannot speak, "she has a lisp"; the dumb is "modest"; the fiery, spiteful gossip is "a burning torch". One becomes a "slender darling", when she can scarce live from decline; another half dead with cough is "frail". Then the fat and full-bosomed is "Ceres" self with Bacchus at breast; the snub-nosed is "sister to Silenus, or a Satyr"; the thick-lipped is "a living kiss".'

PALLADAS

Written in Gregynog in March 1974 and first published as the 'Preface' to *Palladas: Poems* (London: Anvil Press Poetry, 1975).

115 the traditional organisation: this is the arrangement of the five-volume translation of the complete anthology, with facing Greek text, by W. R. Paton (Ed.) (London: William Heinemann, 1927–8).

115 Peter Jay's decision . . . modern versions: Peter Jay (Ed.), *The Greek Anthology and Other Ancient Greek Epigrams. A Selection in Modern Verse Translations* (London: Allen Lane, 1973).

115 Gilbert Highet places: *Juvenal the Satirist* (Oxford: OUP, 1954), p. 142.

115 J. W. Mackail . . . 'one of the most': in his *Select Epigrams from the Greek Anthology* (London and New York: Longmans, Green & Co., 1890), p. 308. The numbering for Palladas used by Harrison (e.g. 1, 40¹, etc.) is, for simplicity's sake, the traditional numbering used in individual collections of Palladas' works, which have been excerpted and assembled from discrete sources. The history of the text of Palladas is complicated, since his poems are scattered across several books of the *Greek Anthology*, now supplemented by papyrus finds. There has been controversy over where poems begin and end and how texts are to be divided.

115 C. M. Bowra . . . 'Palladas and Christianity': published in *Proceedings of the British Academy*, 45 (1959), and reprinted in Bowra's *On Greek Margins* (Oxford: Clarendon Press, 1970).

117 'a Father of the Church': this quotation is traditionally although perhaps apocryphally attributed to Samuel Johnson, an admirer of Palladas who translated several of his epigrams into Latin. See Barry Baldwin (Ed.), *The Latin & Greek Poems of Samuel Johnson: Text, Translation, and Commentary* (London: Duckworth, 1995).

118 'harsh thought': J. W. Mackail, *Select Epigrams from the Greek Anthology*, revised edition (London: Longmans, Green & Co., 1906), p. 330.

119 'divine aphasia': Samuel Beckett, *Waiting for Godot* (English version, 1955), Act I.

PHAEDRA BRITANNICA
This essay was first published as the Introduction to *Phaedra Britannica* (London: Rex Collings Ltd, 1976) and reprinted in *Tony Harrison: Plays Two* (London: Faber & Faber, 2002)

125 Pradon, *Phèdre et Hippolyte*: Nicolas Pradon was Racine's rival, his *Phèdre et Hippolyte: tragédie* (Paris: Henry Loyson, 1677) being published in the same year as the premiere of Racine's *Phèdre*.

125–6 Feuchtwanger . . . 'Adaptations': Lion Feuchtwanger, *Stücke in Versen* (Rudolstadt: Greifenverlag, 1954). On his contribution to the German adaptation of *Edward II*, see V. D. Melngailis, *Leben Eduards des Zweiten von England: Bertolt Brecht's Adaptation of Marlowe's Edward II* (Cambridge, MA: Harvard, 1966).

126 Jean-Jacques Gautier . . . '*la noblesse . . . préservée*': 'the linear nobility, the fire and the grandeur of the original are preserved'. Gautier (1908–86) was a French writer, theatre critic and member of the Académie française.

127 'If we go to see': see 'Racine Spoken', in *On Racine*, translated from the French by Richard Howard (New York: Hill & Wang, 1964).

127 '*Je ne sais pas . . . mort*': 'I do not know if it is possible to play Racine today. Perhaps on stage this theatre is three-quarters dead.'

127 '*Phèdre n'est pas . . . d'acteurs*'; '*Phèdre femme doit . . . tragédie*': '*Phèdre* is not a concerto for a woman but a symphony for an orchestra of actors'; 'The woman Phaedra must be newly incorporated into the tragedy *Phèdre*.' Jean-Louis Barrault, in his *Mise en scène de* Phèdre (Paris: Éditions du Seuil, 1946).

128 most important person in the play: in Leo Spitzer, 'The Récit de Théramène', *Linguistics and Literary History: Essays in Stylistics* (New York: Russell & Russell, 1962), pp. 87–134.

128 Poe's opinion: in Edgar Allen Poe, 'The Poetic Principle', *Home Journal*, 36, August 31 (1850).

128 'classics of our *prose*': Matthew Arnold, 'The Study of Poetry', in *Essays in Criticism, Second Series* (London: Macmillan & Co., 1888), pp. 41–2.

128 Henri de Montherlant thought: 'Racine langouste', *Cahiers de le compagnie Madeline Renaud-Jean-Claude Barrault*, 8 (1955).

128 Jean Dutourd thought: quoted in Martin Turnell, *Jean Racine: Dramatist* (London: Hamish Hamilton, 1972), p. 4.

129 Flaubert thought: quoted in Huntington Cairns, *The Limits of Art* (New York: Bollingen Foundation, 1948), p. 845.

129 *beauté dénuée de signification*: Marcel Proust, *A la recherche du temps perdu* (*nouvelle édition augmentée*) (Saint Julien en Genevois: Arvensa), p. 156.

129 '*semble préparer . . . à Phèdre*': 'seems to prepare the spectator for this character-mix of vices and remorse which the poet

gives to Phaedra'. L. de Boisjermain, *Commentaires sur les ouevres de M. Racine*, vol. 3 (Paris: Panckoucke, 1768), p. 48.

129 R. C. Knight tentatively: R. C. Knight, *Racine et la Grèce* (Paris: Boivin, 1950).

130 Robert Lowell's epithet 'homicidal': in Robert Lowell, *Phaedra: A Verse Translation* (London: Faber & Faber, 1963).

132 first English version of Seneca's play: John Studley in *Seneca his tenne tragedies, translated into Englysh* (London: Thomas Marsh, 1581).

133 George MacMunn . . . 'In the description': *The Underworld of India* (London: Jarrolds, 1933), pp. 203–4.

134 the Yeatsian cry: from the last stanza of Yeats's 'A Dialogue of Self and Soul', first published in *The Winding Stair* (New York: The Fountain Press, 1929).

136 Sir Richard Burton: Richard Francis Burton (1821–90) was an English soldier, diplomat, explorer and prolific author.

137 John Ruskin . . . Theseus: in *Fors Clavigera: Letters to the Workmen and Labourers of Great Britain*, vol. 1 = *The Complete Works of John Ruskin*, vol. 7 (New York: Bryan, Taylor & Co., 1894), p. 316.

137 '*Les monstres étouffés . . . du Minotaur*': 'Monsters strangled and brigands punished, / Procrustes, Cercyon, Scirron and Sinnis, / And the scattered bones of the Epidaurian giant, / And Crete smoking with the blood of the Minotaur.'

138 Sleeman's account: Major-General Sir William Henry Sleeman (1788–1856), a soldier in British India, wrote several books on the subject, including *The Thugs or Phansigars of India: Comprising a History of that Extraordinary Fraternity of Assassins* (Philadelphia: Carey & Hart, 1839) and *Report on the Depredations Committed by the Thug Gangs of Upper and Central India: From the Cold Season of 1836–37, down to Their Gradual Suppression* (Calcutta: G. H. Huttmann, 1840).

138 'that exterminator': *The Works of John Ruskin*, Eds E. T. Cook and Alexander Wedderburn (London: Library Edition, 1903–12), vol. 27, pp. 408–9.

138 'an authority on': 'The morall philosophie of Doni' by Sir Thomas North, in Joseph Jacobs (Ed.), *The Earliest English Version of the Fables of Bidpai* (London: D. Nutt, 1888), p. xli.

139 Walter Pater . . . 'figures, passably': in Pater's *Greek Studies: A Series of Essays* (London: MacMillan, 1910), p. 159.

140 H. Bosworth Smith . . . 'the forbidden precincts': in his *Life of Lord Lawrence* (London: Smith, Elder, 1883), vol. 1, pp. 450–1.

141 'Is there not': Agnes and Egerton Castle, *Rose of the World* (London: Smith, Elder, 1905), p. 103.

141 'news that stays news': Ezra Pound, *ABC of Reading* (New York: New Directions, 1960), p. 29.

142 translation of poet/dramatist Thomas Otway: 'Phaedra to Hippolitus, translated out of Ovid', in *The Works of Mr. Thomas Otway* (London: J. Tonson, 1712), vol. 2, pp. 380–5; *Titus and Berenice: A Tragedy in Verse* (London: R. Tonson, 1677).

143 Alexander Radcliffe . . . 'a Farm-House in Putney in Surrey': in Radcliffe's *Ovid Travestie, a Burlesque upon Ovid's Epistles* (London: Jacob Tonson, 1681).

144 Stevie Smith's poem 'Phèdre': first published in *The New Statesman and The Week-End Review* for 25 December 1964, p. 1001; reproduced in *All the Poems of Stevie Smith*, Ed. Will May (New York: New Directions, 2016), p. 495.

145 Benjamin Whichcote, 'should be the Monarchy': Benjamin Whichcote, *Moral and Religious Aphorisms* (Norwich, 1702), no. 479.

145 'unreasonable things': Dryden's Prologue to Nahum Tate's *The Loyal General* (1680), lines 14–15.

146 'Our Frailties help . . .': John Dryden, 'Creator Spirit, by whose aid', first published in his *Examen Poeticum* (1693).

146 'there are only' . . . 'reason has to': Turnell, *Jean Racine*, p. 7.

147 Philip Vellacott . . . 'no more than': 'Introduction', in Philip Vellacott, *Euripides: Three Plays. Hippolytus – Iphigenia in Tauris – Alcestis* (Harmondsworth: Penguin, 1953).

147 'projections of basic': Turnell, *Jean Racine*, p. 239.

147 'One has to experience': Barbara Wingfield Stratford, *India and the English* (London: Jonathan Cape, 1922), p. 17.

148 '*un de ces orages*': Jean-Louis Barrault in *Mise en scène de Phèdre de Racine* (Paris: Seuil, 1946).

148 Mrs B. M. Croker . . . 'cruel vindictive animal': *Babes in the Wood: A Romance of the Jungle* (London: Methuen, 1910), p. 277.

148 'And finally there is the close': Barbara Wingfield Stratford, *India and the English*, p. 21.

149 'terribly limited': George Steiner, *The Death of Tragedy* (New York: Yale University Press, 1961), p. 8.

152 Bennet Christian Huntingdon Calcraft Kennedy . . . 'We are

here': in 'Carthill' (pseudonym), *The Lost Dominion* (Edinburgh & London: W. Blackwood & Sons, 1924).

153 David Gebhard . . . 'a favourite political': transcribed quotation in the Tony Harrison collection at the Brotherton Library in Leeds. David Gebhard is a much-published American historian of architecture.

153 'not simply impersonal': Turnell, *Jean Racine*, pp. 9, 12.

154 '*Le coeur, qui egrène*': Jean-Louis Barrault, *Le phénomène théâtral* (Oxford: Clarendon Press, 1961), p. 19.

155 'the throbbing tom-toms': Harrison's primary source here remains unidentified, but the phrase 'throbbing tom-toms' was a commonplace in British writing about India. See e.g. Herbert Russell, *Prince in the East* (London: Methuen, 1922), p. 112.

FACING UP TO THE MUSES

President's address to the Classical Association, delivered on Tuesday 12 April 1988, at the University of Bristol. Tony Harrison was president of the Classical Association between 1987 and 1988. The address was first published in *Proceedings of the Classical Association*, 85 (1988).

158 'This Parnassus and Helicon': *The Pilgrimage to Parnassus with the two parts of the return from Parnassus. Three comedies performed in St. John's College, Cambridge, AD 1597–1601. Ed. from mss. by the Rev. W. D. Macray* (Oxford: Clarendon Press, 1886), p. 7.

159 'one of the most unalloyed': E. R. Dodds, *Missing Persons: An Autobiography* (Oxford: OUP, 1977), p. 191.

164 won a tripod for his poetry: in *The Contest of Homer and Hesiod*, for the text of which see *Homeric Hymns. Homeric Apocrypha. Lives of Homer*, edited and translated by Martin L. West (Cambridge, MA: Loeb, 2003).

166 'burned is Apollo's laurel-bough': Christopher Marlowe, in the Epilogue to *Dr Faustus* (first published 1604).

166 'the famous haunt': *A journey into Greece by George Wheler, Esq., in company of Dr. Spon of Lyons* (London: W. Cademan, 1682), p. 460.

166 'so foul that': Paul W. Wallace, 'Hesiod and the Valley of the Muses', in *Greek, Roman, and Byzantine Studies* 15 (1974), pp. 5–24, and also his *Strabo's Description of Boiotia:*

A Commentary (Heidelberg: Bibliothek der Klassischen Altertumswissenschaften, 1979), p. 104.

167 'Is there anywhere': W. Macneile Dixon, *Hellas Revisited* (London: E. Arnold & Co., 1929), pp. 105–8.

168 'must deal': W. Macneile Dixon, *Tragedy* (London: Edward Arnold, 1924), p. 17.

169 'a retreat from the word': George Steiner, *Language and Silence* (Harmondsworth: Penguin, 1969).

171 'sounded like fifteen Arthur Scargills': quoted in 'A Bleeding Poet', an anonymous editorial in *The Economist*, issue 7795, 23 January 1993, p. 95.

171 I think it was Plautus: Harrison's note here reads, 'I have, since my address, received a letter from Dr Peter Jones of Newcastle University suggesting that the lines of Plautus might very well be *"facite totae plateae plateant"* (*Aulularia*, 407).'

173 'Words! Words!': Nikos Kazantzakis, in *Report to Greco*, translated by P. A. Bien (Oxford: Cassirer, 1965).

175 the announcement of her death: Harrison's note here reads, 'Dr. Peter Jones' letter also contained a xerox of the first page of a burlesque of Homer by Thomas Bridges (1797), which has the invocation: "Come, Mrs. Muse, but if a maid, / Then come, Miss Muse, and lend me aid!"'

175 'who deals with': W. Macneile Dixon, *Tragedy* (London: Edward Arnold, 1924), p. 17.

175 'yet without being': F. Nietzsche, *The Birth of Tragedy and The Genealogy of Morals*, translated by Francis Golffing (Garden City, NY: Doubleday, 1956), p. 102.

176 'theatre that can imagine: see Bonnie Marranca's interview with Robert Jay Lifton, 'Art and the Imagery of Extinction', *Performing Arts Journal*, 6.3 (= 18) (1982), pp. 51–66; reprinted in Lifton's *The Future of Immortality* (New York: Basic Books, 1987).

178 Harbage . . . 'an obvious reciprocity': Alfred Harbage, *Shakespeare's Audiences* (New York: Columbia University Press, 1941), p. 160.

178 fire breaks out: Elias Canetti, *Crowds and Power*, translated from the German by Carol Stewart (New York: Viking, 1962), p. 26.

178 'Give us some light': Bertolt Brecht, 'The Lighting', translated by John Willett, in *Bertolt Brecht, Poems 1913–1956*, Eds John Willett and Ralph Manheim, with the co-operation of Erich

Fried (revised edn, London and New York: Methuen, 1987),
p. 426.

178 'a Shakespeare play': W. B. Yeats, *Memoirs* (London:
Macmillan, 1973), p. 276.

180 a British TV documentary: *Paxinou in Athens* by Huw
Weldon (1963).

181 *histēmi*: the first person singular of a crucial verb in the
ancient Greek language, 'I set up', which is notoriously difficult
to conjugate.

182 'first of all': W. B. Yeats, *Memoirs*, p. 276.

183 'The mask challenges': Susan Harris Smith, *Masks in Modern
Drama* (Berkeley, CA: University of California Press, 1984),
p. 9.

183 'tragedy represents': Adrian Poole, *Tragedy: Shakespeare and
the Greek Example* (Oxford: Basil Blackwell, 1987), p. 11.

184 'the portrayal of': Anthony Clare, 'Living Death', *The Listener*,
31 March 1988, issue 3,056, p. 10.

184 'There can be no poetry': Theodor Adorno actually wrote in
his *Prismen* in 1955, '*nach Auschwitz ein Gedicht zu schreiben,
ist barbarisch*' – 'to write a poem after Auschwitz is barbaric'.
Gesammelte Schriften, vol. 10a (Frankfurt am Main: Suhrkamp,
1977), p. 30.

184 an appeal to a Roman general: D. L. Page, *Select Papyri Vol.
III: Poetry* (Loeb Classical Library, vol. 360. London: William
Heinemann Ltd., 1941), pp. 598–9, lines 18–19.

186 '*Theama*' is also: Sophocles, *Oedipus Tyrannus*, 1295; Aeschylus,
Prometheus Bound, 306.

186 'O dread fate': *Oedipus Tyrannus*, 1297–1305, translated by
Richard Jebb (Cambridge: CUP, 1887), pp. 169–71.

189 'total nihilism': Jean-Paul Sartre, *The Trojan Women*, English
version by Ronald Duncan (London: H. Hamilton, 1967), p.
xxi. Sartre's *Les Troyennes* was first produced in 1965.

192 if the *Partisan Review* takes this attitude: Harrison's note
here reads, 'I am glad to be able to report that since my address
another less pusillanimous US magazine, *Agni Review*, has said
it will be publishing my *Lysistrata* later in 1988.'

192 'an excellent selection': Hugh Lloyd-Jones, *The New
Statesman*, 6 October 1978, p. 442, reviewing K. J. Dover's *Greek
Homosexuality* (London: Duckworth, 1978).

199 Lady Falkender . . . 'Before the Election': this anecdote is also

reported in a BBC interview with Sir Hugh Greene broadcast
in 1982 and quoted in an article by Anita Singh in the *Daily
Telegraph*, 4 April 2015, 'Did BBC Help Win Labour the 1964
Election by Cancelling *Steptoe and Son*?'

200 '*Kalo taxidi!*': 'Have a nice trip!'

THE TRACKERS OF OXYRHYNCHUS
This introduction to the text of the play as it was performed
in Delphi was first published in *The Trackers of Oxyrhynchus*
(London: Faber & Faber, 1990), and reprinted in *Tony Harrison:
Plays Five* (London: Faber & Faber, 2004).

202 'I had a dream': Byron, 'Darkness' (1816), lines 1–3.

203 'obvious reciprocity': see note re. p. 178 above, p. 514.

203 'Give us some light': Brecht, 'The Lighting', in *Bertolt Brecht,
Poems 1913–1956*, p. 426.

204 *King Lear*: W. B. Yeats, *Memoirs*, p. 276.

204 'evoked the open air': William Poel, *Shakespeare in the Theatre*
(London and Toronto: Sidgwick and Jackson, Ltd., 1913), p. 4.

204 'exemplary theatre': Harley Granville Barker, *The
Exemplary Theatre* (London: Chatto & Windus, 1922), p. 206;
Dennis Kennedy, *Granville Barker and the Dream of Theatre*
(Cambridge: CUP, 1985), p. 200.

204 terrible image tolerable: Voltaire, Letter 4 to M. de
Genonville (1719), in *Oeuvres complètes de Voltaire*, vol. 2
(*Théâtre*, vol. 1) (Paris: Armand-Aubrée, 1829), pp. 33–9.

204–5 'suffers at': Sophocles, *Oedipus Tyrannus*, 1295; Aeschylus,
Prometheus Bound, 306.

206 'total nihilism': Sartre. Hecuba's last word in Euripides'
Trojan Women is 'life' (1330); see note re. p. 189 above, p. 515.

207 'The problem': Arthur Pickard-Cambridge, *The Dramatic
Festivals of Athens* (Oxford: Oxford University Press, 1953),
p. 285.

208 'lust . . .': D. H. Lawrence, *Apocalypse* (Florence: G. Orioli,
1931), p. 82.

208–9 'sublunary nature': Samuel Johnson, 'Preface' to Samuel
Johnson (Ed.), *The Plays of Shakespeare* (8 vols, London: J. and
R. Tonson, 1765).

209 'Shakespeare should not': Robert Bridges, *Collected Essays*
(Oxford: OUP, 1927), p. 28.

210 'Mere coincidence': Alfred Bennett Harbage, *Shakespeare's Audience* (New York: Columbia University Press), p. 159. Emphasis added.

210 'farmers, craftsmen': W. B. Stanford, *Greek Tragedy and the Emotions* (London: Routledge & Kegan Paul, 1983), p. 17.

211 *Charles I* of 1819: the fragments of *Charles I* were first published in full in *The Poetical Works of Percy Bysshe Shelley*, Ed. William Michael Rossetti (London: E. Moxon, 1870).

213 Dr Hunt . . . 'The piece was': *Dr Hunt's Address to the Annual General Meeting of the Egypt Exploration Society, 1911* (London: Egypt Exploration Society, 1911).

216 Homeric *Hymn to Hermes*: first published in *Shelley's Posthumous Poems*, Ed. Mary Shelley (London: John and Henry L. Hunt, 1824).

217–18 mentioned by Pausanias: Pausanias, *Description of Greece*, 9.29.6–9.30.2.

218 Herodotus says: Herodotus, *Histories*, 2.26.3.

218 Apollo was only reconciled: Pausanias, *Description of Greece*, 2.7.9 and 2.22.2.

HECUBA TO US

Introduction to *The Common Chorus (Parts 1 and II)*, first published by Faber & Faber (London, 1992) and reprinted in *Tony Harrison: Plays Four* (London: Faber & Faber, 2002).

224 'For deedes doe': Edmund Spenser's 'The Ruins of Time' was first published in his *Complaints* (London: William Ponsinby, 1591).

225 'Hippocrates, after': Marcus Aurelius, translation by A. S. L. Farquharson, *Ta eis heauton = The Meditations of the Emperor Marcus Antoninus* (Oxford: Clarendon Press, 1944).

226 'probably gone': J. G. Frazer, *Pausanias's Description of Greece* (Cambridge: CUP, 1898), p. 395.

226 'This year everyone': George Solti, interview with Marc Fisher, *Washington Post*, 5 August 1990.

226 Heinrich Heine was appalled: in the Preface to *Lutèce: lettres sur la vie politique, artistique et sociale de la France* (Paris: Michel Lévy Frères, 1855).

227 'a dozen showers': Joseph Addison, *The Spectator*, no. 592 (Friday 10 September 1714), p. 384.

227 'a common Horace': Lord Chesterfield, *Letters Written By The Late Right Honourable Philip Dormer Stanhope, Earl Of Chesterfield, To His Son, Philip Stanhope* (London: J. Dodsley, 1774), vol. 1, p. 298.

228 'The spectacle of': George Santayana, *Uncommon Sense* (Boston, Basel and Stuttgart: Birkhäuser, 1984), p. 57.

229 'Transience is the backdrop': ibid.

229 'symbolic immortality': Robert Jay Lifton, 'The Psychic Toll of the Nuclear Age', *New York Times Magazine*, 26 September 1982.

230 'negative solidarity': Hannah Arendt, *Men in Dark Times* (New York: Harcourt Brace & Co., 1970), p. 83.

234 spectacular photograph: the photo, taken in 1983 by Raissa Page, was reproduced in her *Guardian* obituary and can be viewed online at https://www.theguardian.com/artanddesign/2011/sep/21/raissa-page-obituary.

234 'of several words': Jeffrey Henderson, *The Maculate Muse: Obscene Language in Attic Comedy* (New York: OUP, 1991), p. 137.

235 *Carry Greenham Home*: directed by Beeban Kidron and Amanda Richardson (1983).

236 'I am so tired': Caroline Blackwood, *On the Perimeter: Caroline Blackwood at Greenham Common* (London: Flamingo, 1984), p. 14.

238 'smelted' into performance: Andrey Tarkovsky, *Sculpting in Time: Reflections on the Cinema*, translated by Kitty Hunter Blair (London: Bodley Head, 1986), p. 134.

HONORARY DOCTORATE, ATHENS

Acceptance speech on receiving an honorary doctorate from the Department of English Language and Literature, National and Kapodistrian University of Athens, December 1998.

244 'we are all Greeks': Percy Bysshe Shelley, Preface to *Hellas* (1821).

244 the Shelley Cyclops: Shelley's translation of Euripides' satyr play *Cyclops* was first published in his *Posthumous Poems*, Ed. Mary Shelley (London: John and Henry L. Hunt, 1824).

PROMETHEUS: FIRE AND POETRY

The Introduction to *Prometheus*, first published by Faber & Faber (London, 1998) and reprinted in *Tony Harrison: Collected Film Poetry* (London: Faber & Faber, 2007).

247 proposed by Gaston Bachelard: in *La psychanalyse du feu* (Paris: Gallimard, 1948).

251 'the vision has dissolved': Richard Holmes, *Shelley: The Pursuit* (London: Weidenfeld & Nicolson, 1974), p. 505.

255 'an English attempt': George Bernard Shaw, *The Perfect Wagnerite* (London: G. Richards, 1898), pp. 218–19.

256 '*Prometheus Unbound* in particular': Timothy Webb is a Shelley and Romantic literature specialist who has published widely. Unfortunately, it has not been possible to identify the source of this quotation.

256 '. . . *Prometheus Unbound*, a drama': Isabel Quigley (Ed.), *Shelley: A Selection* (Harmondsworth: Penguin, 1956), p. 20.

257 'It is easy to conceive': H. H. Anniah Gowda, *Dramatic Poetry from Medieval to Modern Times* (Madras: Macmillian India, 1971), p. 192.

258 'My book *is* poetry': Henrik Ibsen, letter to Bjørnstjerne Bjørnson, written in Rome on 9 December 1867, in *Henrik Ibsens Samlede Verker*, Eds Francis Bull, Halvdan Koht and Didrik Arup Seip (Oslo: Gyldendal 1949), vol. 18, p. 198.

258 'for Shelley was': Karl Marx, quoted in Franz Mehring, *Karl Marx: The Story of His Life*, translated by Edward Fitzgerald (London: John Lane, 1936), Chapter 15.

259 Chartist movement: Paul Foot, *Red Shelley* (London: Bookmarks Publications, 1984), p. 228.

259 'He defied': Heinrich Heine, letter to Rudolf Christiani, 27 May 1824, in *Heines Sämtliche Werke*, vol. 20, Ed. Fritz H. Eisner (Berlin: Akademie Verlag, 1970), p. 163.

259 'had cursed': Adam Mickiewicz, Preface to his Polish translation of Byron's *The Giaour*, *Poezye lorda Byrona tłumaczone, Giaur przez Adama Mickiewicza* (Paris: Alexander Jełowicki, 1835).

259 'never did the': Giuseppe Mazzini, 'Byron and Goethe', which first appeared in English translation in the *Monthly Chronicle*, September 1839.

259–60 'Amid this land': the poem is reproduced in *The Poems of*

Thomas Kibble Hervey, Ed. Mrs T. K. Hervey (Boston: Ticknor and Fields, 1866).

260 'Thanks to fire': Paul Ginestier, *The Poet and the Machine*, translated by Martin B. Friedman (Chapel Hill, NC: University of North Carolina Press, 1961), p. 21.

261 'The Iron Kingdom': Guy de Maupassant, in the fragment 'Le Creusot', published in *Au Soleil* (Paris: V. Havard, 1884) and *Oeuvres complètes*, vol. 9 (Paris: Librairie de France, 1935), p. 328.

261 'primordial figure': Timothy Richard Wutrich, *Prometheus and Faust: The Promethean Revolt in Drama from Classical Antiquity to Goethe* (Westport, CT: Greenwood Press, 1995), p. 8.

261 'the patron saint': George Thomson, *Aeschylus and Athens: A Study in the Social Origins of Drama* (London: Lawrence & Wishart, 1941), p. 297.

261 Karl Marx . . . pleading for freedom: see Marx's 1841 Preface to his doctoral dissertation 'The Difference Between the Democritean and Epicurean Philosophy of Nature'; the cartoon is reproduced in Franz Mehring, *Karl Marx: The Story of his Life*, translated by Edward Fitzgerald (London: John Lane, 1936) and Edith Hall, 'The Problem with Prometheus', in E. Hall, R. Alston and J. McConnell (Eds) *Ancient Slavery and Abolition from Hobbes to Hollywood* (Oxford: OUP, 2011).

261–2 John Lehmann . . . in Sukhum: *Prometheus and the Bolsheviks* (London: Cresset Press, 1937), pp. ii, 254–5.

265 'industrial genocide': Nick Danziger, *Danziger's Britain: A Journey to the Edge* (London: Harper Collins, 1996).

265 'No doubt it has': *La Psychanalyse du feu* (Paris: Gallinard, 1948); English translation by Alan C. M. Ross as *The Psychoanalysis of Fire* (London: Routledge and Kegan Paul, 1964), pp. 55–6.

265–6 'Fire enabled them': Dennis Donoghue, *Thieves of Fire* (London: Faber & Faber, 1973), p. 61.

267 'The atom smashers': Robert S. De Ropp, *The New Prometheans: Creative and Destructive Forces in Modern Science* (London: Cape, 1972), p. 1.

269 'In light-based media': Wolfgang Schivelbusch, *Disenchanted Night: The Industrialization of Light in the Nineteenth Century* (Berkeley, CA: University of California Press, 1988), pp. 220–1.

270 '. . . The main device': Josef Svoboda, quoted in Jarka
   Burian, *The Scenography of Josef Svoboda* (Middletown, CT, and
   Scranton, PA: Wesleyan University Press, 1971), p. 106 (with
   figs 108–11 on p. 107).

271 'Poetry can also': Harrison's note here reads, 'Auden's lecture
   in 1936 to the North London Film Society is included in
   the form of an authorised report as an appendix in Edward
   Mendelson's edition of *Auden's Plays and Other Dramatic
   Writings* (Faber & Faber, 1989).'

273–4 'Milton's imagery of': Marie Seton, *Sergei M. Eisenstein*
   (rev. edn) (London: Dennis Dobson, 1978), p. 380.

274–5 'There is a cinema . . . have to be developed': Victor
   Shklovsky, quoted in Maya Turovskaya, *Tarkovsky: Cinema as
   Poetry* (London: Faber, 1989), p. 10.

275 'I find poetic': Andrey Tarkovsky, *Sculpting in Time*, p. 18.

276 emergent 'prosody': Pier Paolo Pasolini, 'The Cinema of
   Poetry', in Bill Nichols (Ed.), *Pier Paolo Pasolini, Movies and
   Methods* (Berkeley, CA: University of California Press, 1976),
   vol. 1, pp. 542–58.

276 'free indirect subjective': ibid.

276 Rostand's *Cyrano* with Gérard Depardieu: the film version,
   directed by Jean-Paul Rappeneau (1990), of Edmond Rostand's
   1897 play *Cyrano de Bergerac*.

277 'Feeling the rhythmicity': Andrey Tarkovsky, *Sculpting in
   Time*, p. 120.

278 the photograph of the Iraqi soldier: the photo was by Ken
   Jarecke (1991). It was first published in the *Observer* on 10
   March 1991.

THE TEARS AND THE TRUMPETS
A presidential address given to the Virgil Society on 3 June 2000;
published in *Proceedings of the Virgil Society*, 24 (2001).

281 D. W. Blandford: in *Pentekontaetia: The Virgil Society, 1943–
   1993* (London: The Virgil Society, 1993), p. 58.

283 'And thus we see': Franz Werfel's statement in the
   Introduction to *Die Troerinnen des Euripides* (Leipzig: Kurt
   Wolff, 1915), p. 9; translated by Peter Jungk in *A Life Torn by
   History* (London: Weidenfeld, 1990), p. 36.

285 '*delicium est asinus*': the *Copa* ('Female Tavern-Keeper') is a

short Latin poem of unknown authorship which used to be attributed to Virgil.

286 P. J. Enk: 'Appendix Vergiliana', in M. Cary (Ed.), *The Oxford Classical Dictionary* (Oxford: Clarendon Rostand's Press, 1953), p. 73.

286 *pone merum* . . . *'venio'*: *Copa*, lines 87–8. 'Get the wine and the dice, and to hell with anyone who cares about tomorrow. Death demands your ear, and says, "Live today: I'm coming!"'

288 the simile in the *Georgics*: Virgil, *Georgics* 4. 511–16: 'Just as when a nightingale, in the shade of a poplar tree, laments the loss of her chicks, whom a harsh ploughman has spotted and ripped, unfledged, from their nest: she weeps the whole night through, and sitting on a branch breaks out afresh into her song of misery, and fills all the surrounding land with her sad cries: so Orpheus could be touched by no love nor wedding-song.'

288 'either with the clash': Introduction to Ivan Mazarov (Ed.), *Ancient Gold: The Wealth of the Thracians: Treasures from the Republic of Bulgaria* (New York, NY: Harry N. Abrams, 1998).

288 'There is . . .': Emmet Robbins, 'Famous Orpheus', in John Warden (Ed.), *Orpheus: Metamorphosis of a Myth* (Toronto: University of Toronto Press, 1982), p. 18.

290 as Mackail translates it: J. W. Mackail, *The Eclogues and Georgics of Virgil* (London: Rivingtons, 1889).

292 Caecilius Epirota: a poet and grammarian who was teaching Virgil's poetry by the 20s BC.

293 *Parcere subiectis*: Harrison's note here reads, 'The monument has the now discredited reading *pacis*, not *paci*.'

293 '*Superbi* were simply': Geoffrey de Ste. Croix, *The Class Struggle in the Ancient Greek World* (Ithaca, NY: Cornell University Press, 1981), p. 327.

293–4 '. . . a favourite': Robert Graves, 'The Virgil Cult', *Virginia Quarterly Review*, 38 (1962), pp. 13–37.

294 'Five years from now': Benito Mussolini, in a speech made at the installation of the first fascist 'Governor of Rome', in the Hall of the Horatii and Curiatii in the Campidoglio: Benito Mussolini, *Scritti e discorsi* (Milan, 1926), vol. 5, p. 244.

294 'mission to civilise': see Denis Mack Smith, *Mussolini's Roman Empire* (New York: Longman, 1976), p. 59.

295–6 *Res Gestae*: lines 13–15 of the inscription on the

Monumentum Ancyranum, 'Monument of Ankara', which is the most intact surviving version of the *Res Gestae Divi Augusti* ('Deeds of the Divine Augustus').

297 'pass again to triumph': R. D. Williams, 'The Sixth Book of the "Aeneid", *Greece & Rome*, Second Series, vol. 11, no. 1 (March 1964), p. 60.

298 'Most of the people': J. G. Frazer, *Pausanias's Description of Greece* (Cambridge: CUP, 1898), p. 351.

298 'The city of Elis . . .': ibid., p. 634.

299 Dio Chrysostom . . . as Mahaffy puts it: Dio Chrysostom, *Orations* 31.121–2; John Pentland Mahaffy, *The Silver Age of the Greek World* (London: T. Fisher Unwin, 1906), p. 320.

300 a play I staged: *Marcus Aurelius: The Kaisers of Carnuntum* (1995).

303 as Gavin Douglas has it: the Scotsman Gavin Douglas's translation of Virgil's *Aeneid* was first published in 1513.

303 as Ruaeus paraphrases: Ruaeus is the Latinised form of the name of Charles de la Rue, author of an influential edition of the *Aeneid* published in France in 1675.

304 'only rank bad Latin': in Nicholas Horsfall (Ed.), *A Companion to the Study of Virgil* (Leiden: Brill, 1995), p. 107, n. 39.

304 Harry Eyres: in an article headed 'Harry Eyres names a writer whose verse can be read as an elegy for the pain of Kosovo', *Daily Telegraph*, 25 May 1999.

THE FANATIC PILLAGER

Introduction to Tony Harrison's adaptation of Victor Hugo's *The Prince's Play*, published in *Tony Harrison: Plays Two* (London: Faber & Faber, 2002).

310 'Victor Hugo's *Le Roi*': George Steiner, *The Death of Tragedy*, p. 165.

310 'worthy of Shakespeare': Verdi, in a letter of 8 May 1850 to Francesco Piave.

313 Hugo records what Ligier said: 'Ligier told me yesterday at the rehearsal that I was reconstructing the French theatre.' Letter of 22 October 1832 to Mlle Louise Bertin, in *Victor Hugo: Correspondance 1814–1868, édition augmentée* (Saint Julien en Genevois: Arvensa, 2014), p. 257.

314 'As the ingenious': Samuel Taylor Coleridge, *Biographia Literaria* (London: Rest Fenner, 1817), Chapter 18, p. 69.

314 'The example of Shakespeare': in C. C. Abbott (Ed.), *The Letters of Gerard Manley Hopkins to Robert Bridges* (London: OUP, 1955), p. 218.

314 'drumming decasillabon': Thomas Nashe, 'To the Gentlemen of both Universities', Preface to Robert Greene, *Menaphon* (London: Sampson Clarke, 1589).

314 'here and there': G. Gilfillan (Ed.), *The Poetical Works of Edmund Waller and Sir John Denham* (London: James Nisbet, 1855).

315 'Diversity distinguishes': John Dennis, *The Genius and Writings of Shakespeare* (London: Bernard Lintott, 1712), p. 3. Emphasis added.

315 'Every passion': Samuel Taylor Coleridge, *Biographia Literaria* (London: Rest Fenner, 1817), Chapter 18, p. 67.

316 *The Changeling*: by Thomas Middleton and William Rowley (1622), Act I, scene i.

316 'Ha! my brother's murderer?': *The Changeling*, Act V, scene iii.

317 his editor Tottel: Sir Thomas Wyatt's poem exists in two versions, one corrected in his own hand in a manuscript in the British Library (Egerton MS 2711) and the other as printed after Wyatt's death in Richard Tottel's collection *Songes and Sonettes*, often called *Tottel's Miscellany*, in 1557.

317 'As far as the bulk': Coburn Freer, *The Poetics of Jacobean Drama* (Baltimore, MD: Johns Hopkins University Press, 1981), pp. 1–2.

318 the rare perceptive critic: W. D. Howarth, *Molière: A Playwright and His Audience* (Cambridge: CUP, 1982), p. 235.

318 '*Molière est dramatique*': Victor Hugo, *Cromwell: Drame* (Paris: M. de Norvins, 1828), p. lv.

319 'the most beautiful': in the *Deutsche Mercur*, translated by George Henry Lewes, *The Life and Works of Goethe* (London: David Nutt, 1855), p. 140.

319 '*une imitation détestable de*': Frederick the Great, quoted in Alexander Baumgartner, *Goethes Jugend: Eine Kulturstudie* (Freiburg im Breisgau: Herder, 1879), p. 209.

319 'At their most Shakespearean': Michael Hamburger (1926–2007) was a prolific writer, translator and poet. It has not been possible to identify the source of this quotation.

321 'Il nous semble . . .': 'It seems to me that this verse would also be as beautiful as prose.' Victor Hugo, *Cromwell: Drame*, p. xlvi.

321 a wonderfully combatant manifesto poem . . . 'black dogs of prose': from '*Réponse à un acte d'accusation*', 'Reply to an Act of Accusation', translated by Stephen Monte in *Selected Poetry. Victor Hugo* (Manchester: Carcanet, 2001), pp. 109–15.

323 '*Le bandeau!*': 'The Truth of Masks', in Oscar Wilde, *Intentions* (London: Methuen & Co., 1913), p. 233.

324 the scholar M. Descotes: Maurice Descotes, *Le drame romantique et ses grands créateurs: 1827–1839* (Paris: PUF, 1955), p. 217.

325 'The stage is for': Henrik Ibsen, letter to Lucie Wolf, May 1883, quoted by Harley Granville Barker in *On Dramatic Method* (New York: Hill & Wang, 1956), p. 170.

326 Ibsen told C. H. Herford: Herford quoted in Michael Meyer, *Ibsen: A Biography* (London: Hart-Davis, 1971), pp. 783–4.

326 'would have been a': Meyer, ibid., p. 783.

327 'most grotesque': Francesco Lucca, a publisher of Italian music. For his and other outraged responses to Hugo's play, see C. W. Gordon, *From Hugo's 'Hernani' and 'Le Roi s'amuse' to Verdi's 'Ernani' and 'Rigoletto'* (Vancouver: UBC, 1977), pp. 35–53.

327 '*La révolution dramatique . . . Romantisme*': 'The dramatic revolution was defeated the day before yesterday at the Comédie-Française, it is in full rout: it is the Waterloo of Romanticism' (review in *La Quotidienne*, 25 November 1832).

327 The actor Got: in *Journal de Edmond Got: sociétaire de la Comédie-Française, 1822–1901*, Ed. Médéric Got with a preface by Henri Lavedan (Paris: Plon-Nourrit, 1910).

327 '*Le grand poète . . . tableau jacobin*': 'The great poet offers the people, the wretched people, a Jacobin tableau.'

327 'it was the duty of': see Samuel Edwards, *Victor Hugo: A Biography* (New York & London: W. W. Norton & Co., 1997), p. 184.

330 'of these days': Queen Victoria, in a letter of 21 February 1870, quoted in Philip Magnus, *King Edward VII* (London: J. Murray, 1964), p. 143.

330 'a dreadful play': Queen Victoria's entry in her journal for Tuesday 8 May 1860 (vol. 49, p. 121).

EGIL AND EAGLE-BARK

Introduction to *The Oresteia*, in *Tony Harrison: Plays Four*
(London: Faber & Faber, 2002).

334 'Marlowe': Harley Granville Barker, *Prefaces to Shakespeare:
Hamlet* (London: Nick Hern Books, 1993), p. 31.

334 'An actor cannot': Peter Hall, *Diaries* (London: Hamish
Hamilton 1983), p. 247.

335 'in terrific form . . . I started the *Oresteia*': ibid., pp, 242, 418.

335 'from sunlight to': Harley Granville Barker, 'On Translating
Greek Tragedy', in J. A. K Thomson and A. J. Toynbee (Eds),
Essays in Honour of Gilbert Murray (London: Allen & Unwin,
1936), p. 240.

336 'I long to': Peter Hall, *Diaries*, p. 165.

337 'vowelled Greek': John Keats, *Lamia*, lines 199–201.

337 but Robert Browning: *The Agamemnon of Æschylus, Transcribed
by Robert Browning* (London: Smith, Elder & Co., 1877), p. x.

337 'overstocked with consonants': Samuel Johnson, *The Rambler*,
Saturday 19 January 1751, p. 199.

337 'our English': Henry Lawes, *Select Musicall Ayres and Dialogues*
(London: John Playford, 1652), Preface.

338 Aristotle thought: *On the Soul* 2.8.

338 'Consonants are': Osip Mandelstam, 'Some Notes on Poetry',
in Jane Gary Harris (Ed.), *The Collected Critical Prose and
Letters* (London: Collins Harvill, 1991), p. 166.

338 'aural density': George Steiner, *After Babel: Aspects of Language
and Translation* (Oxford, London and New York: OUP, 1975),
p. 314.

341 'He picks you out': Carlyle, in B. A. Litzinger and D. Smalley
(Eds), *Browning: The Critical Heritage* (New York: Routledge,
1970), p. 432.

342 'perverse *tour de force*': F. G. Kenyon (Ed.), *The Works of Robert
Browning* (London: Smith, Elder & Co., 1912), vol. 8, p. xi.

342 'Browning's theory': John Aldington Symonds, in Paul Selver,
The Art of Translating Poetry (London: Baker, 1966), p. 26.

342–3 'Browning's translation': Reuben A. Brower, 'Seven
Agamemnons', in *On Translation* (Oxford: OUP, 1966).

343 'the unwritten *every-other-line*': Robert Browning, in a letter
to James Thomas Fields of 4 February 1856, quoted in Ian Jack,
'Browning on *Sordello* and Men and Women: Unpublished

Letters to James C. Fields', *Huntingdon Library Quarterly*, 45 (1982), p. 196.

343 A contemporary reviewer: in *The London Quarterly* for April 1878, p. 234.

343 'to interpret': Edward Berdoe, *The Browning Cyclopaedia* (New York: Atlantic Publishers, 1892), p. 10.

343 What G. K. Chesterton called: in his *Robert Browning* (London: Macmillan, 1906), Chapter 6.

344 'Metre . . .': Samuel Taylor Coleridge, *Biographia Literaria* (London: Rest Fenner, 1817), Chapter 18, p. 66.

345 'All were totally unspeakable': Peter Hall, *Diaries*, p. 419.

347 Dionysius of Halicarnassus: in *On Demosthenes*, Chapter 39.

348 'megalithic': John Cowper Powys, *A Glastonbury Romance* (New York: Simon & Schuster, 1932).

348 in a letter written in 1876: Robert Browning, letter to his publisher, George Smith, 22 December 1876, in Roma A. King (Ed.), *The Complete Works of Robert Browning* (Athens, Ohio: Ohio University Press, 1969), vol. 14, p. 267.

348 'No Attic dramatist': Bernard Knox, 'Chez Atreus', a review of Andrei Serban's production of *Agamemnon* in New York, *New York Review of Books*, 14 July 1977.

349–50 Stanford: W. B. Stanford, *Aeschylus in His Style* (Dublin: Dublin University Press, 1942), p. 140, n. 3.

350 'Hearken my chant': both poems were first published in Francis Thompson's *Poems* (London: E. Mathews and J. Lane, 1893).

351 'Wiry and white-fiery': Gerard Manley Hopkins, 'The Wreck of the Deutschland' (1918), in W. H. Gardner and N. H. Mackenzie (Eds), *The Poems of Gerard Manley Hopkins*, 4th edn (London: OUP, 1967), p. 55.

352 'Does this not read': D. S. Carne-Ross, *Classics and Translation: Essays*, Kenneth Hayes (Ed.) (Lewisburg, PA: Bucknell University Press, 2010), p. 173.

352 'Sith I loved': *The Poems of Gerard Manley Hopkins*, p. 204.

352 'The sour scythe . . .': 'The Wreck of the Deutschland' (1918), ibid., p. 55.

353 'O then weary . . .': from 'The Leaden Echo and the Golden Echo', ibid., p. 93.

353 'Where, selfwrung . . .': *The Poems of Gerard Manley Hopkins*, p. 98.

353 could himself write a Greek verse: ibid., p. 226.

354 'Tell me where is Fancy bred': translated into ancient Greek in *The Poems of Gerard Manley Hopkins*, p. 225.

355 'Thus if for': Louis MacNeice, in a review of Murray's translation of Aeschylus' *Seven Against Thebes* in *The Spectator*, 10 May 1935.

357 'slices from the banquet of Homer': this was Aeschylus' own description of his works, according to Athenaeus, *Deipnosophists* 8.347e.

357–8 W. P. Ker: *Epic and Romance: Essays on Medieval Literature* (London: Macmillan, 1897), pp. 7, 10.

358 C. D. Locock . . . Esaias Tegnér: C. D. Locock, *Thirty-Two Passages from the* Iliad, *in English Rhymed Verse* (London: Allen & Unwin, 1922); *Thirty-Two Passages from the* Odyssey, *in English Rhymed Verse* (London: Allen & Unwin, 1923); *Fritiof's Saga by E. Tegnér, Translated in the Original Metres* (London: Allen & Unwin, 1924).

358 'kenning': W. B. Stanford, *Aeschylus in His Style*, pp. 61–6, and *Greek Metaphor* (Oxford: Basil Blackwell, 1936), pp. 132–6.

358–9 That great compendium . . . 'Aeschylus himself': G. Vigfússon and F. Y. Powell, *Corpus Poeticum Boreale. The Poetry of the Old Northern Tongue* (Oxford: Clarendon Press, 1883), vol. 2, p. 447.

359 'The Greek language permitted': W. B. Stanford, *Aeschylus in his Style: A Study in Language and Personality* (Dublin: Dublin University Press, 1942), p. 61.

359–60 'so grotesque': W. B. Stanford, *Aeschylus in His Style*, p. 61.

360 Sir John Cheke . . . version of the gospels: James Goodwin (Ed.), *The Gospel according to Saint Matthew and part of the first chapter of The Gospel according to Saint Mark, translated into English from the Greek, with original notes, by Sir John Cheke, Knight* (London: Pickering, 1854).

361 a letter to Robert Bridges: letter of 26 November 1882, in *The Letters of Gerard Manley Hopkins to Robert Bridges*.

361 'continual emphasis': R. P. Winnington Ingram, 'Clytemnestra and the Vote of Athena', *The Journal of Hellenic Studies*, 68 (1948), p. 132.

361 'the clash': Hugh Lloyd-Jones in his translation *Aeschylus: Oresteia* (Berkeley, CA: University of California Press, 1970), p. 23.

366 *'Oreste est le personage . . . maternelle'*: 'Orestes is the symbolic character who must trample under foot all the customs of the maternal family.'

366 Bachofen's *Mutterrecht*: Johann Jakob Bachofen, *Das Mutterrecht: eine Untersuchung über die Gynaikokratie der alten Welt nach ihrer religiösen und rechtlichen Natur* (Stuttgart: Verlag von Krais und Hoffmann, 1861). Translated in Ralph Manheim, *Myth, Religion and Mother Right: Selected Writings of J. J. Bachofen* (London: Routledge & Kegan Paul, 1967).

366 'the world historical': Friedrich Engels, *Der Ursprung der Familie, des Privateigenthums und des Staats* (Hottingen-Zürich, 1884), of which the first English-language edition was published by Charles H. Kerr & Co. (Chicago, 1902).

367 'an advance in': James Strachey's translation of *Moses and Monotheism* (1939), in *The Standard Edition of the Complete Psychological Works of Sigmund Freud*, vol. 23 (London: The Hogarth Press and the Institute of Psycho-analysis, 1964), pp. 113–14.

367 'The notion': G. W. F. Hegel, *The Philosophy of Fine Art*, translated by F. P. B. Osmaston (London: G. Bell & Sons, 1920), vol. 2, pp. 214–15.

367–8 '. . . by nature': *De Generatione Animalium* 1.20.729a and 738b, translated by A. L Peck in *Aristotle: Generation of Animals* (Loeb Classical Library, vol. 366, Cambridge, MA: Harvard University Press, 1942) and *Politics* 1.1254b 5–15.

368 'In nature's plan': Elizabeth Gould Davis, *The First Sex* (New York: G. P. Putnam's Sons, 1971), p. 329.

368 'a puppet': Mary Daly, *Gyn/Ecology* (Boston: Beacon Press, 1978), 'Introduction'.

368 'This is what': Nancy Bogen, *Klytaimnestra Who Stayed at Home* (New York: Twickenham Press, 1980), p. 145.

369 'the personification': Philip Slater, *The Glory of Hera: Greek Mythology and the Family* (Princeton, NJ: Princeton University Press, 1968), p. 137.

SQUARE ROUNDS

Tony Harrison: Plays Five (London: Faber & Faber, 2004).

376 'Their delicatessen': Hudson Maxim, *Defenseless America* (New York: Hearst's International Library Co., 1915), pp. 82–3.

376 'Modern verse': Hudson Maxim, *The Science of Poetry and the Philosophy of Language* (New York and London: Funk & Wagnalls, 1910), p. 66.

376 'poetry and gunpowder': Hudson Maxim, *Reminiscences and Comments by Clifton Johnson* (London: William Heinemann, 1924), pp. 299, 302.

376 'It is perfectly safe': Hudson Maxim, 'The Poet's Uplift', in *Dynamite Stories and Some Interesting Facts about Explosives* (New York: Hearst's International Library Co., 1916), p. 37.

379 'Not having been able': Alfred Nobel, in Edelgard Biedermann (Ed.), *Chère baronne et amie, cher monsieur et ami: der Briefwechsel zwischen Alfred Nobel und Bertha von Suttner* (Hildesheim: G. Olms, 2001), p. 175.

380 'the only American': Hiram Maxim, *My Life* (London: Methuen, 1915), p. 242.

381 James Puckle: see the pamphlet, held in the British Library, by Owen Standidge Puckle, *James Puckle, N.P.: His Books and His Gun* (1974).

383–4 two women doctors: Agnes Livingstone-Learmouth and Barbara Martin Cunningham.

384 'The piercing pain': Adolf Hitler, *Mein Kampf,* translated by Ralph Manheim (Boston: Houghton Mifflin Company, 1971), p. 203.

385 *The Producers*: written and directed by Mel Brooks (1967). *Springtime for Hitler: A Gay Romp with Eva and Adolf at Berchtesgaden* is the name of a fictional musical and its title song within the movie.

386 'In the First World War': William Moore, *Gas Attack!* (London: Leo Cooper, 1987), p. 238.

387 'the chlorine': Robert Harris and Jeremy Paxman, *A Higher Form of Killing* (London: Chatto & Windus, 1982), pp. xi–xii.

403 'Under the Clock': first published in *London Review of Books*, 17 April 2003.

WEEPING FOR HECUBA
Introduction to *Hecuba* of Euripides, translated by Tony Harrison (London: Faber & Faber, 2005).

407 Plutarch tells his story: in his *Life of Pelopidas* ch. 29.3–6. For the relevance to Hamlet's reference to Hecuba in Shakespeare,

cited in Harrison's epigraph here, see E. Hall, 'Trojan Suffering, Tragic Gods, and Transhistorical Metaphysics', in Sarah Annes Brown and Catherine Silverstone (Eds), *Tragedy in Transition* (Oxford: Blackwell, 2008), pp. 16–33.

409 'Tragedy and hapless Hecuba': Franz Werfel, *Die Troerinnen des Euripides* (Leipzig: Kurt Wolff, 1915), p. 11.

412 'All the misery': in Sybil Thorndike and Lewis Casson, 'The Theatre and Gilbert Murray', in Jean Smith and Arnold Toynbee (Eds), *Gilbert Murray: An Unfinished Autobiography, with Contributions by his Friends* (London: Allen & Unwin, 1960), p. 163, n. 1.

EVEN NOW
Preface to Edward Powys Mathers, *Black Marigolds with Coloured Stars* (London: Anvil Press Poetry, 2004).

416 a collection of his best crossword puzzles: in J. M. Campbell (Ed.), *Torquemada-Powys Mathers. 112 Best Crossword Puzzles. With a Portrait and Three Biographical Notes* (by R. C. Mathers, John Dickson Carr and E. Ellen Ashwin) (London: Pushkin Press, 1942).

417 Cecil French: see his *With the Years* (London: Richards Press, 1927).

417 'my rendering was': Edward Powys Mathers, prefatory note in *Black Marigolds: Being a Rendering into English of the 'Panchasika of Chauras'* (Oxford: B. H. Blackwell, 1919).

417 'a melodious and ingenious': *The Chaurapanchâsika, Translated & Illustrated by Sir Edwin Arnold* (London: Kegan Paul & Co., 1896), 'Preface', folio 3.

418 'each beginning with': Arthur Anthony Macdonell, *A History of Sanskrit Literature* (London: Heinemann, 1900), p. 339.

419 Charles Tomlinson . . . Hugh Kenner: Charles Tomlinson, *Oxford Book of Verse in Translation* (Oxford: OUP, 1980), pp. 30–1; Hugh Kenner, 'The Invention of China', *Spectrum* 9.1 (spring 1967), pp. 30–1.

420 'He might have': Edward Powys Mathers, *Anthology of Eastern Love* (London: John Rodker), vol. 11 (1929), pp. 113–38, and vol. 12 (1930), pp. 120–2.

421 'takes his veneration': *Anthology of Eastern Love*, vol. 12, p. 99.

421 an essay on Arabic prose and verse: *Anthology of Eastern Love*, vol. 12, pp. 97–107.

422 'the squibs' of *Red Wise*: Edward Powys Mathers's *Red Wise* (London: Golden Cockerel Press, 1925) is a collection of nineteen short prose pieces featuring or attributed to Abu Nowas. Mathers called them 'squibs' in a 'Note' appended to the stories, following p. 98. Chapter 5 is entitled 'Thanks for Wine'; Chapter 18, 'Hashish Instances', describes eating hashish.

422 'If He made all beauty': Mathers, *Red Wise*, Chapter 9, 'Tavern Scores', pp. 47–8.

423 one of the real 'discoveries' . . . 'in Paris': Mathers, *Anthology of Eastern Love*, vol. 11, pp. 18–21, with vol. 12, pp. 154–5.

424 E. Allen Ashwin . . . His wife Rosamond: in J. M. Campbell (Ed.), *Torquemada-Powys Mathers*, pp. 31–2 and 24–5.

424 'I have not forgotten': Mathers, *Red Wise*, 'Note' appended to the stories following p. 98.

424 'in no way compensated': in J. M. Campbell (Ed.), *Torquemada-Powys Mathers*, p. 25.

425 the Chinese American Julius Wing: Mathers, *Anthology of Eastern Love*, vol. 12 (1930), p. 122.

FLICKS AND THIS FLEETING LIFE
Introduction to *Collected Film Poetry* (London: Faber & Faber, 2007).

427 *Bambi* . . . *Snow White* . . . *White Heat*: Walt Disney's *Bambi* (1942) and *Snow White and the Seven Dwarfs* (1937); *White Heat* (1949), directed by Raoul Walsh.

436 *The Hollywood Hall of Shame*: by Harry and Michael Medved (London: Angus Robertson, 1984).

436 *Lawrence of Arabia* . . . Kozintsev's *Hamlet* and *King Lear*: *Lawrence of Arabia* (1962) and *Dr Zhivago* (1965) were both directed by David Lean; *Hamlet* (1964) and *King Lear* (1971) by Grigori Kozintsev.

437 '*Mirror* is the most': Maya Turovskaya, *Tarkovsky: Cinema as Poetry* (London: Faber & Faber, 1989), p. 66.

437 'The film affected' . . . 'On earth there is': Andrei Tarkovsky, *Sculpting in Time*, pp. 130–1.

438 'At certain periods': Joseph Brodsky, 'Introduction', in

Anna Akhmatova: Poems, translated by L. Coffin (New York: W. W. Norton & Company, Inc., 1983), p. xxx.

450 we developed an understanding: Peter Symes goes into the details of these discoveries in his generous introduction to Harrison's *Collected Film Poetry* (London: Faber & Faber, 2007).

453 'Hello, why he's blue': Maurice Maeterlinck, *The Blue Bird: A Fairy Play in Six Acts* (1908), Act VI, scene ii, translated by Alexander Teixeira De Mattos (London: Methuen, 1909).

454 'Prosody': Joseph Brodsky: 'Introduction', in *Anna Akhmatova: Poems*, p. xxviii.

THE INKY DIGIT OF DEFIANCE
PEN Pinter Prize lecture, 2009, privately printed for Faber & Faber.

462 'Blowing Up the Media': in *Index on Censorship* 5 (1992), pp. 2–3.

464–5 'Inside me contend': John Willett and Ralph Manheim (Eds), with the co-operation of Erich Fried, *Bertolt Brecht, Poems 1913–1956* (translator unspecified) (revised edn, London and New York: Methuen, 1987), p. 331.

466 'To Posterity': the full poem appears in another English translation as 'To Those Born Later' in *Bertolt Brecht, Poems 1913–1956*, pp. 318–20.

470 rare pieces of prose: 'Shango the Shaky Fairy', in this volume, p. 53ff.

472 Yiannis Ritsos: the English translation by Ritsos's devoted editor printed here is an otherwise unpublished partial translation of the poem 'Γαλάζιο Ποίημα. Στον Γκέο Μίλεφ' (Light-Blue Poem. For Geo Milev), written on 27 June 1958 in Sofia. It was first published in Ritsos's collection 'Ανθρώπου και τοπία', *Humans and Landscapes* (1958), and is reprinted in vol. 5 of Ritsos's *Collected Works* (Athens: Kedros, 1987), pp. 369–70. Many thanks to John Kittmer.

474 is regarded by Shelley: Richard Garnett (Ed.), *Select letters of Percy Bysshe Shelley*, with an introduction by Richard Garnett (London: Kegan Paul, Trench, 1882), letter 7 (to Thomas Jefferson Hogg), pp. 15–16.

474 *Pharsalia . . .* Martial: Thomas May, *Lucan's Pharsalia: or the*

civill warres of Rome (London: John Norton and Augustine Mathewes, 1626); *Selected Epigrams of Martial. Englished by Thomas May* (London: T. Walkley, 1629).

475–6 'English literary culture': David Norbrook, *Writing the English Republic* (Cambridge: CUP, 1999), p. 432.

476 'I met Murder': these two lines from Shelley are from the second stanza of 'The Mask of Anarchy' (1819).

477 Dean Herbert Ryle: in *The Tablet*, 26 July 1924, p. 4.

477 'Royalist in politics': T. S. Eliot, 'Preface', *For Lancelot Andrewes: Essays on Style and Order* (London: Faber & Gwyn, 1929), p. ix.

477 'the Senior Churchwarden': Robert Graves, 'The Virgil Cult', *The Virginia Quarterly Review*, 38.1 (winter 1962), p. 13.

478 'Thou gott'st Augustus loue': Thomas May, *Lucan's Pharsalia*, dedication facing the frontispiece.

478–9 'Why Virgil's poems': Robert Graves, 'The Virgil Cult', *The Virginia Quarterly Review*, 38.1, p. 35.

480–1 'Don't hold me back': Primo Levi, 'Pliny', translated by Ruth Feldman with Brian Swann, in *Collected Poems* (Boston: Faber & Faber, 1988), p. 33.

THE LABEL TRAIL TO STRASBOURG

European Prize for Literature acceptance speech, 2010.

483 '*Le coeur bat l'iambe*': Jean-Louis Barrault, *Le phénomène théâtral* (Oxford: Clarendon Press, 1961), p. 19.

490 'One glass and no refill': the poem is a fragment of Amphis' comedy *Gynaecocracy* ('Women in Power'), composed in the fourth century BC. The Greek text reads:

πίνε, παῖζε· θνητὸς ὁ βίος, ὀλίγος οὐπὶ γῆι χρόνος·
ἀθάνατος ὁ θάνατός ἐστιν, ἂν ἅπαξ τις ἀποθάνηι

THE DAVID COHEN PRIZE FOR LITERATURE 2015

Acceptance speech given at the British Library, 26 February 2015.

496 'sounded like fifteen Arthur Scargills': quoted in 'A Bleeding Poet', an anonymous editorial in *The Economist*, issue 7795, 23 January 1993, p. 95.